JUBILATION ZONE

A DRAMATIC TALE OF FRIENDSHIP AND LOVE (1968 – 2008)

JOZEF BANÁŠ

Jozef Banáš
Zóna nadšenia

Jozef Banáš
Jubilation Zone

Text © 2008 Jozef Banáš
Foreword © 2021 Cecilia Rokusek
Translation © 2008 Kevin Slavin
Cover photo © 1989 Ján Lörincz
Jacket design © 2008 Branislav Pavlovič

English edition © 2021 published by Hybrid Global Publishing, 301 E 57th Sreet, 4th Fl, New York, NY 10022 USA and co-published by Global Slovakia, Bratislava Slovakia
Other versions printed in: Germany, Poland, Hungary, Bulgaria, Ukraine, Russia, Syria, Turkey, India, Czech Republic

No part of this book may be reproduced or transmitted in any form or by any means electronic or mechanical, including photocopying, recording or by any information storage and retrieval system, without permission in writing from the publishers.
Jozef Banáš has asserted the right to be identified as the author of this work.

Manufactured in the United States of America, or in the United Kingdom when distributed elsewhere

All rights reserved

Library of congress cataloging-in-publication data available upon request
ISBN 978-1-957013-15-2

WWW.GLOBALSLOVAKIA.COM

Jozef Banáš is one of the best-selling and most translated Slovak writers of the last decade. He is the winner of several national and international literary awards and his 32 books (15 in Slovakia, 17 abroad) have sold a total number of almost 320,000 copies. His work on Milan Rastislav Štefánik has been translated into several languages and 'Jubilation Zone' has been published in eleven countries. Dan Brown has described him as a seeker of truth, and the Dalai Lama blessed his efforts to bring people together.

More about Jozef Banáš at

www.jozefbanas.sk
www.jozefbanas.com

Jubilation Zone
A dramatic tale of friendship and love (1968 – 2008)

Motto I: "You can know someone's past from the way they act today."
(Willy Brandt)

Not all of the characters and events in this novel are real.

Motto II: "The people are happy; it's just that not all of them realize it yet."
(Neumann, Central Committee, East German United Socialist Party)

I dedicate this to my wife, Maria, and my daughters, Maria and Adela, for always standing by me.

Jozef Banáš

Acknowledgements

A writer thinks in solitude, but writes communally with those who help him dig out archive material, criticize him or give reassurance in moments of doubt. I wish to thank from the bottom of my heart all those who helped in the creation of this book. If I have left anybody out, please accept my apology. So, thanks to:

My wife, Mária, and my daughters Mária and Adelka, who at Christmas, 2005, after thirty-seven years, tracked Thomas down in Berlin, and so enabled the writing of this book.

Thomas Angermann, with whom I spent Easter, 2006 in the reminiscences and conversation which became the basis of the novel.

Ola and Michail Obicki from the village of Kolodne, who invited me to a wedding and introduced me to Ivan.

Ivan Ivanovich Pauk, a Soviet army member who participated in the invasion of Czechoslovakia in August, 1968, and who afforded me a look into the soul of a Soviet soldier of those times.

Peter Hartmann, a Berlin librarian, who provided me with a generous amount of archive materials.

Pavol Kuljacek, Ivan Laluha, Juraj Migas and Jaroslav Hlinickz, whose advice increased not only the specialist level of the book, but also my own.

Franz Eder, a journalist from Vienna, who provided me with valuable viewpoints of a person who saw the seventies and eighties from 'the other side'.

Andrea Kralovicova, Martin Cukan and Juraj Soviar, who offered valuable and uncompromising criticism of the early versions of this work.

Jan Lörincz, the photographer who provided the exceptional photograph from 1989 for the cover of the book.

Foreword

Jozef Banáš eloquently radiates his talents as a Slovak novelist, journalist, diplomat, and politician in this non-fiction novel. *Jubilation Zone* is a dramatic tale of trusted and non-trusted friendships and deeply rooted human love that occurred during critical years in Central European history (1968-2008). It is an excellent example of what non-fiction literary genre is all about. The fictional integration of events that truly shaped the events of this time in history are masterfully presented. Mr. Banáš has hit the mark for descriptively outlining in great detail historic events and real people to write a masterful 40-year chronology of both Czech and Slovak history and its threads of impact throughout Europe, Russia, and the rest of the world. The unique style, detail, and attention to the humanness of each individual provide for the reader such intrigue and interest that one cannot put the book down once they start reading it. The contrast that is presented between Central Europe and the Soviet Union leaves the reader to both question and almost despise the corruption and evils of communism that could not even provide people with such basic things as housing, food, and transportation.

This historical setting is filled with love, passion, deception, politics, and the realities of a society as it attempts to balance the infusion of socialism, fascism, and capitalism. The contrasting outcomes of these ideological realities is masterfully articulated. The determination of the Slovak people to be an independent and free nation is integrated throughout the book and presented in the form of a time capsule filled with intrigue, passionate love, sadness, actual historical events, and real people that bring this book to life. It is no wonder that *Jubilation Zone* is the most translated Slovak literary work and that one out of every eight Slovak homes has a copy of the book.

In this non-fiction literary model, there is so much to be learned. This book could be used to teach history in the timeframe described. The 40-year historical span covers not only Central Europe but Eastern and Western Europe as well. Stories connect to a global history span that connects East and West Germany to Ukraine to Russia to the United States to Vietnam to Afghanistan and ultimately to the Czech and Slovak Republics. Not only are events presented for the reader to learn from but in addition key political personalities of the time from Dubcek to Brezhnev, to Gorbachev to Yeltsin to Johnson to Reagan to Havel are brought to light through a description of their real actions for the reader to better understand the times. From Banáš' unique style of writing and attention to descriptive detail, *Jubiliation Zone* provides not only history lessons but in addition it can be a phenomenal resource for discussions and presentations on political and ideological tenets that can be brought into a contemporary and current setting within the 21st century.

The eloquence of the writing and the true beauty of the natural settings that this book captures provides an almost ideal set-up for a movie. In essence, *Jubiliation Zone* captures a time in history that so many know about only from a superficial level. Given the state of the world in 2021, this book is timeless and so much can be taken from it. The book is for everyone from the university student to the mature adult, to the historian, the fiction lover, the avid reader, and anyone, most especially those with European heritage. It is a must read!

Cecilia Rokusek, Ed.D., M.Sc, RDN
President and CEO
National Czech & Slovak Museum & Library
A Smithsonian Affiliate
Cedar Rapids, IA USA

Prologue

No-one is a coward out of conviction. People cave in under life pressures that only the exceptionally brave can withstand. If without evidence someone accuses an acquaintance of cowardice, it is because he himself would back down in a similar situation. It is only by luck that life has not placed him in such a situation. For the unclean, everyone else is also sullied. The former German Chancellor Willy Brandt said to me in 1990 in Vienna: "You can know a person's past by the way he behaves today."

Whoever had integrity under totalitarianism has that same integrity under democracy; whoever was a rat then is still a rat today. In spite of this, those who brand others with the mark of Cain are on the upswing. They boast of lovely deeds to which they have no claim, and cheekily push to the head of the procession. Even that fellow at the back with the crown of thorns on his head gets on their nerves – they prefer to surround themselves with people they needn't be ashamed of.

Our consciences became lazy, but that was all that was needed for a stay in the jubilation zone. We remember it well: in front of the mighty, compliance; among the powerless, refusal. When the zone before the tribune ended, we were ourselves again. Today the tribunes are gone, but the zone carries on – within us.

Both as a politician and as a writer, I have often debated with young people, and for the most part I have been disappointed. They know precious little about our recent past, and what they know they have learned from the owners of truth who after 1989 decided to write their biographies. I had to consider what to do in light of this reality, and I received help from a source I hadn't counted on – life. It wrote my story.

I got to know Thomas in the High Tatras on August 17, 1968. Ivan I met in Mukačevo on August 21, 2007. I spent the month of August 1969 at Thomas' place in West Germany. "Next summer you'll come to see us in Bratislava," I told him. "I'll come," he shouted as my train pulled out of the station at Cologne. In the spring of 1970 the border was closed - for the next twenty years. All I had left were black-and-white photographs and the memories of those fantastic debates with him and his friends about life, politics, socialism, capitalism, friendship and love.

Sometimes I showed my wife and daughters a photo of a twenty year-old German student playing on a banjo. The solidarity and support that Thomas, his friends and family showed us during those times should never be forgotten.

At Christmas, 2005 I found under the tree an envelope from my daughter Maria, who was working in Munich at the European Patent Office. I opened it and found an unknown grizzled man looking out at me from a photo.

"You know, dad, mum and Adela asked me to try and find your friend. I knew only that he was about your age, was from Neuwied, once played the banjo and volleyball, and that you had become friends in August, 1968. When I searched the name Thomas Angermann on the net, hundreds of them appeared on my screen. At first I simply shrugged my shoulders, but then I resolved to phone at least one of them. So I did, and he was the right one," was the way my daughter described tracking him down.

In August, 2007 in Mukacheve, Ivan, a former radio operator in the Soviet occupation army, told me his story. His unit crossed into our territory during the night of August 20, 1968. That was the same night Thomas made his way back over the western border to his home in Germany.

After a thirty-seven year delay, Thomas finally visited me. Our Easter week flowed past like water. We spoke about our individual lives, but also about the fates of Germany, the Czech and Slovak Republics, Ukraine and Russia. We teased each other, we laughed and crietogether, we shook our heads in disbelief. We had been living literally metres from each other and didn't even know it. When we said goodbye in Bratislava, almost the last thing Thomas said was: "This is a story for a book!"

And this is that book. I believe that it will uncover for young people a door to the times their parents lived through: just as they will one day open the door to the times in which they lived for their own children.

Jozef Banáš

Table of Contents

Part I
1

Part II
157

Part III
415

Part I

CHAPTER
ONE

KIEV 2005

THE weather was gloomy in Kiev on October 20, 2005. A light rain fell on the windowsill of the President of the Republic's reception hall. On one side of the long white table sat President Viktor Yushchenko along with his Foreign Minister, Boris Tarasjuk, the head of the delegation of the Ukrainian Supreme Council to the NATO Parliamentary Assembly Oleg Zarubinsky, the interpreter and the minutes-taker. Opposite them were seated the NATO Parliamentary Assembly delegation - the President, Pierre Lellouche, two Vice-presidents, Vahit Erdem from Turkey and the Slovak Jozef Balaz , the general secretary Simon Lunn, his deputy David Hobbs and Svetlana, the Ukrainian responsible for Parliamentary Assembly relations with Ukraine. Viktor Yushchenko signed a few documents which his personal secretary had laid before him, and, looking up, gave his visitors a friendly smile.

"Excuse me for being late, discussions with the Georgian Parliamentary Chair, Mrs. Nino Burjadze, took longer than anticipated. I can assure you that we will have ample time for our meeting." And he favoured them with another small smile. It seemed that his facial muscles were somehow strained, as if from pain. His ashen face was still marked by the effects of the reported poisoning attempt, and his features seemed stiff, wooden. Despite his scars Victor Andrejevic was an elegant man in his black suit with a burgundy tie and handkerchief. His deformed ear was covered by the well-styled greying hair around his temples.

"Mrs. Burjadze is a charming woman so we understand your predicament," commented Pierre Lellouche with the smile that opened doors for the Frenchmen that were closed before many. He informed the President of the arrival of the NATO delegation in Sevastopol, and thanked the Ukrainian side for its gracious welcome. President Yushchenko was evidently in good form. He spoke deliberately, using clear argumentation peppered with humour. Lellouche, Erdem, Lunn and Hobbs paid close attention to the words of the man who from a tribune in Kiev's Independence Square headed the Orange Revolution during the winter of 2004.

Balaz sat as a man enchanted, but not by the President's rhetoric. His head was full of images from August 1968, when the streets of Bratislava were blocked by Soviet tanks. He felt that shiver of fear that overcame him whenever he recalled the concrete barriers of Checkpoint Charlie – the crossing between East and West Berlin. The images came and went through his head, but she remained, sitting opposite him. Balaz could not take his eyes off her.

"Ukraine has an eminent interest in receiving as quickly as possible an invitation to negotiations on entry into NATO. We are expecting that this will come at the NATO summit in Vilnius. We would welcome the support of the Parliamentary Assembly for our position." He stopped and took a sip of his tea. While Lellouche answered at length, Balaz stared as if hypnotized at the minutes-taker sitting across the table from him. She looked a well-preserved fifty with her chestnut rinse, a still-attractive woman. He followed her hand as it recorded a shorthand version of the debate, and he had the impression that she was writing unessential words just so that she would not have to raise her eyes from the page. When she did, he felt as if she was examining him, those green eyes fixing on him for a heartbeat before again being lowered to her work.

The discussions were coming to a close . She was still giving him looks from those green eyes, then looking away. The President had allotted them twenty minutes more than originally planned, and Lelouche thanked him for his consideration. A photographer came into the room to take the customary shots of Viktor Yushchenko and his guests. Except for the interpreter, his aides made their way to the door. Yushchenko called the minutes-taker back.

"Alexandra Josifovna," he said, and whispered something to her before she left the room. Balaz clenched his teeth. The photographer finished his job, the visitors again wished Yushchenko all the best, and the room emptied.

The head of protocol accompanied them to the entrance of the Presidential Palace, where they retrieved their coats from the cloakroom. Passing the Palace ceremonial guard outside, Balaz instinctively looked around. From beside one of the massive marble columns on the first floor he felt the unforgettable turquoise eyes of the minutes-taker looking down at him. When their glances met, he was sure she was smiling. Then she turned quickly away and retreated back onto the gallery.

The trip back to the hotel seemed to take forever. The service BMW had barely stopped before Balaz was dashing up the stairs. With shaking hands he rummaged through the side pocket of his attaché case among photographs and other mementos he held dear – a picture of his wife in her favourite light summer dress, another of his parents, one of his daughters Anicka and Martuska in front of a Christmas tree, and one other. It showed a young Soviet soldier and his mother. For a long moment Balaz studied it carefully. He reckoned the photo must be several years old, in black and white, but he was sure nonetheless that he recognized those penetrating turquoise eyes. He leafed through a pile of papers on his desk until he found the packet which had been distributed by the Ukrainian Supreme Council. It outlined the program for the visit and included the names of the Ukrainian delegates. The last name on the list was that of the President's protocol assistant, Alexandra Josifovna Guseva. It was her.

CHAPTER
TWO

BERLIN 1968

THE auditorium at the Technical University on 17th June street in Berlin-Charlottenburg was so packed that there was scarcely any air to breathe. More than three thousand students from all over Germany had gathered to decry the American aggression in Vietnam. Even though it was still mid-February 1968, it was exceptionally hot in the hall, and there was a fug in the air. Above the stage hung a huge Vietnamese flag with the motto: 'The Vietnamese revolution will triumph'. Below it in smaller letters was written the slogan: 'It is the duty of every revolutionary to make revolution'.

Thomas Ankermann had travelled by train from Bonn just before the beginning of the rally. He was sent by the Social Democratic Students (SDS) group at the University of Friedrich Wilhelm in Bonn. He wasn't able to mask his excitement - today for the first time he would be seeing Rudi Dutschke in action. This idol of the German youth movement sat on the left side of the stage. He looked into the hall with his mild, friendly eyes. He was a charismatic person, of medium height, with an angular face, an attractive smile and long dark hair which curled up in places, and he was a talented speaker. His detractors tried to discredit him among the student body by constantly mentioning his East German background and suggesting that he was of Jewish origin.

Thomas looked him over from top to toe. It occurred to him that the leader of the German leftist youth looked surprisingly meek, to the point of shyness. The excitement rose constantly and when Rudi took the microphone into his hands, the crowd began to chant his name. Smiling, Dutschke began to speak, at first calmly but progressively more combatively and convincing. He called for an organized anti-imperialist struggle while the massed students enthusiastically whistled, applauded and stamped their feet. Next to Rudi sat a Chilean student, Gaston Salvatore, smoking one cigarette after the other. Thomas was somewhat surprised that people were smoking in the hall, but put it down to the excitement. He returned to Bonn full of enthusiasm for the atmosphere and in particular for the man who, in the years to come, would determine the course of his life. He was fascinated by Dutschke. He expressed precisely his own inner feelings and was seeking answers to the same questions in exactly the same way as he did.

Rudi Dutschke worked his way up to become the acknowledged leader of the German youth movement. His slogan, 'In complete surrender to the truth resides the meaning of our lives' completely overwhelmed the new post-war German generation. The student unrest which spread throughout the country from the mid-sixties reached its zenith in the stormy European year, 1968. At first the students protested against the conditions at German universities but gradually the main point of their dissatisfaction moved into the arena of ideology. Alongside their criticism of the German value system, there appeared ever more frequently slogans against the American aggression in Vietnam and against the planned a state of emergency law. A strong extra-parliamentary opposition, APO, was formed, with its core composed of the Socialist Union of German Students.

Dissatisfaction grew, mostly among intellectuals, in the face of the almost miraculous increases in economic prosperity. The reason for this was straightforward – the nation's inability, or rather the unwillingness, to come to terms with the Nazi past. The official West German confession of evil was never accompanied by a genuine individual acknowledgement of personal responsibility. As a result of the absence of an outright acknowledgement of the mistakes of the past, young intellectuals saw the problem of Germany through the prism of the failings not so much of Nazism but more of the Bonn republic. Consequently, for activists like Rudi Dutschke, Peter Schneider or the younger Andreas Baader or Reiner Werner Fassbinder, West German post-war democracy was not the solution, it was the problem. The government, supported by the Americans, wagered on consumerism in the hope that the new generation would forget the failings of their parents in the midst of the rising prosperity. The first supermarkets started to appear in the country, and householders quickly bought fridges, washing machines, televisions and later, cars. Their favourite was the 'people's Beetle' – a car from the Volkswagen company.

The material successes of the parents, German women in particular, who built the new Germany were nonetheless stained by their moral inheritance. If there ever existed a generation whose rebellion was truly based on the rejection of everything their parents stood for – national pride, Nazism, money, prosperity – this generation was 'Hitler's Children', the West German radicals of the 1960s. If we add to all of this the overcrowded dormitories and classrooms, the distant and inaccessible professors who for the most part had had some dealings with the Nazi regime, a superficial education without the encouragement of creativity, it was only a question of time before the pressure exploded.

The most fertile ground was the campus of the Free University in Berlin, founded in 1948 as compensation for the fact that the traditional Humboldt University campus was now located in the communist Soviet zone of East Berlin. A good number of radicals came to study at the Free University - not only for the liberal atmosphere that reigned in the city, but also for a more prosaic reason: this was one way to avoid the compulsory military service. West Berlin, that isolated island at the heart of international affairs, was free in spite of the fact that it was fenced in by a wall almost two hundred kilometres long. It gradually became the centre of the anti-American student revolt; paradoxically however, the whole of West Berlin, including the anti-American students, thrived only thanks to American aid and the presence of the U.S. Army. The War in Vietnam became a substitute topic for the missing debate on Germany's own war crimes. Most of all, the German left-wing youth found no sense in the hypocritical American 'decreed' democracy. With great interest they followed the developments in neighbouring Czechoslovakia, where the new and charismatic leader of the Communist Party, the Slovak Alexander Dubcek, was attempting to reform Stalinist Communism. They were impressed by the fervour with which Czechs and Slovaks supported Dubcek. No politician in 'democratic' West Germany could even dream of such support.

Thomas was therefore surprised by Dutschke's words evaluating his recent visit to Prague where he had explained to the shocked Czech students the senselessness and futility of real capitalism. They for their part explained to him the senselessness and futility of real socialism. All the same, Dutschke himself was a child of real socialism since he was born and grew up in Lückenwalde, which was situated in the Soviet occupation zone, known since 1949 as the German Democratic Republic. He described himself as a socialist brought up in a Christian Evangelist family. Despite his early attempts to support the building of socialism in the GDR, he continually came into conflict with the basic tenets of Marxism-Leninism. Finally, on August 6, 1961, a week before the completion of the Berlin Wall, he added his name to the almost three million GDR citizens who had left the real German socialist state since the end of WWII. He came to the free German state as an anti-Communist and an anti-Fascist, but progressively became an anti-Capitalist. As is the fate of leaders, he was loved by some, hated by others.

On that fated April 11, 1968 Rudi went to the chemist's located about twenty metres from SDS headquarters on Berlin's main street, Kurfürstendamm. He needed to buy some medicine for his three month old son, Hosea- Che, but had to wait fifteen minutes for the lunch-hour closing to be over. Rudi took a walk past the Breusig funeral parlour and a tobacco shop, then headed back to the chemist's. He was sitting on his bicycle, one foot on the pavement, when he noticed a car parking on the centre strip of the 'Ku´damm' directly opposite him. A young man got out, waited for a line of cars to pass, and approached the unsuspecting Dutschke. "Are you Rudi Dutschke?" he asked. Rudi was used to being stopped in the street for debate, and nodded, smiling. This anti-Communist fanatic, Josef Erwin Bachmann, a house painter, had the day before driven from Munich. He drew a pistol from his pocket and in cold blood shot Dutschke twice in the head. Rudi fell to the pavement and felt nothing more - not even the final round that Bachmann shot into him, just to be sure.

CHAPTER
THREE

KIEV 1968

THE Burevestnik Kiev sports hall was filled to capacity. The volleyball team from the Economics University in Bratislava was playing its return match against the Kiev Economics University. It was a hot July day and their uniforms were sodden with sweat right from the opening whistle. Jozef Balaz and most of his team-mates were for the first time in their lives playing before two thousand spectators. From the warm-up on it was clear that this was going to be a difficult match. The Ukrainians were hitting one smash after the other, and so it remained as the match itself got under way. Winter moaned that they were going to get creamed.

"If you're going to carry on like this right at the start, go and sit somewhere in the dressing room and don't destroy our morale. Whether we win or lose is not the main thing; the main point is for each of us to win over ourselves. We have to fight to our maximum and then it's all the same who the winner is. We have to win over our faintheartedness! Do you get it?!" Baca, the captain, shouted at him. Winter simply mumbled something about this team basically being the core of Burevestnik Kiev, the champion of the Soviet Union, and the Soviet Union being champion of the world. "So much the better," said Drsi, bouncing the ball sharply off Winter, "we have nothing to lose."

On the wall opposite the Slovak half, the Soviet and Czechoslovak flags were hanging side by side. The Ukrainians were more experienced but the Slovaks were clearly more determined. Balaz, unexpectedly, was making all his smashes. But one got away from him, and his hard smash hit the Soviet flag and knocked it down. It was clear it had been positioned so as to cover a large hole in the wall behind it. The game was held up and the fans made good fun of the organizing staff, who were clumsily putting it back in place. In the end the Bratislava team lost three times by an identical 13:15 score, but were rewarded with loud applause from the spectators, even from one girl in the front row whose glasses Balaz had accidentally broken with a deflected ball. He went over and apologized to her. She was a little short-sighted and smiled at him with her gorgeous turquoise eyes. "It's all right," she said in Russian, and reddened when he gallantly kissed her hand. She was unsettled; it was clear to him that nothing like that had ever happened to her before. Balaz promised to rush into town and buy her a new pair. "If only it were that simple. Here you have to wait a month to get new glasses," she shrugged.

"So I'll send you new ones immediately after I get home. I only hope you can get along with some sort of substitute till then..."

"Don't put yourself out, I have another pair..."

"No, no... I'll just take a shower and I'll be right back. Wait, please. I'll have to write down your name and address, and most importantly, your prescription."

"It's really not necessary."

"Yes it is," he insisted.

"The address is the dormitory where you're staying."

"You live in our dormitory?" Balaz was delighted.

"You're living in ours."

"Sorry, whom should I ask for?"

She hesitated for just a heartbeat. "Alexandra. Alexandra Josifovna Grycenková. My friends call me Sasha."

"My name is Jozef," he answered in Russian.

"Jozef..." she smiled. "After our Josif... My father is also Josif. And friends say Osja for Josif... You'll be Osja... Da?"

"Da."

The more he looked at her, the better he liked her. They hardly noticed that both teams had gone to the showers and that the sports hall was emptying. Balaz felt the sweat running off his body, but wasn't sure if it was just from the tough match. "Sorry, I really should go and shower. There's going to be a session this evening, I think in your dormitory..."

"I know, but you're naïve if you think it'll be a session. It'll be a blast, a whole lot of fun."

"Will you be there?"

"It's by invitation only."

"You just got invited."

Sasha smiled secretly: "I must be going."

The Slovak team was still in the showers, and the boys teased Balaz that they hadn't even got to Kiev and he'd already picked up a girl. He scarcely heard them; his mind was full of Sasha and their evening to come.

As predicted, the friendly meeting quickly degenerated into a Bacchanalian feast, with forty or so young people gathered around the longest table in the Economics University dining hall. Both nations rivalled each other in singing, drinking and making fun while Balaz discreetly got closer to Sasha. He was possessed by the feeling that they had known each other for a long time. Both of them were intrested in literature; she adored Yevgeny Yevtushenko and was also familiar with Miroslav Valek, a famous Slovak poet. Jozef felt her steady look as he looked into his glass of wine and recited some verses by Yevtushenko. Misha, the President of the Komsomol youth organization at the university all at once stood up and ordered champagne for everyone. Seeing that their host was already half drunk, Cuki commented: "This won't turn out well. We'd do better to stick to vodka."

"Everything will be okay. I need to make a toast, and that can only be done with champagne." Everyone knew that after several rounds of vodka, Ukrainian kvass and Slovak red wine, sparkling wine was not a good choice, but Misha could not be dissuaded. After the glasses were filled he stood up and said: "My friends, we are all closely following the outrages committed by the American imperialists in Vietnam. The whole world is angered by this dirty imperialist occupation of a free Vietnam. Let's drink to the health of our Vietnamese brothers." Everyone raised their glasses, stood up and drank to their health. Misha said something to the musicians standing in the corner. Until then they had been playing Soviet songs plus old hits by Elvis and the Beatles. The band started to play a protest song by Pete Seeger, "We shall overcome". Some of the Ukrainians joined in, as did Balaz and Chochol, who sometimes played this number on their guitars.

"We shall overcome, we shall overcome some day, deep in my heart I do believe, we shall overcome some day." The simplicity of the words and music moved everyone. Then Balaz and Chochol took out their guitars and the session now moved towards a gathering of students protesting the War in Vietnam. When they stopped playing everyone applauded loudly and another toast was called. President Misha got up again. With shaky gestures he asked for silence: "My friends, I thank you for your gesture of solidarity with the Vietnamese p-p-people... hik... Dear Slovak comrades I would like, in the name of all here present, to tell you that we are all closely following what's going on in our brother Czechoslovakia. We can assure you that whatever the hell happens, you can rely on us, your Soviet friends... hik... Always in history we have stood by your side, and so now too. Allow me to drink to comradeship, to friendship, to our supreme representatives – comrades Leonid Ilyich Brezhnev and Alexander Stepanovich Dubcek." The room went quiet, people looked at each other, hesitated then drank without great enthusiasm. The Slovaks didn't care much for drinking to Brezhnev, and it was clear the Ukrainians were unsure what to make of Dubcek. Misha's toast had brought politics into the discussion, and perhaps that was all for the good, since the air needed to be cleared of unresolved questions. Those who were still in good shape entered into a lively debate. Balaz pulled Sasha to himself at the last second to save her from a spray of vomit someone shot in their direction. This was the first victim of the vodka, wine and bubbly.

The band went back to playing Beatles hits again - 'She Loves You', 'All my Loving' - and brought the young Slovaks and Ukrainians to the verge of frenzy. When the singer broke into everyone's favourite love song, 'And I Love Her', Balaz took Sasha onto the dance floor. She was shaking and her hands were a little sweaty. Together they sang: 'I give her all my love, that's all I do...' She moved into him so naturally and spontaneously that they almost didn't notice. He gently stroked her hair and she raised her unbelievable turquoise eyes to him. The band finished and the Ukrainians cheered for Chochol and Balaz to carry on with their guitars. When their Slovak friends joined in, Balaz picked up his guitar. "Play something Slovak," called Misha. "I'll give you something Russian," he countered, and started to play Villon by Bulat Okudzava. He turned to Sasha and sang: "As long as the Earth is turning, as long as the world stays young, Oh God, give everyone what they ask for, but don't forget about me..." Okudzhava, pilloried and loved, Okudzhava condemned, Okudzhava in rebellion. The more cautious pretended they weren't familiar with the lyric while the more daring joined in. Alcohol makes almost everyone courageous. Winter's fingers beat out the rhythm on the tabletop while his eyes carefully checked which students were the drunkest.

'While the world still turns for us and the colours still do glow, my lord, bestow upon us that which we do not have. Leave the wise man his reason, to the spiritless give a horse, grant the happy man his victory... and please remember me'

Finally there was no-one left in the hall who wasn't singing - the Ukrainians in Russian, the Slovaks in Slovak, and those who didn't know the words, humming along. Balaz felt Sasha's look full on him, and so decided on a Czardas from East Slovakia. As he sang: "O my love, let me in, see, I have brought you apples", Sasha unexpectedly sang along. The hall fell silent for a second, followed by loud applause.

"You know our music?" he turned to her in surprise.

"I do. I know your poetry too. 'I sing of a thirst for beauty, besotted with loveliness and the world of my desire enclosed in the echoing of this spirit' ... Sladkovic," she smiled slyly. "I have Slovak roots. My parents were born in Uzhgrorod when it was still in the Czechoslovak Republic. My mother's maiden name was Sidorová. I'm basically Slovak..."

"And now some country music," someone called out. Duro Chochol, a Moravian studying in Bratislava, was the country specialist. His 'Golden Shoes' again brought the crowd into an atmosphere of mass hysteria. The music attracted all the dormitory's inhabitants and so many squeezed into the auditorium it was becoming impossible to breathe.

Balaz felt Sasha squeeze his hand as a signal to follow her out of the room. There was so much noise in the hall that no-one noticed their leaving - in fact very few people were still capable of noticing very much at all. She whispered the number of her room to him; it turned out to be just a few doors down the bend in the hall from the auditorium where they'd spent the evening. He held back for a second but his desire and curiosity overcame his bashfulness. It was clear from her expression that she was thinking the same thoughts as he was. Quickly she locked the door to her room and leapt into his arms, kissing him passionately. He didn't defend himself, quite the reverse: never before had he felt such a desire for a woman as he did for Sasha. Since lovemaking wasn't part of the program for the Komsomol youth movement or for the Czechoslovak Youth Union, neither of them had had much experience and both were a little awkward.

"I give her all my love, that's all I do..." Sasha was amazingly passionate. Out of the blue, Jozef thought of that old soldier Brblos, who on the train had warned the team to be careful around Ukrainian women, that they were intense and desirable, but for them sex was the first step in a more serious relationship. Sasha was his first woman, as he was her first man. Up to now she had just kissed a few boys who were chasing her and wouldn't give her peace. They were all rough and insensitive, and usually drunk and vulgar. Not that she didn't want to make love, quite the contrary; she just hadn't met anyone who she felt respected her. She wasn't asking for love, but she did expect respect and tenderness from a partner. She had spent the entire evening talking to Jozef, and his attractiveness grew stronger for her as time went by. When a strange unknown warm feeling started to possess her body, she couldn't hold back. And Jozef was experiencing the same feelings. When they were dancing to that slow number he pressed her against him and she couldn't ignore his excitement. She looked into his eyes, they both were sweating, and she pressed back.

When they got into her room a wave of pent-up passion swept over the dam and nobody and nothing could hold it back. Even though Jozef had a quick temper, he was gentle with her, lightly rubbing her breasts while she ran her nails softly up and down his spine. The circular movement of her hips was driving him to distraction. Sasha caught herself thinking that here she was naked in front of an unknown foreigner, and she didn't care at all. Their lovemaking was so natural, so spontaneous and mutual it was as if they'd been lovers for years.

Since neither Sasha nor Jozef had ever really been in love before, this torrent of emotion swept them away. Both of them felt that what was happening between them was something more than simple physical love. If this was true love, it was wonderful.

When they went back into the hall an hour later they were met with noise, song and toasts to brotherhood. It seemed that their absence had not been noticed. They danced together for an hour non-stop. They wouldn't and couldn't keep their emotions down. As dawn was approaching, Balaz whispered something to Sasha and they again made their way back to her room. They made love into the morning, not worrying about interruptions since Sasha had explained that her roommates had gone home for the weekend. When he asked what she was studying, she just smiled.

"I'm not a student, I'm a secretary in the military administration service. I come from a village called Kolodne in the Irshava region. I couldn't find my own place in Kiev so I'm living here illegally, with some friends. There's lots of us doing just the same, and as long as we slip the porters a bottle of Moscow vodka from time to time they turn a blind eye."

He leaned over and gave her a soft kiss.

"Do you love me?" she asked.

"I think so... yes... I don't think so, I know so... definitely... Yes, I love you."

CHAPTER
FOUR

NEUWIED 1968

ALTHOUGH it was school holidays, Thomas Ankermann planned to catch the early morning bus from Neuwied to Bonn, where he was a student in the first year of political science at the Arts and Science Faculty of the Friedrich Wilhelm University.

"It's going to be another hot day," his father commented as he sipped his steaming coffee. "Karl called you yesterday. He was asking if you're coming to a meeting of the Committee Against the War in Vietnam or something." Thomas said nothing. "Don't waste your time with such nonsense; let the Americans take care of their own problems."

"If the Americans had shouted at you lot in 1938 after Munich and Kristallnacht, things could be a lot different today. So now we go to scream at the Americans," said Thomas forcefully.

"My God, always the same thing with you. Do you imagine it's pleasant to hear criticism from your own son?" He drank his coffee discontentedly.

"What else do you deserve?"

"Come on, don't start that again..."

"If you at least had the guts to admit it - you all pretend that none of you was ever a Nazi. In the GDR they're at least trying to deal with their former Nazis."

"Don't tell me about the East! If things were really as great there as you claim, do you think I would have left?! And you're also from the GDR. If it seems so wonderful to you over there, be my guest. Go back there. Ulbricht will lay out the welcome mat!" said his father, losing his temper.

"I'm not saying they're perfect, but at least they're making an effort. And here? Two students were expelled from the university for acting honourably."

"Breaking into the rector's office and writing under the name of the Federal President 'constructor of concentration camp' is according to you acting honourably? They were right to expel them. Who deserves respect if not our President? You young people are always going on about honour and respect. How can you expect to encourage respect for values when you applaud the actions of two hooligans who insult the President?"

"And the twenty professors from our university who signed a petition calling on Mr. Lübke to be a man about the whole affair are hooligans too?" Thomas retorted in a raised voice.

"There is no affair, they just made it up in Stern magazine on the basis of information from East German communists, many of whom were in the NSDAP by the way, and are now rewriting history so they look more Catholic than the Pope." His father angrily lit a cigarette. Thomas waved away the smoke with a theatrical gesture.

"I'm not interested in Nazis from the East, but those in the West. Stern is a respected weekly which doesn't print unconfirmed facts. If our best-known graphologists verify that the President's signatures on the blueprints for the concentration camps are genuine, he should act like a man and resign."

"He was only doing what he was told. Hitler locked him up for twenty months and he couldn't get work when he came out. He was glad when Schlepp's office offered him a job. He had no way of knowing the office was working directly for Speer and told to design structures that they later changed into... housing for forced labour conscripts..."

"Hitler sent him to jail for corruption!"

"Stop it, you idiot!!!" his father roared. "You're so biased that you even use Hitler in your arguments! Do you actually believe that those who were condemned and even hanged were being punished for real crimes? It was all made up. And you, aren't you ashamed to take the side of those hooligans?!" His father placed a hand over his heart.

"They weren't housing for workers, they were concentration camps. Nobody is blaming him for doing it if he had no choice. We're blaming him for not stepping down now it's come out."

"You know nothing about life. You're studying politics and you don't know shit about it!"

"The deNazification process is being held back only here. In the GDR they are uncompromising."

"Uncompromising, that's a laugh. All the Nazis now belong to the Communist party!"

"The Communists are conducting an experiment. At least they're trying to achieve something."

"Dear God, you even defend that son of a bitch with the goat's beard who built the Berlin Wall? Now you've really gone over the top!"

"I don't know if things are so bad in the GDR when someone like Wolfgang Kieling went to live there. West Germany's most popular actor wouldn't leave just on a whim. And what about Bertolt Brecht? A world-famous playwright just covering up for the Communists?" Thomas led the debate further.

"That ridiculous comrade of yours, Paul Newman, is just a poser - if not something worse. Maybe he was a Stasi agent, and they forced him to go and live there."

"When you run out of arguments, anybody who says something nice about the GDR is suddenly a Stasi agent. Kieling went over to East Germany after his visit to the United States where, with his own eyes, he saw how they treat the Vietnamese and their own blacks. And our government supports them!"

"Our government can be glad that it is where it is. Twenty years after losing a war for which we are still paying reparations, no state is going to criticize its patron - quite apart from the fact that the Germans are hardly in a position to criticize someone else's war."

"We tolerate a Nazi president, the court awards his wife a painting by Lucas Cranach stolen by Göring from the Cologne Museum! Twenty-three years after the war! Jesus! Heydrich's widow gets a pension of 3,500 marks as a war widow and, instead of imprisonment, twelve thousand concentration camp supervisors get special pensions. It's enough to make you sick!" Thomas shook his head in disbelief.

"I suffered through the Eastern Front," Mr. Ankermann said quietly, and Thomas, somewhat ashamed, said nothing.

"What do you know about this Dubcek fellow?" His father changed the theme with relief.

"He's a wonderful man. He has the whole nation behind him. Here everyone decries socialism, you see it as one huge concentration camp where people can't travel freely or express their opinions..."

"And can they?"

"Of course they can. If they couldn't, everyone would want out of Czechoslovakia. And not only are they not leaving, they support the Communists."

"Just you wait and see, the Dubcek times won't finish well. You don't have to tell me anything. If by any chance you've forgotten, let me remind you. Your father was one of the first three hundred bricklayers who went on strike during the construction of the fortieth block on Stalin Boulevard in Berlin in June, 1953. We marched to the Ministry of Construction and thousands of people joined us. When Minister Selbmann started his speech, someone threw a rock at him. Do you know who that man was? Me, dear boy, me. I wasn't stoning a Communist bureaucrat, but Fritz, my old mate from the construction crew. We were both in the National Socialist German Workers Party, the NSDAP, up to forty-five. And by 1953 he was already a committed Communist! That night the steelworkers from Hennigsdorf joined us, along with twenty thousand railwaymen, ten thousand people from the AEG, from the cable factories in Oberspree, from the power station in Klingenberg, and many more besides. There were at least one hundred thousand of us on Strausbergerplatz. When someone started chanting 'Down with the Communists,' 'We want a united Germany,' and 'Free elections,' I knew it would be bad. And it was." Thomas' father lit another cigarette.

"Do you want to know who was the greatest disappointment for me? That Brecht of yours. We waited for some word of support from some of the authorities like the desert waits for rain. And Brecht was the one. The same day the Russian tanks scattered us, he wrote a letter to Ulbricht I'll never forget. He approved of the action of the Soviet and German Communists against us and called on other intellectuals to support the policy of the Socialist Unity Party, the SED. As a reward for that, he had his own theatre within the year. They gave the famous Theater am Schiffbauerdamm building to that scab."

He then continued in a quieter voice: "Everyone's a hero until they set the tanks on him. That was the second time I'd faced Russian tanks. The first was at Kursk. We messed up that war, but to punish us like that, that was too much... And then on June 16 at Strausbergerplatz they did it to me again. Some of us stayed on there. The night passed without incident and the next day I took you and your mother to your uncle's here in Neuwied. You were five years old at the time. In that year 230 000 people followed us out of the East. And the numbers increased every year..." Thomas Ankermann senior breathed out. "Just don't put too much faith in your Russians; Dubcek won't turn out well."

"If I remember correctly it wasn't the Russians who carried out the carpet bombing of German cities, it was the Americans and the British. And don't worry yourself about Dubcek," Thomas retorted, but without much conviction.

His father stubbed out his cigarette and lovingly tapped his son on the cheek. "Where is it you're going?"

"I don't even know how to say it right. It's written Vyšné Hágy."

"And that's where?"

"In Slovakia. Eastern Czechoslovakia."

"When are you leaving?"

"Tomorrow. We're playing the first game in our group and we have our accommodation reserved from Friday,"

"What date is that?"

"The sixteenth of August."

CHAPTER
FIVE

MOSCOW 1968

KGB Colonel Michail Stepanovich Golubkin stood at attention in the office of the head of the KGB. He knew Andropov well. He had been the Chairman of the Committee for State Security for only a little more than a year, but he had won general respect. He was uncompromising with slackers and cheaters; he did not tolerate snitching or fraud. He fought hard against corruption. He was usually slow to anger, but this was a rare exception. He was nervously rubbing his eyes, his glasses bobbing up and down over his forehead. Golubkin bit his upper lip as Andropov angrily tossed the document the colonel had given him onto his desk.

"This is nonsense. Nobody sends such dramatic reports from Prague as Chervonenko."

"Ambassador Chervonenko is an old and experienced diplomat," said Golubkin in his defence.

"Exactly so. Old experienced diplomats are schooled in exaggeration. They all want to make a career for themselves and so in hope of getting praised they send back reports which are blown out of all proportion. I got the same exaggerations when I was an ambassador in Budapest during the Hungarian uprising. One even maintained that in diplomacy only exaggerated reports are of interest. When he said that, I immediately had him recalled. But that was back in 1956, and *this is 1968. This thing is too serious for such games."* Andropov nervously tapped his fingers on the table top. *Michail Stepanovich, Prague is not Budapest in fifty-six. Then the Hungarians were trying to get rid of socialism. I saw that with my own eyes. The entire leadership was made up of counterrevolutionaries. But this Dubcek is a totally different thing. He is the son of an old Bolshevik, and a true Communist. He comes from a working-class family, and his father was jailed in America because he refused to go to war. When he was five, his family came to the Soviet Union. In March 1925 they went to Kyrgyzstan to help build Communism with the Interhelp cooperative. Then they built automobiles in Gorky. Alexander Dubcek spent thirteen years there and then he fought in the Slovak National Uprising. In short he is a seasoned administrator dedicated to Communism. I refuse to believe that such a person would aim to overthrow Communism, and I don't believe he would like to disappoint his Soviet friends,"* concluded Andropov, shaking his head for good measure.

"*All the reports from our people talk of counterrevolution,"* answered Golubkin with a shrug.

"*What is Dubcek after? Making the economy more efficient, stopping corruption and theft, improving agricultural yields... is this counterrevolution?"* sighed Andropov.

"*Our comrades in the Political Bureau state that there are clear signs of counterrevolution."*

"I imagine we would know about it sooner than the comrades in the Political Bureau. Look here - the latest public opinion survey from Czechoslovakia from July 10. Eight-nine percent of the citizenry state that they wish to live under socialism and only 5 percent support a return to capitalism; 87 percent unequivocally support Dubcek and his leadership, with only 7 percent unsatisfied. So what's Červonenko going on about an overthrow of socialism for?"

"*The reports from Comrade Ambassador are based on information from Comrade Voronin. He is in close contact with Comrades Bilak, Indra and Kolder, plus the chief editor of Rude pravo, Svestka."*

"*Yes, I know,"* Andropov replied sharply. He picked up a photocopy of a letter with Brezhnev's personal comment in the heading: 'For the *eyes of Kosygin, Podgorny and Andropov' and read it silently. "Dear Leonid Ilyich... the political machinery and the instruments of state power are at present to a significant extent paralyzed. Right-wing forces have created the conditions favourable for a counterrevolutionary coup. In this situation we turn to you Soviet Communists... with a request for prompt support and aid, by all the means you have at your disposal. Only with your help can the CSSR pull itself away from the threatening danger of counterrevolution... Consider this letter as an urgent request for intervention and multilateral aid. At the same time we request maximum secrecy for our letter, and for this reason we are writing to you personally and in Russian. Signed Indra, Kolder, Kapek, Svestka, Bilak."Andropov took a deep breath: "Who is this Voronin?"*

"A Counsellor at the Embassy. Our chief resident."

"Do you know anything about him?"

"A classic career agent," said Golubkin, passing Voronin's personnel record to Andropov.

"For such a young man he's made a nice career for himself. He must be very ambitious... The most dangerous spies are ambitious spies," commented Andropov with a bitter smile.

"Comrade Chairman, our reports from Czechoslovakia are confirmed by our sources in the CIA..." Golubkin objected.

"Michail Stepanovich... you know what's going on in the United States. Johnson's over his head in Vietnam. There and everywhere in Europe protests are taking place due to the American activities there. Nothing would suit them more than our potential intervention. Stories about our actions with respect to Czechoslovakia would take the place of reports on American aggression in Vietnam. They need this, and so they're spreading dramatic reports about the Czechoslovak situation."

"Our comrades in Prague are asking for our support..."

"Which comrades? Those who wish to satisfy their personal ambitions and take over the leadership of the Communist Party of Czechoslovakia? They aren't capable of doing it alone, and so they seek our help!" Andropov gave a snort.

"Our French agents also confirm the seriousness of the situation in Prague," the colonel pressed on.

"Ah, the French... they've got their hands full with the student rebellion and also de Gaulle is getting ready to test an atomic bomb in the Pacific in late August. What would deflect world attention better than the Soviet Union intervening in Prague? No, no, Michail Stepanovich... we must be very cautious, very cautious indeed."

The telephone rang. Andropov at first had trouble determining which of the numerous phones on his desk it was. Then he realized that it was the red line. *"Michail Stepanovich, excuse me for a minute, Comrade General Secretary is calling."* Colonel Golubkin saluted and promptly retired. The KGB Chairman picked up the phone; Brezhnev was on the line.

"Good day to you, Leonid Ilyich..." Andropov's initially jovial tone suddenly changed. Brezhnev's shouting was unintelligible: clearly he was not satisfied with the analyses of the secret services. *"Leonid Ilyich, our sources from Washington report that the CIA has no hand in events in Czechoslovakia. I am afraid that our people in Prague are under the influence of their own wishes. The basis of an information service is not to get carried away by their desires and emotions."*

Then Brezhnev lost his temper: *"Yuri Vladimirovich... I'm surprised to be hearing this from someone who was a witness to the events in Hungary. There too Nagy pretended to be a socialist. And look how that finished up! I just don't understand your attitude. I hope you don't sympathize with the Czechoslovak counterrevolution, or want to be held responsible for the return of capitalism to Czechoslovakia? Just look at the weak position of socialism in Romania and the GDR, not to speak of Yugoslavia. We have to be in Czechoslovakia! Do you understand me, Yuri Vladimirovich?! We have to be - and we're not going there just to replace the head of the television!"*

Brezhnev dropped his voice, as if he was aware that he had disclosed something. Andropov tactfully covered up Brezhnev's slip of the tongue. Nonetheless it was clear to him that the top people in the Political Bureau had already decided to invade Czechoslovakia and that Brezhnev needed information from him that would serve as a pretext. In spite of that he tried to use reason.

"Comrade General Secretary," he said in an official tone of voice, "all the information from Czechoslovakia shows that a decisive majority of the population wish to continue with socialism. A decisive majority."

"We know what a decisive majority is. We know what the people of Czechoslovakia want. The Comrades in the Political Bureau are unanimously convinced that in Czechoslovakia the bases of socialism are under threat. Hundreds of thousands of Soviet soldiers did not lay down their lives to liberate the country just for it to fall into the hands of the imperialists!" By now Brezhnev was shouting. "Do I have to tell you, the head of the secret services, what is being prepared for the XIV Congress of the Czechoslovak Communist Party? They're going to sideline all the comrades – Kolder, Indra, Svestka, Piller, Rigo, Kapka – who are sympathetic to us! Comrade Andropov, I'm asking you, please, to furnish for us information in the sense I told you to. Tomorrow we're leaving for discussions with the Czechoslovak comrades. I need proof! Do you understand?" After a moment of silence Brezhnev added curtly: "If we lose Czechoslovakia, I'll step down from the post of Party General Secretary. I don't know who'd replace me, but the Committee for State Security will be the first to have their man in place!"

"I understand, Comrade General Secretary... I understand... All the best... Honour!" Andropov put down the receiver. It was clear that the Soviet incursion into Czechoslovakia was on the cards. Although the head of the secret services was well informed, he was unaware that Minister of Defence Andrej Grechko, after gaining the approval of Brezhnev and Suslov, had been secretly preparing plans for a military operation in Czechoslovakia since April.

He sat back in his favourite winged armchair. He was still deeply convinced not only that an invasion was unnecessary, but also that it would tarnish the good name of the Soviet Union that they had managed to build up since Stalin's death. For a time he mulled over handing in his resignation. Perhaps by doing so he would strike a spark and the generals and highest representatives of the military/industrial complex, with the resignation of the highest member of the secret service, would indeed start to think things over. In the end he banished the thought of resignation from his mind. He was unwilling to risk Brezhnev recalling *him from the key post of head of the secret service. Although he drank only rarely, he poured himself a glass of vodka and flushed his personal reservations down his throat.*

CHAPTER
SIX

PRAGUE 1968

ON Saturday, August 17, a meeting of the leaders of the Communist Party of Czechoslovakia with journalists was held at Hrzansky Palace in Prague. Its purpose was to discuss a joint strategy prior to the upcoming Fourteenth Communist Party Congress. The meeting was of the highest importance since it was well known that Moscow closely monitored the media in Prague and Bratislava. Those present included Government Chairman Oldrich Cernik, Head of Parliament Josef Smrkovsky, and other top officials. The only one missing was Alexander Dubcek. The politicians handled the questions from the curious journalists evasively. Some said he was to accompanying the Romanian President Nicolae Ceausescu, who was ending an official visit to Czechoslovakia, to the airport. This was in fact the second of Dubcek's 'provocations', as Brezhnev referred to this visit, the first being an invitation to the Yugoslav President Josip Broz Tito two weeks earlier. Both of these leaders were given ceremonial welcomes in Prague. They were the only East Bloc leaders to publically support Dubcek's reforms and to reject any kind of outside intervention into Czechoslovak affairs.

In the face of the politicians' reluctance to speak, one of the journalists triumphantly called out: "Dubcek right now is in Komarno; the head of the Hungarian Communists, Kadar, called him urgently." Hearing this, the press looked questioningly at the assembled politicians.

They remained silent. It was clear to everyone that such a meeting could not take place without Moscow knowing about it. Frantisek Kriegel finally confirmed the gloomy speculation: "The sword of Damocles is hanging over us by such a slender thread that it is unimaginable." This was followed by a long silence until one of the journalists concluded, "So they are giving us an ultimatum." Again there was silence.

At that time none of those present at the press conference, nor Dubcek and Kadar in Komarno, could know that the Soviet Union Communist Party Central Committee, meeting at that very moment in Moscow, had unilaterally approved a motion by Leonid Ilyich Brezhnev for the invasion of Czechoslovakia.

CHAPTER
SEVEN

KIEV 1968

SASHA Grycenko stood in her uniform before Major Kozuchin. "Alexandra Josifovna, take the supervisor's stamp, the wax, and the keys to the desk, the safe and your office. At two p.m. you are to be at the Regional Military Administration headquarters. Bring with you only the most essential hygiene supplies. Are you a private?" asked Major Kozuchin of the eighth section of the Kiev military administration.

"No, I am a civil employee."

"Why don't you sit down?" asked Kozuchin, offering a chair. Sasha sat down and gave him a questioning look. "You're single..." He tried to adopt a light tone.

"Yes, I am."

Kozuchin read something from his papers and went on: "Your father was in the army of Ludvík Svoboda..."

"Yes. He participated in the liberation of Czechoslovakia."

"As a soldier of the Soviet army?"

"As a soldier of the Czechoslovak army. His parents lived in the village of Kolodne in the Irsava district. When the village became part of Hungary in 1939, my father went away to Soyuz. There he joined Svoboda's paratroopers as a Czechoslovak citizen in March of 1942 in Buzuluk."

"And you are fluent in..." Kozuchin smiled.

"I'm in fact a Slovak."

"Aha... Well, you're going, so to speak, to find out how your father felt when he liberated Czechoslovakia..."

"Sorry?"

For a long second he studied Sasha. "You have been seconded as administrative support to the operations group of the air force of the Prikarpatsky military circuit, which is part of the Soviet contingent that together with the armies of four member states of the Warsaw Pact is going to Czechoslovakia to help our Czech and Slovak brothers in the struggle against counterrevolution. I needn't emphasize that these orders are strictly confidential..." Kozuchin lit a Mahorka cigarette and puffed on it at length. "It is only a temporary action and there will not be many women involved. You understand of course that we don't want to send married comrades..." Kozuchin said, almost apologetically.

"But I am ready, Comrade Major."

Kozuchin was mildly surprised. From others he would have expected unconditional obedience, but he was a little hesitant about Alexandra Grycenko. She was a friend of his daughter's but apart from that he didn't know much about her. She was a willful girl, always ready to state her opinion in a loud and clear voice. Sometimes she had some problems at the command headquarters. She had some sort of conflict with Lieutenant Vasilyev, who forbade her to read the poetry of Vissotski at Komsomol meetings. She was an avowed admirer of Mayakovsky, Ajtmatov, Dumbadze, Achmatova, Yesenin and Yevtushenko. In her office she kept a copy of Solzhenitsyn's 'A Day in the Life of Ivan Denisovich'. Although it wasn't banned as such, it was not the kind of book her superiors liked to see - but as she wasn't a member of the Party, they let it be. Kozuchin liked her spirit, but was at the same time afraid she would infect his daughter Tatiana with her opinions. He had heard that the inhabitants of Uzhgorod could catch Czechoslovak radio despite the bafflers set up along the borders, and the blocking of radio signals from an allied country was not something easily accepted by Russian citizens. Sasha herself sometimes wondered if this counterrevolution in Czechoslovakia was truly as it was depicted in the Soviet press. Therefore it was a great relief to Kozuchin when Alexandra accepted the order to go to Czechoslovakia without protest.

"Where will the air force staff be settled?"

"They'll tell you that at the military administration. The town is called Sliac, and it has an airport. That's all I can tell you."

"I'll be glad to help the Czechoslovak people in their struggle against counterrevolution."

"Comrade Grycenko, I'm glad you understand our international obligations."

Sasha went back to the hostel. At the porter's desk the janitor excitedly waved a package for her from Bratislava. She looked at the stamp, and found the passage from Slovakia to Kiev had taken two weeks. Once in her room she pressed it to her breast then opened it with trembling hands. The letter was rather crumpled and Sasha smiled to think that someone other than the sender and the receiver had been reading it. As an employee of the Regional Military Administration, she understood that in these difficult times it was necessary to inspect mail coming out of Czechoslovakia.

"Dearest Sasha, I'm sending you the glasses I promised and only hope they're all right. I chose the prescription exactly according to your specifications. I hope they suit you and make your exquisite turquoise eyes even more striking - but not so much so that other people will pay too much attention to them. I don't know what happened to me, but I've been completely different since I got home from Kiev. You really surprised me with your knowledge of Slovakia, our literature and our history. I have taken the liberty of sending you the latest edition of Sladkovich's 'Marina'. Its first verses should read like this:

'I sing of a thirst for beauty, besotted with loveliness... but the centre, the element, heaven, the unity of beauty is, for me, my Sasha'

Forgive me my directness, but I have fallen so deeply in love with you. I hope we will meet again soon."

Sasha pressed the letter to her lips and smiled: 'Maybe we'll see each other sooner than you think...'

CHAPTER
EIGHT

WASHINGTON (WHITE HOUSE) 20.8.1968

IT was a warm August afternoon, 5 p.m. Washington time. The President of the USA Lyndon Johnson was drinking his favourite Cutty Sark scotch whiskey and watching the West Conference basketball game between his team, the newcomers San Diego Rockets, and the favourites, the Los Angeles Lakers. The game was especially dramatic, with the boys from San Diego slightly ahead at half-time, and so the President was in a good mood. He was a little irritated that the Soviet Ambassador had arranged to come by at exactly this time, but the obligations of state had to take precedence over the personal interests of a Texas basketball fan.

The Secretary showed Dobrynin into the Oval Office, with which he had already become familiar in his six years as Soviet Union Ambassador to the USA. Smiling widely, the President came forward to greet him. Then the President's advisors exchanged greetings with the Ambassador. In San Diego the second half has already begun, and Dobrynin noticed as Johnson, against all protocol, stole nervous glances at the television screen. He was aware of the President's weakness for basketball and for cigarettes, but all the same it seemed to him that the President was smoking too much.

"Sorry I'm a little nervous, but our guys have a chance to win against the Lakers. It looks like the Lakers are going to win the West

Conference this year, but we're making it a little harder for them. Still, work is work," the President concluded as, with a sigh, he switched off the set. *"I don't need to introduce you to my advisers— Walt Rostow, head of the National Security Council, and my personal assistant Jack Valetti."*

Dobrynin was unaware that the possible Soviet invasion of Czechoslovakia had not even been discussed at the working lunch the President had shared with his security and foreign policy advisors that day. The Americans placed little importance on this eventuality; their foreign policy was centered on the war in Vietnam and the tense situation in the Middle East just one year after the Six Day War. They had also spent some time on preparations for the upcoming talks with the Soviets on SALT strategic arms reductions.

When the Soviet ambassador arrived in the President's office it was eleven p.m. Central European time, Aug. 20, 1968. He was acting in strict conformity with the instructions and timeline set by Moscow for informing the President of their Czechoslovakia "action". It was meant to coincide precisely with the entry of the first Soviet tank into Prague. Their plans also counted on the enthusiastic welcome of the Czechoslovak population and, hopefully, the speedy formation of a workers and farmers government under Alois Indra.

After observing the usual diplomatic niceties and conveying hearty greetings from the highest Soviet representatives, Dobrynin presented the President a diplomatic note.

"Thank you for the information, Excellency," President Johnson *responded politely after having scanned the message. He had been informed by the Chairman of the Presidium of the Supreme Soviet USSR, Nikolaj Podgorny that the troops of the Warsaw Pact, in the night of August 20-21, 1968, had undertaken a military action for the defence of socialism in Czechoslovakia.*

The President offered the Ambassador a cigarette, which he accepted politely. "Jack, I hope you have noted down everything Mr. Ambassador has told us," he continued, turning to Valetti. *The assistant nodded, his hands shaking slightly.*

The President stood a moment in thought, then looked over at Rostow and once again at the floor. Dobrynin, frowning, awaited a sharp reaction from Johnson; he had been authorized by the Centre to use the Soviet Union's unofficial standpoint, a counter-argument attacking the USA's involvement in Vietnam, in defence against the President's criticism. But still he had been instructed to be circumspect, forbearance before provocation, unless the President really went too far.

Johnson thoughtfully nibbled at some crackers, while Dobrynin spent his time following the sideward movements of the President's extra-large ears.

"Is there any danger of an attack against Romania?" he asked finally.

"No."

"The events in Czechoslovakia should not be allowed to block the arms reductions negotiations. This is a priority of our foreign policy, and I believe the world will understand..." He nodded his head decisively. "Tomorrow morning I'll discuss your information with Dean Rusk and my advisors. We'll give you our answer then." He drank down his whiskey, and Jack poured him another. He noticed that Dobrynin's glass too was empty, and poured the Ambassador a second drink.

The President lit another cigarette, exhaled, and smiled. "Tomorrow morning I intend to announce in public my plan to visit the Soviet Union. I've invited a few friends to breakfast so I could share the good news with them. I would be glad, Excellency, if I could have your government's standpoint on my visit before announcing it publicly. I believe that this visit is extremely important for both our countries. Let's drink to the firming of relations between our two large and powerful countries." Dobrynin's eyes nearly fell out of their sockets. He simply didn't understand. A whole range of the best Soviet-American relations specialists back in Moscow had worked hard on the catalogue of arguments he was holding in his pocket. They wouldn't be necessary. The President drank a second glass in his honour. Dobrynin did not miss the surprise on the faces of Rostow and Valetti., felt their disappointment in the President's reaction. He was looking forward to the congratula-

tory cipher from his "superiors" for his strong defence of the "action". And for doing nothing!

"Of course sir, I shall do all I can to ensure that my country's response to your proposal is on your desk tomorrow at nine. Even now I can say almost with certainty that the reaction will be positive," he reassured the President. Then the President started to tell some amusing anecdotes from Texas. Dobrynin drank down his whiskey, and this time the President himself refilled his glass. Johnson clearly didn't intend to let anything spoil his good mood. Even though he was aware that the Soviet invasion would threaten the arms control treaty, he was just about ready to hug Dobrynin, whose diplomatic thinking had led him to the same conclusion. He was one of the stalwarts of Soviet diplomacy, a disciplined Foreign Service soldier who would never state his own opinion, even if he had one. 'And now those idiots in the Kremlin have played right into their old enemy's hand,' he thought as he looked on Johnson's satisfaction. He smiled ruefully as he thought back to hearing the politburo's definitive decision to go ahead with the invasion, when a kind of down-to-earth good sense had prompted him to consider resigning. Now he could look forward to the congratulations he would receive when he sent off his dramatic message and described how he had defended the Czechoslovakia "action".

"I remember fondly my meeting with your honourable Premier Kosygin in Glassboro not long ago. Please send him my heartfelt greetings..." Johnson continued. Rostow, looking more and more downhearted, was struggling not to interrupt his President. When he was seeing the Soviet Ambassador to the door Johnson repeated his request for a speedy response from Moscow, and again said how much he was looking forward to his visit. As soon as his visitor was out of the office, Johnson immediately switched the television back on. The basketball was just coming to an end, and the Lakers had the game sewn up. Nonetheless he was smiling as he poured drinks for both his advisors. "As of tomorrow, the invasion of Czechoslovakia will replace Vietnam on the front pages of the world's newspapers! Gentlemen, to your health!"

After returning to the Soviet embassy Dobrynin immediately wrote a cipher in which he reported on his reception with the President and *recommended a positive reception to his idea of a visit. He got the response within the hour. He called his secretary and asked him to arrange a call to the Secretary of State, Dean Rusk. While waiting for the connection he poured himself a celebratory glass of pure Moskovska vodka – Moscow had never dreamed that President Johnson's reaction would be so palatable. His only source of irritation was the fact that his secretary still hadn't connected him with Rusk's office, and a few moments later he understood why. The secretary arrived in person to inform him: "Comrade Ambassador, you are to report immediately to the office of the Secretary of State. We have just been handed a note signed by Secretary Rusk himself." Dobrynin understood that the professionals in the ministry had taken a different reaction from the President. After all, Johnson was a simple farmer from Texas, and in America foreign policy was traditionally the domain of Congress. He only hoped that they had not pushed Rusk to support their strong line, and for safety's sake he brought along with him the unofficial standpoint he had not needed with Johnson.*

It was late that night when Dean Rusk received the Ambassador in his office. He announced to Dobrynin that he had just returned from the White House with the authorization to inform him of the position of the government of the United States. In a measured voice Rusk read out a declaration which stated that the United States was unaware of any invitation by the official representatives of Czechoslovakia to the troops of the Warsaw Pact. At its conclusion he recommended to the Ambassador that both parties should consider the matter carefully before publicly announcing a visit by the USA President to the USSR. It was clear to Dobrynin that the visit would be postponed.

A few days later Lyndon Baines Johnson met with the Chiefs of Staff of the American military. They resolved that in no case would force be used against the USSR. In addition, Johnson decreed that there would be no public condemnation of the invasion. Half-jokingly the President concluded: "Let's hope that Moscow appreciates that we here in the United States are not aggressors."

CHAPTER
NINE

BRATISLAVA 1968

His tiny student's room had been infiltrated by a mosquito which, in conjunction with the summer heat, ensured that Balaz would not get much sleep that night. Just before dawn it seemed that he would finally succeed in sleeping soundly, but his alarm clock put an end to that. Still groggy, he dressed himself in overalls still stiff with cement. Although it was only four in the morning, the thermometer showed ten degrees. He was working on the construction of tram lines in the new Bratislava suburb, Strkovec. They were loading Rohozník cement into the huge mixers stationed next to the quarry. A two-lane concrete road to Vrakuna was also being built alongside the new tracks.

Balaz lived on the corner of Belopotockeho and Lehotskeho streets, not far from the main railway station. Every day he travelled by the first local train as far as Trnava, where Feri the driver waited at the station to take him out to Rohozník. Today he was in a great mood since he and Feri had agreed to knock off early in order to attend the Central Europe Cup football match between Spartak Trnava and Red Star Belgrade. He never ate breakfast, but brought with him the two slices of duck fat bread with onion and pepper his mother lovingly prepared. He had a short-cut to the station across Malinovsky street, around the garden restaurant, then up the steps in front of the railway tunnel in time for the four-thirty local. Then, listening to the transistor radio he was so proud of, he would munch on his sandwiches on the wooden benches of the old-timer train.

As usual he was hurrying away from his home when he was suddenly surprised by a strange noise. As a student in the first year at the Economics University he was assigned to the tank brigade for his compulsory military training. He would have recognized the sound of tank tracks ploughing over a hard surface anywhere, anytime. The closer he got to Malinovsky Street the louder was that sound, changing from a noise to a roar.

Tanks, some T-52s and a few old T-34s, were rolling up the main street. Some turned off at Zilinska Street, with the rest continuing up to the train station. He realized that the first contingent had to be heading for Firsnal Square, the site of military parades on Victory Day. On those occasions three tank squadrons and a number of armoured troop carriers rumbled through the streets of the city, but now there seemed to be far too many tanks for a simple parade. And for what parade? The date was not May 9, but August 21. Maybe they were shooting yet another war movie. His train would be leaving in seven minutes, so he'd really have to get a move on. More tanks were standing in front of the railway station. He noticed then for the first time that these tanks did not sport the Czechoslovak emblem, but instead some strange design of white stripes running from the front centre of the body up to the hatch and on to the back, and also sideways over the hatch. He had five minutes before his train left, but noticed that there were very few people inside the vestibule. Then he saw the soldiers blocking the entry with their machine guns at the ready. His thoughts were still concentrated on Feri - if he missed the train he would leave for Rohozník without him, and Jozef would be out a day's salary.

"Let me pass, I have to catch the train to Trnava." The soldiers, cigarettes in their mouths, stared steadily past him. He tried Russian: "Slušajte... Listen, I have to catch my train to Trnava." He automatically raised his voice when speaking in Russian.

"There is no train, nothing is running. Go home. Idi domoj!"

"But... Feri will be waiting for me."

"Idi domoj!!!" a soldier commanded him angrily. Balaz turned and paced back into the vestibule. He turned on his precious transistor radio: 'Warsaw Pact troops during the night from August 20-21 occupied the Czechoslovak Republic. We ask our citizens to remain calm. We will shortly be bringing you the statements of the supreme Party and State representatives..." Mourning music came out of the radio. Balaz ran down the steps and had the feeling that this was all a bad dream. He couldn't believe that the Soviet Union would do such a thing! He hoped that it was all some big misunderstanding which would be cleared up later that day. At that time he was as yet unaware that at eleven p.m. August 20, an invasion with the code name Operation Danube had been launched.

The Czechoslovak Radio interrupted the sad music and the voice of the announcer continued: 'We now bring you a declaration by the Czechoslovak Communist Party Central Committee executive: Yesterday, August 20, 1968, at about eleven p.m., the armies of the Soviet Union, the Polish Republic, the Hungarian People's Republic, the German Democratic Republic and the Bulgarian People's Republic crossed the state border of the Czechoslovak Socialist Republic'.

He sat down on the steps, beside two weeping women. One of them was comforting her friend: "Don't cry, on the radio they said the Americans are coming to our aid". Balaz lit a cigarette and listened to the report on his radio. They announced that the armies of the Warsaw Pact had started the largest military action in Europe since the end of the Second World War: 27 divisions, 300 000 soldiers, 6 000 tanks, 1 000 aircraft, 2 000 heavy weapons and a precisely undetermined number of special missile units, against an enemy which did not exist.

Jozef put out his cigarette and ran back home. At the corner of Zilinska and Malinovsky streets, a Russian tank was just then toppling an electric pole. People were standing around the tank and shaking their fists at the Russian soldiers. He turned on his radio again to hear the announcer read a Call to the Citizens of the Czechoslovak Socialist Republic in which Dubcek, Svoboda, Smrkovsky, Cerník, Kriegel and the other leading state representatives called on the populace to maintain their calm and dignity. "We call on all the inhabitants of our republic to remain calm and not to resist the armed forces which are coming in."

At that moment sweat broke out on his forehead. A Russian soldier, his machine gun aimed straight at him, was blocking his path.

CHAPTER
TEN

PRAGUE 1968

»**T**HIS *has taken place without the knowledge of the President of the Republic, the Chairman of the National Assembly, the Head of Government or the First Secretary of the Central Committee of the Communist Party of Czechoslovakia. The Party Central Committee has been meeting to discuss preparations for the XIV Party Congress. They call on all citizens of the Republic to remain calm and not to resist the armed forces which are at present coming into our country. Accordingly our army, security forces and people's militia have not been given orders to defend our homeland.*

"The leadership is of the conviction that this act contravenes all the principles underlying the relationships between socialist countries as well as the basic standards of international law. All the leading representatives of the state, of the CCP and of the National Front shall remain in the positions to which they were elected as the people's representatives and as members of their bodies pursuant to the laws and other statutes valid in the Czechoslovak Socialist Republic.

"The constitutional representatives are calling an urgent meeting of the National Assembly, and the Government of the Republic and the Party executive is convening a plenary meeting of the Communist Party Central Committee to discuss the situation".

Signed: Communist Party Central Committee Executive."

Party Secretary Cestmír Cisar finished reading the declaration proposal in a somber voice. He placed the document down on the desk and took his seat. Silence reigned in the room. Such was the urgency of the session that those present had eaten only sandwiches while the declaration was being prepared by Cisar and Mlynar. The time was half past one in the morning. Just after midnight, the head of the secretariat had entered the office of Alexander Dubcek and informed him that the Minister of Defence was calling Government Chairman Cernik. A feeling of foreboding swept over Dubcek.

"What is so important that the Minister is phoning after midnight?"

"He says it's urgent."

"So go and talk to him, but be quick about it," Dubcek instructed Cernik. In the meantime they continued with the preparation of the materials for the Party Congress, which would be held in three weeks. This was in fact the final session of the Central Committee before the Congress. Cernik returned in a few minutes and everyone looked at him in curiosity. Ashen-faced, he sat down heavily. Probably everyone knew what to expect.

"They're here... Minister Dzur called to say that the Soviets and four other armies have crossed our border. The Ministry of Defence has been occupied."

The silence was deafening.

"So finally they've done it," sighed Dubcek. He felt like he had just died. His thoughts went back to his father and mother, to Kyrgyzstan in the 1930s, where his family had gone to support the fledgling Soviet Union. He thought of the Russian partisans whom he had fought beside during the Slovak National Uprising in 1945, and of his brother Stefan, who had died during the fighting. His whole life was bound up with Communism and with his faith in the Soviet Union.

The members of the executive slowly got over their initial shock and an emotional debate ensued. Dubcek seemed separated from their words, and was in fact wondering where he had made his mistake. He had believed that the Soviet's opposition to his reforms sprang from their different cultural environment and historical experiences. He had categorically dismissed the thought of the armed Soviet invasion the world press had been trumpeting. After all, it was the Soviet Union which had proposed at the U.N. that 1968 be proclaimed the Year of Understanding Among Nations and had condemned the American invasion of Vietnam. This could not be true; it was surely some cruel joke.

"Alex, we have to react. The Soviet Press Agency is spreading to the world the lie that we invited the Soviets in. We don't have a lot of time," someone suggested. So it was all true.

"Prepare a draft declaration," he requested of the secretaries, Císar and Mlynar, and left the room. Next door, he was heartened to see the Central Committee workers at their desks even though it was two in the morning. He came to the end of the long corridor and turned off into a dark alcove. He looked out over the Vltava River, slowly flowing by as it had been doing for hundreds and thousands of years. Then he raised his eyes to the silhouette of the Hradcany Castle. It occurred to him that he should have listened to the advice of his wife and sons at the end of 1967 not to accept the position of Central Committee First Secretary, but he dismissed the thought as irrelevant at present. He opened the window to let in some fresh air and heard excited voices from below. In the area between Hlavkov Bridge and the Central Committee building, people had begun to gather, and he recognized the need to make the Committee declaration public as quickly as possible. He took a deep breath and seemed to inhale the Dubcek family defiance that had been encoded into his DNA over generations. The Dubceks were a mild-mannered lot, but when pressed to the wall they stood their ground. He walked back into the meeting-room with a defiant step.

"Get me Chervonenko on the line." he instructed his secretary. They were both surprised at the vigour in his voice.

"We've been trying. They're not answering his phone at the Soviet Embassy."

"And Voronin?"

"He's not answering either. Comrade Secretary, the President of the Republic is calling." Dubcek lifted the receiver as everyone looked on anxiously. After a moment he put the phone down. "President Svoboda has just been visited by Soviet Ambassador Chervonenko. They *informed him that the armies of five Warsaw Pact countries crossed the borders of our republic at eleven o'clock last night."*

"It's good they told us, otherwise we'd never have noticed," commented Smrkovsky with his typical sarcasm.

'Bunch of gangsters' went through Dubcek's mind. 'The Kremlin has been occupied by brutes ever since Khrushchev was forced out.' "Is the declaration ready?" he asked Císar and Mlynar. Císar started to read it.

"Thank you," Dubcek said simply. "Let's vote on it. Who's in favour?" Smrkovsky, Kriegel, Spacek, Cernik, Piller, Barbirek and Dubcek raised their hands resolutely and looked over at the four other members of the Communist Party executive.

"Comrades, first we should..." Bilak tied to stall.

"The debate was during the drafting of the declaration," Dubcek cut him off. "Now is the time for voting. Who is against the motion?"

Bilak, Kolder, Svestka and Rigo stared straight ahead then slowly raised their hands.

"Thank you. The Central Committee Executive has passed the declaration by a vote of seven to four." He lifted the document and passed it to the secretary. "See to it that the press agency publishes it immediately. Comrades, I thank you and hereby terminate the Executive meeting. Those who wish to remain are welcome to do so; anyone wishing to leave may do so." Those who had opposed the motion quickly left the room. Dubcek and his supporters returned to his office.

"Alex, listen," Smrkovsky said, coming over to him. "This is serious. If they've already occupied the Ministry of Defence we have only minutes to spare. Don't forget your responsibilities"

"I understand what you're saying, but it's precisely those responsibilities that make it necessary to remain here. He looked at the phone, wishing for someone to call to say this was all a stupid misunderstanding. The phone remained silent.

"If they take you, it'll be the end. You're not just the First Secretary, you're a symbol. And hooligans always attack symbols first!"

"Josef, thank you, but I'll wait for them here."

Then someone opened the window and they moved as one to watch the crowds gathered by the Vltava. The words of the Czech and Slovak anthems seemed to be rising from its turbid water 'Where my home is...' and 'Lightning over the Tatras...' When they'd sung the anthems someone started the International, that worldwide workers' anthem, and other voices joined in. Before they could sing it through, this universal workingman's hymn was drowned out by the sound of tank motors.

They had arrived. The time was three thirty a.m., August 21, 1968. A black Volga led a column of tanks and armoured personnel transporters across Hlavkov Bridge towards the Central Committee building. The crowd in their path dispersed, but too slowly for one Soviet soldier. He opened fire with his machine gun and before the eyes of Dubcek, Smrkovsky and the others, the invasion claimed its first victim, a young student. Smrkovsky grabbed the telephone and screamed down the line to stop the killing. Dubcek initially thought he was addressing the Soviet Ambassador, but then realized he was shouting in Czech. Cervonenko didn't speak Czech.

The tanks came to a halt and paratroopers leapt out of the trucks, machine guns in their hands. The singing of the demonstrators seemed long ago. The Party officials moved back from the window and heard the paratroopers' boots resounding in the courtyard and then in the corridors of the building. As Smrkovsky nervously lit a cigarette, the doors flew back and eight paratroopers burst into Dubcek's office. They covered the windows and communicating doors. Dubcek seemed to think this was an armed robbery and instinctively reached for the telephone; this provoked one of the soldiers to aim his weapon at Dubcek before pulling the telephone cord out of the wall. Again the doors burst open, and four high KGB officers, led by a colonel draped with service medals, made their appearance. They were accompanied by a translator Dubcek recognized from a visit by the Supreme Commander of the Warsaw Pact armed forces, Marshal Jakubovsky, just a few weeks back. He quickly checked off a list of the CPC executive members present and translated the colonel's words: "I am taking you under my protection."

'Protection' was a good word. Each of them had an automatic rifle aimed at the back of his head.

CHAPTER
ELEVEN

KOKTEBEL (CRIMEA) 1968

IN the great reading room of the House of Soviet Writers a feast was going on. The night was ringing with song and exuberant chatter. The hostess, Natalia Vasiljevna once again soaked her aching feet in a basin full of cold water. She had a problem with her varicose veins and continually trotting up and down the stairs wasn't helping any. It was her duty to bring up the bacon, pickled fish, kvass, pickled cucumbers, caviar, salmon, potato piroshky and the other delicacies the guests loved to eat.

„Natalia Vasiljevna, Natalia Vasiljevna," Aksjonov called loudly from the upstairs room. "Bring up some more of those Siberian pelmeni. Yevgeny can't get enough of them."

"Yes, Vasilij Pavlovič... I'm on my way." The hostess sighed, but smiled at the same time. Siberian pelmeni were her specialty and Yevgeny Yevtushenko, a native of Siberia, was especially fond of them. She picked up her tray along with a large stoneware bowl and slowly made her way back up the stairs. The salon was full of noise, smoke and the smells of vodka and kvass. 'My God, this is the elite of Soviet writers,' she thought to herself as she laid the bowl on the table. Sitting in the deep armchairs and joking were Yevgeny Yevtushenko, Anatolij Gladilin and Balter. They were spending their holiday here, although it was ironically described as a 'creative stay'. The fourth member of the party was Vasilij Pavlovic Aksjonov, celebrating his thirty-sixth birthday today, the 20th of August. Yevtushenko's wife timidly stuck her head around the door and asked the partygoers to keep it a little quieter since the other guests couldn't sleep. No-one paid her any attention, partly due to the alcohol and also because of the topic under intense discussion. In fact the whole evening's debate revolved around the same subject, Czechoslovakia. The feeling in the air was that something serious was about to happen.

"I'm telling you, the tanks will be there in a few days," Gladilin opined in a cloud of cigarette smoke. "I'm sure of it. All the papers are writing about a counterrevolution and how they've been shooting Communists."

"And you believe them?!" Aksjonov looked at him reprovingly.

"It's all made up. I've been in contact with some friends of mine in Prague, and nothing's going on there!" Yevtushenko resolutely answered the question and enthusiastically stuffed pelmeni into his mouth. "What do you put into these, Natalia Vasiljevna? They're diabolically tasty."

"Apple vinegar, a little pepper and dill," smiled Natalia as she left the room.

"Dill…" Yevtushenko repeated to himself, since she didn't hear him. "I know that the hardliners in the Kremlin are capable of anything, but I still don't believe they'd invade. I don't believe it," he added for emphasis. "I don't believe it…" he said yet again, but this time with perhaps less conviction. He was aware of the fact that since July they'd been calling up reservists from the western part of the Soviet Union in unprecedented numbers.

The morning after the celebration they were all feeling hung over, so Yevtushenko and Aksjonov decided to go out for a beer. "Hair of the dog," Yevgeny smiled as they walked down the street in the direction of the seashore. Their hope was that, despite the early hour, some pub would already be open, or that some street seller would be doling out kvass for holidaying trade unionists.

"Where are you off to, boys?" Seremet, a Ukrainian writer, called out to them. He was holding a transistor radio up to his ear. "Did you hear? Our troops are in Prague!"

"Where in Prague? What do you mean 'our'?" frowned Yevtushenko.

"Our tanks are in Czechoslovakia. We've been feeding them for years, and now this... We should have done it years ago."

Yevtushenko and Aksjonov listened in horror to Seremet's radio.

"Fuck your mother," swore Aksjonov, while for a long moment Yevtushenko remained speechless. Seremet looked at them uncomprehendingly. Vasilij and Yevgeny went into a snack bar where they bought some vodka, leaned against the counter, poured it and drank. It was really hot outside, so they felt the alcohol's effects almost immediately. They drank from pint glasses, as quiet as mice except for the occasional 'Fuck your mother!' from Aksjonov. They poured an entire bottle of spirits down their throats while the tears ran down their cheeks. Two giants of Soviet literature, adult men, crying like babies – not speaking, simply drinking and crying. Their world was collapsing around them, Dubcek's 'socialism with a human face' was over and done, and with it any hope of anything ever changing in this ossified, crooked and corrupt Soviet Union. The other customers in the pub looked on in wonder.

"What are you staring at?!" cried Aksjonov. "Do you know what has happened?" Silence. "Our tanks have invaded Prague!" Silence. No-one met their eyes, and some retreated outside. "You're impotent slaves!" Aksjonov screamed. "Tomorrow they'll be coming to lock you up." His legs gave way beneath him. Yevtushenko grabbed him under the arms and helped him up the street in the direction of the House of Writers. Vasilij raged along the street, turning on passers-by with loud curses. Yevtushenko took him up to his room. Before he collapsed on his bed and fell asleep, he pulled Yevgeny to him and for long minutes held him close. Both men wept and moaned. Yevgeny went to his own room. He managed to tune Prague in on his radio just in time to hear Zikmund's voice: "Yevgeny Yevtushenko, Yevgeny, can you hear me... Yevgeny, help us... say something... say something!" The voice went silent and Yevtushenko turned to his wife.

"I'm going to send the Government a telegram!" he said in determination.

"Yevgeny, you've been drinking... you know what could happen," his wife Gala tried to reason with him.

"I know."

"So go then; if they lock you up, I'll go to jail with you." Yevgeny hugged her and with a resolute step went down into the street and looked towards the blue post office on Lenin Avenue. But first he sat down in the shade of a linden tree which grew over the House of Writers and scribbled some notes on a piece of paper. His hand was trembling. He was aware of the risk he was about to take. Although he was a celebrated poet and the idol of the younger generation, there were few in the Soviet Union who could get away with such disobedience. But he could not act otherwise. He entered the post office, stood at a wicket and said in a too-loud voice: "To Leonid Ilyich Brezhnev, General Secretary of the Soviet Union Communist Party, Moscow-Kremlin, and Alexej Nikolajevich Kosygin, Government Chairman, Moscow-Kremlin!"

"Are you serious?" was the startled reaction of the young lady behind the counter.

"Completely..." Yevtushenko breathed out. "Write this down: Dear Comrade General Secretary, since yesterday evening, when I found out our tanks had entered Czechoslovakia, I have not been able to sleep, and I no longer know how to live. I know only that it is my moral obligation to express to you the feelings that are ruling me. I am deeply convinced that what we are doing in Czechoslovakia is a tragic mistake and a bitter blow to Soviet-Czechoslovak friendship and to the Communist movement worldwide. It lessens our prestige, both in the outside world and here at home. For all progressive forces, for world peace and for humanistic dreams of the brotherhood of man, it is a step backwards. It is also my personal tragedy since I have many friends in Czechoslovakia and if I ever meet them again, I shall be unable to look them in the eye..."

"I cannot accept this..."

"You'll take anything I can pay you for. I will pay for every word I have spoken." He realized what he had just said. Yes, he would pay for every word. He knew that they would not forgive him for this.

"Yevgeny Alexandrovich…" the clerk pleaded with him. "I have a little girl, I live alone, if I lose my job…"

"Have no fear, I will help you… Just keep writing!" He continued his dictation. The woman dropped her shoulders in resignation and wrote on. "It is my conviction that this is a huge gift to all the world's reactionary forces and we are not able to foresee the consequences of this act. I love my country and its people and see myself as the humble bearer of the traditions of Russian literature passed down to me by Pushkin, Tolstoy, Dostoyevsky and Solzhenitsyn. These traditions have taught me that silence sometimes symbolizes shame. I beg you to understand my opinion on this action as the opinion of an honest son of my homeland and of the poet who once wrote the song 'Do the Russians Desire War?' Signed, Yevtushenko."

"Am I really to send this?" the young woman again tried to object. Then he dictated another, shorter letter to the Czechoslovak Embassy in Moscow, apologizing for this act and declaring his solidarity with the people of Czechoslovakia.

"How much will it cost?' he asked, drawing out his wallet.

"I'm afraid it will be quite expensive."

"That I do not doubt!" He smiled at her encouragingly, turned and went out. The clerk hesitated, gained courage and sent off the telegram. Within the hour she was summoned to the office of the director of the post office and her contract was immediately terminated for a gross infringement of work discipline.

CHAPTER
TWELVE

NEUWIED 1968

"I brought you a Slovak specialty," said Thomas, passing a bottle to his father. "Actually it's gin, but for some reason the Slovaks call it borovichka."

"Slovaks?" his father asked Thomas.

"Dubcek is a Slovak."

"I thought Dubcek was Czech, from Prague."

"Dubcek is Slovak, and he's from Bratislava. Bratislava is the capital of Slovakia, the eastern part of Czechoslovakia. The Czechs live in Prague, the Slovaks in Bratislava and in the High Tatras."

"Suddenly you're so well informed," his father commented irritably.

"Can you believe it? The Slovaks like the Germans, the older generation has fond memories of us."

"Us?"

"Us – Germans," Thomas explained.

"I'm glad to hear you consider yourself a German... Why do the older Slovaks remember us fondly?"

"Because of the army and officers in their smart uniforms. I also heard they had it good under Hitler!"

"Are you being ironic again?"

"No, really quite the opposite. This was the first country where I met people who don't hate the Germans." But his father still thought Thomas was being ironic.

"Even in Germany, not everyone hates Germans." Ankermann senior studied the bottle of Slovak gin with interest.

"You wouldn't have believed the atmosphere there. The people truly love Dubcek. It's strange, but no-one wants to bring back capitalism. I spoke to lots of people and all of them were in favour of 'socialism with a human face' as Dubcek calls it. They're holding a public collection of money for a ski-slope in the Tatras," Thomas continued enthusiastically. "Can you believe they're contributing their own money... I met so many great people there... Jozef even taught me one of their songs." And he started to sing the refrain: 'Dance, Dance, Spin Around...'

"Don't put your sweaty clothes on the table, you know your mother doesn't like it," his dad warned Thomas, who was unpacking his stinky, sweaty uniform from the volleyball tournament in the Tatras.

"How's mama doing?" Thomas asked quietly.

"Better, thank God. She'll be coming home from the hospital in two or three days. I thought in all your excitement about the Czech Communists you'd forgotten about her."

"Sorry, but I'm just so impressed by all that I saw there. I would never have believed there are people who show so much support for their politicians. And they're not just Czechs, they're Czechs and Slovaks."

"Your mum is going to need someone to look after her... I don't know how we'll manage it... home help doesn't come cheap," Tomas' father sighed.

"Can you imagine people toasting Lübke or Kiesinger in restaurants just like that? I could scarcely believe my eyes!"

"If we had the money we could get your mother new hip joints so she could maybe walk again. Otherwise her condition will just get worse." He took a worried sip from his coffee cup.

"That damned house painter Bachmann almost killed Dutschke in broad daylight and the police are almost apologizing to him! He's got his flat covered in pictures of Hitler, and Springer's Bild Zeitung paper is making a national hero out of him!"

"Don't start that again – cut it out! You're getting on my nerves! Dutschke is an East Berlin agent put in place by the Stasi," his father reacted with anger.

"You're the ones who are crazy. Out of fear for your daily bread you bow your heads and say thank you for the charity the nouveaux riches toss your way. I'm going to Berlin; there's a big demonstration coming up against the Vietnam war. We're forming a new Communist Party cell at the university. The founding congress will be in Essen. We'll be standing for election and then things will finally move. Actually, you could stand as a candidate," suggested Thomas, excited by the thought.

"I had enough of that during Ulbricht's communism. No more of that for me!"

"We don't want Ulbricht's socialism, but Dubcek's. Without censorship, without exploitation, without envy... This kind of socialism!" Thomas placed some magazines he'd brought from Czechoslovakia on the table. On the title page of one Dubcek was diving from a diving tower while people looked on smiling; another picture showed Dubcek surrounded by an enthusiastic crowd of people.

"That's just propaganda!" His father tossed the magazine back at his son.

"You don't even want to understand!"

"So it's me who doesn't understand?! Geez, you've completely lost your mind. You hold up Communist politicians as an example for us..." He lit another cigarette and turned on the radio. "Now listen carefully, very carefully." He turned up the volume so that the radio commentator was also shouting."

"According to information from the Czechoslovak Press Agency, last night troops from the Soviet Union, the German Democratic Republic, Hungary and Poland moved into Czechoslovakia. The supreme leadership of the Communist Party, the President of the

Czechoslovak Republic and the country's government declared that the armies were not invited and that the occupation is contrary to all the standards of international law..." announced the moderator in a sombre voice.

"So much for your socialism with a human face. Here's your goatbeard Ulbricht! Just keep this day in mind!"

"That can't be true. It must be some kind of joke..." Thomas put his hands up to his head. He went from one station to the next, but they were all saying the same thing. "But I was there just yesterday! Damn! I was there just yesterday! It can't be true, damn it!"

"It's true, Thomas, all too true. While you were travelling home in the train, their tanks were crossing the border... "

Thomas ran to the telephone and dialed a lengthy number. "Hello, hello... good afternoon, do you speak German? This is Thomas Ankermann calling from Germany. I've just got home from your country... I was in the Tatras with my friend Jozef... could I speak to him please? ... Is this Mrs. Balazova ? Jozef's mother? ... Can I speak to him? ... He's not at home? Do you know where he is? ... Why are you crying? Is it true that... Mrs. Balazova ... bitte, weinen Sie nicht... please don't cry... yes... there are tanks underneath your window... yes... Sorry, please excuse me..."

Thomas replaced the receiver. He sat helplessly on his chair and put his head in his hands. Tears began running down his cheeks. For an instant his father was unsure what to do. "Shit," he said and tenderly stroked Thomas's hair.

CHAPTER
THIRTEEN

BRATISLAVA 1968

AVAJ sjuda! Give me that! Give it here," shouted a Soviet soldier, pointing with his automatic.

"What?" Balaz asked fearfully.

"That radio-receiver," came the command.

"My radio?"

"Da, the radio. Give it here." Balaz obeyed and handed over his transistor radio. The soldier put it into his bag with satisfaction. "No cigarettes?" His hands shaking with fear, Balaz took out a pack of cigarettes and offered one to the soldier. He took a cigarette out of the pack and immediately asked "Mogu bolsche?"

"More?" asked Balaz in confusion.

"Da, more. Bolsche." Balaz sighed and the soldier helped himself to three more. Meanwhile two other Soviets stood nearby and watched Balaz and the other people around him with hostility. One of the tanks was standing next to the sidewalk and some of the young inhabitants were trying to convince the Soviet soldiers of the senselessness of their actions. "Spasibo," the soldier said and passed the cigarettes to his comrades. Balaz stared at them as if hypnotized.

"Why have you come here?"

"Why? Why? To help our brothers in the fight against counterrevolution," answered the soldier who had taken his radio, but without much conviction.

"There is no counterrevolution here," an older woman spoke up in Russian. "Do you see any counterrevolutionaries? Apart from Brezhnev and Kosygin!"

"I don't know, I don't care. I'm just a soldier, I just follow orders!" the soldier shrugged his shoulders.

"You've destroyed everything that your fathers did for us in forty-five when you liberated Czechoslovakia is destroyed..." the occupied Slovaks berated their occupiers in broken Russian.

"We didn't decide anything; the bosses in the Kremlin decided for us... Sorry for that..." Now the soldier was beginning to feel embarrassed. Then an officer stuck his head up out of the tank. When he saw that his men were apologizing to the natives for invading them, he snapped at them in a surly tone. The soldiers quickly climbed onto the tank.

Balaz made his way home, but stopped on the corner of Zilinska and Belopotockeho streets. A soldier holding red flags was standing at the intersection indicating the direction which would take the tanks to Gottwald Square. Their steel tracks were churning up the ground on which he had grown up, played football and dreamed about his future. They were also grinding up his spirit, hope and beliefs; his respect for the wisdom of the nation of Tolstoy was being crushed and killed. Its killers were these soldiers with their dirty uncomprehending faces – fatigued, lethargic, in a way more degraded than he himself was. These unfree conscripts were taking away his freedom.

He was suddenly reminded of the cat that lived and hunted mice in the courtyard of his apartment building. Then it left them in front of the doorway. Sometimes the cat was in a playful mood and play with the mice, which were already half-dead from shock. They would try to escape but had no chance against the greater feline strength. Balaz once stood and watched this uneven contest with the sentiment of a god. With one gesture he could chase the cat away, but some kind of animal instinct held him back. When the mouse ceased to struggle, the cat lost interest, but when Jozef poked it with a stick it crawled away into its mouse hole. It was still alive, but would never be the same free and joyous mouse it had once been. It would live out its life in fear and hatred towards cats.

The gods In the Kremlin had set their cat against Balaz and his fifteen million mousy friends. The difference was that Balaz did not want to hate them.

His father was sitting smoking at the kitchen table. With red eyes his mother was preparing scrambled eggs. His sister Gita was away on holiday in Kysuce.

"Stop that crying!" complained the husband. "Gitka is all right, the Russians just passed through Kysuce. They just asked Granny for some water and continued south to Cadca." He stubbed out his cigarette and immediately lit another, noticing that the pack was almost empty. He turned to Jozef: "Do you have any cigarettes?"

"One of the Russian soldiers took them."

"You'll have to go to Kis the tobacconist before they find them too... This won't turn out well," said his father, stroking his unshaven chin. "For sure this will turn out bad..." he repeated.

"Your friend from Germany phoned about an hour ago. He wanted to find out what's going on..." Jozef's mother choked back her tears. "He asked you to phone him when you came home."

Jozef went to the phone and tried to get an open line, but without success. The party line they shared with two of their neighbours was constantly engaged.

"Please go out to the shop and the market, buy anything you find," asked his mother, giving Jozef her purse and two shopping bags. "You could go too, instead of sitting her smoking and moaning," she told her husband. "When the Russians last came here in forty-five, they cleaned the stores right out."

"I'm going to work."

"You'd better phone first to see if anyone's there."

"I'll go there; anyway, we can't get through on the phone." His father stood up and put the egg sandwiches into his shabby case.

"Listen to me," he told his son, "Don't even think about going into the town and getting into trouble with those soldiers!" Jozef said nothing. "Joe, promise me you won't. On the radio they reported they've already shot some poor student."

"It doesn't matter if I go down into the town or not; the Russians are everywhere. The whole of Zilinská and Malinovskeho is full of tanks. I'll try Vanek's grocery store". He picked up the bags and headed for the door.

Out of nowhere his father came over and pulled Jozef to him. "I know you. Please, don't do anything silly. You don't know what Russians are like when they've had too much to drink." Jozef nodded, slapped his dad on the back and went out.

Kis's tobacco shop was closed and the grating drawn. Luckily, Vanek's was still open, with a long line of people in front of the doors. It was obvious that he would get nothing there, so he ran back to the market on Zilinska. Russian soldiers were trying to remove from the roadway an electric pole knocked over by one of their tanks, which was blocking their way to Firsnal Square and down into the town. Although the street was empty, the locals were keeping an eye on the Russians from behind their curtains. In the market were a few old women from Zahorie who had brought their produce to Bratislava in their old Skodas or even by horse and cart. They seemed undecided whether to stay at their stalls or to escape back home to Zahorie. But they were quickly selling their whole consignment of groceries.

Jozef managed to get five kilos of potatoes, a chicken, three eggs and a loaf of bread. He left his shopping at home and rushed back to the grocery store on Björnsonova. It was closed, with a sign in the window: 'Closed due to holidays. Nearest open shop is on Mytna street.' Off he went to the self-service, hoping that something would be left of their larger stock. Again he saw a crowd of people both inside and outside; again he gave up and turned towards home. Before he went inside his flat he continued up to the fifth floor to Mr. Kis. The old man always kept reserves of cigarettes at home for his regular customers. For ten crowns he was offered ten packs of Detva.

"Don't you have any Bystrice?" Jozef tried his luck.

"For you or for your dad?"

"For my dad."

"For your dad, sure. They're too high-class for students," Kis smiled. "That's all I've got – the rest are for if war breaks out." The tobacconist was a friend of the family, so he allowed himself the joke. Even though he was blind, he was a good-humoured, optimistic fellow.

"Well, it just broke out."

"This is nothing much; they'll threaten us a bit, they'll realize that it was all a big mistake, and then they'll go home."

Jozef started down the staircase, but then turned and called up: "If only!" Back home, he gobbled something down, stuffed two packs of cigarettes into his pockets, and started out for the city. His mum knew her son well enough to realize that any kind of cajoling to stay home and safe would be pointless. He planned to go through Firsnal, officially named Gottwald Square after the first Communist President, past the park on Banskobystricka Street, past the Soviet Bookshop and down to Slovak National Uprising Square. But he had to drop down to Mytna Street on account of the large concentration of Russian tanks and personnel carriers on Firsnal. At any rate, their logistics division was not allowing anyone not Russian into the square. A provisional field camp appeared to have been set up on the cobblestones where generations of excellent football players had learned their tricks, and the self-confident efficiency with which it was being run showed that their plans had been well-laid from the outset.

Jozef followed the lower border of Firsnal, past the Hviezda cinema and the Tatra cabaret, when he noticed a group of about two hundred young people, mostly students, making their way along Banskobystricka. They were chanting slogans in Russian: 'Go back home', 'Lenin, wake up, Brezhnev's gone crazy', 'Kosigyn – son of a bitch', 'Ivan, Natasha's waiting for you'... People were joining the marchers and the crowd was moving onwards towards Firsnal and closer to the tanks. With bitter foresight, some of the locals were locking their entrance doors. As the protestors advanced to Jozefska Street, a line of Soviet soldiers, distanced one metre apart, appeared one block farther on, at Spojna Street. Jozef saw that they were mostly young men, their faces reflecting nervousness and uncertainty. Before them, right in the centre, stood their commanding officer.

When the crowd had come within twenty metres of him, he raised his arm and cried: "Stop where you are. Go home now."

Someone in the crowd shouted back: "You go home, we already are!"

"Stop!" the officer repeated menacingly.

But it was too late to stop. Banskobystricka is a narrow street, lined on one side by apartment buildings and on the other by the three-metre unbroken concrete wall of the Pioneers' Palace. The increasing force from behind was propelling the demonstrators right into the Soviet front line. The noise of the chanted slogans grew and the commander gave an order. The soldiers loaded their Kalashnikovs.

"For the last time, stop!" Now the officer's tone had become more desperate than hostile. Raising his automatic, he fired into the air.

Panic ensued. Those in the front row pushed backwards, but the crowd was immense. Some ducked down Jozefska, while others tried to escape down Spojna Street. This unfortunately brought them a few steps closer to the soldiers, who thought they were being set upon.

Jozef was fortunate to be standing where he was; the flow of people squeezed him down Jozefska, past an ice-cream shop he'd known since his childhood. Meanwhile another shot rang out, followed by yet another. A woman's voice began to cry plaintively. At the sound of the firing, those at the back turned and ran back in the direction of the Pioneers' Palace, so space for retreat was thankfully opened up. People were racing as fast as they could, pursued by Russian soldiers. A hand suddenly grabbed Jozef and pulled him through the ice-cream shop entranceway and into the shop, where a number of people were also sheltering. The owner used a huge key to open a heavy wooden gate. Next to Jozef, a young girl was standing and crying. They were all of them shaking from shock. A wave of Soviet military men swept past the shop window, with their rifle-butts beating anyone who failed to get away. At the corner of the street lay two bodies in a pool of blood. Soviet medics quickly lifted them onto stretchers and took them off somewhere.

CHAPTER
FOURTEEN

ZVOLEN 1968

THE Tupolev with the administration section of the Trans Carpathian military district air force on board landed at the military airport in Uzhgorod at eight o'clock on August twenty-third. The passengers were exclusively superior officers except for three female administrative assistants. One of them was Sasha, dressed in a becoming uniform. During the flight from Kiev, the officers had initially teased the girls, but later they travelled in silence. In confusion, she was on the brink of tears; her father had once liberated Czechoslovakia and now she sincerely desired to help her Czech and Slovak brothers. When she had gone home to bid her family farewell, her sister Olga had also dropped by. Olga had given her a poem Sasha didn't quite understand. It was written by her favourite poet, the man who gave her the strength to live, Yevgeny Yevtushenko. It was entitled, 'Russian Tanks in Prague'.

Tanks are rolling across Prague in the sunset blood of dawn. Tanks are rolling across the truth, not the newspaper named Truth. The tanks are going after the truth; not the newspaper Truth, but the real one... vulgarity has its roots in fear... you've trampled on conscience and honour like hungry beasts, fear rolls in the tracks of tanks and the armour of vulgarity saves it... how to live when they've taken away my faith... here lies a Russian poet, the tanks crushed him in Prague...'

Sasha didn't understand how an authority like Yevtushenko could write a poem condemning the Soviet Union's aid to its brother state, Czechoslovakia. Since her secondment to the air force staff the political staff had presented ample evidence of the West's messing in Czechoslovak affairs. Before they left Uzghorod, the air force commander, Lieutenant General Stepanenko, a twice-decorated hero of the Soviet Union, came to speak to them. It was well-known that he was a sincere old friend of the Czech and Slovak peoples. With her own ears she heard the war veteran telling the embarking troops how their brothers needed their help. So what was Yevtushenko's poem about?

"Here lies a Russian poet, the tanks crushed him in Prague...'

Olga had been working in the post office in Koktebel for five years, and since her divorce Sasha had often gone there to visit her. Before that she worked in Feodosia, but was glad to get a transfer to the quieter Koktebel. Thanks to her sister, Sasha had met almost all the great Soviet writers, but Yevtushenko remained her favourite; she'd read every word he'd written. Just like thousands of other young Russians and Ukrainians, she simply adored him. Yevtushenko had even been introduced to Olga's family, and once brought her some cologne from Moscow. And then something unexpected had taken place: Olga was dismissed from her job because of some telegram Yevtushenko had sent to Brezhnev in which he'd criticized the Soviet action in Czechoslovakia. Surely this great poet too had fallen for the Imperialist propaganda. One or two people could misunderstand what was going on, but thousands? Soviet diplomats, counter-espionage bodies, friends in Czechoslovakia, information from that country, everything showed that they were doing the right thing. But still Yevtushenko was protesting. Sasha sensed that her ardent feelings for this poet were becoming tepid. Her beloved Yevtushenko was preventing her from helping her beloved Jozef! Fortunately Yevtushenko had done the right thing by Ola and arranged with Rubinsky, the local KGB commander in Feodosia, for her to be taken back at the post office. Probably he had gone over the top because he was drunk. Everyone understood that writers love to drink.

Sasha thought all this over and concluded that the worst thing was she had no-one to talk to about her confusion. In a few minutes they would be landing in a central Slovak military airport at Sliac and, according to the information they'd been given, military operations were already in place there. Major Kulikin had told her she didn't have to be concerned for her safety because they would take her straight to staff headquarters. In addition, the Army had orders not to open fire first.

'Hey, the tanks are going after the soldiers sitting inside these tanks... ' 'Hey, the tanks are going after the soldiers sitting inside these tanks... ' The verses of Yevtushenko were running through her mind.

She smiled at the thought that perhaps she really would meet Jozef there. She knew that Zvolen, where she was to be housed, was only 200 kilometres from his home in Bratislava, and she believed that miracles do sometimes happen...

On a chair lay a bunch of Soviet newspapers full of reports on the counterrevolutionaries who wished to pull Czechoslovakia back into the arms of the capitalists. According to the Soviet press agency TASS reporter, in the western part of the country a mob had lynched a Communist Party official who would not allow a drunken teenager to hoist the American flag. Although the report was quite dramatic, there was something a bit fishy about it. She and her colleagues wondered how it was possible that the ordinary people had not intervened in this case. The papers wrote about a 'handful' of discontented people who were being paid by the CIA. It was strange that the Czechoslovak people couldn't deal with a few traitors on their own. The newspapers also showed photos of the Soviet soldiers being enthusiastically welcomed when they'd crossed the border two days previously. Was an elite guard division, and many other divisions besides, along with tanks, aircraft and all kinds of technical support, necessary just to put down a few malcontents? And if they were coming in only to provide that support, why were she and all her fellow administrators being flown in three days after the event? It didn't look to her like they would be going home very soon.

They landed in Sliac on August twenty-fourth at about eleven in the morning. The only planes on the airbase were Soviet MIG jets, a couple of transport Antonovs, and one Tupolev. They climbed into the waiting armoured transporters and twelve minutes later were standing in the courtyard of the military compound in Zvolen. In Latin script on the wall of the building she read: 'Jegorov barracks'. Jegorov had been some sort of Partisan leader, she seemed to recall. The three female staff shared one room. The flight commander, Major Kuznecov, ordered them not to go anywhere until they were called for. Time went by, it was now late afternoon, and still no-one came for them. They had no idea where they were - outside everything was quiet, there was no shooting, only the sounds of aircraft taking off or landing. Luckily they had their emergency supplies with them and so had enough to eat. The water in the sink was also drinkable. After four o'clock local time, Major Kuznecov came and brought Sasha to his makeshift office. Still visible on the walls were pieces of Czechoslovak politicians' photos which had been hastily removed.

"Alexandra Josifovna, they tell me you understand Slovak," he began.

"I understand something, but I don't speak it very well."

"That will do. This is Captain Jurzinov," he said, introducing her to a distinguished-looking officer. "You will accompany him into town to buy some supplies."

"At your command, Comrade Major." Sasha stood, offered the captain her hand and followed him from the room.

She felt her excitement build as they got back into the transporter, which had an escort of six soldiers.

"Is it so dangerous that we need to go with an armed escort?" she asked.

"Not really, but you never know. The first three days were unpleasant; they were throwing stones and Molotov cocktails at us, but nothing more," the Captain answered nonchalantly. The cigarette smoke in the closed vehicle was making her feel sick. When he noticed this, the captain put out his cigarette.

"Thank you. And have you silenced the counterrevolutionaries?" she asked straightforwardly.

"So far none have shown themselves, but we're ready for anything."

She looked forward to her first meeting with ordinary Slovaks. In advance she'd prepared a few expressions she could use with her dear Slovak brothers.

"Captain, we're here," the driver announced. As the transporter drew to a halt, armed infantrymen jumped down.

"We're going to a grocery warehouse. Our Slovak comrades will furnish us with supplies until our own supply lines are established," she was informed by the captain as he disembarked. After looking around and ensuring the situation was calm, he helped her out. She got down with a smile on her face, which faded quickly. They were in the middle of a pretty town, and in the background she could see a Christian church, but the looks on the faces of the local people gathered on the sidewalks were far from friendly. The walls were plastered with posters, many in Russian: 'Ivan, go home', 'Go home to your wives', 'Why are you ruining things?', ' Brezhnev has gone crazy'. Sasha walked like one hyptonized. She didn't understand. Instead of warm embraces and offers of bread, as she had seen in the Moscow Pravda newspaper, they were confronted by stone-faced people. In order to get to the back door of the storehouse by the marketplace, she had to pass in front of a crowd of angry civilians: "Go back home. Don't take our food. Thieves!"

"But we're your brothers..." she tried to object, when some kind of blunt object, perhaps an umbrella, struck her in the face. "Get back home, you Russian swine. You're no brothers of ours!" The force of the blow had knocked her glasses off, and as she picked them up she saw they were broken. "These glasses are from Slovakia,' she sobbed. There was a drop of blood on the glass. One of the soldiers accompanying their party struck a man in the shoulder with his rifle-butt, and he walked away cursing and shaking his fist.

"Come along, Alexandra Josifovna, quickly." They hurried into the warehouse and to peace and quiet. Outside the chanting increased in volume. Sasa realized she was trembling and found a place to sit down. Then her stomach turned over and she threw up. The captain led her into an office and asked a cleaning-lady to bring her some water. The woman did as she was asked, and Sasha managed to drink a little of it. The woman then took off Sasha's military cap and stroked her sweated brow. Heartened by this little act of human kindness, she looked up.

"Where are you from, my dear?" the cleaner asked her.

"From Carpatho-Ukraine."

"And how did you end up here?"

"I came to help you."

The woman realized Sasha was speaking to her in Slovak: "But you know Slovak?"

"My parents are Slovak."

"What's your name, dear?"

"Alexandra."

"Pretty name. I'm Sofia. Like Sophia Loren, you know." Sasha smiled and said nothing. From outside shouting and beating on the metal gate could be heard. Then a shot rang out, followed by silence. Sasha ran to the window. A Russian soldier again shot into the air and the crowd dispersed. She sat back down.

"Why do those people hate us?"

The woman took a seat beside her and gently took her hand. Instinctively, Sasha stroked the woman's. They were wrinkled and cracked, like those of her mother. Hesitantly, the woman began to speak. She told Sasha how her husband's life had been saved in 1945 by a Russian partisan from the Jegorov brigade. For that she had loved Russians all her life, but their invasion of her country was breaking her heart.

"Really, it's breaking my heart. You shouldn't have done this to us, no indeed." The woman talked and Sasha listened until the tears were running down her face. When they got back to the barracks she gave her military rucksack a good kick. Her roommates looked at her as if she'd gone crazy. With shaking hands she pulled out her copy of Pravda with its photos of the Soviet soldiers being enthusiastically welcomed to Czechoslovakia. This time she studied the pictures carefully and at length. The local people were wearing different clothes, different hairstyles. Then she understood - these shots had been taken in May, 1945. She lay on her bed and took out Yevtushenko's poem. She felt that the other girls were still watching her. At first she made to hide the poem, but then placed it openly on the table. Again a wave of sickness washed over her, and she went running to the toilet. When she returned she noticed the piece of paper was in a different position.

She sat on the bedside table, making up her mind to go and see Major Kuznecov and tell him she refused to be a part of this charade. She would demand dismissal from the army. But then she thought about the possible consequences of such an act. 'Good God,' she thought, 'if I had known when we pledged our allegiance to the Soviet Union back in the Uzghorod courtyard...' Lieutenant General Stepanenko had stood before them with the political instructor and given anyone who had any reason for not joining in the international aid effort two minutes to step out of line. No-one had come forward. Indeed, who would step forward - to do so would be seen as acting against their oath, and everyone knew that desertion was a criminal offence. All the same nobody would have come forward because they were all convinced that they were doing an honourable deed. 'If only I had known,' she sighed. But would she have stepped out of line even if she had known? The question troubled her so deeply she dismissed it from her mind.

Again the tears of helplessness ran down her cheeks. 'Please God,' she prayed, 'let me be injured or something, so they'll send me home. I want no part of this!'

CHAPTER
FIFTEEN

BRATISLAVA 1968

Six days after the beginning of the Soviet occupation, the tanks retreated from the streets of Bratislava. In SNP Square, where their concentration had been the densest, there remained only burnt planks, walls covered in graffiti and hollow spaces where the yellow paving stones had been pulled up. Three improvised tombs stood in front of the main university building. In some places dried bloodstains could still be seen. The facades of the hospital, the local government offices and the technical library were peppered with bullet holes. Food supplies slowly returned to normal. Jozef no longer travelled to Trnava for work.

As he walked past the family's post box he automatically poked his finger through the holes of the grill. Again it was empty. It was a month since he'd sent the glasses and his letter to Sasha, but he had still not heard back from her. He thought of her more often than he would like to admit, and sincerely hoped nothing had happened to her. The first woman a man makes love to long remains in his mind.

Upstairs in the kitchen he found a letter addressed to him, with a Zvolen postmark. The sender was someone named Sofia Hola, the address, Radvanska Street, 11. He certainly knew no-one by that name, and opened the envelope curiously.

'My love, forgive me for not writing to you sooner, but a number of things have happened to prevent me from getting in touch. I got your package with the glasses and book all right, even though it took two weeks to reach me. I imagine it was screened by the censors, which is in no way surprising. Our official liars know what they have to look out for! At the same time I volunteered for the administration section of the air force operations group which was being sent to Slovakia, to the city of Zvolen. I was so looking forward to seeing your country and your countrymen, whom I love and respect, which is natural since I too consider myself a Slovak. I also saw it as an honour to be going to Czechoslovakia with the army to help you in your fight against counterrevolution. Believe me when I say I was ready to lay down my life for your homeland. Day after day, our television and papers showed pictures of Czechoslovak counter-revolutionaries, and your countrymen joyously welcoming the Soviet troops. After I arrived in Zvolen, I discovered it was all a fraud, and that the newspaper photos were actually from 1945. I understood then that everything that we were being told was lies, dirty tricks. Mrs. Sofia from Zvolen explained it all to me. Now I feel shame for myself, for my nation and for my homeland.

My dear Jozef, as a result of all this I have no option but to request dismissal from the military. There is no way I can remain in an army that is depriving people of their freedom and happiness. So I don't know where I'll be in the near future. The worst is that though I would love to hold you again I'm ashamed to look you in the eye. I saw a soldier shoot down a young girl of about fifteen. She wasn't doing anything threatening, she just got caught up in the crowd, so maybe the soldier simply panicked and fired off a round. This is a moral weight too heavy for me to bear. Please don't write to my Kiev address because I won't be home for a while, and besides all the mail is opened before you receive it. I wish you all the best, and want you to know that never in my life have I loved anyone as much as I love you, and I never will. For the time being I'm stationed in Zvolen, waiting for permission to return home. How I would love to meet you! Your Sasha.'

Jozef looked at the kitchen clock. It was half past eleven. He consulted the train timetable and found that an express was leaving for Zvolen in seventeen minutes. Quickly he scribbled a note that he would be away for a day or two, that they were not to worry about him, that he'd see them tomorrow. He propped the note on the table, glad that since everyone was out he wouldn't have to do any explaining. Stuffing a few personal items into his backpack along with some bread and salami, he gathered up his summer earnings and hurried off to the station.

The train arrived in Zvolen at a little past four. Since he sometimes came here to play volleyball against the local Forestry and Wood University team, he knew the city a little. He stopped the first passer-by he saw and asked the way to Radvanska. The man guided him, and in fact it was no distance. He found number eleven without difficulty, a three-storey building from the 1930s. Up to the second floor, door number five, Ing. Julius Holy. He rang the bell and the voice of an elderly man reached him through the door. Jozef announced that he desperately needed to talk to Mrs. Holy. The voice told him she wasn't home, but would be there by six.

"Excuse me sir, but it really is urgent. Where am I likely to find her?" The man opened the door on its security chain.

"She works at the grocery warehouse down on the main square. If you don't find her there, come back at six." Flying down the stairs, he realized he hadn't stopped to thank the gentleman. He ran through the square, his head spinning from the happy thought that Sasha was living in this town, that he could soon be meeting her. He was breathing the air of Zvolen, the same air she was breathing. He looked at the faces of passers-by and wondered how they could seem so nonchalant. He quickly located the warehouse with its grey metal gate and loading ramp, but was told that Mrs. Holy had just left for the day.

He returned to the square and collapsed on a bench. It was now five thirty. He looked around and tried to guess which was the lucky road that Sasha walked along. How would she be dressed, in a uniform or in civil wear? Again he studied her letter, trying to find something in it to hold on to. Looking up, he noticed a Soviet military jeep approaching the main gate to the warehouse. Two officers got out, followed by two soldiers.

"Izvinite, Pardon... are you Soviet soldiers?"

"Do we look like Americans... hee-hee-hee?..."

"Sorry, of course you are, but... maybe you could help me... I'm looking for a woman named Alexandra Josifovna Grycenko..." One of the officers was Captain Jurzinov.

"What does she look like?"

"Twenty years old, blond, beautiful."

"And with fantastic turquoise eyes," the captain finished. "You know her?" Jozef nodded. "Where from?" Jozef was taken aback by the question. He hesitated for a moment but thought the officer looked like a regular guy.

"From Kiev. We were there last month on a visit." The captain looked him over, thought for a bit and said: "We're not allowed to talk to any of the locals. Sorry, I have to go."

"But I love her! I want to ask her to marry me," he blurted out in confusion.

"Information concerning Soviet soldiers can only be given out by the Central Command in Bratislava," he confided in a low voice.

The soldiers had meanwhile loaded some boxes into the jeep, and it started off. It was now six o'clock, so Jozef made his way back to the Holys'. Sofia had arrived home and received him warmly. Over tea, she told him everything she knew about Sasha. Essentially she just repeated everything he had read in her letter. He had to admit he was surprised at how much Sasha had trusted this unknown Slovak woman. Sofia told him that they had met a couple of times in the storehouse where she came with some Soviet soldiers from the Jegorov barracks. In her pretty writing, she had checked off a long list of items to be ordered. She was a pretty girl with lovely eyes. Sometimes she looked unwell and threw up - probably from the stress.

Jozef finished the tea, said a thankful goodbye, and made his way back to the train station. He found the next train back to the capital was at eleven, so he had time on his hands. In a vain hope that he might catch a glimpse of her, he set off for the barracks. He didn't know that Sasha had already been back in Ukraine for three days. "I have to find her; even If I have to dig under the ground. I have to find her!"

CHAPTER
SIXTEEN

MOSCOW, 1968

IN the early morning hours of August 21, Soviet paratroopers took Dubcek and the others to Cisar's workroom. After about two hours a KGB officer entered the room and ordered Dubcek to follow him. They went out to the courtyard of the CPC Central Committee building, where tanks and armoured cars stood side by side. Dubcek was ordered to get into one through a circular opening in the top. After a moment Kriegel too squeezed through the aperture. The vehicle moved off. Some twenty minutes later they came to a stop and the two politicians discovered they were at Ruzyne airport. They were taken into a room on the ground floor, and were unaware of the fact that Smrkovsky, Simon, Spacek and Prime Minister Cernik, all captured in Dubcek's office, were in adjoining rooms. When darkness fell, Dubcek was taken first to one airplane then transferred to a second. In a short time they were airborne. After a short stopover at Legnica airport in southern Poland, they arrived at Uzghorod. Cernik and Simon were already there. A division of KGB officers ferried them to a complex of mountain cottages. Shortly before noon on Friday the 23rd a pair of opaque glasses was placed over Dubcek's eyes and he was led to the office of some local Soviet official. He was seated in a chair and a moment later a telephone rang. The KGB man passed it to him. On the other end was Nikolai Podgorny, Head of the Presidium of the USSR

Supreme Soviet and one of the four most powerful men in the Party. In a laconic tone he informed Dubcek that he was expected in Moscow, and then hung up. Dubcek was taken back to the airport, and was soon up in the air again. It was close to eleven o'clock local time when they arrived in Moscow. Dusty and unwashed, he was taken directly from the airport to the Kremlin.

They showed him into a huge room with a long table in the centre. Brezhnev, Government Chairman Kosygin, Podgorny and Party Secretary Voronov were already present. In total silence Podgorny indicated Dubcek to sit in a chair opposite his own. No-one offered to shake hands; Brezhnev rather looked off to the side, as if unwilling to meet Dubcek's eye, and Kosygin's beard hung lower than it usually did. Unknown to him, President Svoboda, along with Government Vice-Chairman Husak, Bilak, Defence Minister Dzur, Justice Minister Kucera, Piller, Indra and others was already in Moscow and had already spoken with the Soviet leadership. In fact Brezhnev had organized a triumphal welcome for Svoboda at the airport followed by crowd-lined streets all the way to the Kremlin. This reception was presented by Soviet television as a sign to the world of their warm brotherly love for Czechoslovakia.

The long silence was broken by Brezhnev.

"Alex, what's going on?" he asked in a jovial and intimate tone. "I hear Comrade Cernik isn't feeling well."

"He's taking it badly," answered Dubcek, staring straight ahead. "Badly," he repeated.

"It's not easy on us either, believe me," Brezhnev continued. Dubcek at first said nothing, then suddenly and resolutely spoke in a loud voice:

"It wouldn't be right if I didn't say to you that sending in the troops was a great political error, which will have tragic consequences!"

"Alex... easy... please take it easy," countered Brezhnev, nervously lighting a cigarette. "I'm not putting the blame on you. You did what you could. We believe that the counterrevolutionaries pulled it all off behind your back..." Dubcek realized the way the Soviets were playing it. They needed him, the symbol of the Prague Spring and of opposition to the invasion. Their idea of a worker/farmer government with

Indra at its head wouldn't wash. Bilak had not been successful in taking over the television, radio or press agency. The whole world was being informed this was a straightforward occupation. Putting a military government into place would mean provoking the total resistance of the Czech and Slovak people. They needed Dubcek. Behind Dubcek's back, Bilak was working with the Soviets to come up with the myth about the counterrevolutionaries.

"Leonid Ilyich, I request to be allowed to speak with my colleagues," retorted Dubcek, ignoring Brezhnev's comment. One after the other, the Soviets attempted to convince Dubcek that a counterrevolution was taking place in his own country, but he refused to react to their absurd lies. When they'd had enough he repeated his request.

Government Chairman Cernik was shown into the room. The Soviets were demanding they agree to the retrospective cancellation of the recently held XIV Congress of the Czechoslovak Communist Party. Now both he and Dubcek were demanding communication with the other Czechoslovak government members. After two hours of fruitless debate, the Russian side remained seated at the table while Dubcek and Cernik were taken to another meeting-room where President Svoboda and the other ČSSR executive representatives were waiting for them. Their reception was hearty and their discussions lasted until three in the morning. Dubcek was exhausted and not feeling his best. Bilak looked him over and concluded that Dubcek was exaggerating his queasiness. One thing was understood by all – the Soviets were demanding their retroactive agreement to the invasion.

Dubcek slept through most of Saturday, August 24, but was finally awakened in the afternoon. Before he was taken back to the Kremlin he was visited by Smrkovsky, who filled him in on the activities back home: "Yesterday a general strike was held throughout the Republic to protest against the military invasion. The XIV Congress is permanently sitting at Vysocany. They're unanimously behind us - in fact the whole world is on our side."

Back in the Kremlin a strengthened Czechoslovak delegation, made up of Mlynar, Lenart, Barbirek, Jakes, Rigo and Svestka, was waiting. The Soviets rapidly moved on to a new round of talks, but Dubcek *throughout was playing for time. He sensed that the longer the negotiations continued, the more upset the Soviets would become. President Svoboda on the other hand begged Dubcek to speak clearly and concisely; he even reproached him for 'just chatting' most of the time. Late in the afternoon the two delegations, led by Dubcek and Brezhnev, again took their places around the negotiating table. This time it was Dubcek who broke the silence. What he had to say froze everyone who was in the negotiating chamber. Looking straight in front of himself, he began:*

"Comrade Bilak, please ask them exactly what they want..." Bilak looked at him in confusion, for he knew that Dubcek's Russian was superior to his own, but he didn't know what he was after. Slowly and clearly he repeated Dubcek's question in Russian. Brezhnev's face fell, but he mastered himself. In a serious tone, he stated it was necessary to prepare a joint document which would in the end be ceremonially signed. Again there was silence. Bilak lost his self-control and raised his voice: "Did you understand, or do I have to translate for you?"

"Fine. This evening at eight we can begin the negotiations," Dubcek said quietly. "Please excuse me," he apologized, then rose from his seat and left the room. The Soviets went out by another door. Then the Czechs and Slovaks gradually made their way out. That was the last time Dubcek participated in the negotiations, which were chaotic and without resolution. On Sunday both delegations met separately in small groups throughout the day. No official bi-partisan negotiations were held.

Dubcek lay in bed the whole day. Part of the delegation believed he was totally exhausted, but another group suspected he was just avoiding his responsibility. In order to make the talks easier he suggested he step down as First Secretary of the Central Committee of the Czechoslovak Communist Party. His proposal was unanimously rejected by his colleagues. It was clear to all that what the Soviets needed most was Dubcek's signature. What they didn't want was to make a national hero and martyr out of him. Smrkovsky, Cernik, Spacek. Mlynar and Simon regularly informed Dubcek of the course of the discussions. He lay in his bed stripped to the waist. On the left side of his chest was a handkerchief folded in four and on his forehead a sticky plaster. He was breathing with difficulty.

The negotiations were led by Cernik, Smrkovsky and Svoboda. That evening Smrkovsky informed Dubcek that the Soviets had arrogantly refused any attempt by the Czechoslovak side to include any of their proposals in the text. They simply stated that the Czechoslovaks were in no position to set conditions. Husak and Dubcek, against the wishes of Brezhnev, put into the protocol a reference to the 'temporary' stay of the Soviet troops. He simply smiled and waved his hand. It was clear to all concerned that the definition of the term 'temporary' would be determined by the strongest party. Essentially he was giving the Czechoslovak side an ultimatum.

Late on Sunday night the Czechoslovak delegation met to formulate a response to the Soviet proposal. Husak suggested everyone speak his mind and cease the fruitless discussions. Then he added: "I'm going to sign it." After Husak had declared himself, the others, one after the other, agreed to sign. Mlynar lamented out loud: "It's too cruel, I won't sign it." Smrkovsky remarked, "If it weren't for my wife and children, I wouldn't sign it either. But since the situation is as it stands, I'll sign." The last to speak was Cernik: "I'll sign it." Then Husak took the floor again, and strongly attacked Mlynar, who did not respond. That left only Kriegel and Dubcek. Cernik took it upon himself to persuade Dubcek.

At breakfast the next morning, Mlynar announced that he too would sign. Dubcek looked as white as chalk, but the plaster was gone from his forehead. He invited everyone into a nearby meeting-room, where they went through the document they'd agreed to sign. The only one not in favour was Kriegel. That evening, on August 26, a plenary session of both sides was held. When the Czechoslovak representatives entered the room, the Soviet politburo was already seated at the long table. They took their places, Dubcek in the centre with Smrkovsky on his right and Cernik on his left. Svoboda spoke briefly: "We are prepared to sign the document." Then after a moment Brezhnev spoke so convincingly he almost persuaded himself. Listening to him, Dubcek couldn't believe what an accomplished actor the man was. This was the man *who had had himself decorated as a war hero despite the fact he had scarcely fought in the war. Dubcek realized he was essentially sitting opposite a band of gangsters. The next to speak was Cernik, and to the surprise of everyone he claimed to be speaking in the name of Dubcek, who wasn't feeling well – and this with Dubcek sitting right next to him. This convinced Dubcek to take the floor. He spoke in his fluent Russian, slowly and somberly, and this served to make his performance all the more affecting. Although he had already agreed to sign, he said, he was beginning to reconsider his position. Brezhnev was beside himself; standing up, he began to shout at Dubcek, his face red, his bushy eyebrows bristling. He screamed that the whole foregoing process of negotiations had been meaningless. Then he stormed from the room, followed by the entire Soviet delegation. Dubcek also stood up, also ready to leave the chamber. "Whether we sign or not is completely irrelevant: in any case they'll do what they want. I'm not signing anything."*

After a moment of silence, President Svoboda said that it was now too late to back out. Surprisingly, Cernik began to urge them to sign - if they didn't sign this wording, there was the risk they'd be forced to sign something even worse. He sincerely believed the commitment Brezhnev had given him face-to-face, that he would remain Government Chairman, would be honoured. Smrkovsky added sadly that they had no choice. He drew a parallel with the situation of President Hacha in 1939 Berlin. "He managed to slow down the Nazification process and so saved many people." It was clear to everyone that his comparison of German Fascists and Russian Communists meant his total resignation as regards Communism. He was a defeated man. Dubcek remained alone. Svoboda sent Bilak with a message for Brezhnev that the opinion of Dubcek was not the opinion of the Czechoslovak delegation.

Dubcek lay on a divan, alone in the room. Leaders always find themselves alone in their most trying moments. He knew that without his own, the signatures of all the others were of no interest. They could sign even ten such documents, but without the signature of the First Secretary the world would know that something was not right. He considered how the citizenry, and primarily the military, would react when they found out he had refused to sign.

Somehow there came into his mind the mysterious death of his onetime Party Leader, Klement Gottwald, who had died in 1953 three days after his return from Stalin's funeral in Moscow. He remembered well the rumours that had flown around the Party leadership concerning their President's death. He was also aware that although the Communist Party was the strongest power in society, and he as Party Secretary was its highest representative, the supreme commander of the military forces was President Svoboda. And he had clearly stated that he intended to sign. Dubcek did not wish to see blood spilled; he could not allow the life of even one Czechoslovak citizen to be wasted. Since all the others had agreed to sign, he would be alone, isolated. In vain he sought arguments that held water against this conviction. If he were to sign, there was a chance the Soviets would leave the country sooner. But still... Hell, they would do what they wanted whether he signed or not. He knew they were quite capable of forging his signature on the document.

An hour before midnight the two delegations met again. Journalists were escorted into the meeting- room. Brezhnev and Svoboda signed first, then Dubcek, followed by the others - everyone apart from Kriegel, whom they didn't even call.

Alexander Dubcek's attempt at socialism with a human face was definitely over.

CHAPTER
SEVENTEEN

BRATISLAVA 1968

THE chief command of the Soviet armed forces was headquartered on Jegorov Square in Bratislava. Jozef saw some symbolism in this: Sasha was in the Jegorov barracks, the Soviet command headquarters were on Jegorov Square. Maybe this Jegorov would bring him luck. At the gate he reported to the soldier at the checkpoint, where he requested a meeting with someone from the personnel department. The soldier didn't show the least sign of willingness; in the end he made a phone call, but no-one answered the call. The soldier shrugged his shoulders. Jozef couldn't believe that his search for his true love would end in the face of such indifference, so he took two packs of cigarettes in flip-top boxes out of his pocket. This kind of packaging was rare enough in Czechoslovakia, not to mention in the Soviet Union. The guard smiled, closed his window so Jozef couldn't hear what he was saying, and again dialed a number. Then he again opened the window: "They'll come and fetch you." After a short time, a young woman in military uniform arrived.

"Who are you looking for?"

"Alexandra Josifovna Grycenko."

"No-one of that name works here."

"I know, but she's a member of your army who was sent to Czechoslovakia. She was in Zvolen, but perhaps she's already gone back to Kiev..."

"We can't give out information about members of our army."

„"She's my fiancée," Balaz burst out.

"What does that mean, fiancée?" the woman asked.

"We're going to be married. Wedding, you understand? Everything was prepared for our marriage in Kiev, but then she was sent on your... action in Czechoslovakia."

"This is not an 'action', it's international aid," the soldier corrected him. Jozef discreetly slipped a bottle of Nina Ricci perfume into her pocket. He'd bought it in the hard-currency shop, and it hadn't come cheap. The soldier looked at him, nodded her head, and indicated that Jozef should follow her. They went up to the first floor. On the walls hung portraits of Brezhnev, Kosygin, and other Soviet potentates. He tried to control the look on his face, but guessed the woman had noticed it. "Wait here. I'll call the major who is in charge of personnel." Jozef sat down. From the adjoining room he could hear wild laughter and the cacophony of voices. It was obvious that serious drinking was going on. After a moment, the 'major in charge of personnel' appeared. Standing up, Jozef introduced himself and briefly explained why he was there. Clearly the major was more than a little drunk. He lit a cigarette and disdainfully addressed Jozef:

"And do you think, comrade, that the Soviet command headquarters is some kind of circus? That we give out information about Soviet personnel to anyone who comes knocking?"

"Comrade Major, I am aware that an action like your... (he swallowed and then forced the phrase out) international aid requires thousands of people. I know that Alexandra Josifovna is just an ordinary soldier, but..."

"Don't babble," the major cut in. "Do you have anything to smoke?" Jozef hopefully pulled out a whole carton of flip-top Spartas, a veritable treasure. The major quickly grabbed them. "Good guy, a really good guy". He eagerly tore the carton open, took out the top pack and lit up."What was it you wanted?" he asked vaguely.

"Alexandra Josifovna... my Ukrainian fiancée..."

"Right, right, I remember. Wait here, I'll send someone out." The major made it to his feet and left the room. Jozef sat down to wait. He looked around the stripped room. It was obvious that the pictures which had once hung on the walls had been removed. A half-hour went by. The shouting, yelling, and occasional drunken singing in the next room got louder. He waited another hour, but still no-one came to him. He got up and carefully opened the door into the hallway. The racket from next door was even louder out there, but the hall was deserted. Jozef thought to himself that if he had a bomb or even a grenade he could blow the entire Soviet command headquarters into the air. He glanced into the room where the drinking party was taking place. Since the hallway was dimly lit, he could see in clearly. There were Russians in uniform and out of uniform, plus a few drunken Slovaks. He sat down on a bench and waited to see what would happen next. After an hour or so the major who had taken his cigarettes rushed from the party room and into the room opposite. The sound of violent retching followed. Then the drunken major staggered out, his eyes bloodshot, and without even noticing Jozef made his way back in to drink some more. The door slammed behind him.

"You don't know what drunken Russians are capable of." His father's words came back to him. Then the words to the famous Russian folk song, 'Kalinka', were screamed out. The last time he'd heard it was in Kiev. He smiled bitterly, then went out into the street. No-one paid him any attention: he was of no interest to anyone.

For the first time in a long time, rain began to fall on Bratislava.

CHAPTER
EIGHTEEN

BRATISLAVA 1968

A N unbelievable mess remained in the city centre after the withdrawal of the Soviet tanks. The scraps of improvised posters hung from the façades of buildings, some torn down by unknowable hands, some by the wind, some fallen under the force of their own weight. Along with those carrying anti-Soviet slogans, one poster with the text 'We demand the replacement of churchwarden Farkas. Signed, the unsatisfied faithful' must have been especially encouraging to the Communist Party's top officials.

With bated breath, the country followed any news from Moscow concerning the Czechoslovak leaders, but the messages coming out were frustratingly inconsistent. Some of the 'reliable information' reported that Dubcek had been hanged, radiated or banished to Siberia.

Jozef sat in the Hron garden restaurant on Suche myto and watched groups of people in intense debate. Everyone was trying to find out what was really going on. The inhabitants of Bratislava were lucky in that antennas capable of catching Austrian television could be mounted on every apartment building. But the Austrians too could only report rumours coming out of Moscow. Then the news spread that the entire Czechoslovak delegation was coming home in full strength. This was a relief since there had been concern for their fate, and especially that of Dubcek. The shots of their landing were eloquent. Jozef would always remember the smiles of Bilak, Husak and Svoboda alongside the gloomy expressions of Dubcek and Smrkovsky. That evening at half past five there was to be an appearance by Dubcek on radio and television. The expectations of the populace gradually turned into a bitter foreboding.

Although he fought against it, Jozef's feelings of disappointment and deception also affected his emotions regarding Sasha. He knew she was not responsible for any of it, but she was the only inhabitant of the Soviet Union he knew and on whom he could focus his immense sadness. She, his darling with her turquoise eyes, was part of the infernal machinery which had destroyed his hopes and dreams. In his heart he reproached her for not displaying at least some form of resistance. If in the USSR there had been more of those who protested against this action, the whole thing need not have happened. The next moment he dismissed this idea - what did the average citizen know about events in Czechoslovakia? He wondered how he would have reacted if the situation had been reversed. He was not too sure that he would have found the strength to resist.

He tried to replace these sad thoughts with hope. He reasoned that perhaps the situation wasn't yet hopeless; the Soviet troops were after all moving back. He hoped that in Moscow things had been explained and that Dubcek would have good news for the nation that evening.

The twenty-seventh of August was a strange day. He waited for Winter in the hope that he could give him at least theoretical hope, even if his curly red hair, sweaty red face, wide nose and dilated nostrils were in fact repulsive. His permanent false smile was the embodiment of his hypocrisy. A native of Kezmarok, he had first come into Balaz's life when the Slovan Bratislava juniors played against Jednota Kezmarok. They were both captains of their respective teams, and Slovan had won. Jozef remembered precisely one smash of his which Winter blocked. It was clear to everyone that Winter had touched the ball, but the referee supported the home team and ignored the foul. Balaz, as captain of his team, challenged the referee to call the touch. The referee found himself caught out and sought a compromise – he challenged the player who had potentially broken the rules to admit his foul. Winter angrily turned on Balaz and categorically denied having touched the ball. But the foul was so obvious that even the hometown fans whistled their disapproval of Winter's dirty tricks. That lie was forever fixed in Balaz's memory. At that time he had no idea that this cheater would become is lifelong nemesis.

When he discovered later that Winter was his classmate at the Business Faculty of the Economics University, he kept a wary distance. Winter quickly became a member of the Union of University Students of Slovakia, along with Jan Husak, the son of Gustav Husak. The students placed a lot of faith in the young Husak, considering him a reasonable fellow. Moreover he was the son of a politician who had been sentenced to prison by the Communists. Winter wasted no time in currying favour with him, becoming in fact his main hanger-on. Jozef was surprised that Husak was pleased with Winter's company since most of those flocking around Ján were weak students. The two of them soon became drinking buddies. Rumours started going around that Winter was a police agent; he acted with an assurance that made the suggestion sound plausible, but Jozef reckoned his arrogance was explained by his friendship with Husak. His main worry at the time was getting some information about Sasha.

"Hello, old chap," said Winter, approaching Jozef from behind and giving him a slap on the shoulder. "Sorry to be late, but getting up here from Solteska dormitory! Those tram drivers don't know the meaning of the word discipline," he joked.

"That's okay, I'm glad you could make it," Balaz answered, feeling like a rat. After a moment he continued, "Listen, Tubby, you're from Kezmarok, what are you doing in Bratislava during the holidays?"

"I have a little job at the Union, we're preparing a big AISEC international student organization conference here... And by the way, don't call me Tubby."

"Oh, sorry."

"So how're you doing?"

"Well, like everybody else I guess," shrugged Balaz . "Pretty blue... we can only hope they won't be here forever. I'm curious what Dubcek's going to say on TV tonight," he said in a measured tone.

"Want one?" Winter offered him a cigarette from a flip-top box.

"Sparta? You've got good connections," smiled Jozef, accepting the cigarette.

"Yes I have." There was silence for a minute. "How come you called me just like that, we're not exactly..."

"Jano... you're friends with Jan, right..."

"Which Jan would that be?"

"Husak."

"Oh him; that's right... It looks like his father's going to be given the top job, he told me yesterday. He met him as soon as he got back from Moscow," Winter said importantly.

"So do you know how things ended up there?"

"No. But as regards old man Husak, Jano let something slip... He's to take over the Party in Slovakia."

"That wouldn't be bad... he's an experienced old workhorse. So Bilak's getting the shove?" Winter nodded meaningfully, like someone in the know.

"And Dubcek?" Balaz asked carefully. Winter thought it over for a second, then shrugged his shoulders.

"What was it you wanted, exactly?"

"Remember when we were in Kiev, I was making a little time with one girl there?"

"Sasha... I remember. Fantastic green eyes. Not bad at all..."

"Yes, Sasha. I kind of fell for her, you know... I sort of feel..."

"You might as well come out and say it. Being in love with a Soviet won't do you any harm," laughed Winter, puffing deeply on his cigarette.

"That's not really what I wanted to talk about. I know she's in Slovakia right now, as part of the occupying army." Winter gave him a sharp glance. "Better be careful. It doesn't matter to me, but it's better not to say 'occupying' in public."

"So what the hell am I supposed to say? Liberating?"

"Say something neutral – Soviet. Things will get cleared up pretty soon."

"She came to Slovakia as a member of the Soviet Army. I managed to find out that she's been seconded to the operational group of the Carpatho-Ukraine military district air battalion in Zvolen... I was wondering... well... if you couldn't..." Under a severe look from Winter, Balaz's voice dried up. He shook his head as if steeling himself to play this one out. "If you couldn't find out through Jan where she is, what she's doing, if she's all right..."

"You know a lot! How did you find these things out? How do you know the Carpatho-Ukraine military district air battalion is in Zvolen?!" Winter snapped the question at him.

"Well... I went up there... they told me that such information can only be given by the Central Command in Bratislava," Balaz stammered out. Winter looked at him critically. Suddenly his tone changed.

"Tell me, Jozef," he said condescendingly, "Do you agree or don't you agree with their coming here?"

"Well... I think... that... hmm... they didn't have to handle it this way... I think we could have managed the situation on our own."

"Do you agree with the intervention of the Soviet forces or not?!" Winter adopted a categorical tone. Balaz remained silent. "So you don't agree!" Balaz's face fell. Winter lost control of himself. "So you piss on our Soviet friends and yet you have the nerve to ask me to find out where some Russian babe you screwed might be?! And to do that I'm supposed to ask Husak's son for help? You must be out of your mind!!! You can forget about that, I really can't help you. You screwed her, you find her!"

"She's Ukrainian... and I didn't 'screw' her... And I'll thank you to speak with respect about a member of our brotherly Soviet army!!!" Balaz spoke the words without knowing where they had come from.

"So they're our brothers all of a sudden. A minute ago you couldn't find anything good to say about them, and now they're our brothers?"

"Jano, don't mix politics into this. Yes, if you must know, I care a lot for her and... it's just that I'm worried and I want to find out if she's all right. I thought you might be able to help me."

"Sorry, I have to be going. Don't overestimate my influence!" said Winter, standing up and leaving without shaking hands. Balaz felt ashamed and diminished. He sorely regretted asking Winter to help him out.

The sun was setting over the buildings across the way, and it was getting cold. He was surprised to find it was getting on for six o'clock and Dubcek's televised speech. Since the Hron restaurant was one of the few with a TV, he went inside just as the commentator was announcing the First Secretary of the Communist Party. The droning hum of voices stilled as Dubcek appeared on the screen. Despite the poor quality of the black-and-white image, Dubcek's paleness was evident. His voice was slow and uneven despite the fact that he was reading from a document held in front of him. It was clear from his face that he was no bearer of good news. "Yesterday we returned from negotiations in Moscow... the Soviet comrades expressed their concern about developments in Czechoslovakia... We assured them that... uh... I do not wish, nor am I able, to build in you false hopes... The freedom of our decision-making and actions has been curtailed..."

"This morning President Svoboda was saying something different. Who are we to believe?" someone called. "Quiet!" rang the answer.

Dubcek carried on: "We promised the Soviet comrades that we would undertake everything possible to make the stay of the Soviet military forces as brief as possible."

"What are you doing making them promises, they should promise to leave!" called some anonymous daredevil.

"Bugger that. When a half-million of them come, they're not here just for a visit," someone else offered their analysis.

"All of our activities will be constrained within a context that will not depend solely on our will..." Dubcek had trouble finishing his sentence.

"So we're fucked," someone declared.

"Quiet!!!"

Dubcek continued in a shaky voice: "The complete and most expedient withdrawal of these forces will be the paramount goal of all our efforts. It is explicitly stated in the protocol that the stay of the Soviet troops is only temporary..."

"So that means forever," chipped in another barroom analyst.

"Quiet!!!"

"The unity of our actions alone will ensure the success of our future policies." Dubcek paused to take a breath; he seemed on the brink of tears. The populace felt that he had more to say, much more, but he could not. It was clear to everyone that this was the end.

"Pour us all a vodka," a man seated at Balaz's table ordered.

"No-one's drinking vodka in here today. Bring us Slovak gin!" insisted a guy in a "USA" t-shirt, and his suggestion was met with a round of loud applause. Balaz looked at his countrymen as they began to get drunk; he listened to their words getting bolder the more they drank. He had the feeling that in this state the Slovaks would be capable of starting a worldwide revolution. Drunken heroism was a Slovak specialty.

"So they're here for just a short time. Like hell they are. We'll bow down before them, just as for long generations we've bowed down to someone... and we'll brag that we handled the thing so well that they didn't kick us in the teeth, but just up the ass!" Again the guy in the USA t-shirt was holding forth.

Jozef went out into the darkening night. Despite the problems it might cause them both, he needed to write Sasha a letter.

CHAPTER
NINETEEN

UZGHOROD 1968

THE KGB officer in Uzghorod watched Sasha's attractive figure with undisguised pleasure. She sat before him hunched over in a chair. She wasn't feeling very well; her period was five weeks late, and the pregnancy test showed that she was almost certainly expecting. The only man she had ever been with was Jozef, and she even remembered the date: July 28. Her condition left her feeling torn between joy and sorrow; her affair with Jozef was over. Even if the Soviet invasion of Czechoslovakia was somehow legitimate, she personally could never look Jozef in the eyes again. When she wrote him that letter from Zvolen that she was ending their relationship, she had imagined her only remembrances of him would be the pair of glasses and the poem Marína by Sládkovic. And now she was expecting his baby. Somehow she felt glad about this turn of events. Tomorrow she had an appointment with the commander of the military personnel division at which she would hand in her request to resign from the army. The officer looked at her and in her sadness and poor health, and felt sorry for her.

"We have called you here for one reason: we have seized a letter addressed to you from Bratislava, Czechoslovakia. Naturally you understand that due to the counterrevolutionary activities in that country and your status as a member of the Soviet Army, we must be cautious. This letter is not the best thing that could happen to you, quite the contrary. It doesn't show either you or the Comrade who wrote it... what's his name, ah, Balaz..., in a good light." Sasha looked at him directly and sincerely with her penetrating eyes. The officer dropped his stare.

"I'm not a member of the Soviet Army, I'm simply a civil employee," she explained through pursed lips. She thought to herself, 'If you saw with your own eyes what's going on in Czechoslovakia, you'd not utter such stupidities about some counterrevolution.' Her heart was racing, her breathing short and shallow. She'd never before been summoned to a hearing with the KGB, but it was an experience no Soviet citizen would welcome. In fact, throughout the Soviet Union there were very few official institutions one would enjoy visiting, but the Soviet State Security was definitely at the bottom of everyone's list. Sasha was frankly afraid, although she felt sure Jozef would not be naïve enough to refer to her straightforward comments on the political situation in his homeland. He knew as well as she did that if the KGB learned about it, it would mean more than her dishonourable discharge; a trial and a prison sentence would almost definitely follow. She was only twenty, with her whole life ahead of her. 'Oh God, please let there be nothing compromising in what he wrote. Why did I even put such things on paper... why couldn't I control my emotions... Sophia warned me not to write it... I got what I deserved!'

Her fate was in the hands of God and the KGB.

"Can you explain this code to me? 'I, possessed by beauty, sing of sweet desire, the desire for beauty'. The officer read the rough and literal translation of the Sládkovic poem. Sasha couldn't help smiling. "I don't see what is funny in this..."

"I don't know what it is. I don't understand..."

"You don't understand? Well, if that's the way you want it. But what is the meaning of these numbers: 1, 3, 6, 8, 9? What, Comrade Grycenko?"

Sasha realized that Jozef was giving her the numbers of selected verses from Sládkovic's Marína. She had no idea that these numbers had so intrigued the Soviet secret service that her Ukrainian commander Lieutenant General Tichonov had called a special meeting of his operational staff to discuss them. They had discovered that administrative assistant Grycenko had been seconded to the air force staff in the town of Zvolen in central Slovakia. The top Ukrainian code-breakers had analysed the set of numbers in Balaz's letter and come up with various interpretations of them. Some enthusiastic KGB analysts had even reached the conclusion that deciphering the combination of numbers was the key to uncovering an anti-Soviet conspiracy in Czechoslovakia. This could be the evidence that the Soviet leadership desperately needed! The KGB boss Yuri Andropov had sent all the KGB section leaders the order to find at any price evidence of anti-Soviet and anti-socialist activity in Czechoslovakia. The chief KGB commander in Uzghorod, Lieutenant Colonel Mosul was an ambitious man. When he was shown Balaz's letter, he immediately seized his opportunity. Right away he contacted his superior officer, General Tichonov, another officer with high ambitions. They decided that they would present Moscow with the evidence it was seeking. Mosul already had visions of himself as a full colonel, Tichonov as a major general.

"So you have Slovak roots?" the KGB man probed.

"My origin is Ukrainian. I was born in the Soviet Union."

"But your parents are Czech," affirmed the interrogator, consulting a document.

"Slovaks. They were born in Czechoslovakia."

"Aha..." the officer was taken aback for a second."How did they wind up in the Soviet Union? "

"Comrade Stalin brought them here."

"What Comrade Stalin?"

"The former General Secretary, Josif Vissarionovich Stalin, who annexed Carpatho-Ukraine, along with my parents, to the Soviet Union." It was clear that history was not the officer's strong suit.

"Comrade Grycenko, we are not in a history classroom. Carpatho-Ukraine has always been part of the Soviet Union!" The officer strengthened his tone. "Who is Jozef Balaz?"

"A student at the Economics University in Bratislava."
"How do you know him?"
"From Kiev."
"From Kiev?"
"He was in Kiev two months back."

The officer saw his chance and took it. "Really? And why was he in Kiev? Was it connected to the counterrevolution?"

"There's counterrevolution here too?" Sasha was surprised.

"No, but there could be if we're not vigilant!"

"There's something going on?"

"Don't be flip, Comrade Grycenko. You're at KGB headquarters! Who invited him here?"

"The Komsomol Central Committee at Kiev Economic University."

The officer fidgeted and scratched the nape of his neck. Then he asked Sasha for more details. She told him how she had met Jozef at a party, that they had discussed Yesenin and Mayakovski, and that they had traded addresses. She spoke sincerely and truthfully about everything – except for their lovemaking. When she finished, the officer looked her up and down. Her explanation seemed logical, and the facts could easily be checked. The girl wouldn't dare lie to the KGB; she'd know what the consequences were. The only problem was that Lieutenant Colonel Mosul was expecting the dramatic unmasking of a counterrevolutionary plot.

"Do you expect me to believe this fairytale?" he turned on her sharply. "Do you maintain that what you're telling me is the whole truth?" Sasha remained silent. She wondered if after all she should have told him about that wonderful night with Jozef. Then she reckoned that even if she told him, it really wouldn't change anything.

"Have you told me everything?" the officer asked again.

"Everything," Sasha responded after a slight hesitation.

"As you like." The KGB officer pressed a buzzer and two men, dressed in uniforms Sasha didn't recognize, entered the room. "Take her away!"

CHAPTER
TWENTY

BERLIN 1968

IT was still early in the morning on a day near the end of August when the first students began to gather near the ruins of the Gedächtniskirche on Kurfürstendamm in West Berlin. Thomas was one of them. He had come up from Bonn the day before with a group of ten other student radicals. The trip along the rail corridor through the GDR was surprisingly pleasant. He had the feeling that the East German soldiers and inspectors were being especially friendly to them, probably because they knew why they were travelling to West Berlin. Along the way, the students discussed the situation in Germany, Vietnam, and of course Czechoslovakia.

"Did you see those shots on TV of the American President, Johnson, greeting the Russian Ambassador? They were almost hugging each other!" said Hans in disgust. "How the powerful understand each other, even if they are enemies."

"The Russian was telling him they'd invaded Czechoslovakia, and all Johnson could manage was a formal protest. He said the United States would protest this aggressive action at the United Nations," Hans continued with a scowl. "That's tantamount to saying, 'Boys, do whatever you like with those Czechoslovaks'."

"Why would the Americans want to stop them? They're more than glad the Russians are making the same mistake they made in

Vietnam: now the world won't point its finger at them alone!" was Peter's analysis.

"It reminds me of the situation in 1938, when Chamberlain and Daladier signed the Munich Agreement forcing Czechoslovakia to cede Sudetenland to the Nazis. I'm not sure we Germans have the right to condemn the Russians," Karl remarked.

"Good you brought that up. I personally think that's exactly why we have the right. We're a new generation and we're not going to keep quiet just because we're ashamed of our fathers. How long must we carry that burden?! I'm here to protest not as a German but as a free man!" Thomas said forcefully.

"Can you believe that as the Russian forces were crossing the Czechoslovak border, the American Foreign Minister was telling the Foreign Office of the Democratic Party what good relations the United States has with the Soviet Union... it makes me want to puke," said Hans, shaking his head.

"It's obvious that those two are not going to do anything to harm each other – and the poor Czechs and Slovaks are waiting for the Americans to come to the rescue. The same thing happened to my father in '53, when he burned the Russian flag in front of the Brandenburg Gate. When the Russian tanks rolled in, the Americans stood on their tanks one hundred metres away, watching them and smoking their Marlboros. That's why we're protesting against invaders, whether it's the Russians in Czechoslovakia or the Americans in Vietnam. If we do nothing, in a few years nobody will take us seriously. Let the Americans call us Fascists if they like. We're fighting for justice, and that's what's important!" By now Thomas had really lost his temper.

"That's it exactly," agreed Karl, pulling out his guitar. In a moment the train carriage was afire with Pete Seeger's protest song: 'We shall overcome, we shall overcome some day, deep in my heart I do believe, we shall overcome some day'. The song was taken up by all present – even the East German officials, of whom there were surprisingly many, did not try to quiet them down.

Rudi Dutschke was recovering slowly from the serious injuries he'd suffered in the assassination attempt last April. He had gone so far as to write a letter to the twenty-three- year old house painter who had shot him, Bachmann by name, saying that he forgave him and asking him to join the German protest movement and fight for socialism and against American imperialism.

Bachmann had, however, hanged himself in the holding cell. Officially it was called suicide, but the students were convinced that he had been silenced by those who'd put him up to the job. Everyone was disappointed that Rudi was not going to appear at the largest anti-American demonstration ever, organized by the Fritz Teufel Commune of the Free University in Berlin. Together with his wife Gretchen and their son, he had quietly left West Berlin and gone into exile sometime in June. Thomas carried in his pocket the letter from Dutschke he intended to read at the demonstration. They had been in frequent contact since the April meeting of the Young Socialists, where he had met and befriended Rudi. In reference to the Warsaw Pact invasion of Czechoslovakia, he had written to Thomas: 'They are dirty pigs, barbarians and traitors'.

It was getting on for eight o'clock, and Thomas already couldn't see to the end of the march. Above their heads the students were carrying placards condemning American aggression in Vietnam. The person next to him was holding a large photo of a Vietnamese woman with the barrel of an American's rifle at her temple. Under it was written: 'Put down your gun, buddy, and go home!' Other people were carrying portraits of Che Guevara, Ho Chi Min, Rosa Luxemburg and other revolutionary heroes. The New York Times later estimated the size of the crowd at over ten thousand. It was truly the greatest anti-war demonstration ever held on German soil. The crowd moved past the Opera House, the site of the fatal police shooting of Benno Ohnesorg, and then proceeded towards the offices of the Axel Springer Verlag publishing house. The nineteen-floor steel and glass construction, located in the Bohemian quarter of Kreuzberg, right next to the Berlin Wall, sported a neon sign on its top floor: 'Berlin bleibt frei' (Berlin remains free). Day and night, the message shone over East Berlin.

The building was surrounded by barbed wire and guarded by heavily armed emergency police units. Thomas sensed that the breaking point was fast approaching. Bachmann, Rudi Dutschke's would-be assassin, was an avid reader of the venomous right-wing newspaper Bild Zeitung, published by Axel Springer, the most powerful press baron in Germany. The tabloid staunchly defended American policy and frenetically attacked anything on the left. Bild Zeitung explicitly called on German citizens to join in the repressive actions against the radical students. Thomas had today's edition of Bild Zeitung, featuring on the cover page in big bold letters: 'Don't leave all the dirty work to the police'. With a print run of four million, Bild Zeitung was far and away the best-selling daily in Europe. But it was more than the students who were enraged by Springer's media; two hundred of the country's leading intellectuals officially called on the population to boycott Springer's publications.

From their windows, the local residents followed the demonstration, the more timid from behind their curtains. The march was being accompanied by mounted policemen, who for the moment calmly looked on as the students chanted: 'Springer is a murderer!' and 'Springer is a Nazi!'

Thomas and his comrades had no idea that among the ten thousand protestors were a couple of hundred well-trained and organized Stasi agents from the East German secret police, who were nonplussed when the group around Thomas held up photos of Alexander Dubcek and pictures of the Soviet tanks in Prague. Then the chant 'Hands off Prague!' was taken up. Photos of Dubcek were handed around. The secret infiltrators looked around in confusion and then backed away from Thomas's group. So as to remain inconspicuous, some of them even joined in calling out anti-Ulbricht slogans. Perhaps this was the first, and also the last time these East German secret service men could give vent to their true feelings regarding Party Leader Walter Ulbricht, a key supporter of Brezhnev's decision to invade Czechoslovakia. The anti- Soviet calls spread quickly. It is a fact that in a crowd like this, all it takes is for two or three people to take up a slogan and soon everyone else will be shouting it. In front of Springer's building the most popular chant was: "Ulbricht, Brejnew sind Schweine." (Ulbricht and Brezhnev are swine).

Peter Greiner was bursting with laughter. From his office in the Springer publishing house, he looked down at the students chanting slogans against Brezhnev and Ulbricht. He was familiar with the practices of the East German secret service and knew that any large demonstration in West Berlin would be infiltrated by a number of shadowy persons from the East. He had had no idea that such a journalistic scoop would soon fall into his lap. If he knew which of these young men in the crowd had come with the idea of decrying the Soviet occupation of Czechoslovakia and thus inadvertently revealing the GDR agents, he would have kissed his feet. Quickly picking up his camera and tape recorder, he raced down the stairs in search of his exclusive story. When in the next day's paper his editors saw his report from the demonstration at which Stasi agents were shouting slogans against their own leader, they would surely grant him his sought-for permanent placement in Berlin. So far he had been allocated a two-year assignment as Berlin and East German correspondent and his wife was a native of Berlin. Greiner had acclimatized himself to life here, and his wife was meanwhile able to care for her ill mother. Full of expectations and élan, he burst into the vestibule of the building and found it full of police. One of them advised him against going out into the crowd because things could rapidly get rough. Greiner assured him that he was going out at his own risk, then joined the heaving crowd. He headed straight for the group chanting Dubcek's name. He had already noticed Thomas from his office window.

"Hello, I'm a journalist with Bild Zeitung and I'd like to ask you a few questions," he said, approaching Thomas.

"There are no journalists at Bild Zeitung, just scandalmongers!" Thomas brushed him off. For a second Greiner was offended, but he kept at it.

"We can talk about that some other time, but I can guarantee you that your opinion on the Russian occupation of Czechoslovakia will be on our front page."

"I'm not interested."

"Doesn't it bother you to be part of a demonstration full of Stasi agents? Perhaps the Stasi even organized it!"

"What agents?" Now he had Thomas' attention.

"East German. Give that portrait of Dubcek to that guy over there and I'll photograph him with it. Come on..." Greiner was succeeding in provoking Thomas, so he actually handed the poster to a good-looking fellow wearing snow-white Adidas sports shoes. When he saw what he was holding and that Greiner was taking his picture, he immediately threw the portrait to the ground and disappeared into the crowd. "What do you think of that...?" asked Greiner with a laugh. Then he tried to get another 'demonstrator' to pose with a picture of Ulbricht decorated with a swastika, and when that failed, another. Confusion erupted as the spies in the crowd realized that they could be featured in tomorrow's newspaper or newsreel as participants in a demonstration against their East German boss, a circumstance it would be hard to explain back home. Their assignment was to provoke as much anger against the Americans as possible, not to be photographed chanting against their own leader. Hundreds of young men in identical footwear began to ease out of the crowd.

"Yes," said Thomas into Greiner's microphone, "we are protesting not only against the American aggression in Vietnam but also against the Russian aggression in Czechoslovakia. Aggression is aggression, no matter if it's carried out by our allies or our enemies." The moderator waved to Thomas from the podium, urging him to come up and say something. Meantime things were heating up – the moment had arrived for the provoker and the police agent, Urbach. Together with his accomplice Baumann, they removed a number of 'mollis' (Molotov cocktails) from the boot of a car standing nearby and threw them at a van with Springer written across it. In the heat of the action, the students failed to notice that all the vehicles standing near the building were old and clapped-out.

The cries got louder; the cars burned brightly. Sirens from fire engines, ambulances and police cars filled the air with noise. Water cannons and green police vans parked close by in readiness sprang into action. The police had been ordered to suppress anti-American manifestations at any cost.

The previous day, the American Ambassador had visited the German Chancellor Kurt Kiesinger and politely requested an adequate response by the authorities should anti-American slogans or banners be registered.

Someone from the stage was shouting: "Tell the Americans if they don't put a stop to imperialism, the day and hour will come when we do it for them." He could say no more, for the police were advancing in response to the simple order: 'In the case of anti-American slogans...' and even the dimmest policeman understood that such sentiments were in no way pro-American. The police took out their truncheons, the police horses neighed nervously, stones flew and the megaphone-bearer on the stage urged the students to go home. The crowd responded: 'Swine, Fascist pigs', 'America go home', 'Hands off Vietnam', 'Hands off Prague', 'Long live Dutschke'... Glass shattered, and Thomas looked on as the crowd tried to force their way into the Springer publishing house. The glass building shook and splintered. The police pressed forward. Thomas got a sharp crack over the head with a truncheon. As blood poured down his face he felt his legs give way. He saw the reporter Greiner, saw a policeman bang his head with the edge of a plexiglass shield and knock the tape recorder from his hands. Then he was hit again and the sight of a bloody pavement was the last thing Thomas remembered.

CHAPTER
TWENTYONE

BERLIN 1968

SLOWLY he opened his eyes. He was staring at a white ceiling from which the plaster was peeling. When he tried to turn his head, he felt a prick of pain in his neck. He was lying in a hospital bed covered in a fluffy white quilt. Beside the bed was a stand with an upturned bottle from which a transparent liquid dripped. This was the first time in his life that he had been in a hospital except for a couple of days when as a boy he had his tonsils removed. He had no idea what day it was, and only a faint memory of what had happened to him.

"It was a pretty good cut," he heard a voice as if from a distance, but saw a young man, his head bandaged, sitting at his bedside. He had the feeling he should know him. "They hit you right in the neck with a truncheon."

"Who hit me?"

"A policeman at the demonstration... Two days ago in front of the Springer building..." his visitor informed him. Little by little Thomas began to remember. "You were lucky. He lost control of his horse and it almost trod on you. You fell to the ground, and when I tried to get you back on your feet I took a hit on the forehead. The doctor tells me I got a concussion and six stitches," the man smiled bravely.

Thomas studied him and again felt he had already met him somewhere.

"I'm Peter Greiner, the reporter who was trying to interview you. I didn't finish writing it, and I guess I never will. I have the feeling it isn't worth the bother. I wanted to write an article on the anti-Communist demonstration but they stopped me... there's irony for you... capitalist cops... their assault was pure brutality. Nothing special was going down. The people would have gone home and that would have been the end of it, but the government needed to show the Americans where they stand. It was all out of order, uncalled for. I wrote it all down and dictated it to my secretary; this morning she called to say my boss spiked it. He said a daily like Bild Zeitung was not about to call into question a justified incursion by the Berlin police against disturbers of public order... What's your name by the way?"

"Thomas Ankermann."

"Are you from Berlin?"

"No, from Bonn. More exactly, from Neuwied."

"Studying?"

" Political science at Friedrich Wilhelm University."

"Students at Bonn have always been radicals... Almost as radical as those in Berlin! The Free University is at the epicentre of the student unrest... Hurt?" This last was in reaction to the grimace that crossed Thomas' face.

"Think you could find me a glass of water?" Thomas asked. Greiner poured one out and Thomas greedily drank it down.

"These infusions always make you thirsty. The doctors came to look you over this morning. They X-rayed your head. They said you'd better pray none of the neck vertebrae are damaged. Later the doctor brought in a normal civilian. I pretended to be sleeping. He asked the doctor a few questions about you, and asked him to call when you're better. It was clear the guy was from the BND."

"The what?"

"The national security service. If I were you I'd get ready for some questioning. They're all hot to find some anti-American elements.

And I can assure you they're taking it all seriously. When they come back, better tell them you were there to protest the Soviet invasion of Czechoslovakia. The doctor told me they'd be sending me home tomorrow morning. I'll print off a few of the photos I took of you at the demo where you're holding a picture of Brezhnev and Ulbricht with the letters SS across it. In another you have a portrait of Dubcek in your hand. I'm sure if you show them these pictures they'll leave you alone. If that doesn't work I suspect you may face expulsion from the university.

"And what about you?"

"What about me?"

"Won't you be kicked out of your work?" asked Thomas.

"I was just doing my job. I'm a journalist and we're always at risk,"

"I meant, won't they fire you on account of that article you wrote about those bastard police?"

"Careful," Greiner warned. "You never know who's listening. They won't fire me, but...I must admit I've been doing a lot of thinking these last couple of days... looks like I'll be leaving the paper of my own accord..."

"Are you really not happy at the paper which offers the best benefits package in Germany?"

"That's right. Old Man Axel knows how to look after his people. But that makes you the best paid reporter/prostitute in Germany. Besides, I'm really not prepared to keep pushing the line of primitive anti-Communism and at the same time blindly defend American aggressivity and racism. Not long ago I wrote something about the way they deal with the blacks in Chicago, and the boss threw me out of his office."

"Springer maintains that his papers say what most of the German people don't dare to say out loud," Thomas commented.

"With his racism and Nazism, Springer is waking up a beast in Germany which was starting to be tamed; at least I would like to think so. He makes a show of supporting Israel so that he can attack the left at will. I'm no socialist - quite the reverse - but his pro-American servility and antipathy for the student movement get on my nerves."

"For him we are terrorists who can be beaten and shot," nodded Thomas.

Just then the door opened and in came the doctor and another man.

"Well, I see you're feeling better,'" said the doctor in a kindly tone.

"What happened to me, doctor?"

"I guess you got caught up in the trouble at that demonstration. You had a wound at the base of your skull and your head was without feeling..." The doctor rotated his head and tried to move his neck until Thomas hissed in pain... That's good, you're reacting. Thankfully the X-ray showed no injury to your vertebrae. I imagine in two or three days you'll be able to go home... or at least out of the hospital," the doctor corrected himself with a look at the man at his side. He looked to be between forty and fifty, with a meaty face and pronounced creases around his eyes, and he immediately began his questioning.

"You're Thomas Ankermann, resident in Neuwied... born...?"

,"Yes."

,"Did you write this?" The man showed him a copy of some paper. Thomas glanced at it briefly and shook his head.

"I have no idea what that is."

"That's interesting, since we found it in your trousers pocket. After you get out of the hospital, report immediately to the Kreuzberg police station. Here is your summons. Immediately, understand? Don't even think about disappearing. We'll send you home from West Berlin only after you've explained a few things to us." With a sarcastic grin he added, "If you are able to..."

The two visitors left together; Greiner immediately picked up the photocopy they'd left behind and began to read it out loud. "Our Father, who art in the West, hallowed be thy name, Capital. Give us this day our daily profit, may the interest rates rise, both on Wall Street and in Europe. Give us our turnover and raise our credit rating as we raise the credit rate to our borrowers. Lead us not into bankruptcy and deliver us from the unions. Yours is half the world's kingdom, the power and the glory. Mammon." As he neared the end Greiner began to smile and then to laugh - "so finally I get to read that famous student Our Father. Not bad, not divine, but not bad. Did you write it?"

"I truly don't know it came to be in my pocket. I swear it's the first time I've laid eyes on it."

"What you say isn't important, but rather what the police investigator believes. If he says you had it in your trousers pocket, so it was in your pocket, even if you've never worn trousers in your life!" Greiner stared at his new student friend with a fatherly expression. "Thomas, I'm older than you and I know from experience this story doesn't necessarily have a happy end. They need to lay a few leaders of the student demos at the feet of the Establishment. They've already got rid of Dutschke so now they need new scapegoats. It's all getting out of hand; the Americans are unhappy. I'm afraid it won't be as easy for you to get out of this as I'd thought. I'm giving you fair warning. Don't make a move until I've brought you those pictures from the demonstration. When they're grilling you, don't hesitate to mention my name. I wanted to hand in my notice at Bild Zeitung right after they let me out of here, but I see it would be better if I hang on for a few more days. The testimony of a Bild reporter might do you some good... But I can assure you that for the next couple of days I'll be walking into the newsroom with my teeth clenched!"

Thomas smiled his thanks and, coming over to his bed, Greiner firmly shook the hand of the young idealist from Neuwied.

CHAPTER
TWENTYTWO

KIEV 1968

SASHA was seated in a creaky chair at the main Kiev KGB headquarters. She had been summoned here for questioning almost every day for three months. Fatigue was visible on her face and she almost always felt sick. An officer whose name she didn't even know was standing over her and shouting in a voice shaking with rage: "Now I'm going to read this to you for about the fiftieth time: 'I can't sleep, and I don't know how to go on living. All I know is that it is my moral duty to express to you the feelings that engulf me. I am completely sure that what we have done in Czechoslovakia is a tragic mistake and a bitter blow to Soviet-Czechoslovak friendship and to the worldwide Communist movement. It diminishes our prestige before the world and at home. It is a step back for all progressive forces, for world peace and for humanist dreams of future brotherhood. It is also my personal tragedy, for I have many friends in Czechoslovakia and I have no idea how I will be able to look them in the eye if indeed I ever meet them again'..."

Sasha wept softly. She had been carrying her child for four months now. The investigator took a drink of water, pursed his lips and, after finding his place, continued: 'It is my conviction that this is a huge gift to all the world's reactionary forces and that we are not able to foresee the consequences of this act. I love my country and its people and see myself as the humble bearer of the traditions of Russian literature passed to me by Pushkin, Tolstoy, Dostoevsky and Solzhenitzyn. These traditions have taught me that silence sometimes symbolizes shame. I beg you to understand my opinion on this action as the opinion of an honest son of my homeland and of the poet who once wrote the song 'Do the Russians Desire War?' Finishing his reading, the officer slammed the sheet of paper down onto the desk. "These words could only have been written by some pig who hates our socialist homeland." Something snapped inside her. She was physically small and light, but her words rang loud and clear: "That was not written by 'some pig', they are the words of Yevgeny Yevtushenko!"

"I don't care what the bastard is called, I want to know how this paper got into your handbag!"

"If I was carrying it in my bag I'd tell you so openly. But it was never in my possession!" Now resignation and apathy dominated her almost inaudible answer.

"Water?" the officer offered, sensing she was on the verge of vomiting again. Sasha just nodded. She had trouble drinking, her hands were shaking so much. "Okay, let's forget about this... Yevtushenko... But you still have to explain this code to me. What is the meaning of this series of numbers: 1, 3, 6, 8, 9?"

"I told you before, they are the numbers of the verses from the poem by the Slovak poet Andrej Sládkovič."

"Right, simply poetry! But they add up to 27. And do you know what the number 27 means? It's the number of Soviet divisions which are in Czechoslovakia! Do you mean to tell me that this is just a coincidence?"

Hardly had he finished speaking when an officer Sasha had not seen before burst into the room . He screamed at the investigator that he was a complete imbecile, and if he ever again revealed state military secrets he'd be sent straight to jail. Then Sasha realized that her interrogation was being monitored from outside the room. The number of Soviet divisions in Czechoslovakia was at this moment the last thing on her mind. The investigator was sent away by the angry officer who, noticing how pale Sasha looked, handed her the glass of water.

"Sorry, Alexandra Josifovna... they are idiots... let's try and put an end to this silly misunderstanding. Such fools... What the hell is going on here?!" To Sasha's surprise the officer seemed clearly contrite. She had not expected such a display of humanity from the KGB.

"Please let me be, I can't take any more of this. You have the book, just read it through, it's nothing more than a love story... Don't you understand... it's about love... love..." Sasha fell forwards, and if the officer had not caught her she would have landed on the concrete floor. The service doctor was immediately called. He took her pulse and realized it was too slow and faint. They had her taken at once to the military hospital.

CHAPTER
TWENTYTHREE

NEUWIED 1968

THOMAS' mother was sitting rather than lying on her bed. Her legs were very swollen and the pain was getting worse. The trouble with her legs had started just after the war, when Annemarie Ankermann was one of a million 'Trümmerfrau' (women of the ruins) who literally rebuilt the devastated country. It would have been impossible to count the thousands, tens of thousands, hundreds of thousands of bricks she'd moved with her bare hands. Slowly and with great patience she chipped away at them with a little old hammer before passing them to the bricklayers, usually old men who had not been called up to serve in the military and were now building shelters for those who had lost their homes in the senseless bombing raids carried out by the creators of the new world democracy. Most of the younger men had either died in the fighting or were rotting away in Soviet and American prisoner-of-war camps. Her husband was one of the more fortunate: near the end of the war he had been captured by the British in Hamburg, and had fortunately made his way back home.

Through the open door to the living room Annemarie could hear some television debate over which of the two Germanys was more coming to terms with its Nazi past, the West or the East. They were dealing with that eternal theme – 'Schuldgefühl' (guilty conscience).

A man's voice was reading: 'Beate Karlsfeld, a non-Jewish woman of German origin, the wife of the French Jew Serge Klarsfeld, who survived the concentration camp and became known as a Nazi hunter, came to Berlin on November 7 for a social democratic congress, made her way up to Chancellor Kiesinger, called him a Nazi and slapped his face.'

"She should have slapped him again, kicked him in the bum, and pushed him off the podium!" was the comment of Annemarie's son Thomas, who was in the living room getting ready for his afternoon shift. He had an after-school job making prefabricated concrete slabs in the factory where his dad was a foreman. His mother said nothing, and the voice continued: 'Up to the end of 1968 the German Federal Republic imprisoned 6,221 Germans for crimes committed under the Nazi regime. Last year only 30 Nazis were convicted, most of them insignificant figures. Not one judge from the Hitler era has ever been convicted of a war crime.'

"Close that door!" his mother called out. "I can't listen to any more of that! I was never in the Nazi Party, I never killed anyone, I ruined my health to rebuild the country but I'd never point my finger at anyone. We were all of us silent and afraid, yet nowadays everyone is a hero. I hate a Johnny-come-lately!"

"You don't get it, mama. It's not a question of revenge for... (he almost said 'your,' but stopped himself in time) behaviour during the war, it's about making sure it never happens again. If we don't come to terms with our past, it could well repeat itself."

"You're just lucky I won't be around in fifty years to ask you about your own failings."

"I'll do everything in my power to live in such a way that I'll be able to look my own children straight in the eye."

"Do you have the feeling your father and I can't look you in the eye?"

"Sorry, I wasn't thinking about you in particular."

"About who, then?"

The doorbell rang. The postwoman Hilda came with two letters for Thomas: one from Peter Greiner in Berlin, the other a registered letter from the Rector's Office at Friedrich Wilhelm University. Thomas impatiently tore Peter's letter open.

"Hi, Thomas! Sorry for the delay in writing, but I've been busy moving from Tiergarten to Wilmersdorf. It's a quieter area and Ingrid is closer to her mother here. I finally signed a contract with my new employer, Das Leben Publishers. Starting November 1, I'm officially their new correspondent for West Berlin and the GDR. I finally had enough of prostituting myself at Bild Zeitung. In my new workplace I have more freedom about what, how and when I write. Paradoxically, even though West Berlin is surrounded by that horrible wall, the atmosphere here seems a lot freer than elsewhere in the FRG. The students are much more courageous. Partly it's because the Free University only came into existence in 1948 and isn't so bound by the past. Maybe you should think about whether it would be worth your while studying Political Science here. I could find out the details and send them along to you.

"I'm really glad that my photos were of some use to you in your interrogation by the police. I have to say I was really afraid they'd send you to jail for a few months. Did you know that as of May there's been a new law on a state of emergency here. Do you have any news from your friend Jozef in Czechoslovakia? I send you my best wishes. Let me hear from you soon! Peter"

Thomas looked at his watch and saw he had six minutes to catch the bus from Ischl to his job. He stuck the other letter into his shirt pocket, kissed his mother goodbye and headed off to the bus stop. He was glad it was Friday, and he looked forwards to going to the new covered swimming pool the next day with his girlfriend, Helga. It was a beautiful sunny start to December. The hectic year, 1968, was slowly coming to an end, and Thomas' thoughts turned to Christmas. Then he had three exams upcoming in January and hoped to complete the semester successfully.

That thought reminded him of the letter in his pocket. He opened it as the bus took him to the factory. The University Rector was sorry to inform him that on the basis of information from the West Berlin police he had taken part in an unlawful demonstration which, according to the law declaring a state of emergency, forbade students who had participated in such actions from studying at universities in the Federal Republic of Germany. With regret they informed him that the University Council had decided that, with immediate effect, he was expelled from the university.

CHAPTER TWENTYFOUR

BRATISLAVA 1969

JOZEF'S little sister Katarina was so pleased. Her mother had bought her a bouquet of yellow chrysanthemums at the market. It was nothing extraordinary, but taking into account the poor selection it was a success and would surely please her homeroom teacher, Miss Baranyiova. It was International Teachers' Day, and this was an opportunity for the parents to show their gratitude to the teacher, who was celebrating forty years in the classroom. She had earned her teaching decree at the Sorbonne in Paris in the time of the First Czechoslovak Republic and was well-liked by the pupils, their parents and her fellow teachers. Some of her younger colleagues rolled their eyes, but secretly they respected Baranyiova's quality. It was her students who won the top prizes at the mathematics, physics and language Olympics. The principal was glad to have her on his staff.

Katarina came home confused, still carrying the bouquet. She hadn't been able to present it to Comrade Teacher because she was no longer employed at the school. Principal Hornacek himself had informed the students of the sad fact that yesterday Miss Baranyiova had retired. When some of the students decided to go to her home with their flowers, no-one answered the door, even though the house lights were shining.

The children had no way of knowing that their teacher was one of the first victims of the 'cleansing' that was slowly beginning throughout Czechoslovakia. She hadn't yet been dismissed, but the principal had informed her that her name appeared on the preliminary lists. The reason for this was straightforward: she had refused to sign a declaration that the Soviet occupation was an act of international aid. Baranyiova did not wish to complicate the situation for Mr. Hornacek and requested retirement, effective immediately.

At his university, Jozef and his schoolmates were informed that starting in their third semester a new subject would be introduced: 'Theory of Marxism-Leninism'. It was to be taught by Associate Professor Liseckova from Moscow. It was rumoured that all their teachers would gradually be replaced by staff from the Soviet Union.

The Czechoslovak Socialist Republic had been declared a federation on October 30, 1968 by President Ludvík Svoboda in Bratislava. A dental technician named Samuel Babulic had glued together his broken false teeth, so the President was able to declare the new federation without lisping.

From the Business Faculty campus to Belopotocka Street was not a great distance, so Jozef usually went to school and home on foot. Today, March 28, 1969, he stopped at the school dormitory to agree with his friends on where they would watch the big hockey game. The week before, at the World Hockey Championships in Stockholm, the Czechoslovak team had surprised everyone by beating the world champion Soviet Union 2:0, and now the two countries would meet again, in the semifinals.

Just as he was about to go into the dormitory he heard the loud noise of a low-flying helicopter. From its cabin, leaflets were falling over the town's roofs, streets and squares. A few of these fluttered to the earth in front of the dormitory entrance, so Jozef bent down and picked one up. On it was the news that the Central Committee of the Czechoslovak Communist Party was officially informing the citizenry that the counterrevolutionary forces in Czechoslovakia had been definitively defeated. The flyer condemned Smrkovsky and praised the 'healthy forces' represented by Bilak, Husak, Svoboda, and a few others. Dubcek was not mentioned. After having read a few lines it came to Jozef that the leaflet was printed in Russian. From this he surmised that they hadn't found anyone willing to translate this rubbish into Slovak. He threw the leaflet back on the ground.

In his friend Brblos's room things were merry as usual. His Sony Duo tape player was playing the newest hit by the Beatles, 'Revolution'. A picture of Jan Palach was taped to the wall. When Palach set fire to himself in Prague on January 16, Brblos organized a student march to SNP Square the following day. They lit candles and sang the song, 'Run Home, Ivan'. The demonstration had scarcely begun when the police showed up and ordered them to break it up. It was Brblos' bad luck that even when he whispered his voice sounded like it was coming through a megaphone, so one policeman took him for the ringleader and tried out his new truncheon on his back. It turned out that it was of such exceptional quality that even a month later Brblos was still earning cigarettes in the shower room by showing the other students the 'sausages' on his back.

The boys gathered in Baca's room to watch the game. Since he was a senior student he had a special privilege – a television set. Although the room was designed for four, there were now about thirty squeezed into it. At that moment all across Czechoslovakia - in living rooms, stations and pubs - similar overcrowding was the norm. The inhabitants of the country were particularly aroused because originally the World Championships were to be held in Czechoslovakia, but the country's new leadership, the 'normalizers' had refused the honour since it could lead to unforeseen reactions by the fans. In other words, they understood that for Czechs and Slovaks hockey was a powerful moral weapon. And so it turned out, because for the second time in the tournament Czechoslovakia beat the Soviet Union, 4:3. When the team captain Jozef Golonka threw down his helmet at the end of the game, it was the signal for a hearty cheer from fifteen million throats. The television moderator Vladimir Vacha finished his broadcast with the words, 'Now you at home, celebrate'. For these words, he was dismissed from the TV station shortly thereafter.

Spontaneously, the population hit the streets; over a half-million people in Czechoslovakia's seventy cities and towns rejoiced on that March evening. The hockey victory served as a sort of plaster on the wound that the nation had received nine months earlier. The less the people dared to undertake any action against their occupiers, the more they projected their anger and helplessness onto their hockey players, who had represented them by beating the Russians. The Slovaks had always been fond of showing someone something 'representationally'. For a thousand years they lived in subjugation, landless, at best asservants and flunkies. Those thousand years had taught them how to bow and scrape. The backs of the Slovak people had been bent by all that bowing down to their greater or lesser overlords. Thus they were taught to genuflect by masters, reeves, priests, policemen, innkeepers: the powerful, high and low. How well they had learned to scrape! They were so used to it that it was all the same to them who they bowed down to - landowners, the church, communists, democrats. They all knew that it was enough to cleverly sneak in a new regime and the nation would keep on obeying. The worst that would happen was that they would grumble at home under the covers or after a few shots in the pub, maybe even throw a few rocks at someone safely from behind a rock, but that was the extent of it. They didn't dare do more; they wanted to stay alive. Under the Soviet occupation too they had to survive, to stay alive - with their backs bent. As the saying goes, nothing is so bad that it can't get even worse. Now the nation was revelling in the victory of their hockey team, and the tension was so thick you could cut it with a knife. The supreme leadership of the occupation forces warned their Czechoslovak puppets that if they couldn't handle the situation, the Soviet troops were prepared to go into the streets and restore order themselves.

When a couple of hundred spirited and enthusiastic students approached the U Tvarozka building which housed the Soviet division headquarters, they were unaware of the Soviet decree. They were headed for SNP Square, so U Tvarozka was only a short detour. They had been fortifying their resolve at the U Hasicov pub and as a result were in a wild mood. The day before, Jozef had by chance gone past the Tvarozka building, and the cobblestone pavement was unbroken and certainly not dug up. But when they approached it that evening Jozef was surprised to see that the part in front of the building had been removed and a few wheelbarrows of broken pavement left standing nearby. The students gathered under the building's windows and chanted the names of Golonka, Dzurilla, Nedomansky, Suchy and the other players who had brought about the glorious 4:3 victory. Then they turned to ridiculing Ragulin and other members of the Soviet team. This somehow continued led into cries against Brezhnev, Kosygin and Podgorny. Suddenly someone started the call: 'Russians go home! Russians go home!' The chant caught on. Someone gleefully unfurled a Czechoslovak flag, which was followed by another and another. Then a large portrait of Dubcek was displayed. Then came the splintering of glass; a stone had broken a window in the Soviet division headquarters. The police stood on the pavement in close formation. "Bloody Russian pigs," a familiar voice near Jozef screamed out. The guy who shouted proceeded to pick up a rock and threw in with all his might in the direction of the building. It was Winter. Others copied his daring exploit and soon the building's windows broke in a shower of glass. The police moved forwards. Jozef looked around, but Winter was nowhere to be seen. A loud shout rang out, some police official ordering the students to disperse. But the stones continued to fly. Truncheons out, the police began their work. That was enough for the students, and their protests transformed into the emptying of bottles of liquor in their dormitory rooms.

When Jozef got home just before midnight, he was sweaty and dirty and stinking of alcohol. After taking a shower, he joined his family at the table. His father was watching the news on Austrian TV, an advantage of the family being trilingual. As Jozef spread lard on a slice of bread and sliced an onion, he followed the special report being read by an Austrian newsman. On the screen were shots from Prague showing demonstrators in front of the Soviet air company Aeroflot celebrating the result of the hockey game. There too stones were breaking the company's display windows, but the police reaction was delayed until all possible damage had been done. The moderator commented on this strange behaviour, thus confirming Jozef's impression that the whole thing was a put-up job. The next day, the same Austrian station would carry a report that the whole event was stage-managed by the Czech Interior Minister, Grösser. Secret police agents had provoked the over-excited students into the violence. He thought back to the hot-headed Winter and the curious pile of stones that had appeared from one day to the next...

A few days later Alexander Dubcek resigned from the post of Communist Party First Secretary and was replaced by the pro-Moscow Gustav Husak.

CHAPTER
TWENTYFIVE

KOLODNE (UKRAINE) 1969

IN the village of Kolodne, in the Ivanovo-Frankovsk area in Carpatho- Ukraine, everyone was watching the Soviet Union versus Czechoslovakia hockey game. A great majority of the villagers were supporting the Czechs/Slovaks. The older inhabitants well remembered when they were a part of Czechoslovakia. Those were the golden years for the community. Even now the town's lone asphalt road was called Masarykova. It had been laid in the times of the First Czechoslovak Republic. After 1945, without asking anyone, Stalin annexed Carpatho-Ukraine to the Soviet Union. The elders' strong emotional relationship with the country of their birth still remained. The people of Kolodne had always felt themselves to be more Slovak than Soviet. No-one was able to completely explain what 'Soviet' actually meant.

After the referee's final whistle, they jubilantly opened bottles of homemade alcohol and toasted the victory. They were able to celebrate openly, without fear that some stranger could overhear them – they were among 'our' own people, and they knew who was 'ours' and who was not. The only real risk was the great quantity of illegally distilled alcohol on hand, and that too was only dangerous on account of strangers. The locals knew that the militiaman Vasja and even the head of the village committee distilled their own drink.

Homebrewed solidarity was a stronger bond for the proletariat than Marx and Engels put together.

Everyone was celebrating except for Alexandra Grycenko. She had returned home four months earlier. The KGB had finally realized that the 'code' they had hoped would lead them to some secret underground in Ukraine was simply an innocent notation of the verses of a love poem by a Slovak author. When they checked the alibi of a certain Andrej Sládkovic they found that he could not be the leader of an anti-Soviet conspiracy since he had been dead for almost one hundred years. They let Sasha go home. They didn't have to expel her from the army since she herself had requested to be dismissed. She was just an administrative worker, so the only thing she had to do was sign a pledge of silence.

Alexandra did not toast the hockey victory. That afternoon, on the day of Czechoslovakia's glorious victory, she had given birth to a son in the Irsava hospital. Despite the fact that he came into the world a month earlier than expected, he was healthy and full of life. She named him after her father: Josif. Since the child's father was unknown he was registered as Josif Josifovich Grycenko. Some people maintained that she had given him the name in honour of the captain of the Czechoslovak hockey team, Jozef Golonka.

But Sasha knew which Jozef she had named the baby after.

CHAPTER
TWENTYSIX

NEUWIED 1969

On the last day of June, Balaz passed his exam in Marxist philosophy. This meant that only statistics stood between him and the successful completion of his second year. His teacher, the strict Mr. Benko, advised him to spend the summer reviewing certain concepts in the subject and to come for the make-up examination in September. Jozef wasn't too bothered by this schedule since the only major event planned for his summer was the Economics University volleyball team trip to West Germany. Despite the strong rhetoric about closing the borders, Czechs and Slovaks were so far still free to travel anywhere in the whole world. Jozef felt both excitement and curiosity in equal measures. This would be the first time he'd see a so-called capitalist country. In fact, it would be one of his first trips anywhere beyond the boundaries of Czechoslovakia. His first time abroad was when he was eighteen. He'd travelled to Budapest to visit an uncle there. His parents had tried a couple of times in vain to get a hard-currency allowance, which was the necessary precondition for applying for permission to travel to a capitalist country or even to Yugoslavia. There were no rules governing this hard-currency allowance; mostly it depended on the strength of one's connections in the Czechoslovak State Bank. Such contacts were mostly built on the basis of bribes. But now everything was being arranged by the Slovak Students' Union, the team's guarantor.

When the Prague-Cologne express arrived in the West German border town of Schirnding, Jozef was overcome by a strange and powerful emotion. An enamel sign at the station read: 'Willkommen in Bayern!' (Welcome to Bavaria!) So this was West Germany. His head was full of the thoughts which, mostly in elementary school, had been drummed into his brain. Bavaria, where the prime minister was the reactionary Franz Josef Strauss, the man who wanted to arm West Germany with nuclear weapons.

This was the area from which in the 1950s, so they had been told, the imperialists had floated balloons full of potato bugs over Czechoslovakia in order to undermine socialist agricultural production. This was the West, which he had thought he would never visit in his entire lifetime. Since he spoke German fluently, he had no trouble deciphering the announcement that the train would remain in the station for fifteen minutes. He couldn't resist the urge to get off the train. He had the feeling that his legs were about to give way under him. For the first time in his life he was standing on 'Western' soil. Once, as a child, he'd visited Bratislava Castle and looked out across the Danube into Austria. On that occasion, he had lamented that for him Austria was as far away as the moon - a place he would never get to. Once, when his uncle Emil and his seven year old son were visiting from Cadca in the north of Slovakia, they had made a bicycle trip to Devin Castle. The whole castle area was strung with barbed wire and big signs that warned: 'Border zone, no entry, danger of death!' Behind the barbed wire, guard towers had been erected at regular intervals. Since little Paul needed the toilet, they got off their bikes. A guard up in his tower kept an eye on them. Seeing him, Paul asked his dad what those towers were for. His father, a teacher, answered soberly: "Those are guard towers. The border guards in them are protecting us from our enemies." Paul thought this over for a while and, still looking at the guard, asked: "Then why is he looking in our direction?" Without answering, Uncle Emil got back on his bicycle and started pedalling back to Devin. Although Jozef was only two years older than Paul, he never forgot that day.

And now he was standing in Schirnding, West Germany. He smiled to himself. Today was the first time he had ever been on the other side of that barbed wire. He breathed in deeply. The air felt and tasted the same as on his own side of the border. He and Dezo each bought a pack of cigarettes, John Player Specials. They came in a black bakelite case, which he held in his hand like a sacrament. If they came back home with such cigarettes they'd be really cool.

The Slovak students were discovering the so-called Western lifestyle. For some their biggest problem with capitalism occurred in their hotel bathrooms. Laco refused to run water into the tub, claiming the tap set reminded him of a nuclear power station control unit, while Šaňo discovered a small tank with its own tap next to the toilet bowl. He was quite merrily using it to wash his feet until someone explained to him what a bidet was for. Luckily he figured out how to let the water out of the bathtub, otherwise it would have remained there until they checked out of the hotel,

Another slight misunderstanding arose in a restaurant in Duisburg, where they were each served a bowl full of acidic water. The boys wondered why they didn't serve it in glasses but assumed this was a quirk of this particular establishment - at least until the waiter, seeing someone about to drink from it, advised them that a fingerbowl is served to clean one's hands after eating. On the other hand, in the shops no-one shouted at them, the staff treated them politely, and Balaz almost fell over when the chemist even came and opened the door for him as he was leaving.

Winter was the group leader, even though he had put on a lot of weight recently and no longer played on the team. But he was happy to act in an official role, and was head of the international relations section of the Slovak University Student Union. Although this was a full-time position, he somehow managed to combine it with a regular class load at the Economics University. This had been arranged for him by Jano Husak, so no-one enquired any deeper into it. Winter appeared relaxed, even jovial, during the trip; he made jokes about politics and even, at a reception hosted by a Deutsche

Bank director in Duisburg, went so far as to state that the incursion into Czechoslovakia by Warsaw Pact troops was a mistake. During the debate that followed, the other students unanimously supported this opinion. Jozef chose not to participate in political discussions when Winter was present. He had been cautious about what he said to him since their exchange of opinions in the Hron restaurant and what had happened in front of the military headquarters in the U Tvarozka building. He also advised the other students not to say too much. At the end of the Deutsche Bank reception it was Winter who delivered the thank-you speech. He spoke without notes, in very good German, and was rewarded by spontaneous applause.

"Where did you pick up your German?" he was asked after his speech. Curiously, Winter appeared embarrassed and answered in some confusion: "I attended a German secondary school in Kezmarok...and I learned a little bit at home..." he added.

"You speak it as if it was your native language. Congratulations!" Jozef was sincere in his praise. Winter just smiled.

After a week of wandering around Germany the Slovak students split up; some returned home while others wanted to travel some more across Europe. Jozef got on the train at Duisburg, the last place the team slept together, and headed for Cologne. Thomas and some of his friends met him at the station. Their reunion was very emotional for both of them. They immediately carried on to Illrich, where Thomas lived with his parents.

The year before in *Vysne Hagy*, where they had met playing volleyball during the Slovak National Uprising Cup, Thomas had invited Jozef to visit him. The volleyball team from Neuwied, a small town on the banks of the Rhine River between Koblenz and Bonn, was participating for the first time in a socialist country. Both teams were accommodated in the same hostel. Thomas played banjo, Jozef guitar, and together they had entertained their friends at evening gatherings.

Jozef had wanted to earn a bit of money for his studies so Thomas' father had found him a summer job in a factory making concrete panels for new houses. They became accustomed to travelling together early in the morning from Illrich to Neuwied. In reality Illrich no longer existed as such since its five thousand inhabitants had been incorporated into Neuwied in June, 1969. In spite of this, the locals still proudly called themselves Illrich, and kept painting over the first part of the Neuwied-Illrich sign at bus stops.

After work, Jozef played for the local volleyball team, which the year before had been promoted to the top German league. The owner of the club, Mr. Wellner, was also the owner of the concrete panel factory. In those times Czechoslovak volleyball was among the best in the world, and they had even been world champions three years before. When Jozef mentioned that he'd played against Slávia Bratislava, the Czechoslovak captain Golian's home team, he was treated with great respect.

Jozef had entered an entirely new world. He saw colour television for the first time in the Roland club where the team regularly hung out after practices. He heard the newest hits by the Beatles, the Archies and Barry Ryan. He saw the hit American film 'Bonnie and Clyde' with Faye Dunaway and Warren Beatty in the lead roles. This marked the first time he had experienced wide-screen cinema. When he drank Coca-Cola from its traditional pear-shaped bottle, his hand actually shook. Thomas commented on this with a wide smile, and all Jozef could do was shrug and say: "For the first time in my life I'm drinking the real thing!"

'Sepp', as his German friends now called him, quickly adapted to life under capitalism in the shops and pubs, but not so well on the job site. Along with Germans there were also Serbs, Turks and Portuguese working at the factory. Lunch break was strictly from twelve to one in the afternoon. That August was very hot, so the workers generally ate lunch out of the sun in the cool cellar. In one of the rooms they stored the textile insulation sheets, which made a nice resting-place. The manager ate lunch in a nearby restaurant, and was sometimes late in returning. Balaz didn't see why the men always got up precisely at one o'clock and went to work in the hot sun. He was comfortable on his mattress and found himself drifting off to sleep.

"What's up young man? Aren't you feeling well?" the manager Karl asked in a concerned voice.

"Just having a little lie-down."

"What do you mean a lie-down?" Karl didn't get it. "The break is over."

"Well, the boss isn't around."

"Now I understand why it's taking you so long to build that socialism of yours, " Karl laughed. "What does it matter if the boss is here or not? It says in your contract that you work eight and a half hours per day, and for that you get the money agreed on. I assume you want to get all of that money."

"Of course."

"So old man Wellner, the man who gives you that money, expects that you're going to work those hours."

"Yeah, but... but..." Balaz objected, but uncertainly. "He's not here to see us." Karl and the rest of the men who were standing around broke out laughing. "Hey, Marx would call this exploitation," Balaz tried a little humour.

"Who's he, a teacher of yours?" Karl asked.

"He's your teacher - a German theoretician who described the exploitation of the working class by the capitalists."

"Well I've never heard of your favourite German, but keep on lying there if you want to. But first tell me how much a worker earns per hour back home," and he gave Jozef a questioning look.

"Oh, about ten to fifteen crowns... about fifty pfennig..."

Loud laughter filled the air.

"Good then; we'll give you those fifty pfennig and you can keep on lying around... that's about one-fifth of what we get paid. Agreed?"

Jozef stood up and shamefacedly went back to the workshop. He never again tried to extend the break-time. Once, on the way to work, he saw a group of unemployed men carrying banners demanding jobs. 'If our employed people looked so well-dressed and well-fed, they'd be so happy they'd never think of going on strike,' he thought to himself.

From then on he became an enthusiastic worker. He kept thinking about the dress he'd buy with the money for his true love, Sasha. He wasn't sure how he would give it to her, but that wasn't important. He hadn't heard from her in almost a year, he didn't even know if she was still in Czechoslovakia or at home in Ukraine. He'd sent her a few letters and postcards, care of the student dormitory at the Economics University in Kiev. Although he never got an answer, he continued to write her romantic letters. When he went to the Karstadt department store to buy the dress, he realized he didn't know her size. He found a woman who had the same build as Sasha, and she was glad to help him out. He wondered which dress would make Sasha happy, and they were glad to assist him in his choice. He told them that the girl the dress was for had beautiful turquoise eyes, and immediately the saleslady found a wonderful dress in a combination of ivory and a soft turquoise colour. It wasn't exactly cheap, but when his model tried it on, he knew it was the right choice.

He didn't want to admit to himself that maybe he'd never again meet Sasha to give her his gift. Although they had met each other only once, and that over a year ago, the passing of time did nothing to erase her memory from his mind.

CHAPTER
TWENTYSEVEN

KOLODNE 1969

THE house of Josif Josifovich Grycenko stood near the main street in the centre of the village. He and his sons Josif, Ivan and Michail had built it together ten years ago. Like the rest of the houses in this district, it was built of unbaked clay.

When Josif Josifovich found out that Sasha was expecting a child by an unknown man, he wanted to disown her. Sasha heard this only later from her mother, who had managed to convince her outraged husband that despite everything that had happened, Sasha was still their daughter, and that after being discharged from the army she had no place to live. For Josif Josifovich, a former officer in the Soviet army and the Czechoslovak Liberation Army, no-one had the right to bring his honour into question – not even his own daughter. Out-of-wedlock children were nothing rare in the Soviet Union, but not in the family of Josif Grycenko. He finally gave in to his wife's insistence and Sasha was sheltered in the family home, which she'd returned to after leaving the army. She was released on medical grounds. His condition for her returning was that she would give up her child. She refused adamantly, even at the cost of leaving their house and never seeing her parents again.

In the end, the situation was saved by Major Michail Obicki, who asked Sasha for her hand. They had known each other from the days when they'd both worked at the District Military Administration in Kiev. Even then he had had a crush on her, He wasn't a bad fellow. But Sasha was still young and didn't wish to end up like many other eighteen year olds, with three children by the age of twenty-five, and whose major social activity apart was dragging their husbands out of the pub late at night. In the Soviet Union, being without a man meant being exposed to the sneers of decrepit married women who – often beaten and degraded by their husbands – had one last refuge: they were not alone. 'The more you beat your wife, the tastier your soup will be,' the men said to each other toughly, at which the women giggled in embarrassment. When Michail proposed to Sasha, she didn't stop to think it over. Little Josif needed a father, Mišo was a nice enough guy, and so she accepted him. He was ten years older than her, but he looked good in his uniform and was the dream of many women.

The three-room house would have been sufficient if Josif Grycenko and his wife Olga, Grycenko's eighty year old mother, her son Ivan and his wife, Larisa, plus their son, did not all live there. On hearing that Sasha and her son would be moving into the house, Larisa started to talk openly about going back to her mother in Irsava. That house was no larger, but her mother had recently been taken into the local mental hospital and, according to the doctors, there was no chance she'd ever be able to go back home. Thus, they would have two rooms for themselves. But in the end they didn't have to decide, since Major Obicki, on his first visit to the Grycenkoes to discuss the wedding arrangements, announced that after the ceremony they would be travelling to the city of Komsomolsk in the Far East. A new two-room flat was already prepared for them there. The major was being transferred to the Far East military division due to the growing incidence of hostile actions by the Chinese People's Republic on the Soviet-Chinese borders.

"So you're going off to war," commented Grycenko thoughtfully. Suddenly he began to feel sorry for Michail and his daughter.

"Not to a war, but to local armed actions in Ussuri…"

"I know what 'local armed actions' means," declared Grycenko.

Then they drank spirits until they were both legless. This was how Major Obicki definitively won his father-in-law over. Sasha's mother cried all night and throughout the following day. She realized that her daughter would be moving to practically the other end of the Soviet Union, about twelve thousand kilometres from home. It was even farther than Western Siberia, where their neighbour, Serioz, had been sent for eight years for killing his wife.

CHAPTER
TWENTYEIGHT

NEUWIED – BRATISLAVA 1969

ALTHOUGH the parliamentary elections in Germany were to be held on September 27 (Jozef easily remembered when, because the German elections almost always fell on his birthday), the street furnishings and buses were already plastered with the faces of the various parties' candidates. He listened with enthusiasm to the heated debates of his German friends as they passionately commented on the programs of the individual political parties. It seemed funny to him that after practice the guys from the volleyball team would fall out at the Roland pub over their political favourites.

"Do you really need so many parties? If you had only one like us you wouldn't be arguing so much," he teased the others. The television was always on at the Roland, and the news was just beginning. The American astronaut Neil Armstrong, the first man to step on the moon, was on a visit to Germany. After shots of Armstrong waving to the crowds came some footage from Prague, where a protest demonstration had greeted the first anniversary of the Soviet occupation, August 21.

"Police and military divisions were set out against the citizens. In fact, tank brigades were called out in the centre of Prague and Brno. This tank operation marks the largest military engagement of

the Czechoslovak army since the Second World War. In Prague, Brno and Bratislava, the armed forces' reaction was particularly strong, and order was restored only late at night. The show of force was made possible by a new law on the maintenance and preservation of public order, or in popular parlance, the 'law of the truncheon'. This law made the citizen susceptible to a fine of up to 5,000 crowns, a prison sentence of up to three months, and dismissal from work or school. What was surprising about the law was that it was signed by the Chairman of the Federal Assembly, Alexander Dubcek.

On the 20th of August, the militia shot two people dead in Prague, then another two in Brno the following day. As a lawyer, President Husak realized that these violent acts were not protected by the law, so on August 22 he quickly summoned the Federal Assembly Executive, who recommended the plenary approve the 'law of the truncheon'. The only one not to support the bill was Dubcek, but in the end he signed it into law."

Following the report the place grew quiet. All heads turned towards Jozef. 'So Dubcek signed a law against the people...' he thought in disappointment. It came as a shock to him. Svoboda, Dubcek and Cernik, the three men of the Prague Spring, were now signing its death certificate.

"That's the way it happens here too. When the people stand up and say something, they set the police on them. But look here, things aren't looking too good back home," Hans turned to Jozef. "Thousands of your countrymen are staying here. Wellner promised you the chance to play for our team, and you could study at the university in Bonn. You speak great German, they'll give you a little flat, a sports scholarship, and you could keep working at the factory. I spoke to Wellner about you, and he'd be glad if you took him up on his offer..." urged Hans.

"That's a great idea; Seppi, stay here. We're in the top division, you could help us." The boys set to persuading Jozef to stay in Germany. He said nothing but thought to himself: when Alexander Dubcek signs laws making it legal to beat demonstrators and kick students out of school, things are bad indeed.

The television was turned off, and on the radio a young Dutch singer called Heintje was singing about his mummy, who had made it possible to fulfill his childhood dreams. He promised his mama that when she needed him to, he would give her back that love.

Jozef stared in front of himself. The boys kept quiet, sensing what was going on in his head. He thought about his own mama, his dad and sisters, his friends at Uni and in the city, about Bratislava his beloved if shabby home town. He was born there, as well as under the Tatras, in fact anywhere in his native land. He remembered his father's words: 'You're Slovak, and no matter what, you'll never leave your country. If things get bad for you, go up to see the monument to General Stefanik on Bradlo, look out over the four poles of the compass and everywhere you'll see a wonderful country with lovely people who need you - just like you need them. Bradlo, family, friends, his dear Tatras, everything was drawing him home. The borders were still open, and the Czechoslovak government was negotiating with the Soviets about removing their troops. He politely turned down their generous offer. In two days he'd be going back home.

The whole team, as well as Thomas' parents, came to bid him farewell at the Cologne train station. His friend's mother was being pushed in a wheelchair, but she came all the same. As a souvenir, Mr. Wellner presented Jozef with a Lamborghini wrist watch, which even today he has stored among his most treasured possessions. The conductor was waving 'all aboard', so Jozef finally got on the train. Thomas had taken off his glasses and seemed to be rubbing his eyes. They embraced one last time, and neither tried to hide their tears. Jozef had invited Thomas to visit him in Bratislava, but both realized it might not be that simple. The Slovak and the German didn't want to be separated: 'Auf Wiedersehen,' Jozef said, 'Till next time'. Thomas thrust into Jozef's hand as a last-minute gift a book he knew the young Slovak really wanted to read. It was by Johannes Mario Simmel and was titled, 'Alle Menschen werden Brüder' (All Men Will Be Brothers). "This will stop you from forgetting German at least. Dofidenja," Thomas smiled through his tears. When the train began to shunt, neither of them imagined it would take thirty-seven long years for them to meet again.

In the spring of 1970, the Communist Party leader Husak announced that 'the frontier is not a boulevard', and that Czechoslovakia was closing its borders. Censorship and the control of letters and parcels were reintroduced. Jozef and Thomas wrote to each other for a time after Jozef got back home, but it was clear that letters from capitalist Germany were being opened. He was called in by the Faculty Vice-Dean and gently told that it wasn't right for him to be writing to a citizen of a capitalist country. They suggested he find a pen-pal from the Soviet Union. Jozef had a brainstorm. He asked the Vice-Dean if the University couldn't help him locate Alexandra Josifovna Grycenko, an administration worker for the Soviet Army; of course it would be a lot easier for an institution to find someone than for an individual. The Vice-Dean liked the idea. It would be good if at a time when students were unwilling to travel to the Soviet Union, there was at least one student in the school who was befriending a citizen of their brother country. The Vice-Dean promised Jozef the complete support of the school administration, and he kept his word. Just before Christmas 1969, in the presence of the Secretary for Foreign Affairs of the Business Faculty and the Consul from the USSR Consulate in Bratislava, he read out a letter from Kiev. The sender was the Personnel Office of the District Military Administration in Uzghorod. In response to the request of the Dean's Office of the Business Faculty of the Economics University and the USSR Consulate in Bratislava, they announced that Alexandra Josifovna Grycenko, resident in Kolodne, Carpatho-Ukraine, Irsava District, had married an officer of the Soviet Army, Major Michail Borisovich Obicky, who, on 1. 9. 1969 was seconded to the staff of the Far East Military Administration headquartered in the city of Komsomolsk.

Jozef wrapped the ivory and turquoise dress in a plastic wrapper with the logo of the Karstadt firm on it and put it away in the farthest corner of his old wooden cupboard.

Part II

CHAPTER
ONE

BRATISLAVA 1970

A band called Istropolis, with Karol Solenský singing, played at the Bernolak student hostel entertainment evenings. Jozef enjoyed going there with his friends, and in its repertoire the band played international hits that Jozef loved. He had learned to play a few of them on the guitar he had bought in his last year of secondary school. To get it he had skipped lunch for a month and saved the one hundred and forty crowns for the cheapest 'Spanish' guitar available. 'Memphis Tennessee' by Johnny Rivers, 'Shake Hands' and 'Marmor Stein und Eisen bricht' by Drafi Deutscher, 'Yesterday Man' by Chris Andrews, 'Sloop John B' by the Beach Boys and his all-time favourite, 'Massachusetts' by the Bee Gees were among the first tunes he learned to play on his new guitar.

Cuki, Dezo, Baca, Selo, Jozef and the others were discussing the Skiing World Championship now taking place in the High Tatras. It was hard for them to hear each other since the dance-floor was full of twisting bodies and the band obviously had quality amplifiers. The whole of Czechoslovakia was caught up by The World Championships, if not for the skiing then due to the fact that the opening gala was the first ever colour transmission by Czechoslovak Television. Jozef enjoyed looking at his countrymen's gaping faces and thinking back to his own reactions a year before at the Roland pub in Germany.

The boys laughingly toasted the delayed arrival of colour broadcasting in Czechoslovakia. It was good news, in spite of the statistic that only one in ten households in the country owned a television set. This statistic translated into some kind of bond among the citizenry, since the neighbours, if not the whole building, tended to come to watch programs of great general interest in the flat of the fortunate owner. On the other hand, this made the state apparatus nervous, since neighbours gathering to watch the news and political commentaries were sure to have something to say to each other about the 'official story'. Watching television together came to be an unofficial Czechoslovak version of Hyde Park.

Karol and his band finished their set and the dancers made their way back to their tables. The guys were in the midst of discussing the dismissal of Professor Fidrkus from the school; he was one of many who had refused to sign a declaration that the invasion of the Warsaw Pact troops was an act of international aid. The debate centred on how to get him reinstated. He was a very popular teacher; a Czech by birth, his Slovak was more melodious than that of many natives. Then Jan Winter came up to the table, his arm around a nice-looking girl. They'd just left the dance-floor and the girl was happy for an excuse to get his sweaty arm off her. Jan Husak too came over with Winter. Although he never mentioned that his father was the most powerful man in the country, it was something the others never forgot. Winter had been drinking, and tried to pull the girl down onto a chair beside him. She had a refined expression, pretty blues eyes and wonderful slim legs. It was clear that Winter had designs on her, but equally clear that she wasn't interested. Politely but firmly, she excused herself and moved off to another table. Jozef made sure he remembered which table she was sitting at.

"Listen Jan," Dezo started right in, "isn't there something to be done about Fidrkus? If your dad was behind him, for sure they'd let him stay here."

Husak took a deep breath then nodded his head: "Naturally there'd be no problem. I already talked to him about it. The School

Committee is ready to overlook the condition he sign the declaration, but only if he stops agitating against the Soviets. But... he just won't listen."

"But why did they get rid of Zeman? He was the best in the whole faculty – without politics, just a physical educator instructor and volleyball coach."

"Zeman had bad luck precisely because he was in Phys. Ed. Listen guys, you have to understand that my father doesn't think these things up, it's Moscow putting the pressure on him." Husak junior said in a disgusted voice. "When he gave Brezhnev a list of those to be expelled, it was less than two percent of the Communist Party's rank-and-file. Moscow insisted that at least twenty percent be dismissed. Brezhnev presented it to my father as an ultimatum. He also threatened a return to the fifties. I don't have to tell you how Bilak, Indra, Jakes, Salgovic and the rest are waiting for my father's resignation. I was present when he had his meeting with Kadar. He told him how much repression, how many executions and prisoners, was the result in Hungary after 1956, and my father didn't was willing to pay any price to avoid the same thing here. He didn't want to see innocent people put behind bars, didn't want to see the Party stripped of all of its intelligent members. But he had to sack a good number of academics from the universities. So, instead of specialists, he kicked out gym teachers. And by the way, we've arranged for Zeman to have a part-time contract; they're not even going to chop his salary." Husak downed his glass of wine at one go. "Try telling Fidrkus to stop with the politics and stick to his subject. I know we need him here, and so does my father," Jan concluded.

Istropolis came back on stage and Karol Solensky broke into 'Let´s Twist Again' by Chubby Checker. Jozef had already noticed what a good dancer Winter's partner was – far too good for such a clumsy guy. As soon as the music started he went over to her table and asked her to dance. She didn't look exactly thrilled.

"I didn't come over here to propose to you – that can wait till later," he joked. "I'm Jozef." She took his arm as they made their way onto the dance floor. "Marta," she smiled back.

Her lithe body rippled to the rhythm of rock and roll; she backed away from him only to move forward in graceful movements. From the start he was so fascinated by her that instead of thinking about his dance steps, he just watched her move. Then he began to put everything he'd picked up in dance class into his dancing. In fact they were so obviously into their own space that the other couples moved back a little to give them room. Then the students surrounded them, clapping along with the rhythm. They fit so well together that it seemed like they'd been attending dance lessons for years. Their energy reached right up to the stage, where Solensky encouraged them with his gestures. When the song ended, the hall broke out in spontaneous applause. Only Winter was not clapping. He left with a sour look on his face. Solensky gave Jozef the thumbs up, and started a slow song, 'Strangers in the Night'. When Jozef put his arms around the girl, she didn't pull away. They were both sweaty and out of breath. The lights dimmed, as befit the mood of the song. The couples on the dance-floor silently moved into each other's embrace. Jozef was aware of the beating of Marta's heart, and she could feel his in return.

"May I call you Marta? You're the lady but I'm clearly older than you..." he asked.

"Of course. I'm Marta. My friends call me Mata."

"Joe." He guessed she was waiting for the ritual kiss normal on such occasions, but he just smiled.

"You're from Bratislava, right?"

"How did you guess?"

"You can't hide an accent like that. You can spot a native a mile away," she laughed.

"And you, where are you from?"

"Uhadni."

"From your beautiful Slovak, I'd judge that's in Central Slovakia."

"In Eastern Slovakia, Presov in fact. But I was born in the Spis area, in Podolinec."

"So I should apologize that I'm a full-blooded Bratislavian."

"What are you studying?" he led the conversation on.

"Ceramics. At the SUP."

"What's SUP?"

"The Arts and Crafts secondary school. On Palisady. In the third year."

"So you're not eighteen yet?" He couldn't hide the surprise in his voice.

"Six more months," she laughed. "And you?"

"I'm doing foreign trade at the Economics University. Third year." Jozef answered, confused. He couldn't believe that such a confident and mature girl wasn't even eighteen. "Really, you're not eighteen yet?" She shook her head. "So I can't even give you a kiss," he said in mock sadness.

"You couldn't even if I was eighteen!" Now she was laughing at him.

"Are you seeing someone?" he asked as the song ended and he saw her back to her table. When she shook her head, he asked if he could invite her for a dance later. She nodded.

From then on she was his only partner – not just that night, but on other nights to follow, until the summer holidays, when Marta returned home to Presov. Those holidays were the longest two months in Jozef's life. In September Marta entered her graduation year. She was already a little worried about what she'd do after that; she couldn't face being back in Presov with a hysterical mother and a dispirited father. But these gloomy thoughts were chased out of her head when she thought about meeting Jozef again. He was waiting for her in front of her dormitory, from where they usually went to 'Tea at Five'. They were always the first on the dance floor and would dance until they were worn out. When the evening discos were just getting going at about nine thirty, they'd be on their way back to Marta's dormitory. Because of this, their friends called them "The Model Youths'. The secondary school residence closed at ten sharp, and a couple of times Marta had already been put on report. The director warned her that if this happened again, her parents would be informed, and she would be forced to leave the dormitory.

One balmy evening in mid-October, the inevitable happened. That autumn was pleasantly warm, the wonderful Indian Summer calling lovers into each other's arms. After their standard chocolate cake and Kofola at a café on the Korzo, they went out into the night. On the corner of Leningradska and Sedlarska streets, a colour television had recently been installed in a glass display window, and a crowd of people were watching the evening news. But the world held little interest for the two young lovers. They walked the warm streets of nighttime Bratislava. The birds who had delayed their winter flights to hotter climates were singing sweetly to them. They kissed and hugged their way across Bratislava and found themselves near Ondrej Cemetery. The time was quarter to ten, street lights had replaced the light of day, but the young lovers noticed none of this. Jozef was too busy kissing Mata every two steps. They held nothing back; the stares they drew from passers-by meant nothing to them. When you're in love, the moment of parting for the evening is almost as painful as saying goodbye forever. It was now ten o'clock, and Marta knew she wouldn't be going back to the hostel that evening. There existed a silent solidarity among the girls in the dormitory – if one of them for some reason didn't make it home for the night, the others would tell the matron she was staying at her auntie's, her uncle's, or her granny's. Usually the matrons, remembering their own younger days, would accept this feeble alibi with tolerant understanding.

Matron Slusna caused no problem in the case of Marta Balecka, even though she was somewhat surprised. It had never happened before, and Balecka was a girl with an excellent reputation. 'Oh well,' she thought to herself, 'everybody has to start sometime.'

Both Jozef and Marta were surprised to see it was already ten thirty. It was getting cold, and there was no way they could go to Jozef's – his mother didn't even know he was going out with Marta. And even if she did know, her strict Catholic upbringing would never allow her to welcome into her home a girl who her son was not married to.

"Hang on a sec," Jozef whispered to her and, going across the road, he tossed a couple of stones at a lit-up window. A young man's face appeared, a quick conversation took place, and the head disappeared, to be replaced by two flying sleeping bags. Jozef caught them and returned to Marta. "Luckily, two boys I used to play volleyball with in high school live on the ground floor," he grinned. Marta only now realized that the building was another student hostel. "The guys lent me their sleeping bags, come along." They made their way back towards Ondrej Cemetery.

"To the cemetery?" Marta was taken aback.

"That's one place we're sure to get some peace and quiet. Unless some others like us are already there," he smiled. "Don't worry, this won't be the first time I've slept in a cemetery... You just have to get used to it," was his advice.

"Yes, but..." she started to protest but, seeing how calm and collected Jozef looked, she followed him trustingly.

They found their place between two tombs. Little by little they adjusted to the dim light coming from the nearby street. 'Here in the arms of God lies City Councillor Franz von Züller,' Jozef read the German notice on the crypt. "This man died when he was twenty-two years old. My age..." They laid one of the sleeping bags on the grass and covered themselves with the second one. "I can't imagine having never met you..." He pulled her closer to him: "The mosquitoes are biting!"

"You don't have to make up reasons for holding me..." and she cozied up even closer.

"Why do people fear the dead? It's the living they should watch out for..."

"They're afraid of the unknown, and death is the great unknown," she responded. "If people were sure that the afterlife would be pleasant, they wouldn't be afraid of it. The priests threaten the fires of hell, so Catholics are afraid. I think that death is life, but from the other side - just as there is no dark side of our planet, but only shadow when we're on the far side from the sun. Death is the reverse face of life, and just as the sun returns, so too does life. It's all for the best that we don't know how things are in the shadow. Can you imagine how people would behave if they knew that everything that follows death is pleasant? Living on earth would lose all its meaning."

"Do you know that you're saying exactly what I think? The interesting thing is that the one who created all this has given us no idea of whether things there are bad or good!" Jozef continued the philosophizing. He was impressed at how thoughtful Marta was for her age.

"Or whether there's anything at all over there."

"But it's logical that something must be there. Nothing simply cannot exist. That's why death cannot mean the end of everything, but is only the passage to another form of being. The way I see it, dying is nothing more than the direct opposite of birth. When we're born we come here from another dimension, and when we die we go back there."

"Maybe we move to even other dimensions..."

"Do you think that City Councillor von Züller ended up in another dimension?" Jozef wondered out loud.

"Who is Town Councillor von Züller?" Marta was lost.

"The gentleman who is spending his time here with us. We're lying beside his precious tomb," Jozef laughed.

"Stop it..."

"Excuse us, Mr. Councillor; I hope we won't disturb you too much.." Jozef made a small bow in the direction of the headstone.

"What did you say?"

"I was just apologizing to Mister Town Councillor in his own language. Actually, I think he's quite pleased with our company..." Marta squeezed his hand.

Just then the ringing of the bell from the cemetery chapel made itself heard, as subdued and unassuming as the chapel which sheltered it.

"Midnight."

"You still want to sleep in a cemetery?" Hesitation had returned to Marta's voice.

"Do you have any other idea? There's the option of pretending to be out of our minds and shouting at the top of our voices so they'll take us to the drunk tank. But we wouldn't have the money for the fine. They won't let you into the dormitory, and you run the risk of your poor mother out in Presov finding out how her darling is spending her nights." Marta said nothing. "Are you afraid?" he asked her.

"Who of?"

"Of me."

"I'm just cold," she murmured and cuddled up closer.

"I'm feeling the cold too." They both were trembling, but not from the cold. Silently they looked up at the heavens, outlined on one side by a stone angel and on the other by a cross, both planted on great marble monuments. In an old run-down house right over the cemetery's wall, someone began to play Beethoven's 'Moonlight Sonata'. They looked at each other, then found there actually was a moon up there among the stars, and that it was shining on them with love.

"It feels so nice to be with you... I think... I think I'm falling in love with you..." In their four months together this was the first time she had said those words.

"I know I'm in love with you," was his answer.

It was as if the moon above had stopped in its course to look down on them. They kissed passionately. The moon wondered if these young people were going to make love. They both wanted the other so much. They felt each other's trembling body. The moon, the stars and the mosquitoes were the only witnesses to their shy embraces – perhaps along with Town Councillor von Züller. If so, this was probably the most pleasant moment of his two hundred years in Ondrej Cemetery. Marta rolled herself up into a ball and in a moment was asleep. For a long time Jozef looked up into the night. It struck him that Sasha would never see this constellation in faraway Komsomolsk.

CHAPTER
TWO

BERLIN 1970

ANDREAS Baader who, in April 1968, together with Gudrun Ensslin, set fire to a department store in Frankfurt, was serving a three-year prison sentence in West Berlin. They had burnt the store as a protest against the decadence of German consumer society and against the War in Vietnam. Germany was shocked by this act. The Baader and Ensslin trial was covered by the journalist Ulrike Meinhof, writing for the Hamburg newspaper Konkret. Later she would join up with him to form a terrorist organization, the RAF – Red Army Faction. Baader and Ensslin lodged an appeal against their three-year sentence on political grounds. They both remained temporarily at large and quickly disappeared into the flats of their sympathizers. It was only in 1970 that the police, completely by chance, came across Andreas Baader. He was transferred to Berlin, where he began serving his sentence at the Tegel prison. On account of his good behaviour he was permitted to visit the German Central Institute for Social Issues, where he wished to study some literary records on youth crime. Together with Ulrike Meinhof, he was supposedly working on a book about youth criminal behaviour. On May 14, 1970, during one of his visits to the Institute, an armed and masked group attacked the two police officers accompanying Baader. An employee of the Institute was seriously injured in the shooting. During the confusion Baader and his *accomplices, led by Meinhof, managed to escape through a window and to melt into the Berlin underworld.*

Shortly after Jozef's departure, Thomas called Greiner in Berlin. Peter had found him a one-room flat for rent in a rear courtyard on Kochstrasse, not far from the Wall. It was the end of August and the new school year was to begin in a month. He had applied to the Free University and, thanks to Greiner's contacts in the study department, a response came to Neuwied in short order. He had been accepted into the first year program in the political science and sociology department, and registration was to take place on October 1. He decided to travel to Berlin as soon as possible, to use September to involve himself in reviving the student movement which had become substantially weaker after Rudi Dutschke left the country. On his arrival in Berlin, he immediately got in touch with the city's student radicals, whom he'd met at joint actions during his studies in Bonn. After the collapse of the SDS, student activities had quieted down, and their interest in their fellow students had increased – the miniskirts they had previously ignored now engaged the revolutionaries more than Marxist theory. Their revolutionary energy was now channeled into sex and drugs and rock and roll. Thomas himself felt isolated and unacknowledged, so he considered letting his hair grow in the style of the Beatles in order to attract girls.

At that time, the big hit on television was called Dalli, Dalli, with the popular moderator Hans Rosenthal. Thomas was watching it and drinking beer and cheap vodka when someone banged on his door.

"What, is the house on fire?!" he called and slowly made his way to the door, while the banging continued. As soon as he got the door open a young man with thick eyebrows and long sideburns burst into his flat.

"My name is Andreas Baader. I was sent to you by Rudi. I just broke out of jail and I plan to get out of Berlin tomorrow. Right now I need a place to sleep tonight. You're new here and they don't know about you. Can I stay the night?"

"You don't need to ask! Of course," Thomas indicated to Andreas that he should come in. He closed the blinds on both of his windows and turned up the sound on the television. Andreas sat at the kitchen table and nervously lit a cigarette. "Got any beer?" Thomas passed him a can and Andreas thirstily drank from it.

"Vodka?" Baader nodded and Thomas poured him a drink. Andreas drank it down and Thomas offered him a refill, which he refused.

"I should stay sober, just in case. I'll be out of here by dawn – you don't have to worry. Where's your telephone?" Thomas pointed to where the phone sat on top of the fridge. Baader dialed a number. "Hi, is that you? Are you okay? I'm with a friend, everything's in order. Tomorrow, at the place we decided. See you then." He hung up and lit another cigarette, but this time more calmly. "Is it okay if I clean myself up a bit?" Thomas directed him to the shower and gave him a towel and some soap. While Andreas was getting washed, Thomas pulled down the couch and made it up. He himself would sleep on the divan in the kitchen. The evening news came on the television, but the first story about the construction of the new parliament buildings was interrupted. On the screen appeared the Berlin Police Commissioner, who announced that a dangerous criminal, Andreas Baader, a member of the RAF terrorist group, had escaped from custody that day. He assured the public that the police were tracking him down. A photo of Baader was shown. The Commissioner announced a reward of 10,000 marks to anyone who provided information leading to his apprehension. The news then continued with a report on the progress of negotiations among the ambassadors of the four occupation forces – from the USA, USSR, Great Britain and France – on the status of the divided city.

Andreas came out of the bathroom clearly refreshed.

"They just announced that if I turn you in they'll give me ten thousand marks," laughed Thomas.

"Big money. If it wasn't so serious, I could wait here for you to get back with the money, and we could split it..." The idea struck Andreas as hilarious. "So, pour me another one!" Between the vodka and the cigarettes, they were pleasantly groggy when it came time to sleep.

The sun was just rising when Thomas was awakened by insistent banging at his door.

"Police, open up! Do you hear me?! Open this door immediately or we'll break it down!" The voice, accompanied by the barking of dogs, came through the door. Tumbling off the divan, he went to warn Andreas, but found his bed empty. He ran into the bathroom, then to the pantry. The window, overlooking a large chestnut tree, was open. The sun was winking at him through its branches. He opened the door; masked policemen wearing bulletproof vests and helmets rushed into his flat.

"Where is he?" growled one of them.

"Who?" Thomas decided to play dumb.

"Don't jerk us around. A blind man can see you have two beds made up. Where is he?"

"I don't know. Last night we overdid it, I fell asleep, and now he's not here..." The canine brigade went into action, the dogs quickly reacting to Baader's smell. They turned the flat over, but of course came up with nothing. The officer in charge opened the window, saw the tree, and understood how Andreas had eluded them.

"Get dressed!" he commanded. "You're coming with us."

"I didn't do anything. Where are we going?"

"Don't talk back, get dressed." One of the policemen threw a pair of pants and a shirt at him. In a few minutes they were on their way to the Kreuzberg police headquarters in an armoured police van. The station was full of Turks and blacks, who had moved to Berlin en masse and settled primarily in Kreuzberg. It was a dangerous part of town that sheltered all kinds of people on the run from the police. The officer who questioned Thomas was a healthy fifty year-old with an amiable expression on his face.

"So you're telling me you'd never seen this guy before..." His smile was a trifle sarcastic.

"Never met him. I had no idea who he was. He phoned about a half an hour before he came by. He said only that he got my number from Rudi Dutschke in case he needed some place to sleep in Berlin. I used to be friends with Dutschke, but I haven't seen him since he went abroad. I had no reason to turn this man away; I've only been in Berlin a few months and I don't know many people here yet..."

"Was this the man?" The commissioner showed him a photo of Baader. Thomas nodded. "Do you know who he is?" Thomas shook his head. "You're the only idiot in Germany who doesn't know this face, right?" The policeman laughed in his face.

"No, I don't know him. I'm from a small town called Neuwied, close to Koblenz and nobody cares much about politics there..."

"Don't give me that. What about your participation in the protests against the Springer newspaper chain?!" A bunch of papers were waved under Thomas' nose. "Here's your file, dear Mr. Ankermann. Just in case you think the police in Berlin are stupider than the Federal police. So, one more time – where was Baader going when he left you?"

"Really, I don't know. He only said he'd be gone before morning, that I needn't be afraid. When you came he'd already left, I guess down that big chestnut tree."

"Now we're getting somewhere. Do you want a coffee? "

"No, thanks."

"You don't need to tell me you're not connected to the RAF, we already know that. That's you'r ace in the hole so far. We'll call you in again, so don't try to leave West Berlin. All the border points have your picture. Try to leave and you'll land in jail for sure. If you're a good boy, you'll get out of this. You can go now."

Thomas went as far as the first telephone box, from where he called Peter Greiner. They met up at a café on the corner of Nollstrasse. He told him what had happened and Peter, who had good relations with the Kreuzberg headquarters from the time he was working for the Berliner Zeitung, promised to find out what was going on.

Several weeks went by. Nothing new had happened and Thomas had more or less forgotten about the Baader incident. It was two days after St. Nicholas Day; the streets were filling up with snow. He had just arrived home from a seminar and turned on the evening news on

TV. They were reporting a visit to Poland by Chancellor Willy Brandt. After signing a treaty recognizing the Oder and Neissa rivers as the borders, the Chancellor attended a ceremony at the Monument to the Heroes of the anti-Fascist Uprising in the Jewish Ghetto. According to the protocol, Brandt was to lay a wreath, straighten the ribbon on it and, still facing the memorial, back down the steps.

The Chancellor carried out the protocol up to the moment when, instead of going back down the steps, he fell to his knees. Thomas watched, together with the entire German nation, fascinated by the unexpected gesture. Brandt then bowed his head, knelt forwards and stared fixedly at the ground – at the snowy wet Polish soil. This was, after all, the same soil where twenty-five years before German soldiers had executed Warsaw's defenders, both Polish and Jewish. The whole world was rendered speechless by this astonishing expression of conciliation.

It was as if something shifted inside Thomas. Nervously he lit a cigarette. He thought about his father, a champion of conciliation and tolerance. Nobody is perfect; no-one has the right to judge. Now here was his Chancellor on his knees to the Polish and Jewish people. The strength of Willy Brandt knocked him off balance. He realized that such a gesture would not please everyone, but he himself approved of it with his whole heart and soul. He was proud of the Chancellor. He switched off the television and thought about things – about his own values, about the meaning of politics, about what he wanted to do with his life. Willy Brandt, the son of a poor family, was showing the whole world that the Germans too had a soul, that this nation condemned by the world knew how to come to terms with a nation who had been their enemy for ages gone by. Thomas had the feeling that the Chancellor was asking him to help his cause, the cause of truth and justice. It seemed to him that love, forgiveness and understanding could achieve more than throwing rocks and Molotov cocktails, or burning down department stores and police stations.

He remembered that he hadn't checked his mail that day, so he went down to the post boxes. There was an envelope with the stamp of the Free University in Berlin. It informed him that, on the basis of a new law regarding this institution passed on 9. 7. 1970, the first-year political science student Thomas Ankermann, on the basis of suspected cooperation with anti-state activists, was temporarily suspended from his studies for the 1970/1971 school year.

"So that's that," he thought laconically while eating the scorched beans he had left heating on the burner.

CHAPTER
THREE

PRESOV 1970 – 1971

MARTA suffered very painful periods, with cramps radiating out to the tips of her fingers. From her weakness and pale complexion, her mother always knew when it was time to prepare some marjoram broth, so when Marta came home for Christmas her mother had a good supply of the herb on hand. She also kept a record of the days when her daughter's periods were due.

"I'm telling you, she must be pregnant!" Mrs. Balecky shouted to her husband, who was peacefully doing the vacuuming. Up to 1968, Balecky had worked as the assistant to the manager of a household goods outlet. Although he wasn't a member of the Communist Party, he was nonetheless removed from his post for refusing to sign a declaration that the Soviet invasion was an act of international aid. Thanks to his fluency in German, Hungarian and Russian, he'd found employment at the reception desk of the new hotel Saris.

"Can you believe that today some German reserved a room by teleprinter in the LONG LIVE THE CPC Hotel. The Communist Party of Czechoslovakia Hotel! Can you believe that?"

"It's all your fault!" his wife accused him.

"How can it be my fault that on the roof of the hotel there's a big neon sign reading, 'Long Live the CPC', and under that in smaller print, 'Hotel'. The man evidently thought that was the name of the hotel..."

"She should never have gone to school in Bratislava!"

"What can those foreigners think of us?"

"What are you saying?" Mrs. Balecky shouted over the screech of the vacuum cleaner. It was a ten year old ETA and roared so loudly that the glasses in the cabinet rattled. They'd also rattled when the Russian tanks had rumbled under their windows in 1968.

"That the German must think we're a weird country."

"What German?"

"The one who booked the room..."

"I swear there's something wrong with your head! Your daughter is pregnant by some boy we don't even know and you're going on about the Germans! But that's the way you brought her up, sending her off to play sports, take piano lessons, and all sorts of other things. If she'd sat quietly at home, this would never have happened!"

Balecky realized that his wife had reached what he called her 'boiling point'. It was a stage where the only way to communicate with his wife was by ignoring her. He started to sing one of his favourite arias from The Bartered Bride opera. He was an amateur operetta singer, and if it wasn't for his suspicious wife he could have sung professionally in the Presov operetta theatre. His wife had forbidden him from attending rehearsals because there were too many young female singers and ballet dancers. So nowadays he did his singing while he was cleaning the flat. He well knew that his stentorian singing drove his wife mad. Opera arias were his small revenge, and he knew lots of them.

"If it wasn't for you this would never have happened. I was dead against her going to Bratislava. If she was in the high school here, I could keep an eye on her!"

"We shall remain faithful, We shall remain faithful, Faithful to each other..." Balecky brought his aria to such a ringing tremolo that the humming of the vacuum cleaner seemed like the sighing of a summer breeze.

"Stop that wailing! She's pregnant I tell you."

"Can't hear you," he worked his comment into Smetana's melody. He knew that his wife was only waiting for a reaction from him in order to launch into one of the thousands of quarrels that marked their conjugal cohabitation. Her husband's singing and the thud of the children's feet from the flat above were surefire methods of driving her to distraction.

"That's just like you. When things are bad, you start singing." Going over to the vacuum, she emphatically shut it off.

"What's up now?"

"Your daughter's pregnant, and you don't know by whom."

"How do you know she's pregnant?"

"She hasn't had her period! Oh God, what did I do to deserve this? It's all because you pushed her to go to Bratislava!!!"

"She's got a talent for painting, and besides, if she'd stayed here sooner or later you'd have driven her crazy!"

Mrs. Balecky went out, slamming the door in her rage. Balecky smiled. Those times when the wife stormed out and stayed away from home for an hour or two were among the small pleasures of his married life.

'Shining eyes, lips saying I love you, Wherever I go, there I sing how I love you...' With joy he began to sing Lehar. The idea of being a grandfather somehow pleased him. Marta, who had come home for Christmas with her sister Eva, a university student in Olomouc, returned from shopping. He asked her the question directly.

"Yes, my period is late."

"Are you telling me you're not... what do you call it these days... a virgin?"

"Dad, where've you been living?" interjected her sister Eva, coming in from the kitchen where she was baking Christmas cookies. "Nowadays you'd be hard pressed to find a virgin even among fifteen-year-olds... And Marta is eighteen."

"And who's the father?" Balecky enquired. Marta showed him a couple of letters from Jozef. Her father, seeing the love this unknown man was showing his daughter Marta, calmed down.

"And will he marry you when he finds out about your... condition?"

"He already knows."

"And?"

"Even before this happened he wanted to get married. He's finishing university next summer, and I'm graduating too, so we'll manage somehow."

"When the baby's born you could live here, with us." Marta did not react. "I know, I know, because of your mother..."

"First we have to finish school and besides..."

"Besides, what?" her father looked at her questioningly.

"Jojo" (this was Marta's pet name for Jozef) would like to come and talk to you. Dad, can't you talk to mum first? We've already decided we're getting married. I'm afraid she'll make a scene." Fondly her father hugged her to him. "Yes, she'll make a scene, but we're used to her scenes aren't we?" They smiled at each other mischievously. "I'd better get started learning that Smetana properly... I imagine you'll let me sing at your wedding..."

Two days later, Jozef travelled down to Presov. He brought his future mother-in-law a huge bouquet of flowers, and this went a certain way towards softening her up.

"This must have cost some money..." Then, for form's sake, she got angry. Not realizing how she was poisoning the atmosphere, she turned on her husband: "And when was the last time you brought me flowers?" Balecky was at a loss for words, unable to imagine that he would ever bring the old girl flowers.

Mrs. Balecky was offended because Marta had first talked the situation over with her father, and so she resolved to take the initiative. When Jozef, in a shaky voice, asked for their younger daughter's hand in marriage, she broke into the obligatory sobbing, crying that her daughter was too young, that she hadn't even finished school, that she had her own life to lead. But Jozef had been well prepared by Marta and kept repeating that he would take good care of her, that even though he was still a student, financially they weren't so badly off. Due to his grade point average, he received an allowance of two hundred crowns plus a small stipendium, a further two hundred as a player on the university volleyball team, and five hundred more from his part-time job as a reporter for the TIP sports weekly. When he had laid it all out before Marta's mother, she began to take him more seriously. In fact, as the head of an accounting unit with thirty years' experience, she was paid only four hundred crowns more.

"But where are you going to live?" she asked next.

"We haven't decided yet, but we'll work it out," Balaz promised.

The Baleckies finished their questioning, except for the mother's occasional sighs and sobs. Perhaps her sadness was in part caused by the thought that her elder daughter had a boyfriend in the Czech region and the younger one wanted to get married and live in Bratislava, which would leave her alone with her husband in Presov.

"Marta turned eighteen just two months ago... I wouldn't like to see her at her wedding with a big belly. It's not something we'd like everyone see. You know what people in the east are like..." she thought out loud.

"Ha-ha-ha..." Balecky laughed. "What do you imagine they'll think when an eighteen-year-old gets married just before her graduation?"

Mrs. Balecky thought it over and came up with a suggestion: "We know the priest in Stary Smokovec. There's a lovely historic church there... It's where my husband and I were wedded..."

"Maybe we should get Marta's opinion on this," Balecky added his comment.

"We'd be very happy if your wedding was held in a church... well in a church as well" she stuck to her guns.

"That might be a problem for my father, but I think I can convince him," Jozef said finally.

"A marriage in the town hall is just a meaningless formality, but a church wedding is a ceremony that stays with you throughout your entire life. It would mean a lot to me," she repeated.

The Ascension of the Virgin Mary Church in Stary Smokovec was little more than a large chapel, and getting a date in such a historic location was not easy. One of the main reasons why so many more marriages were celebrated there than in other churches was the advantageous position of the church. It was concealed beside a large amphitheatre, far from the eyes of curious people, and the priest was known for his wisdom and discretion. Church weddings at this time of frequent checks on members of the Communist Party also required a good dose of civic courage.

For Jozef's father, remaining in the Party was a question of his existence. He had seen what had happened to his colleagues who had refused to approve of the 'international aid of the USSR and the Warsaw Pact countries'. Without exception, they had all been shifted to factories, warehouses or farm cooperatives. Not that he was afraid of hard work, being as he was from Kysuce, where life was never easy. What he was afraid was what would happen to his three children if he was kicked out of the Party and his pay reduced by half. Clearly they'd have to leave the city and start afresh in some village, growing vegetables to feed themselves. His son, who was in his final year at university, would have to give up his studies. When Jozef told him that the Baleckies wanted a church wedding, at first he frowned and said nothing.

"Bloody bastards," he burst out, slamming his fist down on the table and the Pravda newspaper, where there was a four-page article entitled 'Lessons from the 1968 Crisis'. It was a neo-Stalinist lecture inspired by Bilak, Indra, Jakes and other neoconservative survivors, and it was causing a storm of debate throughout Czechoslovakia. At sessions of the Communist Party, at Revolutionary Workers Union meetings, in organizations of youth, fishers and writers, just anywhere where people attended meetings (and that was everywhere), the citizens had to raise their hands in favour of this 'scrap of paper which a normal-thinking person would not even wipe his bum with' as Balaz senior expressed it. The 'Lessons' was a document inspired by Moscow and the collaborationist leadership of the Czechoslovak Communist Party dictating to the people how to lead their lives. It was an evil edict which would set the liberties of the Dubcek era back by two decades.

"They've disgraced me and blackmailed me enough. All my life I've done what I was told, covered my back and held my tongue.

All so that you, Gitka and Katka could have a decent life, study, marry and have your share of happiness. To hell with living like this..." Just before his dad covered his face with his hands, Jozef thought he saw a tear in his eye. "Yesterday at a meeting I filled in a form that I have no problem with the Communist Party policy on religion... They think that when they force someone to join the Party and forbid him from attending church services, he instantly ceases to be a believer... My whole life I've hoped that one day this would all change – that Bilak and his idiot followers would one day simply disappear and we could start to live as decent people. Is it possible that here I am at the age of fifty and the only times I've been across the border were to Budapest and Krakow?! My childhood dream was to travel the world..." Jozef only listened; never before had his father spoken to him so openly. Only now did he realize what a tortured, downtrodden soul the man had. "They kicked out Mraz, Snajder, Pohanka... all the best people. They named some guy who used to work as a night porter to be the leader of the union just because he's from the east and claims to know Bilak. Again they've made a laughing-stock out of us." All at once he took a deep breath and stood up from the table: "No way, no more surrendering, at least not on things which matter to my children. Tell Balecky he can go ahead with his church wedding, even if they use it as proof of my doubts about the policy on religion..." Then he pulled his son to him: "When is it to be?"

"Marta's mother booked a date for the last Saturday in January..."

"I was asking about the baby's birth..." his father said with a smile. "You're the last of the Balaz clan, you have to have a son... The last Saturday in January? Well, that's just over a month from now." Now it was Jozef's turn to smile. "What will your mother say, I wonder?"

"She already knows, but she hasn't got up the courage to talk to you about the church wedding. Dad, I want you to know I really respect you and that... I love you."

The wedding feast took place at the House of Slovak Writers which, even though it was two kilometres away from the church, was not as expensive as the Hotel Bellevue Mrs. Balecky suggested.

Balaz knew the manager there, and when they found out they would be able to reserve beds for twenty, they decided on it.

The 'Marína' music group, founded and led by Mr. Balecky, provided the entertainment. The small reception room was airless, but just outside the doors was the wonderful Tatra winter, ten below zero. The non-smokers eventually had mercy on those who kept popping out onto the tiny terrace for a cigarette. It got so smoky inside that Jozef could hardly make out Winter, who was standing by the open glass doors and waving to him. He indicated that the bride and groom should come outside for a second. He and Marta looked at each other in surprise.

"Excuse me for disturbing you, but I heard about your wedding and had to come and congratulate you. I'm at home in Kezmarok, so it's just around the corner. It occurred to Jozef that Winter must have seen his school-mates Cuki, Dezo and Brblos behind him at the party. Winter hadn't been invited; the silence was embarrassing. His greeting, "I wish you all the best, happiness, health and all you wish for..." came across as stiff and unnatural, and as usual he was sweating heavily. "I brought you a little something as a wedding gift," he continued, and took a picture wrapped in paper out of a large plastic bag. He tore off the paper and revealed an antique oil painting of a church with a bell-tower. He thrust it into Marta's hands and awaited her reaction.

"It's Podolinec..."she said, surprised.

"Right, Podolinec. I remembered when we were dancing together the first time..." His voice broke. "Sorry, you told me then that you were from Podolinec. I hope you like it..."

Marta didn't have to pretend her pleasure. "Thank you so much, really you have made me so happy." She planted a kiss on Winter's cheek. Watching the two of them, Jozef had an uneasy feeling. A sense of foreboding overcame him when, on leaving, Winter asked Marta a question whose significance he would understand only many years later. "I have to get going, but there's something I've been wanting to ask you... was your father once the post-master in Podolinec?"

"Yes he was, during the Slovak State and just after the war..."

"Right, right, thank you. I wish you both all the best..." Delighted, Marta went to show the painting to her father. Winter gave Jozef a friendly tap on the shoulder, and said "You always seem to be a step ahead of me... up till now." For a long moment Jozef stared at the door Winter had left by. The words 'up till now' continued to ring in his ears.

CHAPTER
FOUR

KOMSOMOLSK NA AMURE 1971

THE Soviet Union's economic situation was getting steadily worse. According to the official statistics however, the citizens of Russia and the other Soviet Union members were doing fine. Nobody believed the statistics of course; everybody knew that lying and cheating were a way of life right down to the most humble workplace. When the population saw how those at the top were stealing and denying, they followed their example. Even though Khrushchev had long ago been relegated to the ashbin of history, his slogan was still in use: 'catch up and overtake the United States'. But whereas in the U.S. the five percent of the active population engaged in agriculture managed to feed the nation and also export goodly amounts of grain, vegetables and fruit, in the USSR the twenty-five percent working in the agricultural sector could not even feed themselves sufficiently. Under the system of state subsidies it was impossible to achieve any sort of effectiveness. The philosophy of providing the basic foodstuffs to all at a cheap price led to the paradox that bread was cheaper than the wheat from which it was produced. The farmers regularly bought much more bread than they needed for themselves – they fed it to their pigs. The upshot was that in the cities bread was available only in the early morning, and even then only in insufficient quantities. The only joy for the Soviet citizenry was the private allotment, which the state put up with because the productivity of these individual plots was many times higher than on the state cooperatives.

Agricultural machines wore out and the replacement machinery supplied to the state and collective farms by the factories was often inoperative. Theft, fraud and camouflage were a normal part of life for the citizens of socialist's premier country. The Economics Gazette reported that of ten thousand musical instruments manufactured in the factory in Kirovsk, nine thousand were damaged, and this after passing through inspection. From the 133,000 televisions sold per year in Moscow, there was an average of three repairs needed per set. In the mid-1970s there were 25 cars per thousand inhabitants; in the United States, the figure was almost 600. There was no mention of the difference in the quality of the automobiles, which was a strictly confidential statistic available to senior Party and state officials alone. Under these conditions of society-wide shortages, corruption naturally flourished. The only sector to which investment flowed was to the military, giving rise to the so-called military/industrial complex, which Khrushchev had once referred to as a 'metal-eater'. Nine ministries and about 50 million people served the military/industrial complex.

Thanks to cheap subsidized flights, the Soviet company Aeroflot became the largest airline in the world – not in terms of turnover of course, but as regards the number of travellers. A ticket from Komsomolsk to Moscow or Kiev by way of Vladivostok cost 18 rubles. But for the average citizen, getting one was unimaginable.

Sasha had been living with her husband Michail and her son Josif in Komsomolsk for almost two years. Apart from Kiev, she had never seen a bigger city. She'd known only Mukachevo, Uzghorod and Irsava, the last of which she considered 'the biggest hole' she'd ever seen until then. Komsomolsk surpassed even her worst fears however. She was lucky that her husband was a professional officer in the Soviet army. Thanks to this and to the cheap Aeroflot air flights she was able to go home to Ukraine twice a year. Although she hated the military after her experiences in Kiev and Czechoslovakia, she calmed herself with the thought that being the wife of a major in the Soviet army carried with it many advantages.

After their arrival in Komsomolsk they were allocated a shared two-room flat, a dream at that time. It didn't bother her that they had to share the bathroom, toilet and kitchen with the family of Major Kuzma, who had been sent to the Far East at the same time as the Obickies. The Kuzmas, who luckily had no children, had one room to themselves, while the Obickies lived in the other one. The men stayed with their divisions during the week, only coming home on the weekends; this was based on the specious reasoning that the Chinese army too had weekends off. Sasha got to know Natalia, Major Kuzma's wife, who worked as a clerk in the district library for ninety rubles per month. Sasha was at home with young Josif, and to earn a little extra money taught German at home. In this forgotten corner of the world, her students consisted mostly of the wives of other officers, who lived in the hope that their husbands might one day be transferred to the GSVG (Group of Soviet Armies in Germany). In the German Democratic Republic there was an occupation army of over a half-million Soviets. Since 1968, Czechoslovakia had become a second dream for these military wives, who only hoped that the Soviet presence in both these countries would go on for as long as possible.

Less than a week after moving in to their military housing block they were visited by the militia member responsible for their individual building. It was necessary to refer any problems to him. 'Referring problems to him' essentially meant turning in neighbours whose behaviour or speech could raise suspicions of anti-Soviet activity. Sasha couldn't really understand what kind of anti-Soviet activity could arise here in the Far East, so far removed from the centres of Soviet life, but all the same she resolved to be careful – which meant being non-communicative. Apart from Natali,a she had almost no relations with the neighbours, whom she met only on the stairs or at work sessions. People simply didn't trust each other.

The officers' wives, together with the members of the intelligentsia, took part quite often in such work sessions. According to the official propaganda, members of the intelligentsia lived off the work of the workers and the cooperatives, and so it was their socialist duty to help them out. They mostly liked helping with the potato harvest – not just because of the opportunity to be out in the fresh air, but principally because with a little cleverness, they could get some potatoes for themselves. When Sasha first took part in the potato harvest she noticed the metal buckets used to collect the potatoes had holes in them.

"Why are there holes in these buckets?" she asked the supervisor.

"This is your first time on a collective farm, isn't it?" Sasha nodded. "They're so that no-one will steal the buckets," the supervisor said laconically and handed her a plastic sack. While the members of the intelligentsia began to collect the potatoes, someone noticed the workers looking on, overseeing them.

"This didn't happen a few years back," commented Professor Lebedev, a lecturer in the basics of geophysics at the Polytechnic. "The harvest is poorer, so they're keeping an eye on every potato."

The fact that they were under guard was taken by the work party as a challenge to get around the coop workers. Since the people had to get to the fields in their own cars (no-one cared that a great majority of the volunteers didn't have cars), they didn't imagine they would be checked on their way back.

"Be careful. The sacks you want to take from communal to private ownership – in other words take home, mustn't weigh more than twenty kilos," one of the professor's younger colleagues warned them with a smile. "Up to twenty is a simple offence with a fine of about thirty rubles which, at fifty kopeks per kilo, is worth the risk. In no circumstances should Party members steal the potatoes. We've had cases where people have been expelled from the Party for that." After this wise advice there was almost nobody who didn't hide full sacks of potatoes in his car. The collective workers whose potatoes they were stealing were suspicious because there were relatively few potatoes collected. They didn't hesitate and called in the militia, who simply confiscated a couple of sacks for themselves and imposed a few tiny fines. Then a few more sacks were bought off them by the workers from the collective. The result was that practically no potatoes were left for the consumer market.

In front of the entrance to the buildings stood the ever-watchful 'grannies', wrapped up to their ears in winter clothing. In vain they tried to report the volunteers to the militia; it was enough for the volunteers to show confirmation of payment of the fine and the matter was settled.

Their cohabitation with the Kuzmas, after the initial mutual toleration, turned into a series of daily quarrels. As the tension on the Sino-Soviet border decreased, the atmosphere in the shared flat became tenser. Both soldiers spent more time at home and of course spent more time drinking together. A drunken person is more inclined towards quarrels and recriminations than to calm debate, especially when egged on by his wife. Sasha couldn't help noticing that Natalia was now marking her food in the fridge. When it was Natalia's turn to buy toilet paper, there was cut-up newspaper in the washroom instead; Sasha's freshly-washed linen was now taken down above the stove in the kitchen before it was dry. Major Kuzma hinted to Major Obicky that Natalia suspected that some of their food was disappearing from the fridge. Sasha refused to believe their three-year old Josif was taking things from the neighbours' saucepans.

More and more often Natalia found reasons for quarreling. Sasha was teaching German to the wife of the butcher on the next street, so, while the other shoppers found bones along with the meat in the newspaper their purchases were wrapped in, she was sold pure meat. Noticing that Sasha was putting meat into their shared fridge while she was cooling mostly bones was hard for Natalia. One day Sasha found a new fridge in the corner of the small kitchen. Natalia coolly announced that from now on she was going to store her things in her own fridge. Sasha took this stoically, as she did when the lids from her preserving jars started disappearing. There was always a ready supply of jars, but finding lids in the Far East was harder than shifting the Chinese from the Ussuri River.

The pot boiled over when Natalia, seemingly by accident, spilt ink on the Obickies' new carpet. A citizen who found a new carpet in Komsomolsk experienced a feeling comparable to the feeling of pride when Yuri Gagarin was launched into space, or when he managed to buy a few oranges. Soviet citizens felt pride only rarely. Sasha shed tears over the damaged carpet. She recalled how she had come by it. She had the good luck to be the wife of a soldier, but then most of the inhabitants of Komsomolsk were military, and also the daughter of a war veteran. In the Soviet Union veterans enjoyed many advantages. For example, they didn't have to stand in lines at restaurants, although almost none of the Victors over Fascism could afford to eat in restaurants. But they also needn't stand in line at grocery stores– for this it was worth fighting and winning the Second World War. The veterans also had their own lines for low-supply goods; it was enough to show their identity cards as veterans of the Great Patriotic War. One of these advantages was that they could request hard-to-get industrial goods.

When the Obickies had saved 800 rubles for the carpet which Sasha had found in the home furnishings central warehouse, they completed the request form in the name of her father, the war veteran. Then they wrote his pass number in the relevant column. Three months later they received a notice that the carpet was in the warehouse and that they could come and pick it up. Her husband took leave for the occasion since he didn't want to miss the moment when she would lay the brand new carpet in their room. Arriving at the warehouse, Sasha presented the notice to the saleslady with a shaking hand. She took them into the back room, where they took possession of the sought-after carpet. When Sasha prepared to pay for it, the saleslady asked her to show the veteran's documents.

"My father is the veteran, I wrote in the number of his pass," Sasha insisted.

"But anyone can write in the number my dear. I need his papers; otherwise I can't let you have the carpet."

"But my father lives in Carpathian Ukraine, fifteen thousand kilometres from here..."

"So you should have written to him to send you his papers."

"He needs to have them with him every day. Without them he couldn't even buy his bread. You can check it through the military administration!"

"We don't have time for that. Put the carpet back where you got it!" The saleslady had adopted the cutting tone used by people who are used to being obeyed. Sasha stood there helplessly. At that second an uncharacteristic anger took hold of Major Obicky.

"You horrible bitch, you have the nerve to refuse a damned carpet to the daughter of a hero of the Great Patriotic War, a man who conquered Berlin?! Get me your superior immediately!!!" Sasha looked at her husband with a newfound admiration. They could almost hear the saleslady's knees shaking. Not only did she let them buy the carpet, she even went so far as to open the door for them, the first act of courtesy towards a customer that Sasha had ever seen in the Soviet Union. The cowed saleswoman again apologized, and whispered: "If you want to sell the carpet, I can give you two hundred rubles more than you paid for it..." Major Obicky nearly caught her head in the closing door.

Sasha sat in her room on the carpet she had tried in vain to get the ink-spot out of. She was sorry she had ever given Natalia the key to the room so she could come in and watch the television when they weren't home. Down her cheeks streamed tears of impotence – even war veterans only had the right to one carpet every ten years. What kind of life was this? Her look fell on little Josif, who was sitting on the damaged carpet playing with a wooden train. He was her only joy in this forgotten part of the world. What kind of society would her young boy grow up in? What future could he look forward to in a country where it was a problem to get bread, toilet paper or butter, let alone a precious carpet? She tenderly stroked her son's head. He was developing the features of his faraway father, a man Sasha remembered less and less.

She and her husband Michail had been trying to have a child of their own, but somehow without success. She poured some vodka into a glass and drank it back in one swallow. Today was Wednesday and Friday, when her husband would come home to her, was so terribly far away. She thought about their life in this city, in this building, about having somehow to communicate with Natalia, then heard a key turning in the lock. Natalia! She made up her mind to tell her she would have to get them a new carpet. But the footsteps in the hallway did not go to the Kuzma's room, but to hers. The door opened and there stood Michail, beaming. Sasha jumped up and hugged him tightly.

"Michail, my dear Michail, what are you doing here?!"

"Have you been crying?" He looked at her questioningly. She nodded.

"Why? Has something happened?"

"Oh Michail, if you had any idea... what happened... I can't, I won't stay... I'm suffocating here... we're rotting away in this god-forsaken place... I can't put up with Natalia any longer. Maybe it was an accident, but I suspect she did it to us on purpose... look..." she pointed to the stained carpet. "She poured ink all over our carpet!"

"Ink?" Michail smiled in confusion. She smelled alcohol on him.

"You think it's funny?"

"Pour us a drink – we have to celebrate!"

Sasha, looking at him in curiosity, poured vodka into two glasses.

"Celebrate the destruction of the carpet?"

"Celebrate... aha... look!" Michail got to his feet and came to military attention before his wife. "Well, do you see anything different?" Sasha looked her husband over and noticed nothing. Miša leaned down and showed her his shoulder-pips. "I'm no longer a major, I'm a lieutenant-colonel!" Proudly he came to attention, but Sasha showed no great enthusiasm. "They've given me an extra thirty rubles in pay!"

"That's good," she said absently.

"Yes, but there's more. Don't stand up, you could hurt yourself..." The new, slightly tipsy lieutenant-colonel slowly drew a large envelope out of his pocket and from it produced a decree written on paper with the official stamp of the Soviet Union. The Commander of the Far East Military Administration, General-Major Dolgorukov, informed him that the General Staff of the Soviet Union had decided on the seconding of Lieutenant Colonel Obicky to the staff of the Tenth Armoured Division headquartered in... Moscow!!! Sasha couldn't understand what she was hearing. "Don't you get it Sasha? We are going... to... Moscow... to Móóóoscow!!! Now do you understand??!"

Sasha seized the piece of paper and when she'd read the report with her own eyes, her head began to spin from the excitement. Michail poured more drinks, lit a candle, picked up his guitar and, to comfort their fatigued souls, began to play something by Bulat Okudzhava. Little Josif sat with them and looked on with a big smile on his face. He felt fine - whenever his dad started to play his guitar it was a sign that something good was going on. It didn't happen very often.

'In the world lived one soldier, brave, fair, and new,
But without respect, since he was made of paper.
He wished to change the world and live there happily,
But in a child's room he had to stay, he was only made of paper.'

He kissed his son on his coal-black hair and squeezed his wife's hand, then continued in his rough, pensive but pleasant voice:

'Ready to leap into flames, prepared to die for us.
Who would force him into a fire? He was only made of paper.
You want me in the fire? Okay, then. Bravely he marched on
He burned up – a cheap victim of death – he was only made of paper.'

Sasha looked at her husband, whose eyes had reddened. She felt in her heart something she had never before known in her relationship with Michail. It struck her that now, for the first time, she truly loved him. She cuddled up closer to him. Michail put one arm around her, the other around their son, who had never seen his parents so happy. In his ears he heard the words of Okudzhava's song: 'He wished to change the world and live there happily...'

CHAPTER
FIVE

BRATISLAVA 1971 – 1974

"Has it arrived?" the older Balaz stared at his son, who had just phoned with the nurse at the maternity ward. Jozef nodded. "A boy?" he asked, hoping that this third birth would bring him a grandson.

"Another girl," Jozef laughed.

His father pondered the news a moment, then asked "Healthy?"

"Two and a half kilos. A little small, but they're both doing fine."

"Thank God for that. I guess the next one will be a boy," he said ruefully. "Congratulations, my son." "Thanks, granddad...ha-ha-ha." They both shared a laugh. The news of the birth of baby Martina spread quickly to Presov, Cadca, Parnica, Sternberk and Prague - everywhere the Balaz and Balecky families were to be found. Jozef ran to the maternity hospital on Zochova street as quickly as he could while carrying the large bouquet an acquaintance at the Zilinska market had reserved for the occasion. He got to the hospital faster than the trolleybus would have done. He handed the flowers to the nurse and asked her to have his wife come to the window. Almost an hour later Marta stood looking down at him from the second floor, holding her bouquet. Her fatigue, but also her joy, was clearly written on her features. The proud father would be permitted to meet his new daughter the next day. From fear of infection, the regulations forbade visitors on the ward itself. Jozef thought how to express his thanks and gratitude and finally knelt on the pavement and rubbed his head into the warm June lawn. This provided Marta and also some passers-by with amusement at the antics of the crazed new father.

Three days later Marta came to the Balaz's flat, where they were living for the time being. Jozef's older sister was already married with two children of her own and although his younger sister was still living with her parents, there was a small room next to the kitchen for the newlyweds. Originally it was designed as the maid's room. 'Lucky this building was built during the capitalist era,' Jozef thought to himself, 'otherwise there'd be no maid and we'd have no place to sleep'. He thought it was a bit funny that his sister lived alone in a room that was four times larger, but his mother's opinion was: 'You wanted a bicycle, so now just pedal'. The three of them were squeezed into a space of less than five square metres, but Marta managed to do miracles with it.

They both finished school, the principal of Marta's secondary school being most accommodating towards her. Although some of the members of the graduating committee shook their heads at her bulging belly, he stood by her. Probably at some other institution she would have been forced to leave, but Mr. Bagar was a fair man. It certainly helped that Marta had always been at the top of her class during her whole studies. Her graduating subjects were all straight As. It was two weeks after her graduation that the baby was born, and the principal was among the first to send his congratulations. One more advantage of Jozef's being a father was that the law in certain circumstances allowed conscripts to serve their time in the town of their residence. Now that he had graduated from university he was drafted for one year. Thanks to little Martina he was able to attend the Klement Gottwald Military and Political Academy in Bratislava as a graduate sergeant. There were a further forty graduates also attending the academy, half of them married and three with children.

Jozef's military service meant there was now space in their room for the cradle they'd stored in the basement. Little Martina had slept with her parents on a mattress which during the day folded up into a couch. Marta was even able to find a place for a hot-plate in that little area. This didn't exactly please her mother-in-law, who had looking forward to showing off her culinary skills to Marta. However Mata had been advised by her more experienced friends to maintain a certain distance from her mother-in-law, especially around the stove. The kitchen, and the stove in particular, is the most frequent setting for potential problems. Since Marta would be living with her in-laws until the end of Jozef's service she was taking great care around his mother. She had tried a few times to give Marta some cooking tips, but in the end figured that her daughter-in-law would best learn from her own mistakes.

Jozef was an easy time at the Military Academy. It was now three years since the Soviet invasion, and although most Czechs and Slovaks had been in favour of socialism before 1968, nowadays it would be hard to find a single supporter of the Russian real socialism model. This was with the possible exception of Bilak and a few of his fellow-travellers, who were dedicated to leading the nation to socialist paradise with a big stick. It was however necessary for everyone to pretend belief. They adapted, they simulated, they cowtowed. Hypocrisy became the daily bread for fifteen million people, along with a good dose of self-mockery. Like Captain Jezek, who at the academy was in charge of PSM – political schooling of the men. His goal was to convince the officers that the best thing for their future was friendship with the Soviet Union and the other socialist countries. 'As far as possible, forever' he would say with a mysterious smile. Captain Jezek was not very committed to convincing the soldiers of something he himself didn't believe, so he gave them free reign on the condition that they not leave the classroom. He in the meantime went to see Anicka, the pedagogical faculty accountant, who had her little 'hideaway' in the back of the munitions store. Since they were never issued live ammunition, no-one ever went there. The Academy was for learning, not for fighting.

At the political schooling lessons the graduate soldiers spent their time watching Austrian television. The Academy must have been well-situated since they could catch the ORF signal with only a fairly long wire. Thanks to their instructor's sexual appetite and the proximity to Austria they were able to witness an obviously drunken Brezhnev trying to conduct an orchestra playing the International during a Communist Party congress in Poland. From the BBC, Voice of America and Free Europe the soldiers, students and ordinary citizens found out what was really happening in Czechoslovakia. Most often the time passed quickly, but there were also occasions when it seemed to stand still. Military service was one of the latter. The university graduate officers lodged in their wooden barracks found various ways to make the time go by. Miki the lawyer drank, sociologist Jano studied underground literature, Elo the Romantic composed verse, Duro and Svito played chess, Fero practiced his karate by breaking planks into splinters, Monopoly, smuggled into the barracks by Mici, became a big hit.

One evening the President of the Socialist Youth Union at the Academy, Sergeant Guca, came into their smoky room and tossed a bunch of forms onto the nearest bed: "Guys, this is your big chance!" he called out in his typically Bratislava accent. Guca was single, and it was clear to everyone that he was stationed there due to his connections. "Here are applications for the Communist Party. After the 'cleansing' they need new members, and soldiers have it easier. If you wait until you're back in civil life they have to accept three members of the working class for each of you. That's the new regulation. But as soldiers you're counted as workers." Guca looked around in expectation.

"Shove it up your ass," was the first reaction from Fero, while the others acted as if nothing had been said and carried on with their activities – smoking, reading or playing cards.

"Don't be such idiots. You'll never again have such an opportunity. Here am I trying to help you guys out, I got the commander to agree to this scheme, and all you do is..."

"Get them off of my bed," Miki raised his voice.

Red in the face, Guca quickly gathered the forms together and stormed out. From the forty potential Communist Party candidates, not one had accepted his application forms. So far.

During the second half of his military service Jozef gave ever more thought to the question of where they would live when he came home. His mother had made it amply clear that she was expecting them to move out. His service was to finish in August 1973. In May Maros Fajnor, an old friend from the university, visited him. Maros had been working as a trade officer at Chirana Export Piestany, but was now leaving to work for a foreign trade enterprise in Brno. Approval for his departure from Chirana was granted on the condition that he find a replacement. Finding someone to take his place wouldn't be such a big problem since he was on the list of those who would be allocated a service flat in the summer of 1974. Jozef saw the offer almost as an intervention from the hand of God, and didn't hesitate for one second. He took a day's leave and travelled to Piestany to meet personally with the head of the cadre section at Chirana. They agreed to his employment and in addition got it in writing that after the completion of the block of flats in the Piestany-Sihot estate he would be given flat number 11, on the sixth floor of block 6A.

On Friday August 31, Balaz was released from his military service. Over the weekend they packed their bags, wrapping their wedding gifts, mostly pillows and quilts, in a big sheet. They packed everything they could in the little Renault his father-in-law had driven from Presov. Luckily the car had a roof rack, so they were also able to carry boxes full of kitchen accessories and other things that wouldn't fit inside the Renault. Leaving the flat where he was born and had grown up, where he had spent the whole twenty-three years of his life, gave him a funny feeling. At the last moment his mother gave him three hundred crowns and he still had some savings from when he worked at TIP editors, so they wouldn't be arriving empty-handed.

They travelled up to Stara Tura, the headquarters of Chirana, national enterprise. Through his rear-view mirror, Banaz could read Chirana 'national enterprise'. "Let's see what this 'esirprente lanoitan' brings us" he thought to himself as he parked at the main entrance.

They were temporarily housed in a workers' building with the horrible name 'House of Specialists'. Two iron beds and a wooden baby's version were squeezed into a room of about 4 x 3 metres. It was nothing great, but in contrast to the corner they had inhabited at his parents' it was nothing short of luxury. And best of all, they were alone together. Chirana Export Piestany didn't have its own lodging-house and so, after approval by head management they were able to offer their employees flats in Stara Tura. Balaz now understood why his schoolmate Miro had called the town the 'rear end of the world'. He himself had lasted three months there.

Chirana Export was part of a manufacturing factory based in Piestany. Just like the shift workers, the trade department officers started their working day at six in the morning, finishing at half past two. Until nine a.m the export department caught up with their administrative tasks or basically just passed the time. Despite their constant objections that their business partners In Paris, Bern or Essen didn't come to work until nine, the directive on working hours in the manufacturing/management unit was never changed. This meant that when the department went home at two thirty telephone calls from their foreign partners were left unanswered. When Balaz criticized this nonsense, he was told by the Chairman of the Revolutionary Workers' Movement that "we are not going to adapt to the capitalists."

At the House of Specialists the toilets and bathrooms were shared communally. The Stara Tura workers, similarly to the 'leading social force' in other sectors of Czechoslovak socialist society, were famous for their consumption of alcohol. When someone drinks a lot he tends to pee more frequently; vomiting is also a frequent phenomenon among this class of person. That meant that the smell of urine and vomit in the communal sanitary facilities could often be overpowering. Since their toilet paper kept disappearing, the Balaz family took to using cut-up Pravda or other newspapers to wipe themselves.

One cold November afternoon, after Jozef's return from Piestany Marta came back from the toilet in a foul mood.

"Be so good as to go down to the paper goods store and pick up some normal toilet paper. I've had enough of wiping myself with newspaper sandpaper!"

"But that's the only thing the workers won't steal..."

"So I won't leave it in the toilet, I'll carry it with me."

Balaz put on his quilted jacket, popped his cap onto his head and, seeing that his wife was not about to back down, went out into the rain mixed with the season's first snow. "Don't forget your umbrella" was Marta's final message.

"I won't need it, I'll be back in a second."

"Just don't come back without that toilet roll!"

"Don't worry, I'll bring joy to your bourgeois backside." To this quip he added a forced smile.

And he would have been back in a second if the only paper goods shop in Stara Tura hadn't been closed for inventory-taking. The hand-printed sign glued onto the shop door advised him: 'The nearest shop in Nove Mesto will be glad to serve you'. – Nove Mesto was twenty kilometres away, but Jozef was in luck; the shop was near to the inter-city bus station, and one was leaving in three minutes. He didn't know Nove Mesto well, but found out the town had two paper goods shops. The thought that the odds in favour of getting toilet paper had just risen by one hundred percent brought joy to his heart. He didn't get through the door of the first one - on the door was written 'Out of toilet paper, expecting more on Monday.' He got to the second one at three minutes past four, just as the assistant was locking up.

"Excuse me please, we desperately need toilet paper!"

"Don't you see the time? It's gone three minutes after four. We close at four."

"I'll pay you as much as you want, I just need that toilet roll. Please."

"I'm sorry, but at any rate we don't have any toilet paper, it's coming on Monday."

"Where else could I try?"

"There's a new shopping centre in Piestany that's open until six."

"Thanks anyway." Balaz put his cap back on and pulled it down over his ears. It had turned colder and the snow was thickening. The train station was only ten minutes away; if he was really lucky he could make it to Piestany in time to get to the shopping centre. After a wait of twenty minutes the local to Piestany came into the station, and he arrived in that town at half-past five. He found out where the shop was and started running. He was in luck - the shop was still open. Here his luck turned bad - they were out of toilet paper.

"The delivery's coming on Monday. We should have it stocked by noon," was the message, accompanied by a sweet smile of condolence.

"Do you have any serviettes? That would work just as well!"

"We don't have any; they ran out just after the toilet paper."

"What can we use instead of toilet paper? It's got to be something soft" His request was delivered with a sorrowful expression. Maybe the sales assistant would take pity on him.

She winked at him conspiringly: 'I'd go to the newspaper shop and ask for 'Voice of the National Committee'. It costs only 12 halliers, it's almost as soft as toilet paper, and when you slice it up it'll last you a lot longer than toilet paper that costs one crown. The shop's just around the corner, but you'll have to hurry. They close at six."

He made it to the newspaper stand before six, to find they had closed early. He made his way back to the station. The train to Stara Tura was finished for the day, but another one took him back to Nove Mesto, then he made it home to Stara Tura by bus. At ten minutes before midnight he stood at the entrance to the lodging-house. The porter had bad news for him...

"Your wife phoned the police, and they've just left. I'll phone the station, let them know you're back. Out with the boys, eh?"

He raced up the stairs and found Marta seated at the table. Seeing him safe and sound, she burst into tears of relief. He told her the story of his paper chase, but neither of them saw any humour in the tale. They had to be up for work the next day at four-thirty, so they went right to bed.

At the beginning of March, Jozef got a call from a customer, a dentist in Marseilles, that the spit-bowl in the dental set sold him by Chirana was cracked. After filling in the prescribed form, Jozef sent it to the material/technical department with a request for express dispatch to France.

"Where do you think you are?" Vilo Drzík, the head of supplies, asked sarcastically. "Spit-bowls aren't slotted in for manufacture until the third quarter."

"But this man needs a bowl right away, otherwise he'll go out of business. He's losing patients every day. He doesn't care what quarter it is!' Balaz kept pushing.

"What can I tell you? These are the advantages of a planned socialist economy... I know how you feel... Know what? Go and see old Smalik, he'll help you out. Just don't tell him I sent you."

"Who is this Smalik?"

"The head of the warehousing department. He's got about a hundred sets slated for shipment to Angola. They spit on the ground there anyway, so they say."

This wasn't the first time someone had come to Smalik in despair. For a bottle of gin he separated a spit-bowl from a read dental set and gave it to Balaz, who immediately took it to Bratislava to clear customs, then sent it to Marseilles. He paid for the shipment out of his own pocket, partly since he didn't want the firm to know he was supplying his customer with stolen merchandise.

If Balaz needed to phone a client in a capitalist country first he had to submit a detailed questionnaire regarding when, where, why and with whom he wanted to telephone. When he received a signed notification from the head of the export section, he was allowed to use the phone. In emergency situations the signature of the assistant director could suffice, but if both were away on business, he simply couldn't make the call. The same procedure applied to the sending of telex.

Copying texts was also a tricky business. He had to go the head of SB (Special Branch), which was essentially the local branch of the State Security office. The copying machine was kept locked in the office of the SB head. When the head of the trade department signed his copy application, the the SB head put on a pair of rubber gloves, poured some ink into the copying machine and printed off the requested number of copies with a carbon printer. The copies usually came out smudged and anyone who touched a copy came away with blue fingers. So Special Bureau required the ordering party sign the reception receipt before actually touching the copies.

Balaz and the rest of his department were constantly criticizing the bureaucratic obstacles and general nonsense that complicated and delayed their work. He went so far as to mock the director of the enterprise, JUDr. Cernak, an older businessman who had been working in foreign trade since the times of the first Czechoslovak Republic. He heard him out and then replied sadly: "What you're telling me is completely logical. I also get angry about these idiotic rules, but... unfortunately... there's no way around it. I have personally brought it to the attention of the general director in Stara Tura. He's an old Party hack who was brought in to replace an experienced specialist, Ing. Turan. Surely you've heard his name before. Turan could still be the director today if he had not refused to agree to the 'Lessons from the 1968 Crisis". I'm truly sorry, Mr. Balaz." His tone was almost fatherly, and Balaz noticed that he'd not been called 'comrade' as was the usual salutation. "Be careful what you say and where you say it - the Chairman of the Party organization, Okruzny, gets to hear every one of your criticisms, and you're making him uneasy... and watch who you tell jokes to."

"Have you heard this one?" Balaz burst out with a sparkle in his eye, and before the director could react he launched into one of his jokes: "Husak asks the American president how much the average worker makes. 'One hundred and fifty dollars a week,' says the president. 'And how much does he need to live on?' 'Somewhere between fifty and seventy dollars,' comes the reply. 'And what does he do with the difference?' Husak continues. 'That's not our business, America is a free country!' Now the president asks the same about Czechoslovakia. 'Workers in my country earn about two and a half thousand crowns a month.' 'And how much does he need to live on?' 'If he has two children, at least three thousand.' 'And where does he get the difference from?' 'That's not our business, we are a democratic country'. . . "

Cernak laughed. "Thanks for that sign of trust. From what I've been told you'll be getting your flat within the month. It would be too bad if Okruzny started making problems for you..."

Jozef left the director's office saddened. He was aware that the Party dominated the professional management. From that time he went home more and more downhearted and bitter, and waking up at four thirty every morning didn't help his mood. Marta worked in the advertising department at Chirana and her thousand crowns per month was a necessary supplement to Josef's starting salary of one thousand seven hundred.

The occasional sharp debates with Okruzny didn't bother him that much. They were getting their flat and behind its closed doors all the Communists in the world and Okruzny in particular could go piss up a rope. The Sihot flat was just waiting for official approval and there was to be a kindergarten just across the road from 6A. Marta had received a recommendation from her boss and little Martuska was enrolled in the play school. It seemed that finally a more joyous life was awaiting them. Their salaries would be increased a little, enough that they wouldn't have to buy apples individually but by the kilo! Marta bought a new dress that emphasized her splendid figure. After the birth she had regained her original weight and beauty. After a long time they began to go to the cinema again. Again they were enjoying their life.

On April 1 he was summoned to a meeting with Comrade Placha, the secretary of the Party factory Chairman. Comrade Chairman was asking him in for a friendly conversation - if possible, right away.

"That doesn't sound so friendly" his colleague Aranyi forecast.

"Comrade Chairman doesn't call in the rank and file just like that. I sense a problem of some kind. Have you been shooting off your mouth again?" worried Filkova.

"Either that or they're giving him a promotion," joked fat Grajtak breathlessly. His self-confidence had increased since he had joined the People's Militia. It wasn't that he was a star candidate, just that he was the only suitable candidate in the office. As soon as the commander of the factory militia Remenar came into the office, everyone kept their eyes on their work.

"People, don't be naïve, someone has to join up. Haviar and Cerny have retired, I need two new recruits," he almost pleaded.

"Surely you don't want the iron fist of the proletariat to be a woman's?" Filková said in her own defence. Everyone was surprised, since this was the first time she'd made such a thing of her femininity. Until then she'd only cursed out men, who in her opinion abused and exploited women.

"I wasn't even thinking of you," Remenar retorted, and turned to the other three men. "Aranyi, what about you?"

"Me? I'm the Military Cooperation Association treasurer."

"Right," Remenar had to admit when he checked the employees register.

"And I'm the chairman of the Trade Union cultural commission," Balaz added. Remenar again checked the register. "Julo!" he said, turning to Grajtak, who was looking at him with the expression of a small trapped animal. "I don't see anything for you. The Party, the Union, the Soviet-Czechoslovakia Friendship Association, the Military Cooperation Association, the gardening committee... you're nowhere. You're going to join the militia!"

"But I'm a peace-loving guy. I've never in my life held a gun. And I have a military exemption..." Julo was trying his best to refuse.

"What do you think the militia does?" Aranyi came into the discussion on Remenar's side, afraid that somehow Julo would wiggle out of it. "They shoot air guns!"

"That's about it, and once a month they go on weenie roasts. You can manage that, and you were just bragging about your new grill. So you're in; now at least you'll be exempt from other activities. Sign here." Grajtak shrugged, signed the form and became a member of the worker's armed unit.

Balaz put on his jacket, straightened his tie and a moment later knocked on Chairman, Okruzny's door. He had been in the enterprise for six months and had never yet been in his office. The rumour about Okruzny was that at the time of the Soviet invasion he was the commander of the Piestany airport. In spite of the calls by Dubcek and Svoboda for the army not to show any resistance to the Soviets, he had ordered his heavy guns into a state of alert. It was said that he announced that the 'Ruskies' would come into the Piestany airport over his dead body. Following the reclassification of the invasion as international aid, Okruzny's heavy guns were not forgotten. Moreover, since during the investigations he himself had confirmed that he had issued the order, he was thrown out of the army after being demoted to a simple soldier. For a time he mooched around Piestany without a job, but his heroism lasted only until he had run out of money. When his savings were gone he took to drinking - on credit. By chance just when his savings had hit rock bottom he ran into the plain-clothes colonel of security, Kyska. As one of the senior members in the Piestany State Security he was a man of wide influence. He and Okruzny had been friends for many years, and when Kyska offered him the paid position of Chairman of the Party organization at Chirana Export, Okruzny didn't hesitate to accept it. He had never quite understood how they could kick him out of the army but not of the Communist Party. In all likelihood this oversight by certification committee was simply the result of the confusion which reigned at that time. Okruzny underwent self-criticism, by which he regained the trust of the comrades. And so he found himself in the position, below Kyška, of the second most powerful person at Chirana Export.

"Come in," was the jovial response by the secretary to Balaz's knock. "Comrade Chairman is expecting you. Would you like tea or coffee?" Balaz did not immediately answer, being busy studying the portraits of Marx, Engels and Husak decorating the walls. "So what will it be?" the secretary repeated her offer.

"Maybe just a glass of water, thank you very much."

"Comrade Balaz is here," the secretary informed Kyska, signalling to Balaz to enter. Okruzny welcomed him with a wide smile on his face, a firm handshake and a place on a big comfortable armchair.

"So how are things, Comrade?" he asked cheerily.

"Fine. We're happy about the flat," Balaz answered carefully.

"That's fine that you're getting a flat. The Party knows how to look after its young comrades, qualified comrades in particular. And you, comrade Balaz, are qualified, as is your wife. We've had our eye on you for quite some time. I'm very pleased with your constructive criticisms. The Party needs more comrades like you."

"But I'm not a Party member..." Balaz reminded him.

And that's exactly what I want to talk to you about. What about a glass of vodka? Or gin if you prefer."

"Well I wouldn't say no to a little gin..."

Okruzny poured it out. "I'll come straight to the point. As I've already mentioned, we in the Party leadership are quite impressed by your active attitude to your job. Your results are first-class. Your wife too has been fitting in well in her new position. Her superior, Comrade Gabor, has given her an excellent reference. We've discussed the two of you at a Party leadership meeting and we've come to the conclusion that... you'd be valuable members of our Party organization..."

"Me, in the Communist Party?" The words were out of his mouth before Balaz had time to reflect.

"Why ever not?" the Chairman asked, puzzled. "Your father is in the Party," Okruzny reminded him.

"That's true."

"So why not you?" While Balaz sat stunned, Okruzny looked him over closely.

"You've taken me a little by surprise. I'm still young, I don't have much experience as yet; I've never been a member of anything apart from the philatelic club and the volleyball team."

"You have to start sometime... What about another little drink?" Without waiting for an answer, Okruzny poured them both a glass. "Look here, Jozef, allow me to address you by your first name, we are colleagues after all. I'm Laco." He put out his hand.

"Jozef, pleased to meet you." From now on they would be on a first-name basis.

"I won't keep you. I only want to tell you we've already gotten approval from the Party District Committee in Trnava. They've already accepted three workers into the Party, so as a result we have a place for one member of the working intelligentsia. Don't think getting management professionals into the Party is an easy thing. Other people would be jumping for joy if they got such an offer. Listen...talk it over with your wife and let me know tomorrow. Honour to Work!" With that, Okruzny stood up and limply squeezed Jozef's sweaty right hand.

That evening he and Marta talked it over. They were well aware of the trap they'd be stepping into. When Okruzny had mentioned three workers and not six, it was clear that the offer was for him alone.

"My mother would die if I ever joined the Party, and I feel the same way about it," were Marta's final words on the topic.

"And me? I know what it all means. My dad and I discussed it a couple of times, and he never suggested I join up. He himself was basically forced into it, blackmailed. They offered him a flat. My God! I just realized! We're waiting for a flat like we're waiting for the Second Coming. If we both turn them down we can kiss that flat goodbye. It would be like spitting in their face. That's why Okruzny waited until now, two weeks before signing the flat over to us, to bring it up. Damn it all!" Jozef slapped his forehead while Marta stared gloomily into the air. In his stomach he felt the same way he had back in the Hron restaurant when Winter asked his opinion on the Soviet's 'international aid'. He had absolutely no idea where they'd live if they didn't get that flat. One look at his wife told him she was thinking exactly the same.

The next day Balaz got in touch with Okruzny. He explained that he had a young daughter who was often ill and that his wife had to spend a lot of time at home with her, which would make it hard for her to fully participate in Party activities. For himself, he agreed to the Chairman's suggestion. He would be proud to become a candidate for membership in the Communist Party of Slovakia. "I knew you wouldn't let me down." Okruzny stood up and put out his hand.

CHAPTER
SIX

BERLIN 1971 – 1972

THOMAS, along with Michael, Bodo, Reiner, Walter, Dieter and a few other comrades from the Radical Social-Democratic Faction Stamokap were squeezed into the kitchen of his Berlin bachelor flat. They were smoking Camels and drinking cans of beer with chasers of their favourite spirit, Korn. One bottle was already dead and it was clear that some of them were feeling its effects. Thomas and Michael were holding a lively debate, with the others chiming in only sporadically.

"So everything's ready for tomorrow!" Michael, the de facto leader of the group, was clearly looking forward to the action. He was quite a handy fellow, especially when it came to making Molotov cocktails. He was a student of chemistry, and explosives were sort of a hobby. Michael always seemed to have a ready supply of money and it was rumoured that he had a lucrative sideline in making bomb charges. Whenever anything in Germany was blown up, Michael could be seen with a mysterious smile on his face. He was respected, but at the same time feared. No-one was asking where he found the components to make the bombs and grenades. It was sure he wasn't buying them on the open market since all demolition companies using explosives were under strict government control. The same regulations covered mines and other workplaces using blasting materials. Another rumour within Stamokap had it that Michael enjoyed connections with the East German secret police, Stasi, and that they were the source of his supply. He was in fact from East Germany and had grown up with Rudi Dutschke in the town of Lückenwald. Thomas well remembered how Rudi would warn him about Michael's aggressiveness and hot temper. At that time he had the impression that Rudi knew more about Michael than he was saying out loud. Since Thomas had started meeting with the journalist Peter Greiner he was becoming better oriented in these matters. Greiner was now working as the West Berlin and East Bloc correspondent for the weekly 'Das Leben' and had great contacts and reliable information. Thomas remembered one conversation when Peter had mentioned that the radical youth organizations of West Berlin were saturated with Stasi agents, and that they were exceptionally well paid for their undercover activities.

"Boys, I'm really looking forward to tomorrow, we'll ready let the Kreuzberg police have it. I'm glad that at least we are carrying on from where the APO (non-parliamentary opposition) left off. If it wasn't for Stamokap, the German youth movement wouldn't have the least trace of the old fighting spirit." It was clear that Michael was proud of his own role within the faction.

"As for me, I'm considering forgetting about our socialist youth movement and the Stamokap faction in particular," Thomas said thoughtfully. The others looked at him in surprise.

"Have you gone out of your mind? You want to leave us in the lurch just when the public is starting to really get nervous? Is that your game?" Walter joined in the debate for the first time.

"The public is starting to get royally pissed-off," was Thomas' comeback to that.

"Well, is that a good thing or a bad thing?" Michael demanded.

"It's basically a pile of shit," said Thomas coolly. "The more active we are, the more the public is fed up with us!"

A silence fell over the room, which Michael took advantage of to fill everyone's glasses right to the brim. "Hey, hey, take it easy with that stuff. You think I get it for nothing?" Thomas protested angrily and poured most of his glass back into the bottle.

"You act like you're on the edge of starvation!" Michael drank his down in one go.

"I sure don't have as much spending money as you."

"What do you mean by that?!"

"That so far I'm not starving, but maybe I will be soon. Ever since they tossed me out of university I haven't been able to find a job. That bloody regulation forbidding employers to take on anyone who is either active in radical politics or is even suspected of it was the last straw. I've applied for about twenty jobs and been turned down every time," Thomas complained, shaking his head. Michael thoughtfully stared in front of himself, occasionally stroking his chin. He nervously lit a cigarette.

"So why don't you help Karl out?" Reiner asked.

"Karl has bled my drier than the average capitalist does. And he claims to be my friend."

"Listen... I'm getting a strange feeling that you're becoming... apathetic or something... is that it?" Walter looked at him questioningly. Thomas didn't answer for a bit, then said:

"I don't know if any of this makes sense any more. We wanted to engage the public but we've done exactly the opposite. All of our actions, all these groupings, whether it's Stamokap or the Spontis, the Marxists, the Maoists, right through to the RAF, are having no effect. We're completely excluded and isolated from the political debate. We all recognize this, but nobody wants to say it out loud. Even the parliamentary SPD keeps away from us. No-one can deny the fact that the SPD has expelled more than 10 000 young people who refused to retract their so-called revolutionary standpoints."

"I don't recognize you any more - Thomas Ankermann, one of the people closest to Rudi Dutschke, shitting in his pants!" Now Bodo too was shaking his head.

"If Rudi was here, he'd kick you right in the ass!" Michael got back into the debate.

Thomas hesitated and then said in a quiet voice: "When Rudi was here, he kicked all of you in the ass."

"What? The last I heard, Rudi was in Norway," Michael seemed confused.

"We were together a few days ago; we met at Gollwitzer's. There were five of us - Rudi, Gollwitzer and me, along with President Heinemann and his wife."

"President? What president?" Walter couldn't believe what he was hearing.

"Gustav Heinemann, the President of the Federal Republic of Germany," Thomas answered nonchalantly.

"You must be out of your mind!" Michael was taken aback. "Are you saying a leader of the German radicals was meeting with the president of this country?! Do you take us for idiots?!"

"The meeting was at the express request of the president of the republic. The meeting was secret and I'm sharing it with you because I have full faith in you." Thomas said emphatically. "We discussed everything - Germany's post-war history, the country's role in Europe and in the world, the mission and future of the SPD, the East zone, our revolutionary activities, and life in general." A cold silence fell over the kitchen; the boys understood that Thomas was not lying to them. "I came away with two impressions - that the President was disappointed yet powerful and Rudi committed but powerless..."

"But I don't understand why Rudi didn't call me? I'm his closest friend after all." It was clear that Michael was offended. Thomas gave him a long look but said nothing. Michael's upset showed on his face and the boys noticed how sad he seemed.

"What did Rudi say about the movement?" Walter leaned closer to Thomas in his eagerness to hear.

"Do you really want to know?" Thomas' answer was put as a challenge to them, and they all nodded. "That all our actions are well-meant stupidities!"

Silence reigned.

"He would never say that! You made that up!" Michael was almost screaming. "You're just saying it to cause dissent and doubt among us!" The others, on his prompting, nodded their heads. "It's interesting that you're saying it now, just before tomorrow's big demonstration. Doesn't it seem strange to the rest of you?" Now Michael was actually shouting. "Your opinions lately don't make sense to us..." Again Michael looked around the room, searching for confirmation and support.

"Really, Thomas, you ought to tell us what's going on with you. Lately your opinions have been kind of strange, defeatist." Now Bodo was speaking for all of them. Thomas sat and thought.

"It doesn't mean anything for me anymore," he finally responded in a cloud of cigarette smoke.

"Ah, it doesn't mean anything to you! Out of the blue, now that things are starting to get serious. Well I'll tell you why it's lost its meaning, why you're demoralizing us and stepping back from our activities!" Michael raised his voice dramatically. Immediately after that he seemed to be trying to control himself. It looked as if he thought he'd gone too far and didn't want to say any more, but the expressions on the others' faces urged him to continue. "Okay, I'll tell you what's being said behind your back, and that nonsense you made up about some meeting with Rudi and Heinemann just confirms it. The members for some time have thought you've been cooperating with the Secret Service!"

Thomas nearly dropped his glass of Korn. But looking around at the men's sullen stares, he saw that this really was what was being said about him. Michael again took the floor: "Tell him, guys. Why do I always have to be the spokesman?!"

"That's the way it is, Thomas. That's what we're all wondering," Walter said, quietly and sadly. Thomas sat and smoked on, saying nothing. There was a kind of thunder in the atmosphere.

"Well, I guess I'll get going." Bodo stood up, and the rest of the comrades followed his lead.

"Rudi and I really did meet with the President. You can ask him yourselves. Right now he's living in Grünewald, at Hohenzollerndamm 91," Thomas was revealing a closely guarded secret, staring right into Michael's eyes. "If you don't know where that is, it's right next door to Axel Springer's villa. You'd better write it down so you can give your people the correct information!"

"What people?!"

"The Stasi - the East German Secret Service. They give you your money, your explosives, so you can spread them around and make a profit for yourself." Michael couldn't hold himself back and jumped at Thomas. That was when the fight started. The table was turned over, splashing beer and spirits onto the floor. Both cursed the other as a swine and a traitor. Finally the others managed to pull them apart.

"You shouldn't have said that, now you've really gone too far. You'll regret that, you can count on that. You have no proof!!!" Michael was howling and shaking with rage.

"He won't have to prove anything," said a voice coming from the entranceway. During the fight nobody noticed a strange man had come into the flat.

"My name is Peter Greiner. I'm a reporter," he smiled. "I'm a friend of Thomas'. Excuse me for coming in unannounced; I did call but nobody heard me... How are you doing, Hans?" He was addressing Michael. The men looked at him in surprise.

"I'm Michael... Michael Neumann..." Michael stammered his name to Greiner.

"I know you're Michael, Hans is just your codename." Michael's legs buckled, the blood ran to his head, and he had to sit down quickly. It was clear to all those present that if asked to undergo a lie detector session he would have to refuse.

"Excuse me, there's too much smoke in here, cigarettes are not good for me..." he said weakly. "What did you say? That I'm a Stasi agent? That... that's absurd," Michael attempted to convince his comrades.

"Major Kuhlkampf sends you his warmest greetings."

"Major who?" His voice had begun to crack.

"Your commanding officer from the II/9 Department of SIC – Supreme Intelligence Command? The man you meet at his home in Karlshorst, East Berlin... Not far from the main headquarters of the Soviet Military Group in Germany..."

The lads looked at each other in amazement. Michael started to deny it, but then he quietly pulled himself together and left without another word. There was a long moment of thoughtful silence, then Walter stubbed out his cigarette and turned towards the door. The others followed his example, and Thomas and Peter were left alone. They looked at each other until Thomas shook his head.

"For me that's the last straw! I'm had it up to here with this revolution," Thomas spit out.

CHAPTER
SEVEN

PIESTANY 1975

FROM the moment Balaz became a candidate for membership in the Communist Party, he was allowed to travel to capitalist countries. The allowance in marks or francs wasn't generous and so trade representatives economized as much as they could before heading west. The bellboys in the hotels they stayed at were always surprised at the weight of their suitcases. This of course was on account of the tins of fish and pate, the bread and salami, in some cases even hot-plates and potatoes, they brought from home. The thriftiness of the travellers was matched by that of their companies. It was usual for two reps to share a room, so Balaz found himself sharing a single room in Milan with the despised head of the trade group, Bolejuch. The hot September weather forced them both to shed their modesty and parade around in their red and white underclothes. They sat on the double bed with their backs to each other and embarrassedly ate their rations.

"Comrade Balaz, do you have any sardines?" Bolejuch asked without turning around. "I've got some ham, want to trade?" Now, Balaz was no big fan of sardines, but since they were cheaper than ham his wife Marta tended to overstock them. He was a little surprised that his thrifty director was proposing such an unequal exchange of goods. 'I guess he's getting a little tired of ham day in and day out,' he concluded, and accepted the deal with joy. These basic food stocks of socialist businessmen were duly swapped. It took only one bite for Balaz to discover he'd been swindled - the ham had gone off. Again Bolejuch had tricked him. He didn't have the nerve to confront his boss, and so he ate the putrid meat; at least the smell of the sardines masked its odour. 'If I get sick, at least I'll be able to save on food for a couple of days.' He comforted himself with the thought. The smell of sardines and onions filled the close room, so Balaz stepped out onto the balcony and gazed down three storeys onto the street. He noticed a number of lightly-dressed women in front of the hotel chatting with men and sometimes accompanying them into the hotel. After a time Bolejuch joined him outside, burping as he came out. Outfitted in their red vests and white pants they looked like Czechoslovak athletes. Fortunately they were high enough up not to cause a shock to any of the millions of Italians crossing below them.

"Have you been in the West before?" he asked meaningfully.

"Once, as a student."

"Comrade Balaz, you're still a young comrade." He paused to consider how to go on. "Those women down there are whores." He looked down at the prostitutes for a moment until he found the words. "Those Czech bastards have lodged us in a brothel!" Balaz thought back on the first thing the trade delegate, Svoboda said when he welcomed him to Milan: "Couldn't you leave that prick at home?!" It was obvious to Balaz that Bolejuch's reputation was as 'good' in international business circles as back home in Piestany.

The evening cooled down nicely and they went walking in the city centre. Bolejuch suddenly stopped in front of an antique shop in one of the city's many small squares where busts of composers filled the display window. Beethoven, Mozart, Verdi, Wagner, Mendelssohn and others stared out at them as if they were seeing Slovaks for the first time.

"Comrade Balaz, look how clever we Slovaks are!" he cried out, pointing at one figure. "That Mendelssohn was an engraver where

I'm from in Kicina, and now he's on sale here in Italy!" Balaz felt his stomach turn, and knew it wasn't only due to Bolejuch's ham.

Back home in Bratislava he came out of the lift on the sixth floor of his building and smelled the pleasant aroma of chamomile; he knew that his child was again having bronchial problems. She was ill frequently, as were a lot of her classmates in her newly-opened prefab kindergarten. It was said that the building was put up in a hurry, and among the materials used in its construction was asbestos. But no-one complained, since to do so would be pointless. In fact they were pleased they had been able to get their children into the kindergarten, where applications far outstripped capacity. This left the mothers free to go to work and thus supplement their family income.

Usually in those times people had two kinds of problem with money - they didn't have enough and there was almost nothing to buy. At the greengrocers there was only rarely fruit or vegetables on sale. At the small improvised stands in the housing estates bread could only be found if you went early enough, so working mothers were usually out of luck after work. Accordingly good relations with the shop assistants played a key role. Jozef's mother worked at a home decorating shop in Bratislava, and this helped keep her family stocked up. If she wanted mandarins or bananas at Christmas - workers in Czechoslovakia didn't see them during the rest of the year - she went to see her friend Julia at the butcher's, who had asked her for some curtains from Bulgaria. The most reliable source of information was the butcher shop cashier Eva, who told her that Jolana in the grocer's wanted some roast beef. Now roast beef was top-quality meat, and without the necessary connections people could only hear about it, smell it, and dream about it. So Mrs. Balazova told Jolana that Julia had a nice bit of beef put away for her in exchange for the curtains, and that she would gladly pass it on to Jolana if she could get her some mandarins for Christmas.

Joy from the victories of 'real socialism' could be enjoyed by the workers on certain occasions during the year - during the celebrations for the Great October Revolution (celebrated In November),

Consumers' Day, Miners' Day, Teachers' Day, Cooperative Farmers' Day, Liberation Day, Railway Workers' Day, Public Safety Day, Army Day, the anniversary of the Slovak National Uprising, Harvest Festival, and most of all, Workers' Day. May Day was looked forward to as long as it didn't fall on Saturday or Sunday. In general, though, the working people enjoyed this celebration. First of all, they got the day off work, so if the weather was decent they could spend it in their allotment gardens. Before the May Day parade, the younger workers had to make up posters with the faces of the Party leadership or banners with slogans written across them. Since Balaz was now a member of the Communist Party, participation at the parade was obligatory for him. The banner he worked on was 'In Unity There Is Strength'. Of course he had to suffer teasing from his friends on account of this; the only shop open on these occasions was the Unity department store. After the end of the parade everyone rushed there in the hope of finding some bananas. The lines were long, the people's tempers short, and the chance of finding the sought-after tropical fruit about fifty-fifty. Under a banner reading 'The Customer Is King', the workers slowly shuffled towards the sales counter. This time Balaz was lucky - he got some bananas. In his excitement he raised his bananas, along with his Unity/Strength poster, up in the air. Immediately the shop guard was on him, asking for his identity papers and warning him against causing a public disturbance.

"The baby's got bronchitis again." Marta's sad voice rang out from the bathroom when she heard Balaz's key turn in the door. He found her sitting on the toilet bowl with her daughter in her arms. Under her, in a pot on a hotplate, chamomile tea was steaming. The bathroom's flimsy walls served only one purpose - to provide visual isolation for the user. Sounds and smells penetrated not only throughout the home, but carried through to the flats of the nearest neighbours. Once when Balaz had drunk too much at his birthday party his friend Duro was kind enough to play his accordion outside the bathroom door until the vomiting ceased.

Young Martuska's coughing bouts seemed to spark up at regular intervals, and the local children's doctor was starting to get fed up with Marta's frequent visits. She simply wrote her another prescription for penicillin and sent her away. As she sat on the toilet bowl it was clear to Jozef that his wife was close to tears - not only on account of her daughter's illnesses but also due to the horrible cockroaches which all the newly-built apartment houses shared communally. Marta had a real aversion to these unpleasant insects. Luckily when you turned the lights on, they hid themselves away. In consequence she preferred the cost of lighting the bathroom permanently to the idea of swarms of disgusting insects crawling behind her back when she sat on the seat.

"Please put some more water in the pot and boil up some more chamomile. Then you can take my place for a while if that's all right with you." Good husband Jozef obediently fetched the pot to fill it with water.

"Damn, the tap's off again!"

"Get some water from the bathtub. Perhaps you've forgotten that up here on the sixth floor during the summer we get water only between two and five in the morning. Don't use too much, I'm going to stew some plums in a minute and I'll need plenty of water."

While the water and chamomile was heating up, Jozef read Pravda. He was drawn by the first page, which consisted of lengthy excepts from the speech of the CSSR Government Chairman Lubomir Strougal at the XV Communist Party Congress. He couldn't believe his eyes. Strougal was for a change sharply criticizing the situation in the machine engineering sector, to which the manufacturing/management unit of Chirana belonged. The official was pinpointing the identical issues that Balaz and several of his colleagues had complained of. In fact he complained so much that he was known as a constant moaner. He was deep in the article when Marta called out if the water was boiling yet. He quickly finished his reading and stuck the paper into his attaché case. There was to be a meeting of the enterprise Party branch the next day, and it would definitely come in handy.

A minute later he opened the door to the bathroom. Marta handed over his daughter and hurried out, dressed only in her panties and bra. Both she and the child were covered in sweat from the steam, but the good news was that she had stopped coughing. Jozef took his place on the toilet seat and gently took the child into his arms.

"Hell!" He clearly heard the angry voice of his wife through the flimsy wall.

"What's up?" he asked curiously, for his wife was not much given to cursing. "I want to take a shower but I need the water for my preserves. Now I'll have to work covered in sweat..." Marta wiped herself down and silently and carefully transferred the water from the tub into her pots. When she'd drained all the water, she hopefully tried the taps but in vain. The water would only run again in twelve hours. "This is driving me crazy!" she muttered.

"Perhaps you've forgotten that up here on the sixth floor..." Jozef tried to make a joke of it.

"I'm in no mood for jokes!" She proved this a minute later when she found Jozef heading out of the toilet with the child still in his arms. "You have to stay there longer than that. You've only been there twenty minutes!"

"I have to go. We had beans at lunch and I'm going to burst..." He popped the baby into her arms and went back to the toilet. When he'd finished, he discovered that the toilet paper had run out. He knew new supplies would not be in the shops for another month - he'd read it on the door of the shop. He called Marta to bring him the newspaper.

"Where is it?"

Jozef remembered that instead of cutting the newspaper into toilet-sized strips he'd put it into his bag.

"I didn't cut it up."

"So wipe your bum with your fingers!" They both laughed but Jozef sensed they were laughing through their tears.

"Where did you leave it?"

"In my bag, but I need it. Get me another one."

"What did you find so interesting?"

"Strougal made a good speech."

"They all make good speeches and it ends there. If only they'd talk less and do more. They haven't even had onions in the shops for two weeks. You'll have to go to old Rolko and get some from the cooperative." She opened the door and handed him a few pieces of cut-up paper, with the instruction: "Don't use it all up."

"I've already talked to Rolko; Jules and I are going to meet him this evening. He's got a couple of kilos for us."

"Try to get a whole sackful. What good are a few kilos of potatoes for two families?"

"He's only the night watchman at the cooperative, not the chairman, and he can't take too much. Besides, we're not the only ones he's helping out..."

Even though there generally was a sufficient supply of onions at the market, the Balaz family's combined monthly salaries of one thousand eight hundred crowns didn't allow them to invest too much in this wonderful vegetable at one time. They needed the money for things other than onions. Every crown was important - that was why he had entered a nation-wide Czechoslovak Television in Slovakia competition for writing an original screenplay for children. Even though he had never read a screenplay in his life, he'd written a story on the basis of his experience at Chirana. The prizes were twelve, ten and eight thousand crowns!

"I shouldn't count on first prize, but second would suit us fine," he told his wife resolutely. In the end he was awarded first prize and began to write screenplays on a regular basis.

The next day immediately after the end of work, the meeting of members of the enterprise Communist Party organization took place. There were only two points on the program – a proposal for accepting Comrade Remenar as a candidate for Party membership, and the resolutions of the XV Communist Party Congress. Balaz had already done some thinking about what he would say. He was frankly surprised that they were considering accepting Remenar. Everyone knew he was an unscrupulous career-builder who was incompetent at his job. On the other hand, his father was the department chief with the Slovak Communist Party regional committee in Bratislava.

Out of fear his colleagues avoided him whenever possible. Perhaps if Balaz hadn't been charged up by the article he was carrying in his attaché case, if the water was flowing up to the sixth floor, if his daughter hadn't been coughing all night long and he'd been able to get some sleep, he would have been passive during the meeting and said nothing. So he was not in the best of humour, and when the candidature issue was raised he felt his jaw set. In his presentation Remenar had passed himself off as an expert on foreign trade and claimed to have advised his older superiors Bognar and Horsky on how to fulfill the export plan for their territories. When the Chairman called for discussion, neither Bognar nor Horsky said anything; Balaz on the other hand lost his cool. He stated not only his own opinion, but that of most of his co-workers. When he revealed that due to his incompetence Remenar had cost the company hundreds of thousands, that he didn't speak any world languages and that he had sent a shipload of dental equipment to Egypt instead of to Morocco, he felt as if someone else was speaking out of his mouth. When he really got going he didn't hesitate to mention Remenar's driving under the influence accident, in which one person was injured. That was another situation his father had cleared up for him. At the conclusion of his speech, Balaz stated that he was not in favour of Remenar's acceptance into the Party. His words were followed by a stony silence – the Chairman was frowning, Remenar was grinding his teeth. Then the Chairman asked for comments on Comrade Balaz's remarks. He looked around the room and found everyone looking at the floor. Finally Bognar took the floor and promised 'to do everything possible to fulfill the export plan on his territory'.

"Thank you, Comrade Bognar. Does anyone else have something to say?" he asked in a challenging tone. No-one else had anything to say. The Chairman called for a vote, and was himself the first to raise his hand in favour. This was a signal for the others to follow his lead. The only one against Remenar's appointment was Balaz.

The second point on the program was the implementation of the resolutions of the Communist Party Congress as it related to the foreign trade section of Chirana Export. Chairman Okruzny reported with satisfaction that the enterprise was fulfilling all indicators concerning both export and import. But he couldn't omit a remark regarding exports to capitalist countries: with the exception of the excellent cooperation with the West German company Dentaltechnik, export lagged behind the planned quotas, in particular with French-speaking territories.

"This cannot only be put down to subjective reasons as the officer responsible for these territories, Comrade Balaz, is always trying to convince us. Sometimes it is also necessary to look at oneself critically, Comrade Balaz."

All the members of the committee were glad that Okruzny's newest victim was none other than Engineer Balaz. With his hot temper they were expecting a battle of words between the naïve university graduate and the former army officer. They were aware that in the last few weeks Okruzny had turned red at the very mention of his name. Balaz's reaction was even fiercer than they had anticipated. He had been 'preparing' for this meeting by sitting in the Drlicka pub with his friend Duro Lesko, and naturally the sharpness of his commentaries increased according to the number of glasses of gin consumed. Scarcely had the Chairman stopped speaking before Balaz's hand shot up. Mentally the others shrank back, fearing the worst, but Balaz's statement still outstripped their expectations.

"Mr. Chairman, you're out of your depth," was his opening sentence. "You've never studied foreign trade nor even worked in the field. If Mr. Director criticized me that would be one thing, but you have no right to!"

"Comrade Director!" Okruzny corrected him.

"We pretend and let on that everything is under control. So that the management doesn't find out what we're up to, we secretly slip off to Trnava or even to Bratislava and send spare parts to our customers. And why? Because our fantastic planned economy deliberately produces these parts exactly when our clients don't need them. When they do need them, we're not producing them. Do you actually believe that our clients understand that our everyday spit-bowls are only manufactured in the third quarter when they need them in March? How can I fulfill the export plan when I'm not even allowed to phone France?" Now Balaz was under full steam. He was aware he was going too far but he didn't care. The solemnity, the cheating, stupidity, two-facedness and plain incompetence of these party hacks had gotten under his skin, and the time had come for him to get it out. The week of rehearsing with gin had surely given him the courage he needed.

"Comrade Balaz, I'm not saying that some of the things you've mentioned don't have their merit, but I would perhaps have chosen other words," his director, who the day before had agreed with everything he was now saying, interrupted him in an attempt to calm him down. Then he timorously looked towards the Chairman, who answered him with a cynical smile: "Leave the comrade alone, let him finish," he urged.

"Now I'd like to read something to you." He opened his case and began to read from some papers. This was surprising because never before had he used notes; at Party meetings spoke always without prompts. In a cutting tone he applied his criticisms in a society-wide context. "Shifting Czechoslovakia's industrial production from light to heavy was a mistake. Our industry was a world leader, particularly in light industry branches. Yes Comrades, we have built a lot of factories, mainly in Slovakia, but these were all heavy machinery plants. The plan to rebuild Czechoslovakia as a world power in heavy engineering has proved to be wrong. Metallurgy and engineering create false profits in the economy. The large investments in these branches have not brought the expected profit – in fact without subsidies they would be in the red. And I won't even discuss the damage to the environment. We're not managing to face the technological challenges of the modern world. Essentially Slovak factories are manufacturing only basic components that are sent to Czech enterprises or, even worse, abroad, for finishing. General engineering with a wide product range on a low technological level is simply unable to compete on the world's markets. In addition to this, the incompetence of planners within the Council for Mutual Economic Aid has shown that the socialist economies, far from complementing each other, are actually competing with each other. The only competitive manufacturing branch in Slovakia is armaments. To state it plainly, if Slovakia wasn't manufacturing tanks, gunnery and weapons systems it would be hard to find practically anything of quality in the Slovak economy."

He finished reading and took his seat. Silence again reigned in the meeting-room. Uncertainly the Party members looked to Chairman Okruzny for direction.

"Dear Comrades," he began. "I'm finding it hard to find words. Over the years I have heard various critiques, but such an attack on our Communist Party and even the supreme bodies of our fraternal Council for Mutual Economic Aid in such a direct way is unprecedented!"

The Chairman stopped to take a drink of water, but instead of continuing he simply shook his head from side to side. Balaz again asked to speak and Okruzny, anticipating that he would retract his statement, gave him the floor. Balaz, however, pulled out his notebook once more and began reading: "Party members must extend self-criticism and criticism from the top down. Criticism is the duty of every Party member. It is unthinkable that shortcomings are covered up and avoided by saying nothing. Every member has the right to criticize any Communist Party official, even the most senior. In the case that his critique is not accepted, he may turn to the Control and Inspection Commission of the Central Committee of the Czechoslovak Communist Party. The right to criticize is a basic condition of intra-Party democracy. Anyone who suppresses criticism has no right to be a member of the Communist Party!"

"Comrades, this is truly strong medicine. I don't know who's been filling your head with such ideas, Comrade Balaz. We have to understand, Comrades, that Comrade Balaz is a young comrade, and that youth has the right to sharper words, to stronger criticism. All the same, what he has performed here today is not the constructive criticism we all seek, but an out-and-out condemnation of the bases of socialism. Comrade Balaz, I believe you owe all of us here an apology!"

Balaz frowned and slowly stood up. "Comrade Chairman, forgive me, I thought you were a conscientious member of the Communist

Party, and as such would keep up with your reading of Party documents. Nobody is putting ideas into my head, I've only been reading an article on the regulations of the Communist Party. The critique wasn't my own; I was quoting the words of a member of the Central Committee of the Czechoslovak Communist Party and the Chairman of the Federal Government, Comrade Lubomir Strougal."

A buzz travelled round the room. Balaz pulled the daily Pravda out of the packet he'd been covering it with. 'Socialism has its advantages,' he thought to himself, 'If it hadn't been for the shortage of toilet paper I would never have come into contact with such good arguments.' He looked at the Chairman – "It would seem, Comrade Chairman, that you're not keeping up with your reading the Party newspaper." The silence that followed was heavy with ill foreboding.

Balaz had scarcely arrived at work the following day before he got a call from the secretary of the Chairman of the company Party organization asking him to immediately come to his office. He smiled to himself as he thought that ordinarily his knees would be shaking in such a situation, but now he was calm and determined. He had decided to leave the company at the first opportunity. He knew that idiots were everywhere throughout the country, but he hoped they weren't such total idiots as those at the head of the Party organization at Chirana Export.

Okruzny was nervously pacing his office. "You are a total prick!" was the first thing he said when Balaz entered his office. "That kind of behavior is not what I took you into the Party for. I thought we understood each other and that you would prove to be a real Communist. But you're not a Communist; you're just a provocateur filled up with the ideas of your business partners in the West. I told the director not to give you the Western desk, that he should put you in charge of socialist countries. And that's how we got where we are. And then there's your wife. Instead of fulfilling her responsibilities at work, she's always off sick. She has more absences than anyone else in the enterprise." As Okruzny stopped to take a drink of water, Balaz reflected that this marked the first time he hadn't been offered a drink. "Just listen here, you fighter for truth and justice – so that you can't say that Laco Okruzny is a bastard, I'll give you a fair offer.

If you get out of here I'll give you a good cadre assessment; if you stay, I'll liquidate you. Got it?!"

"Got it. Will that be all?"

"That's all."

When Jozef came home, his wife didn't have to ask a single question – everything was clear at one glance. She said nothing.

"Anything good on television?" His question took her by surprise. "I need to get my mind off things – if I start talking about work now I'll end up killing someone. Sorry....Do we have any cognac?" Marta poured him out a glass, then poured one for herself. Their daughter was already sleeping. They turned the television on just as the Young People's Television Club, with the popular host Jan Vala, was starting. In contrast to almost all the senseless propaganda programs on Czechoslovak TV, this one was actually worth watching. But Jozef hardly noticed what was on the screen, his head was so full of the events of the last two days.

"That could be something of interest for you," Marta said, breaking into the train of his thoughts. Jan Vala was in the middle of a debate on diplomacy featuring two Czechs and one jovial, appealing Slovak. He was Doctor Kramar and worked as the director of the press department of the Federal Ministry of Foreign Affairs. He was talking about his ministry's need for educated young people, preferably from Slovakia. Immediately Jozef decided that when he finished the business that was to take him to Prague on the following day, he would drop into the Foreign Affairs Ministry.

For the first time in his life he found himself at the Cernin Palace. He asked the porter to connect him with JUDr. Kramar.

"Good afternoon. My name is Jozef Balaz. Excuse me for interrupting you, but I saw you on television yesterday. You said you were looking for new staff. I wanted to ask if I could work in your ministry..."

There was a long silence on the other end of the line. "Where did you say you were from?"

"From Bratislava."

"I'll send my secretary down to get you."

While Jozef was showing his identity papers to the porter, a charming young woman came to accompany him up to the office of the press section director.

Kramar indicated where he should seat and immediately started in: "What is your educational background?"

"The Economics University in Bratislava. Foreign trade."

"Are you a Party member?"

"Yes,"

"Is there anyone in your family who has emigrated to the West?"

"No."

"What languages do you speak?"

"I work at Chirana Export with the French and German territories. I speak good English and Hungarian, and of course Russian."

Kramar stared at him in thought and smiled mysteriously. Then he went over to his telephone. "Give me the language department." While he was being put through, he asked Balaz if he knew where the Tuscany Palace was. Balaz shook his head. "Go out of here in the direction of Hradcany. That's where our language department sits." The telephone rang. "This is Kramar. I have a man here who claims he speaks five languages, and I need someone to test him. Orally, please - just have a discussion with him and give me your findings on paper. Thank you. Goodbye." Then he looked Balaz up and down. "Go over there, and when they're done testing you, come back here. I should be leaving for a reception at the Bulgarian Embassy, but I'll wait for you first."

In a little over an hour Balaz was back. His JAK 34 was just taking off for Piestany from Ruzyne airport, but he didn't care. This venture was well worth the price of the night train through Bratislava home.

Kramar looked at the language department results and sat there shaking his head. Finally he addressed Balaz in German and was answered fluently. He wasn't sure when the language switched to English, but that was enough for Kramar. He took the candidate papers from his desk and passed them to Balaz. "Fill these out and have your employer fill out the cadre evaluation – I hope it will be positive – and then send it on to me." Again he gave his personable smile: "This has never happened before you know. If it all works out, you'll be the first diplomat who was ever hired right from the street! And I'll be doing my best to make it happen."

Balaz took tram 22 to the Main Railway Station.

All the way home on the train Balaz was consumed by impatience and curiosity. He took the cadre report form of the Ministry of Foreign Affairs from his attaché case. There were exactly thirty carefully numbered boxes to be completed. He began by quickly filling in his name, surname, date of birth and residence. He reckoned that since he had already shocked Kramar once he might as well shock him again by sending the completed form back to him as soon as possible. In box number eight ('Class Origin') he wrote 'socialist intelligentsia,' and number ten ('Property Holdings') didn't take him long at all to fill in. He wrote in a dash. He did the same for box number twelve (State, Party, Ministerial and Other Awards), seventeen (Party Positions), nineteen (Public Positions), and twenty (Political Affiliation before 1945 and after 1948). In box eighteen ('Membership and Positions in Social Organizations) he wrote 'Revolutionary Trade Union Movement' since almost everyone was a member, 'Socialist Youth Association', since almost all young people belonged to it, and the 'Czechoslovak-Soviet Friendship Association'. He'd never attended a single meeting but was quite sure nobody would check it, and it might come in handy for him. He had never had a position above that of member anywhere. In column twenty-eight ('Stays Abroad, Country, Purpose of Visit, Length of Stay, Year') with satisfaction he wrote in the first place 'the Soviet Union, sports, 1968'. A positive relation to the Soviet Union was, along with membership in the Czechoslovak Communist Party and good language skills, among the decisive factors for career advancement in the world of diplomacy.

CHAPTER
EIGHT

BERLIN 1972 – 1979

THOMAS had been going out with a dark-eyed brunette named Angelika for three months. She was a salesgirl in a small grocery on Kurfürstendamm, an exclusive shop with a solid client base. Angelika made good money working there, and since Thomas had been looking for work for several months and his situation was getting desperate, her pay helped out. It was a little embarrassing for him to be supported by his new girl-friend, but Angelika was clearly in love with him and had enough money for them both. It also interested Thomas that her father was an assistant manager in the office of the Berlin mayor, the socialist Klaus Schütz.

It was a raw Sunday in December, and they were comfortable just lying in their warm bed. They had a candle burning on the desk, and were watching T.V. and drinking Merlot wine. On the screen the German Chancellor Willy Brandt was giving a live interview from Oslo just prior to receiving the Nobel Peace Prize for 1972. 'This is encouraging not just for me but for the whole German nation. I am glad that after the horrors of war that we have lived through in our recent past and for which the German people bear and will continue to bear moral responsibility, we can claim with satisfaction that the granting of the Nobel Peace Prize to a German Chancellor is our rehabilitation in the eyes of Europe and of the world.' At the end of the interview he looked steadily into the camera and condemned those young Germans who were engaged in senseless violence, kidnappings and killing of innocent people. He called upon them to put their shoulder to the wheel and to do their part in the conciliation policy the Bonn government had started to apply towards their Eastern neighbours. "Anyone who has a clean heart and clean intentions is welcome. It's not important whether these young people are Christian Democrats or Social Democrats. The important thing is that they are engaged for their country, for peace, and for friendship among nations.'

"What are you thinking about?" asked Angelika, nudging him as she spoke.

"Sorry..."

"Am I really so unattractive?" she asked, cuddling up to him with a smile.

"Not at all, in fact you're so fantastic that I'd like to have you for my wife!" The words were out, but he didn't know where they'd come from. Angelika just cuddled tighter into him. "I'd just like to lead a normal life, have an ordinary job, and help this country to be a little more normal."

"My dad said that job in the Senate office is looking promising. He's even mentioned it to the Mayor." Angelika stopped to take a breath and continued carefully: "But it would help if you were a member of the Social Democrats..."

Thomas felt bad that his girlfriend's father was getting involved on his behalf, but soothed himself with the thought that he was a fine man and was anyway looking for a way to help his 'future son-in-law' out.

"You want to know what I was just thinking? I was thinking that being in the same party Willy Brandt leads would be a great honour for me."

Two weeks later he entered the Senator's Office as an officer for youth, sport and education. He remained there for just a short time because such an ambitious, organized and capable young man, a graduate of political science at the Free University, was sure to catch the eye of Senator Dietrich Stobbe. He asked Thomas to be his assistant, a position that was the dream of every young person in the SPD. Stobbe himself was a young, dynamic deputy who had won the respect of his colleagues and of the people of Berlin. In the May1977 elections to the senate he was elected and then appointed as the Berlin mayor by the local assembly. Stobbe selected Thomas to be the Senate secretary.

After his appointment he and moved to Wedding, a comfortable quarter not far from the centre; again Angelika's father was instrumental in securing for them a three-room flat on the top of a four-storey house on the corner of Triftstrasse and Sparstrasse streets. From their apartment they had a lovely view over Leopoldo Square and the Virchow Colony.

Angelika left her job at the grocery store and started work at a newly-opened KaDeWe department store in Tiergarten, which meant a fifteen-minute walk to work. She was given the position of manager of the grocery department, at that time one of the largest of its kind in the world. Thomas felt as if his life was beginning to turn in the right direction; he surprised himself by the equanimity with which he received the news of the suicides of his old comrades Andreas Baader and Gudrun Ensslin in the Stuttgart prison on 18. 10. 1977. It was perhaps telling that he was more shaken up by the news that his football hero Franz Beckenbauer was leaving Bayern Munchen to play in America for the New York Cosmos.

Also at this time Stern magazine shocked not only West Berlin but the entire nation with the serial confessions of a sixteen-year-old girl Christiana under the title, 'We the Children from ZOO Station'. It concerned Christiana and a group of children from a children's home who'd become addicted to heroin and supported their habits by selling their bodies at the well-known railway station. The serial was accompanied by the chilling fact that 84 young people died from overdoses in Berlin alone in 1977.

When Mayor Stobbe invited Thomas to elaborate a plan for the engagement of Berlin's youth population in a program to include sports, learning and culture, he set to work with enthusiasm. He and his team went out to Kreuzberg and came up with a plan for getting a youth centre in a factory building belonging to the Berthold AG Company in Mehring. Through their positive energy the young people began to enlist sponsors for the program. Among the first to contribute was the mayor. The factory was transformed into a vast youth centre with lots of activity units - and the essential thing was that the youth themselves managed it. Thomas's plan was gradually reproduced in cities throughout the republic.

Thomas found great favour with the young people and with his fellow politicians. The mayor encouraged him to become a candidate for the city senate, and in March 1979 he was elected as a senator for SPD. At the age of thirty-two he was one of the youngest deputies in Germany. A great political career was opening up before him.

CHAPTER
NINE

MOSCOW 1977

SASHA and her husband walked through the streets of Moscow as if they were in New York or Paris. For the average Soviet Union citizen Moscow was the centre of the world, but getting a job or, more significantly, housing was no easy thing. The capital was for the chosen. Sasha couldn't stop staring at the wonderful, shining marble metro stations. They were built in the times of Stalin when the ambitious goal of the Soviet leadership was to make this city the centre of the proletariat world. The huge arcades with their crystal chandeliers were more reminiscent of a royal palace than an underground transit station for the workers. Sasha had never in her life seen as many cars as there were on the boulevards of Moscow - but then again she had known only Kiev and Komsomolsk. One of the trickiest situations she had to solve occurred at streetlights. When the light turned green people didn't walk but ran across the road. This was because Moscow drivers recklessly drove on the red signals too. The GUM department store near to Red Square also took her breath away - woolen sweaters from Czechoslovakia, kitchen appliances from the German Democratic Republic, toilet paper, soap and toothpaste from Poland, even Hungarian sweets were available - all you had to do was spend a few hours standing in line!

At the time when the Czar's architect Pomerantsev designed one of the largest shopping centres in the world, he could have had no idea that his two and a half kilometres of sales counters and forty-seven thousand metres of shop floor would be such a successful idea. A few decades later the people of Moscow could wait in their never-ending lines under a solid roof and with a modest amount of heating. Perhaps in part due to their society of shortages, the Russian people ranked among the most well-read peoples in the world. In the Soviet Union it was possible to discuss Dostoyevsky, Pushkin or Scholochov not only with the educated but also with building engineers, metal workers, or crane operators. But not with coop farmers - they didn't have the time to stand in long queues, so there were no bookshops in their villages. The ever-present lines were a feature of urban life in the Soviet Union. The customers were truly comradely and you could even reserve your place in line. Clever people stood in line for a time, then asked those in front of them to hold their places while they went to arrange things at the post office or to pick up their kids from their kindergarten.

The lines in which few people read were those in front of shops with alcohol. These opened at eleven o'clock but their thirsty clients were already queuing up at ten. At ten thirty the workers discretely left their workplaces to stand in line. Standing in these lines was also helpful in the case that someone was looking for someone to share the purchase of a bottle of vodka with. Someone holding up three fingers was indicating they were looking for a third partner for their shopping expedition.

There were other advantages to standing in queues. It was an opportunity to meet new people, sometimes resulting in life-long friendships. Even when the lines were shorter it didn't mean that the waiting time would be shorter too. If for example a group of war veterans showed up at the last minute, those already waiting were out of luck. The newcomers had fought for victory over fascism so that they wouldn't ever have to wait in line. Pregnant mothers and those with small children also took precedence over normal shoppers, so it came to be normal practice for women without children to borrow those of their neighbours so as not to have to wait in line.

Pensioners were also big fans of lines. They would stand in a line and when impatient shoppers came by the retirees would show with their fingers their price for surrendering their place in line for them.

Queues had such an attractive force that people would join the line without even knowing what was on sale. When people saw a line it was clear to everyone that some rare commodity had just arrived. If after an hour of waiting they discovered that the product on offer was a non-corrosive frying pan, they would buy it even if they already had a complete set at home. They could rest assured that they could either sell it on or trade if for a cassette recorder, a flannel shirt or a good book. When the shopper finally got to the desired counter in any Soviet shop they could read the optimistic sign: 'Socialism means a satisfied customer!'

The Obickí family got a two-room flat in a lovely part of town, Jasenovo, surrounded by woods and meadows. Initially it felt strange for them to be alone with their son in the flat; they could now walk around in pajamas or even underwear without the fear of unexpectedly bumping into anyone else. For the first few weeks they felt isolated, but in the Soviet Union a person can even get used to privacy if they have to.

Jasenovo was designed as a quarter for selected workers, mostly from the ranks of the military, the police and a few scientific institutes, universities and government offices. There was also a smattering of the best workers to motivate their luckier neighbours. The panel buildings were a little unimaginative but compared with the decrepit buildings in Komsomolosk they were just about perfect. A shopping network, cinemas and a metro extension were promised in the next five-year plan. In the meantime Sasha could tolerate without complaint the hour's travel in the packed buses that took her to her job at a translation institute. It sometimes happened that the bus was so full that she couldn't get on, but she used the waiting time 'usefully'. She and the rest of the people in the line watched in amusement as the bus drivers siphoned off petrol into canisters at the final stop. The complex guards were so polite they even helped the drivers load the canisters into their cars parked inside the bus yards. Neither Sasha nor the others would even think of intervening -

the solidarity of silence and pretence ruled because everyone helped themselves as best they could. The former leader Nikita Sergejevich Khrushchev once said in an interview for the Voice of America that if the citizenry would stop stealing for at least one day, socialism could finally be built in the Soviet Union.

She was happy with her job at the translation office. She earned a little over one hundred and fifty rubles which, together with her husband's three hundred, made for a comfortable monthly income. All the same she was thrifty and saved wherever possible. Their dream was to be able to afford a car - the average Soviet working family had to save for about twenty-five years for such a luxury.

Sasha was thankful her mother had taught her to sew and knit. She shortened her husband's shirts and trousers for young Josif and unravelled old sweaters to reuse the wool for new ones. Several of her colleagues regularly earned a little money from selling these woolies at their place of work. Her neighbour, Vorsilova, the widow of a pilot who had crashed somewhere in the Urals, supported herself through this cottage industry. In fact she was so enterprising that she pasted advertisements on lamp posts for people who wanted to buy such pullovers. Such selling was not against the law in the Soviet Union, but the posting of ads outside of designated areas was. The fine for this 'crime' was beyond her means, so Vorsilova proposed to the local militiaman that she would pay him a regular small sum for turning a blind eye to her activity. She was told that the Soviet militia could not accept bribes, but if she wanted to knit the odd pullover as a gift for his children he could not refuse them. Vorsilova worked fourteen hours every day of the week so that her two daughters aged sixteen and seventeen could dress as nicely as their classmates and have winter boots from Romania, jeans from Hungary and tape players from Estonia.

One day, Sasha came home beaming: "I'm going to Germany!"

"To a conference in the GDR?"

"To the Federated Republic! To the West! My boss has officially nominated me as the translator for our institute's delegation to an international congress of translators of German literature, in Frankfurt. Misha, Misha, do you understand? Do you get it? I'm going to

West Germany! I've never even been to Budapest and here I am going to Germany. To the capitalist world!" Her eyes stared somewhere into the distance, as if she was getting ready for her own reincarnation. The dream of every Soviet citizen, to visit the West, was, against all odds, coming true for her.

She threw herself into fulfilling all the formalities related to her trip. She filled in countless forms regarding her acceptance of the Party religion policy, family relations abroad, state awards, and membership in social organizations. When filling in the box regarding Communist Party membership she regretted for a moment that she was not a member since it would have sped up her acceptance for the congress. On the other hand, Michail was not only a Party member but also an officer in the Soviet Armed Forces. She attached the recommendation of her department head to the form. Her boss liked her, but at the same time he was a cautious man. He gave her a lengthy interview, wrote everything down carefully, and convened a meeting of the works collective where he read out loud what he had written about Sasha. Next she took this recommendation to the chairman of the trade union who, after seeing that her application was backed by the entire collective, simply added his signature. The Chairman of the Soviet Union Communist Party at the institute was a more difficult case. He weighed his responsibility and also a certain risk factor. If Comrade Obicka were by any chance to fail to act properly abroad, or God forbid remained there, the punishment would also fall on his head. Still, the Comrade's husband was after all a senior army officer, and her young son would be remaining behind. After a few additional questions, he finally signed it. Sasha went in person to hand in her signed application at the district Communist Party headquarters and waited patiently for her appointment. One colleague who had visited Italy advised her to prepare for this by studying facts about Germany, in particular the economic and social problems of West Germany. But the main thing would be her knowledge of the Soviet Union, its policy of peace, the names of the supreme representatives and the latest victories of Soviet science and culture. Sasha became a regular reader of Pravda, she watched the news on television and studied West Germany's problems. When the day came for her to appear at her interview before a commission of the Party district committee, she felt a little nervous. The commission was made up of twelve people, who regarded her with undisguised envy. She was given two questions. The first concerned the main points of the resolutions of the XXV Communist Party Congress, and the second was about the current problems of workers in the FRG. She answered both to the evident satisfaction of the commission members. They congratulated her and asked her to send along the results of her complete physical health examination as soon as possible. Two days later she returned with the results. And then she began to wait. Since she was an employee of the Central Literary Institute, the decision on her trip abroad fell under the competence of the culture section of the Communist Party Central Committee. Since the Frankfurt conference was two months away she breathed easier. Then came the day when two comrades called her in for a discussion, asking how she liked living in Moscow, how life was in Czechoslovakia, hinting that they knew something of her problems with the KGB, and finally granting her permission to travel. Then they gave her a brochure with tips on how a Soviet Union citizen should behave in a capitalist country. They required her to confirm in writing that she would not discuss the contents of the brochure with anyone. Finally they wished her a pleasant trip. Sasha shone with happiness; even the enormous cold building of the Communist Party Central Committee looked good to her all of a sudden.

Her departure date was just around the corner when the institute director suddenly called her to his office. "I'm terribly sorry, but for political reasons the trip has been cancelled." He hesitated in reflection then went on: "It would seem that NATO has unilaterally decided to locate American nuclear missiles on FRG territory. In protest the Soviet Union has frozen relations with NATO countries in all areas."

CHAPTER
TEN

PRAGUE 1977

OKRUZNY kept his word. When the request from the Ministry of Foreign Affairs for a cadre assessment came to Chirana Export, Comrade Ing. Jozef Balaz received a positive report. Then nothing happened for a long while. Okruzny, worried that Balaz would not be leaving the enterprise, made his life unpleasant whenever he could. Due to the influence of the almighty Okruzny, and because she was often off work with her sick Martuska, Mrs. Balazova was laid off. This made the family's economic situation more precarious, but luckily Marta's family helped them out. They bought them new furniture for the living room plus a fridge and washing machine. Her mother was a clerk with the forest administration and her father worked as a receptionist in a hotel, so Balaz could not understand how they could support two daughters from their relatively low salaries. But when he saw the paper-thin slices of salami and the thinly spread butter on a sandwich his mother-in-law was preparing for him, it began to make sense. The Balaz family was also eligible for a non-repayable state loan of thirty thousand crowns for young families, and this substantially eased their economic situation.

Martuska had had a number of bouts of bronchitis. Her parents were at the end of their tether and money was still tight. The work situation was also unpleasant for Balaz. After almost six months, the head of the personnel department finally called him in and when he saw his broad smile Balaz hoped that the news he'd been waiting for had come. Along with a comment about how much the enterprise would miss him, he announced that as of January 1, 1977 Balaz would be an employee of the Federal Ministry of Foreign Affairs. Although he as yet had no idea where they would live, he signed a commitment to return the company flat to Chirana Export within six months. Balaz immediately called Drlicka and the rest of his friends and they went out for a few drinks.

On the second of January he took the train to Bratislava and spent the night at his parents'. The following morning at four o'clock he got on the bus which regularly ferried groups of Slovak diplomats up to Prague from Bratislava and its surroundings. Then on Friday afternoon it made the trip back to Bratislava. Only diplomats from the east of the country were authorized to travel by airplane. In Prague Balaz headed directly to the press section, where he was welcomed heartily by Milan Kramar, who had convened a short meeting for the section employees. He wished them all a Happy New Year and introduced their new colleague. Balaz was seconded to the foreign journalists department.

Everyone there operated on a first-name basis. Balaz began the prescribed trip round the ministry, visiting the key sections in order to get an idea of how the ministry worked. He also took the official language examinations, which he completed with 'excellent' or 'very good' results. This meant that his basic entry salary of 2,800 crowns would be augmented by a language premium of a further 600 crowns, so in total he would be earning one thousand crowns more than at Chirana. He felt like a king. He was looking forward to his new career and to getting to know the federal capital, Prague.

On the first Monday in February, the deputy director of the section, Ing. Kaderabek, called a meeting. He announced a session of all the ministry employees at two o'clock, at which they would adopt a standpoint on Charter 77. Since Jozef had just completed his tour around the ministry's sections and studied various documents of all sorts, he imagined that Charter 77 too was some kind of official document. So he asked Kaderabek if he might read the charter before the session. Kaderabek looked at him in surprise and said haughtily: "Comrade Balaz, you seem to have too little work to do." After he had left, the colleagues explained to Balaz that Charter 77 was an anti-state declaration written by Havel, Patocka and Hajek, dissidents and enemies of the state. Balaz immediately regretted his request - he knew that Kaderabek would think he was provoking him.

For Kaderabek, even saying 'good morning' was almost a provocation. His customary greeting was the official 'Honour', short for the Party-inspired 'Honour to Work'. In short Kaderabek was a die-hard hardline Communist. He was a former journalist who, during the Soviet invasion, had from his position at Free Czechoslovak Radio roused the nation to resistance against the Soviets. When all functionaries were being forced to agree the invasion was 'international aid' he preferred to head for the West. However, his seriously ill wife was unable to undergo the stresses of forced displacement, so he stayed, gritted his teeth and adapted to the new reality. In the end his brother and his family emigrated while he stayed behind. After the ideological 'normalization,' the Ministry of Foreign Affairs needed new reliable staff members; Kaderabek signed the 'aid' declaration, performed his contrition, distanced himself from his brother, and was rewarded with a position at the Ministry. The hiring commission had learned from experience that such penitents often turned out to be the most grateful and ardent Communists.

When they were back in the office his colleague Marik discretely passed Balaz a French newspaper. "Page four," he murmured. Opening the paper, he found there the complete wording of Charter 77. He took the newspaper with him to the Ministry reading-room. Since there was no-one there at the time, he was able to study the document at his leisure. The more he read of it, the deeper grew the frown on his face. He found that the opinions of its authors corresponded very closely to his own thinking; in fact their conclusions regarding the economic and social situation were completely the same as what he himself had outlined in that infamous Chirana speech. He had left Piestany precisely because he was disgusted with their unwillingness and inability to do anything to make the situation better. Moreover, what he had said out loud was what the others had been whispering for the longest time, all the while outwardly accepting the nonsense, theft and fraud of the system in place. Finally the people behind the charter were speaking out in the open. They weren't demanding the dissolution of socialism, simply its improvement. He sat and pondered what he should do. The session was set to start in two hours and he knew everyone would be expected to sign a document condemning a charter they all secretly agreed with. He felt like a beaten dog - he had escaped from Chirana only to find himself constrained to commit new, even bigger, absurdities.

He decided to go to the nearby Tuscany palace where, in addition to the language departments the Ministry's medical and dental clinics were also located. He knocked on the door of Doctor Jurosova, who was also from Slovakia. He explained that he wasn't feeling well, he had a scratchy throat, and he thought he had a fever. As he tried to think of other symptoms she interrupted: "Don't try so hard. You don't want to be there, right?"

"Where?"

"At the anti-Charter 77 session." Balaz said nothing. "You're the second such case today. I'll put you on sick leave for a week, it'll look better. But remember it will still seem suspicious. Today you arrive from Slovakia full of health, and then you develop a sudden illness."

"Put me on sick leave." The doctor gave him confirmation of his unfitness to work. Balaz took advantage of the lunch break, when the section head was out of the office, to leave his sick note on the secretary's desk. He told her he had to hurry to catch his train and, stopping only long enough to grab his attaché case, he left the building.

While at the end of the meeting the chairman was calling on the diplomats and staff to vote on a resolution condemning Charter 77, the Prague – Bratislava express was pulling into the station at Kolín. The anti-Charter 77 movement had begun throughout the republic. Workers from all professions, and particularly among the ranks of the intelligentsia, signed the resolution. The most widespread reaction was the Declaration of Artistic Unions, which came to be known as the Anti-Charter. At the end of January in the hall of the National Theatre the foremost Czech and Slovak artists, in return for a promise of the chance to continue to publish, act, create, in short, to practice their professions, signed the 'Declaration of Czechoslovak Committees of Artistic Unions, Towards New Creative Acts In the Name of Socialism and Peace.' Gradually hundreds of artists from all parts of the country followed the example of the National Theatre assembly. Everyone who was anyone in Czechoslovak science, art or culture signed it. The artistic community allowed itself to be bullied into supporting the policies of the Czechoslovak Communist Party, its leading role in society, the Great October Revolution and the indispensable and eternal friendship with the Soviet Union. They signed with grave faces, ashamed and browbeaten. They signed it because, like the other fifteen million citizens of Czechoslovakia, they could not conceive that one day totality would collapse and that they would be brought to account for their corruption. They comforted themselves with the thought that those fifteen million others were equally immoral. They bowed their heads and settled for the material benefits that the Communist Party leadership and the republic's government offered them... within the possibilities of real socialism.

After his return from his week's 'sick' leave, Balaz felt that his colleagues were looking at him anxiously and knew it was due to his absence from the session. When on his return from Bratislava he had called in on his section head, he was nervous, expecting repercussions. But the director hadn't even mentioned the incident, and had instead told him: "I want to tell you in all secrecy that I've been nominated as Ambassador to Austria. There are twenty-one Czechs in the Embassy, and I'd like to have at least one Slovak there." He stopped for consideration and then added: "Someone I can trust..." He gave a conspiring smile. "When I'm there they're going to change the press secretary. Would you be interested in coming with me?" Balaz gasped. To go to neighbouring Austria was the dream of every Czechoslovak diplomat - to be stationed in a capitalist capital city where he could easily watch Czechoslovak television, listen to Czechoslovak radio and have Bratislava a stone's throw away! "Well, of course I would... I hadn't even dreamed... Certainly, Comrade Director..." Balaz breathed the words out.

"Forget that Comrade stuff. My name is Milan." Kramar put out his hand.

"I'm Jozef," Balaz stuttered out. After being employed for only a month, to be on a first name basis with a member of the minister's collegium, with one of the most influential men in Czechoslovak foreign policy, was almost unbelievable.

"Why don't you take a seat?" the director offered. "I just want to say that the way you got into the ministry really impressed me. And the minister is also impressed."

"You... you spoke to the minister about me?"

"The minister is a normal type of man, one of the most normal in this government. He also has a background in public relations, just like you. I'm a bit of a writer myself. But he isn't having an easy time of it. We need more Slovaks in the diplomatic corps. To be more precise, capable Slovaks." Going over to the radio, he tuned in some opera aria, a loud opera aria. "Unfortunately they're rather thin on the ground," he continued in a lowered voice. "Even though Chnoupek is the minister, the real decision-maker in foreign policy is Bilak. And he's a disaster." He gave Balaz a long meaningful look. "Whenever you want to say something in this building you don't want other people to know about, it's a good idea to turn the radio on. If you don't have a radio in your office, run the water on in the sink at full stream." Balaz continued to listen, knowing this conversation had a point. "Husak is behind Chnoupek, but Bilak has Moscow behind him. You know of course that Chnoupek is from Bratislava, just like Husak. And you're from Bratislava too of course." Again that long, thoughtful glance. "Bilak is sucking Husak's blood. Unfortunately, not even the General Secretary or the President can shift someone who has the backing of Moscow. The majority of Slovaks at the ministry and on the Party Central Committee are from the east. Most of them are dependable men, but look out for Stefan, Jarenka and a few others. These are Bilak's spies at the ministry."

Kramar looked at a document in his hand and then continued: "I mentioned your potential secondment to Vienna to the Minister. He knows about your background and agreed to my proposal. My nomination is about seventy percent sure; it's just waiting on Bilak signature, which hasn't come yet. For you there's one condition - it's April now, and you have until the end of the year to bring your German up to level four. It's a hard exam, but I know you'll manage it... I guess that's all for the moment..." He smiled and shook Balaz's hand.

"Thank you. And thanks most of all for your faith in me."

Everything that we've discussed is strictly between ourselves of course," Kramar reminded him as a matter of course.

When he got home for the weekend, a summons from the Trnava District Court was waiting for him. The Chirana Export Foreign Trade Enterprise was prosecuting him. According to mutual agreement the service flat in Piestany was to be returned within six months of his resignation. Balaz hadn't returned it. They couldn't. They had nowhere else to go. "What are we going to do?" Marta wanted to know.

"What can they do to us? The case hasn't been heard yet. They'd probably pass an eviction order, but I know that in such cases the law forces the company to provide substitute housing."

"Substitute housing?! That's what they did with the Lukac family... You know what the substitute housing was? A one-room flat in a dormitory in Stara Tura." Marta began to sob. "I talked to my mother, and if it came to that, we could have a room in their two-room flat in Presov."

"Do you think my parents in Bratislava wouldn't offer us the same in their three-room flat?"

Mrs. Balazova said nothing. "Don't worry," he reassured her. "We won't be going to stay with anyone. I'd prefer that one-room place in Stara Tura." She sobbed some more and Jozef searched for a way to calm her fears, especially when baby Martuska started crying too.

"Don't cry... come on, don't cry... I have some news for you... but please, don't tell a soul, not even your mother. I talked to my section head yesterday. Imagine, we're calling each other by our first names."

"Well, great, that'll really help us out!" Her tears kept flowing.

"He told me he'd been talking to the Minister. If everything goes as planned, by next January at the latest I should be transferred to Vienna. As a press attaché. But please, Marta, I'm begging you, not one word to anyone! Kramar's appointment isn't definite yet."

His wife's expression brightened a bit, but cautiously. "I know you. You always think up some bombastic tale to calm me down, and then nothing comes of it..."

"This time it's almost a sure thing. All I have to do is bring my German up a level by the end of the year... So from today on we're all going to speak to each other in German. We'll buy some tapes and everything – washing the dishes, cleaning the flat, doing the washing, ironing... making love, everything will be in German! Thankfully we can catch Austrian television and radio up here."

"Jozef, Jojo, if only it could be true..." Suddenly she hugged him with enthusiasm. "Chirana can have their stupid flat and we'll be out of here!"

Balaz went to see his former director, Cernak. He asked him to let them keep the flat to the end of the year, when they'd be moving to Prague.

"The summer holidays are coming up, so nobody will be making any big decisions. Then I'll find a way to stall to the end of the year," Cernak said encouragingly, "but after New Year's I can't guarantee anything."

"Director, I give you my word of honour that we'll return the flat right after New Year's. Thanks very much for this!"

"It's a pity you left the enterprise. I miss you, as do the other normal people who are still working here. Just after you quit, Malý, Pastier, Chodák and even Onderka went. He was the one who could tolerate Okruzny the most, but it became too much of a strain for him. As for me, I'll hang on until the end of the year, and then I'll take my retirement...So you've got till then to work something out with the flat. And don't let them push us Slovaks around up there in Prague!" Cernak offered him his hand, and Balaz noticed it was trembling. All of a sudden he got the feeling that this could be the last time he'd meet Cernak.

He was gradually getting used to the ministry. By now he knew who belonged to which group, who was intriguing with whom against whom, who he had to watch out for, who would look after something right away and who would only act when forced to do so. Kramar managed his role perfectly, playing up to Bilak at every occasion, and sometime in October word went around the Ministry that Bilak had approved his appointment. It was in early December that Austria gave its consent to the new Czechoslovak Ambassador, Milan Kramar. At a small reception at the Ministry just before Christmas he took Balaz aside.

"The Minister has given his tentative agreement to your secondment. When are you taking that German examination?"

"Tomorrow."

Kramar looked at him sincerely. "So I'll cross my fingers for you. Come and see me as soon as you get the results."

The next day at two Balaz came out of what that day seemed to him the most beautiful building in the world, the Tuscany Palace on Hradcany Square. Not just this palace, but also the Hradcany Castle, Prague, Piestany, the whole world in fact, seemed a wonderful place. In his pocket he had confirmation of having passed the German language exam at the highest level. He headed straight for Kramar's office. There he was warmly congratulated and then Kramar made a phone call. "Go to the back annex, to the special tasks section. They just want to finalize some formalities with you. They know you're on your way."

This upset Balaz for some reason. He hadn't even known there was a rear annex to Cernin Palace; he knew only that at Chirana Export the special tasks section meant the State Security workplace. He breathed deeply and carried on, feeling like he was walking towards his own execution. Arriving at the rear block he rang the bell. A secretary opened the door and looked him over. They went through a first and then a second barred door. This took them to the secretary's office.

"Comrade Director is expecting you. Go in please."

She opened the door for him. Behind a desk turned away from the door sat a heavy-set man, writing something on a piece of paper. "Sit down, Comrade." Balaz sat down. Despite the overhead fluorescent lights the room was dark. The man seemed familiar to him, his voice most of all. He finished writing and turned to face Balaz.

"Welcome!" With a broad smile on his face and an outstretched hand sat Ján Winter.

CHAPTER
ELEVEN

BERLIN 1981

THOMAS got married on the second Saturday in September, 1981. The marriage took place in the luxurious Kempinski hotel. Thomas' mother, despite her difficulties in walking, shone with happiness. Her only son was taking for his bride the daughter of the Mayor's Director of Operations, and Thomas was himself one of the youngest deputies in Germany - so far only in the city senate, but everyone foresaw a brilliant career ahead for him.

His father however, unused to the splendour of one of Berlin's top hotels, was clearly nervous. The wedding was attended by many of Thomas' colleagues from the senate as well as several national members of parliament. From among his old friends only the journalist Peter Greiner showed up - no-one from Stamokap or the other radical groups. To tell the truth, Thomas wasn't surprised, and was in fact relieved. He was afraid that they might cause a scene in the setting of a snobby hotel like the Kempinski.

He would meet up with them again sooner than he might have expected. Two days after his wedding there was a street riot in the Schöneberg quarter. Several hundred young squatters refused to give up a number of houses the city had decided to demolish. The originally peaceful demonstration escalated into a street war between the police and the youth after an eighteen year old student, Klaus

Jürgen Rattay was fatally injured by a bus. When the news of his death spread, almost the whole Schöneberg quarter turned into a battle zone. The young people barricaded themselves into about one hundred and fifty houses and pelted the police lines with old iron, toilet bowls and any handy pieces of furniture. Over a hundred police officers had been injured, 450 activists arrested, and the street-fighting was spreading to many other places. Thomas thought that as a young senator with many acquaintances among the demonstrators he could be of assistance, although his wife Angelika had tried to dissuade him from going. He arrived without protective equipment, dressed in a sweater and jeans, but followed by a group of riot police. As a result his arrival was met by a shower of rubbish tossed down from the houses. In the end he managed to be allowed to approach a building draped with the sign: 'For 22 years the Church has done nothing but collect rent, and now they want to take the roof from over our heads!!!'

The leader of the occupying group in the house was Reiner, a former friend of Thomas' from Stamokap. He was aware that Thomas had voted against the destruction of the houses in the Senate. Thomas hoped that since they had let him be, he could agree an end to the rioting with the radicals. As the police stepped back, he walked up to the entranceway, surrounded by photographers and cameramen. Live and direct the whole of Berlin watched the brave act by the young senator, who was known to be against the evictions,. He made his way into the kitchen of one of the flats to meet the group. He tried to shake hands with Reiner, but his gesture was refused. As he was about to speak, Rainer growled: "We don't negotiate with Fascists!"

"Reiner, for heaven's sake, don't use such strong words. Even those who voted for the evictions aren't fascists."

"They want to fix them up because property prices have risen and you in the senate want to line your pockets when they're sold!" an obviously drugged-up youth screamed at Thomas. If it wasn't for Reiner, Thomas would likely have thumped him.

"Shut your mouth!" Reiner snapped at the boy. "And get out of here. All of you, out of here, leave us to talk alone. Do you hear me?" He started to shove the others out of the room, than after they'd gone he slammed the door shut. He sat across from Thomas, and they stared at each other for a time. "So you have the nerve to show up here spouting morality, eh? First you betray our ideals and then you come here in the name of the opposite side?!"

"I didn't betray you; sorry but I just couldn't stay in a group that was riddled with agents of the East German Secret Service!"

"We got rid of Michael, and he's not even in Berlin these days. But that's not the main thing - have a look at this..." He pulled from his pocket a creased black-and-white photograph. It showed a man of about thirty in the uniform of the Nazi SS, standing with ordinary soldiers beneath a sign reading 'Konzentrationslager Majdanek'. Reiner passed Thomas the photo. He looked at it and shrugged his shoulders. "I don't know why you're showing me this..."

"Have a good look at the face of the SS officer. And then look at the names on the back of the picture."

Frowning, Thomas looked closely at the faces. Then he began to read the names on the other side until he came to Karl Joachim Lammer. He nearly dropped the photo in shock. Again he checked the face. Now he recognized it - he was looking at the smiling face of the father of his wife, the former Angelika Lammer.

"Do you have a copy of this?"

"No, it's the only copy I have. Take it, and do what you like with it. And now, get out of here!" Thomas sat like a log on the chair until Reiner smacked him on the shoulder and repeated: "Get the hell out of here!"

Slowly he descended the stairs. When he came through the doorway he was immediately surrounded by reporters.

"There's no talking to them. They're a bunch of violent criminals who don't care about solving their need for housing but aim only to destabilize our democratic political system!" he declared. Reiner and his followers heard Thomas' words on their television set.

"You'll pay for that!" Reiner hissed through his teeth.

CHAPTER
TWELVE

MOSCOW 1979 – FEYZABAD 1982

cold wind was blowing through Moscow in mid-December1979. Josif was in the third grade at his elementary school, which specialized in the German language. Sasha tried hard to encourage him to learn foreign languages, but since Russian citizens did not have easy access to even the German Democratic Republic there didn't seem much point to mastering foreign languages. When Josif complained how hard it was, she could only tell him it would surely come in handy one day. Her husband Michail had been transferred to some high position at the Ministry of Defence, but he hadn't told Sasha much about his new position. He had less time now for his family, but when he got leave he could spend two or three days at home.

Due to Michail's being a high official in the Army General Staff the Obicky family experienced fewer of the usual worries, frustrations and joys of average Soviet citizens. Still, even after three years the metro hadn't reached their new suburb and because of the ongoing building there the buses were more and more packed. Sasha had to carry their groceries in her net shopping bag from the centre of Moscow. There were more shops nowadays in the area where they lived, but by four in the afternoon the only thing left on their sad-looking shelves was tinned fish. A normal life depended on having a car - most people therefore lived abnormal lives. Military officers were registered on special waiting lists which were of course shorter than for the general population, and the Obickíes received notification in March that a new Lada passenger car would be allocated to them in the fourth quarter of the year. They would be informed of the specific date of delivery in good time.

Since Michail had a service vehicle and driver, they planned for Sasha to use the new family car most often. One of the conditions for eligibility to own a car was the successful completion of a driving course. Purchasing a car required systematic preparation, so she went and put her name down for a course in their area. After ten minutes of chatting on her telephone, the clerk found time to inform Sasha that the course was booked up for the next two years. Luckily the head of the military administration for the fourteenth zone was a friend of Michail's, so an extra place was found for his wife. The same clerk grudgingly gave Sasha the required forms to be completed and told her a recent photo and a medical certificate would be necessary. She took a day off work to undergo the medical examination, prepared for a wait of seven to eight hours. Finally she was seen and the coveted confirmation received, but it mentioned a vision problem which would require glasses. She visited almost every optician in the city and got the same answer - glasses would not be delivered from the factories to the shops before July. Now it was the beginning of April, and her driving course was set to begin in three days. Since she was short-sighted she tried to get away with wearing her old pair, but the sourpuss clerk rejected her photo because she wasn't wearing glasses. This meant another trip to the photographer and then back to the office for the final stamp on her application. She could then begin her three-month driving course. Well, she could have if the auto-school's cars had been operational. Yet another nonchalant official told her the repairs would take all summer, so she could begin her course on the first of August - five months later. Sasha didn't know if she should laugh or cry. She consoled herself with the thought that by then her new glasses would be ready and she would be less of a threat on the road.

On the first of August the instructor was waiting for the excited candidates with the news that since there were so many of them the course time would be reduced by one-third. He advised them to find somebody who would be willing to take them out since the regulations stipulated a set number of hours behind the wheel. When someone asked timidly if that meant they would get a percentage of the course fee back, the instructor told him to take it up with the director of the school. Everyone knew what that meant, and resigned themselves to the conditions.

Two months later Sasha had her fresh new driving licence, with the instruction to apply to the compulsory Club of Amateur Drivers. She was told that one of the advantages of membership in the club was easier access to spare parts. She wasn't quite sure how this would be an advantage since all Soviet drivers of all Soviet cars requiring spares were members of the mandatory 'club'.

The December handover date was fast approaching, so Sasha and Michail busied themselves buying windshield wipers, reserve bulbs, brake pads, exhaust pipes and anything else they could think of for their new automobile. Soviet car owners planned for the arrival of their new cars as carefully as they would for the birth of a new child by buying all the equipment necessary. It was generally known that the quality of Soviet automobiles was shocking and so they stocked up on anything that could be missing from the 'new' vehicle and would later have to be installed by the state garages. Or perhaps uninstalled - as they were the best source for spare parts the garages often kept up their stocks by swapping their customers' working components for worn-out or nonfunctional ones. To be a garage employee was to belong to an elite.

Finally, a week before Christmas, the postman brought the long-awaited announcement that the following day at ten in the morning they were to present themselves at the Lada showroom on Kyjevsky Prospect. By now it was five p.m. and Sasha realized she'd best draw the money out of the bank, which was open until eight. She was nervous about dealing with such a large amount of money and phoned her husband so that they could go to the bank together. Michail was an honourable and honest man, so he first went home to change out of his uniform into civilian clothing. They took both of their account books with them.

Arriving at the bank at six o'clock, they explained to the bank clerk they wanted to withdraw money from both accounts and to write a cheque for the 7,419 rubles mentioned in the letter. The lady complained that they should have come earlier because such a large transaction was not as straightforward as they imagined. When they answered that they had just received the notification that day and couldn't get away from work any earlier, she sighed and got down to work. Michail asked her to make the cheque out in his wife's name.

"Your wife's name?" the clerk asked in surprise. "The car will be in your name?" She looked at Sasha, astonished.

"Is that not allowed?" Sasha was puzzled.

"Yes, yes" she answered, failing to understand how one of the most luxurious and sought-after consumer products in the Soviet Union could be in the ownership of a woman. When she got over her confusion she explained that according to government regulations a cheque could only be drawn on a sum ending in zero.

"So write it out for 7,420 rubes." In his frustration, Michail raised his voice.

"Please don't shout at me, I'm only doing my job! And you're aware that you'll lose one ruble by rounding it off..." Offended by his tone, she became standoffish.

"Sorry, I didn't mean to shout, and I'd be glad to donate that ruble to whatever cause the Soviet state would like to use it for," Michail said, looking her straight in the face. Some of the people in the line behind them started to laugh.

"I don't think you should be making fun of the Soviet state."

"Our government deserves my ruble, our government is wonderful, but unfortunately some of its citizens don't fully understand its regulations, and even some of its institutions don't understand them or even try to understand them. The government is fine, but some government officials are not worth that one ruble!" Michail had by now completely lost his temper. The clerk turned red.

"Excuse me, I'm not obliged to deal with arrogant clients..."

"And I'm not willing to deal with incompetent clerks!" He banged his pass as an officer of the General Staff of the USSR Ministry of Defense onto the counter. "Call your superior officer. Immediately!" Seeing the state emblem with its hammer and sickle, the clerk looked like she was about to have a heart attack, stuttered out an apology and had the cheque ready in record time. It was a huge piece of paper. As the Obickies came out of the bank, they felt as victorious as many veterans must have felt the day they conquered Berlin.

The next day Sasha and Michail went by metro to the car showroom.

While they were living one of the most exciting days of their lives, a few kilometres away in the bowels of the Kremlin a debate was taking place which would soon change not only their lives but those of tens of millions of people.

Raised voices rang out from the office of the General Secretary of the Communist Party of the Soviet Union. Over the last few weeks select groupings of the politburo had been meeting in Brezhnev's office. Most often Brezhnev was joined by the Minister of Foreign Affairs Gromyko, the Minister of Defence Ustinov, the head of the Secret Service Andropov, the head of the General Staff of the Soviet Army Marshall l Ogarkov, his first deputy Achromejev, the Afghanistan expert Colonel Nikolai Tservov and a number of advisors on foreign and security policy.

"What would we want to go there for? There's nothing for us in Afghanistan. We can't establish real socialism by sending tanks into such a huge country," protested Brezhnev, shaking his head emphatically.

"Leonid Ilyich, I know that establishing real socialism by sending in tanks is never easy, but we're not interested in bringing socialism to Afghanistan. It's... it's a matter of defending socialism in our country, General Secretary. The Mujahidin are constantly being armed by the United States, Saudi Arabia and Iran. On the east, China and Pakistan are becoming involved in the conflict," was the objection of Ustinov.

"It's entirely possible that after the loss of Iran the Americans are seeking a new base in Afghanistan..." Now it was Gromyko attempt-

ing to convince Brezhnev, who simply frowned and poured vodka for all present.

"Thank you, Leonid Ilyich, none for me." Andropov said in refusal.

"What do you mean none for me?! The General Secretary can and you can't?!" Brezhnev forced him to take a glass. "What you're telling me here is nonsense. You yourself gave me an analysis according to which the Afghanistan government is exaggerating the significance and influence of America and other foreign powers in their affairs. They want to create the impression that the situation there is so dramatic that we have to send our lads in to fight for them!"

"I would make bold to mention," commented one of the advisors, Andrei Agentov, "that the Afghanistan leadership is making political blunders. They've broken up large holdings and divided them among poor farmers. They've turned the landowners against them and haven't done anything for the peasantry because without technology it's impossible to farm the land. The result is that corn and grain supplies have grown short and famine has broken out in many parts of the country."

"That's bound to happen when socialism is run by idiots," Gromyko growled. Agentov almost forgot where he was and had to smother a smile. To cover it up he went on:

"I would also like to add that implementing Marxism-Leninism in one of the most fundamentalist Muslim countries is simply not possible in the short term. It's questionable whether it's possible to implement any kind of ideology there by force..."

Brezhnev looked at him appraisingly. Agentov had the impression that the General Secretary was thankful for his viewpoint.

But Andropov was not so pleased: "This is possible, Comrade Agentov, but the situation there is changing rapidly. Since this imbecile Amin overthrew our man Taraki, all the Soviet investments we've been making in Kabul for quite some time are under threat."

"Jurij Vladimirovič, Taraki was a nationalist and a Communist," Ustinov added.

"Sorry, but Amin is a fanatic who applies our ideas in such a way that he eliminates thousands of landowners, clerics, professionals and *artisans if they don't agree to give up Islam,"* Agentov commented politely.

"So you see, Andrei Alexandrovich, one more reason for us to go in and get rid of this crazy man," said Ustinov with a laugh.

"Excuse me Minister, but practically all members of the General Staff and the supreme command of the Soviet military are against dispatching our troops to Afghanistan. Occupying this country long-term is practically impossible from the military point of view. We could take a lesson from the English, who twice tried to subdue the country and each time left with a bloody nose and huge personnel losses." Marshall Ogarkov's opinion obviously represented the feelings of the armed forces.

Ustinov gave him a dirty look. *"Comrade Marshall, I can only agree with the General Staff as regards the military side, but we have to also be aware of the political aspects of our possible intervention."* Ustinov looked to Gromyko for support and was rewarded with a nod head from the Minister of Foreign Affairs.

Brezhnev turned to Andropov: *"Yuri Vladimirovich, isn't it the case that many of these alarming reports are produced by Soviet agents who tell us what they think we politburo members want to hear?"* Brezhnev looked long and hard at the KGB chief. *"As I recall, you once confessed that the same thing happened during the Czechoslovakia crisis..."* This came as a revelation to many in the room.

"Leonid Ilyich, Comrade General Secretary... the situation in Afghanistan is diametrically different. Not only our intelligence officers but also the Indians have gathered information regarding an American build-up on the Pakistan border. Moreover, the photographs we have obtained of our agents being roasted alive by the mujahidin tell a clear story..."

Brezhnev rubbed his chin. Andropov knew that the fate of the individual soldier carried more weight with Brezhnev than a load of statistics. Ustinov gave him an encouraging wink.

"Civil diplomats also confirm the agents' reports," Gromyko added.

"So now there's a difference between diplomacy and spying?" Brezhnev joked.

"In Afghanistan we won't be fighting against the mujahidin, Comrade General Secretary, but against the United States. A war against the Americans in Afghanistan is preferable to fighting them in Leningrad or Moscow!" Gromyko was playing on Brezhnev's famed hatred of Washington.

The head of the General Staff, Marshall Ogarkov, tried to object that on the basis of intelligence reports the concentration of Americans was not substantial, but Ustinov cut him off.

Neither Ogarkov nor anyone else from the General Staff was willing to put their careers at risk. The discussions on a potential intervention in Afghanistan carried on for a few more days, but Ogarkov and the military staff were absent. In the end Brezhnev was talked around by Ustinov, Gromyko and Andropov. The USSR Communist Party Central Committee decided that the Soviet Union would send its troops in fraternal aid to the people of Afghanistan. On December 27, 1979 the invasion of Afghanistan by 50,000 Soviet soldiers began.

Sasha and Michail followed the instructions given them by post, and walked over to wicket number 4. They joined the line-up, but when after an hour nothing had happened, Michail went up to a clerk standing nearby and asked why, an hour after opening time, nobody was being served.

"Wicket number four is closed today," he was informed.

"And you couldn't have told us that earlier? Don't you see these people standing in line for nothing?" Again Michail was losing his temper.

"Nobody asked me," scowled the clerk. "You can stand at wickets 1, 2 or 3." Grumbling, the line-up shifted to the other wickets. They were upset with the clerk, and ashamed that none of them except Michail had complained. This was precisely the reaction typical of the downtrodden, browbeaten and abased Soviet citizen. They were used to the permanent degradation, and took pleasure in the thought that the clerk envied them because he himself probably didn't have a car.

They were in luck since their queue moved along quite smoothly. Soon they found themselves only one step away from the window.

"Sign here," was the instruction given to the gentleman in horn-rimmed glasses standing in front of them.

"Could you lend me a pen?" the man politely asked the clerk.

"I have to lend you my pen? Who wants the car, you or me?" was the response from behind the window. The clerk stood waiting for the client to sign the form. The man simply looked around helplessly. "Come on, come on. Do you think you're in the West where they'll even wipe your bum for you if you ask?!"

"Here you are," said Sasha, giving her pen to the man. The man thanked her and signed the form. "Cheque!" bellowed the clerk.

The man rapidly produced the cheque from an inside pocket and, handing it to the clerk, asked: "Excuse me, but why are you already asking for the money? Do I have to pay for something I haven't even seen? What If I don't like the colour or something?" He was probably hoping his audacity would gain the support of those waiting behind him.

Instead of that, one man grumbled impatiently: "Stop holding things up, I have to get to work!"

"Sorry, but my wife and I have been saving all our life for this... thirty years... you know, a university professor doesn't earn a whole lot." The bespectacled gentleman had turned to the others to explain himself.

The clerk seemed to be sorry for the obviously unworldly client. "Unfortunately, sir, we can't guarantee any specific colour; it could turn out that the factory produced only red cars this quarter."

"You're right, the colour isn't that important, but what if the car is defective?" He was still waiting for an explanation as to why he had to pay up front.

"None of the cars are perfect; you'll have to choose the best available. If you buy a pair of shoes, you can't expect they'll be comfortable the first time you put them on. You have to wait until they're broken in... giving the mechanic a bottle of something would probably help," he added with a wink.

"My dear sir," Michail said pleasantly but firmly. "I understand your hesitation, you're completely in the right, but to tell the truth you should thank your lucky stars you're going to get a car at all... And we really have to get a move on."

"You're right, sir, forgive me." The professor finally vacated the wicket.

Someone farther back in the line couldn't resist a final comment: "You should be used to life in the Soviet Union by now. All the same, we have it easier than in the West!" Nobody bothered to take him up on that.

After paying and getting the required confirmation, Sasha and Michail were allowed to continue to the pick-up area at the back of the warehouse. On the way, Michail phoned an engineer friend of his who'd promised to join them at ten o'clock. He was a car specialist, and they had agreed he'd help the Obickies pick out a reliable vehicle. Unfortunately he wasn't able to meet them after all, and so they were left to their own devices. But he'd told Michail the basic principles of purchasing a car in the USSR. Perhaps the most important thing was checking the exact date of manufacture - if it was made near the end of the quarter-year there was a great risk it would be of poor quality. Under pressure to meet the pre-set quota, the workers tended to be less careful than they should be. Another no-no was buying something manufactured just after payday, when the crew would still be recovering from their hangovers.

Their first glimpse of the selection boosted their spirits - there were five different colours available! Mindful of the advice given to the professor, they sought out a mechanic standing nearby. His initial unwillingness was dissipated by the bottle of vodka Michail had brought along for his engineer colleague.

"All of these cars are available; just choose the colour you like." Sasha opted for orange, and even though the mechanic warned that even a drunken policeman would notice such a loud colour, she was adamant. So they headed over to the orange zone, and there their problems started. One had a flat tire, the second was missing the rear-view mirror, the third had no windshield wipers, and the fourth, scratches on the bodywork. When they finally found a complete model the mechanic sat at the wheel and turned the ignition key.

Nothing happened. In vain he kept trying, and then got out to look under the hood. The new battery had been removed and replaced with an old one. There were no acceptable orange models, but the mechanic located a working blue one. By this time both Sasha and Michail were tired, so although blue was a far cry from orange, they didn't protest. At least no drunken policeman was likely to notice such a nondescript colour. After almost twelve frustrating hours sorting it out, they got into their new car and drove off towards home.

Since they were used to travelling by public transit, the trip took them longer than they'd thought, and it was midnight before they got home. Their son Josif was spending the night at the neighbour's. To celebrate, Michail took a bottle of vodka out of the cabinet and they sat down to relax. They drank the first glass down in one go then, while Michail began to study the owners' manual, Sasha went to prepare something to eat. She took out of the fridge some salted fish, garlic piroshky, pickles, preserved mushrooms, cheese, sausage and a good supply of bread - a celebration feast!

Today was Thursday, and the plan was to drive to some friends' house on Saturday to show off their new car. Sasha felt that after the birth of her son, this was the happiest day of her life. She looked at her husband and realized how much she loved him. As if feeling the warmth of her glance, Michail returned her gaze. He put aside the manual and went over and gave her a hug. After such a long time they were home alone together, and they both felt the other's excitement. Michail slowly dropped to his knees and buried his face between his wife's breasts. She undid her blouse and Michail keep on nuzzling. Although it was two in the morning neither of them was thinking of the time. They made love more sweetly than they had for the longest time. Then they drank one more glass of vodka and looked at each other tenderly.

"I love you so, so much!" The words escaped from Sasha's mouth.

"I love you too," he responded, again pulling her to him and kissing her on her lips, throat, neck, and down to her breasts. Again they made love, and held each other close until morning.

"I have the feeling that our happiness is truly beginning."

"I feel it too, my love. If we had the joy of having our own child... but all the same... Josif is growing into a fine young man... I do love him, you know."

"I know that," said Sasha and hugged him more tightly.

The New Year's celebrations were fast approaching. To the extent possible in Moscow shops, people were out buying gifts. Michail had managed to get a large poster of Inspector Colombo from a colleague on the General Staff. Since Soviet Television had been airing this popular American series, the Inspector had become the hero of many Soviet youths, including his son Josif. At the same time he admired Michail, the steadfast and brave Soviet soldier. A ten-year-old boy could ask for no greater protection against the cruel world than Colombo and his stepfather.

Sasha was in the bathroom and Josif in his bedroom doing his homework when Michail arrived home with his Christmas shopping, so he was able to hide their gifts in an old box in the pantry. He looked forward to the joy his carefully-chosen presents would bring his family, but when he saw his wife's face as she emerged from the bathroom he knew something was not right.

"What's up? Has something happened? Has the car broken down?"

Sasha ran right into his arms. He had the feeling that it was more than car problems. He had no idea what it could be, but he was a firm believer in women's intuition.

"Sasha, my dear, what's wrong? What's happened, for heaven's sake?" Now Michail too was worried.

"You got a letter from the Ministry." She nodded towards the kitchen table.

"From what Ministry?"

"From the Ministry of National Defence, where else!"

Michail went over to the table and picked up an envelope bearing the stamp of the USSR Ministry of Defence. Suddenly he had a bad feeling. He knew what was being whispered not only at the Ministry but throughout the country in the last few weeks. It was as if his hands didn't want to open the packet. Sasha stood at his side, saying nothing. Michail began to read: 'In conjunction with the command of the USSR Minister of National Defence, Marshall Dmitrij Fjodorovich Ustinov, I have decided that as of January 1, 1980 you will be transferred to the Supreme Command of the Soviet Armed Forces in Kabul, Afghanistan. Signed, Marshall Nikolaj Vasilievich Ogarkov, Commander of the General Staff,'

Tears began running down Sasha's face. "They couldn't even wait until after the New Year," Michail sighed, and pulled Sasha to him. Little Josif, seeing his mother in tears, took hold of her skirt and looked up at his parents. There they stood, one small family whose fate, just as thousands of years in the past and probably thousands of years in the future, would be decided by someone else.

Obicky didn't remain long at the headquarters in Kabul, but was dispatched right away to the staff in Feyzabad, the capital of the north-eastern province of Badakhshan. In his tours of duty inside the Soviet Union he had seen much deprivation, but nothing prepared him for what he was confronted with there. Afghanistan was one of the world's poorest countries, and Badakhshan was its poorest region. For the most part people lived in one-room clay shacks without windows or doors; only the better-off had such luxuries. It was fortunate that the peasantry slept together with their donkeys and goats - they helped them get through the minus-fifteen temperatures.

It would be something of an exaggeration to call Feyzabad a town. The ten-thousand- strong settlement was connected to the capital of the neighbouring province by a strategic road. Jokingly referred to by the Russian troops as the 'motorway', it was a wide forest road full of potholes and serving almost exclusively tracked tanks and personnel carriers. These slow-moving vehicles were easy prey for the mujahidin operating on the peaks and precipices above the roadway. Due to a lack of helicopters, the key task Michail and his men were assigned by General Gromov was to construct a runway for supply and fighting aircraft. Colonel Michail Obicky threw himself into the task with his customary dedication. He was pleased that the planes which would be landing at the new military airport would also be bringing food and medicines to these desolate people.

They situated their landing strip on a plateau above a bend on the Kokcha River, about ten kilometres north-west of Feyzabad. Heavy rollers pressed tons of gravel into the rocky ground and then the men put in place the steel plates which would make up the runway. Although it was only provisional it was sufficient to provide safe landing even for the heavy Antonov transporters. The first time Obicky landed, he had to clench his teeth as the plane bumped along the steel 'ladder'. With time both the men and the machines adapted to the provisional runway.

When a Mi-8 helicopter with Michail Obicky on board took off on Its standard flight to Kabul there was no way for the crew to know the mujahidin in the Rabbani fortress at elevation 1 140 were preparing to test one of the first Stinger missiles supplied them by the CIA. They were aware that Soviet helicopters regularly flew above the perfect cover of their highland headquarters, and the increasing noise of an approaching helicopter alerted one of them to start aiming his weapon...

CHAPTER
THIRTEEN

PRAGUE 1978

WINTER turned around at the desk and, nodding his head, looked Balaz up and down. His smile was that of a winner who has in his hands the power to determine the fate of someone he's conquered.

"How's it going?" he asked in Czech, still with that smile.

"Fine."

"I was glad to hear you'd come to our Ministry. We need capable and loyal comrades from Slovakia up here. We Slovaks have to show the Czechos what we're made of. A few more like you and they'd soon stop making fun of us!" Winter took out a bottle of Slovak gin and poured two glasses out. "So, welcome!" Out of a sense of duty, Balaz raised his glass. "I've also heard you're just one step away from going to Vienna. Everyone here is jealous. Who wouldn't want to be sent there?! I imagine you're quite looking forward to it..." Balaz simply nodded. "Well, that's not what I would call enthusiasm." He tapped Balaz jovially on the shoulder.

"If we Slovaks are to show those 'Czechos' what we're made of, maybe we should speak Slovak..." His glance at Winter was reproachful.

"Right!"

"So why do you keep speaking Czech? I imagine the Czechs are intelligent enough to understand your Slovak."

"Holy cow, sorry... I'm really sorry..." Winter actually blushed. "You know, when a guy sits here day after day in a Czech environment, he stops thinking about it..."

"I sit in a Czech environment all day too, and it hasn't happened to me yet."

"I automatically speak Czech to Czech people."

"But they do understand Slovak..."

"I've just got out of a meeting... anyway, I said sorry." Winter responded irritably and then put a big smile back on his round red face. "Looks like that Kramar has really taken a shine to you. Ever since he was seconded to Vienna back in October he's been asking for you." Winter let his breath out audibly and shot Balaz a meaningful glance.

"Any problems?"

"Not really... no, no, quite the reverse... we know you're an exceptionally capable man, you speak five languages... even the old-timers are saying they haven't seen your like in eons... Incidentally, and just between us, I was at a meeting at the Central Committee International Section and Comrade Bilak himself came over at the end to ask me about you... We're really glad that it's you who's being sent as the press attaché to Austria. There's a sizeable Czech and Slovak community in Austria we'd like to have good relations with; Comrade Bilak depends a lot on Austrian- Czechoslovak friendship... we invest quite a bit there." Winter paused for thought, then carried on: "But that's all information of a slightly secret kind. Again his appraising look. Balaz clearly had no idea what Winter was on about.

I don't know why you're telling me about Austria. I attended seminars at the second territorial section and spent a month at the Austrian desk..."

"Why are we talking to you? Well, well... because we trust you." Winter was clearly taken aback.

"Glad to hear it." A silence fell, finally broken by Winter. "Jozef, it's important for all of us that you be the one going to Vienna..."

"And where's the problem?" Balaz still didn't know where all of this was leading.

"Okay, I'll say it right out. Here where I'm working is the special personnel workplace, but we're under the Ministry of the Interior, its secret branch, to be specific... we're a branch of state security." Winter stared at the silent Balaz and couldn't figure out if he was bluffing or really didn't understand what he was trying to tell him. He had heard from his older colleagues that when some of the new diplomats had their first contact with the secret service, the StB, they were stunned.

"You do know what the StB is, don't you?!" Winter was finding it hard to keep his nerves under control.

"What the hell have I done to get called in here?"

"Wait a minute; of course you haven't done anything wrong... The truth is you have every chance to be a great diplomat and to build up a successful career. I've already said that for Czechoslovakia and for our allies, Vienna is of key importance. Austria is a hotbed of espionage and counter-espionage for practically every country. You must see that as our neighbour it has special significance for us..."

"That's clear, but what I don't understand is what all this spying stuff has to do with me..."

"Counter-espionage! We have to send our very best people to such a delicate position. You must see that being sent there is a great honour. And I'm sure your wife will be very pleased to be in Vienna, plus she'll have more time to take care of your child. I hope she'll be able to get over her health problems..."

"For Christ's sake, tell me what you want from me!" It was Balaz's turn to lose his temper, and he was beginning to have an inkling of what Winter was after. In his mind he saw Kramar's gloomy face when he sent him back here to this rear annex.

"It has been decided to postpone your appointment for a few months. During this time you'll undergo special preparation by the top specialists from our country... and from the Soviet Union." Winter went on talking, but Balaz couldn't hear him. He was thinking about Cernak from Chirana, and the commitment to hand over his flat by the end of 1977. Now it was January, 1978 and it looked like nothing was about to change.

"... you'll be taught to work with drop boxes, with the latest technologies, with..." He noticed that Balaz was lost in thought. "Are you listening to me?"

"I'm listening," Balaz answered, almost inaudibly.

"When you've completed your training, you'll sign an agreement to cooperate with us, and the next day you can take up your position. When you're there, we'll give you the name of the comrade who's in charge of you."

"Would you mind opening a window? It's a little hot in here."

"There is no window," Winter snapped. An antique table clock on his desk swung its pendulum from side to side. Balaz followed its eternal back and forth motion as if hypnotized.

"What if I don't go for training and don't sign the cooperation agreement?"

"We don't force anyone into anything... Anyone who has signed has done so willingly... Jožo, don't be stupid. Everyone would give their eye-teeth to be in your place. With Kramar in Vienna you'll have an easy life. We're not asking anything extraordinary of you; everyone there has already gone through this... From what I hear, you've received a court order to give up your flat in Piestany... Do you know how wonderful the service flats are in Vienna? In Penzing, one of the city's most attractive quarters... And when you come back here after four years, we'll find you something equally desirable. That's what we've done for everyone... who signed our agreement."

"Do I have to decide right away?"

"You don't have to, but I don't understand your putting it off. If you're thinking about discussing my proposal with someone, I wouldn't advise it... To be more exact, it's forbidden. If we find out you have, there'll be big trouble." Winter stopped, considering his words. "Jozef," his tone and facial expression grew softer, "practically everyone who's sent to the West signs this agreement with us. It's up to you if you sign or not."

"Jan, I'm... I'm a conscientious and disciplined representative of socialist diplomacy... I know where my duty lies," Balaz stammered out.

"No-one doubts that. But if you aren't one of us we couldn't give you tasks and take full advantage of your position... "

"I need time to think it over. I need room to breathe. The weekend's coming up; I'll give you my answer on Monday..."

"That would be fine."

Balaz stood and buttoned up his jacket. Only then did he realize his back was soaked with sweat. Winter squeezed his hand. "But remember, not one word about our discussion. Not at the office, not at home!" Balaz nodded.

He made his way out of the building, around Hradcany Square, and down Nerudovka Street. When he came to his senses he found himself standing in Malostranske Square. The doors of Saint Nicholas Church stood open. He went in and sat down in one of the pews, then raised his head and stared long and hard at the huge vaulted dome ceiling. After a time he went back to the Ministry. Since it was Friday, the service bus would be leaving for Bratislava in a half an hour.

Back in the flat in Piestany, the pressure got to be too much for him and he told Marta everything that had happened. His conscience was easy – either way he would have had to explain why they wouldn't be going to Vienna after all. It was clear from Winter's words that if he didn't sign that blasted document he could forget about the appointment to Austria. He would have liked nothing better than to call Kramar in Vienna and beg him to come over to Bratislava for a meeting, but he couldn't risk Winter finding out about it.

On Monday morning there was a bad storm that delayed their arrival in Prague. He kept thinking of Marta sitting on one of the large cardboard cartons holding the clothes she'd already packed for Vienna. She'd greeted him with the news that she'd already learned to count to ten in German. To his surprise he found a smile spreading over his face. He realized that if a person takes a clear moral stance he suddenly feels cleansed, at peace, and free. When Marta told him she'd rather be a simple worker in a factory than have him sign something so compromising, his smile widened. He had no intention of signing up to cooperate with the secret service; his only regret was not being able to provide a roof over the heads of his wife and daughter.

Once in Prague, he went directly to the press section, where he found a note from Winter telling him he was expected at half past eleven. He immediately called Kramar's office in Vienna. Kramar's secretary informed him the Ambassador had left for Prague. The Austrian section said they were expecting Comrade Ambassador at twelve o'clock.

Winter asked Balaz to take a seat. "Thank you, that won't be necessary. I only wanted to tell you I appreciate your offer and... your confidence in me, but I can't agree to your terms."

For a few seconds Winter just looked at him. "Why don't we sit down and have a cup of coffee?" Balaz sat down but refused the offer of coffee. "Well, it's your free decision of course, but you'll have to accept the consequences. You know what the housing situation is like these days. There's no guarantee you won't be turned out of that flat... Your daughter will want to go to university... Your wife is a talented artist, I've seen her catalogue. She'll naturally want to put on some exhibitions..."

Balaz realized there was nothing they didn't know about him and his family. "You've got your parents and sisters to consider. I could tell you everything will be all right, but who knows how my superiors and the Central Committee comrades will see the situation." Winter broke off to light a cigarette. As Balaz lit his, he was aware his hand was trembling. For that matter, so was Winter's. "You can imagine we don't believe your absence at the meeting against Charter 77 was due to illness..."

"I have a doctor's certificate."

"Yeah, yeah... but you weren't ill... you just didn't want to be there... but you got the note from the doctor right enough. We also remember your attitude to the Warsaw Pact intervention ...It took you a while to acknowledge that it was a case of international aid, but finally you did... Not long ago you caused a disturbance at the Jednota department store in Piestany," Winter scowled disapprovingly. "And even now you don't get it... you just don't get it!" He sighed and shrugged his shoulders: "Is that your final word?"

"You know, a person would have to deceive and lie; me, if I try to tell a lie, I turn red immediately... and so the enemy would see right through me." Balaz surprised himself with the lightness with which he had spoken. He smiled at the thought.

"So you think this is a laughing matter?! Okay, if that's the way you want it," Winter said dismissively.

Balaz's first stop after leaving the rear annex was the 'Black Bull' restaurant, where he quickly downed two glasses of Slovak gin. The 'Bull' was a favourite watering-hole for Slovaks working in Prague, since it was one of the few places in town serving Slovak gin. Suitably fortified, he made his way to work. He remembered he wanted to contact Kramar .

"Yes, I know," Kramar cut him off before he could say much. "Be in the washroom on the third floor of your wing at exactly two o'clock.

"In the washroom?" Balaz was slow to understand.

"In the washroom... The toilet, understand?"

The men's toilet on the third floor of the wing where the press section was situated was a relatively unfrequented place. When Balaz came in, Kramar was already standing at the wide old-fashioned urinal with his trousers unbuttoned. He signalled for Balaz to stand next to him. Balaz just stared, feeling like he was in Wonderland. But the Ambassador's gesture was clear and forceful. He too unbuttoned his flies. At regular intervals Kramar activated the flush mechanism and indicated that Balaz should do likewise. He finally understood that together they were creating a sound barrier, and that in the Ministry of Foreign Affairs even the washrooms were bugged.

"Don't worry, I'm not gay or anything. I know everything. Winter reported it to me right afterwards. I'm really sorry. I'm more than sorry, I'm bloody angry. The whole office in Vienna is full of spies.

I was so glad I could bring in at least one person who was on the level. I knew when you first came to me that you were a normal guy and not a plant from the Central Committee or the secret police. I guess you know that you're appointment to Vienna is out the window now... That was your free choice, and I respect you for it. My only hope for you is that you'll be able to get out of the situation with the least damage done to your career...Winter was furious. I got the feeling that something must have happened between you two in the past. He was so eager to get you into the network, unbelievably so. What's been going on with the two of you?" Kramar was puzzled and curious.

Balaz thought about it. "That was my impression too. I got the feeling he was looking for a way to compromise me so he'd have grounds for blackmailing me... the only thing I don't know is why."

"That's basically what I thought. When you find out why, please let me know!"

They both washed and dried their hands in the only wash-basin. Kramar put out his hand and firmly grasped Balaz's. "If our paths don't cross again, I'd like to say how glad I was to meet you. You're one of the few people in this place I wanted to have at my side. I hope life will be kind to you. Just so you know, that Winter guy..."

He had no chance to finish his sentence. The door opened and Moravek, a colleague from the press section, came in, staring at them both in surprise. Kramar waved to him nonchalantly and went off in the direction of the lift. What he had wanted to say about Winter, Balaz would wait ten years to find out.

CHAPTER
FOURTEEN

MOSCOW 1982

THE Soviet Union Communist Party General Secretary Leonid Ilyich Brezhnev was sitting in a deep armchair in the salon next to his office. It was the only place in the Kremlin where he could get any sort of peace. His son Yuri, his daughter Galina, his nurse Nina Korovikova, his wife Valeria, and the supreme commander of the KGB Andropov were the only people allowed in his sanctuary. Each of these had their own way of communicating with the most powerful man in the Soviet Union; most often he was visited by Nina, a forty-year-old brunette beauty, and most infrequently by his wife, Victoria. She had long since resigned herself to her estranged relationship with her husband and essentially also with her children.

The once proud, slim and charming Major General, who had promoted himself to Marshal of the Soviet Union, had become a drunkard whose only reasons for living were his collections of state decorations and exclusive automobiles. He was said to have some fifty luxurious vehicles in the Kremlin's garage. His personal favourites were his luxury Cadillac Eldorado and his Lincoln Continental, both of which he had received as gifts from the American President, Richard Nixon. New display cases were constantly being built in his office to house his decorations, which he derived great pleasure from viewing. The larger they were, the more he cherished them. One of the most powerful men in the *world was in essence a senile old man who was incapable of speaking without a script. His charmingly flirtatious nurse, Nina, was gaining more and more power over the Old Man of the Kremlin. His love for her was all-accepting, and he listened to no-one but her. The Marshal's bodyguards would look down at the ground whenever she emerged from his salon doing up her blouse and with her hair dishevelled.*

Brezhnev was taking ever stronger does of barbiturates which, on the advice of the Minister of the Interior, Schelokov, he washed down with vodka. He was told his organism would better handle them in this form. Despite a clear command from Andropov to limit the excessive amount of drugs Brezhnev was taking, Nina regularly gave him strong sleeping tablets. She had taken the care of Brezhnev into her own hands. First she had had to overcome the influence of Brezhnev's former caregiver Dzuna, a talented Georgian folk healer. Many senior bureaucrats and artists swore by her gift of healing. Andropov had helped Brezhnev out by having Dzuna employed as a researcher and radio technologist at the Soviet Academy of Sciences, where she would be close by should he require her. But Nina was prettier, more communicative and, according to rumour, a great masseuse. Some even went so far as to suggest her massages were not limited to Brezhnev's back and shoulders. Nowadays his senility was exhibiting itself more often, and the KGB had trouble pinpointing the supreme leader's lucid moments in order to display him in public. During one official visit to Moscow by the West German Chancellor Helmut Schmidt, Brezhnev repeatedly addressed his guest as Herr Willy Brandt. Actually, the negotiations were conducted by the man sitting next to him, Foreign Minister Gromyko.

Enfeebled by age and decimated by alcohol, Brezhnev made practically no decisions himself. The country was being run by Gromyko, Andropov, Ustinov and Suslov. In 1977, this quartet had the Supreme Soviet approve the so-called Brezhnev constitution. The General Secretary was as happy as a child when he discovered a law would be named for him. What could be a greater joy for a senile geriatric, the survivor of a number of heart attacks, than to have something bear his name while he was still alive?

JUBILATION ZONE

The Soviet Union was almost in a state of being without a government, and when a country has no ruler, it leaves ample room for crooks, cheats and gangsters to prosper. From the top level, through the associated republics, down to the regions and communities, the biggest crooks were running things - the result was that the country was steadily sliding into bankruptcy. This was not so apparent to the ordinary citizen since the standard of living was maintained at the price of alarmingly increasing foreign debt. The Kremlin's superman was indirectly supported by Egypt and Syria when they attacked Israel on the feast of Yom Kippur, October 6, 1973. In the course of 24 hours the greatest oil exporters announced a radical decrease in oil extraction and, due to its support for Israel, an oil embargo against the United States. The most worrying of their sanctions was an increase of 70 percent in international oil prices, which were shortly thereafter boosted to twice the price at the beginning of the year. It was America's backing of Israel which caused the greatest joy to the Kremlin, which naturally welcomed the inflated oil prices. It meant an unexpected windfall for the Soviet Union, allowing it to support domestic living standards and to finance Communist Parties in the rest of the world more generously. From 1971 to 1990 Soviet agencies subsidized French Communists to the tune of 50 million dollars, the Italians, 47 million, and they even 'pumped' 42 million into the miniscule American Communist Party.

Given the lack of systematic controls, state functionaries robbed the USSR of its national wealth. The majority of Communist Party potentates in the various republics sent literally wagonloads of gifts to Brezhnev personally. Since these First Secretaries had been in power for twenty years and more, they had learnt how to rechannel the funds coming to them from Moscow. Requests for funding for commercial building or industrial reconstruction related in many cases to non-existent entities. The most legendary of these swindlers was the 'Uzbek Khan with party membership', Shariff Rashidov, who, on the basis of machinations with cotton which did not exist, defrauded Moscow of millions of rubles. When he died mysteriously in 1983, he was buried in a mausoleum with a dome made of gold.

Even Brezhnev's closest confidant, Interior Minister Schelokov, did not lag behind in the corruption sweepstakes. When a delivery of nine luxury German Mercedes arrived at his Ministry, Schelokov quickly signed vehicles over to himself, his wife, his daughter and even his godmother!

High officials' wives became collectors of jewellery, fine art, luxury goods, houses and villas. They did not even bother to hide their ill-gotten gains from the eyes of a public which was also swept up in the extreme flood of theft, fraud and corruption. A mood of resignation dominated the social climate.

Brezhnev's neglected wife Valeria spent most of her time in the family cottage ten kilometres from Moscow. Their son Yuri used his position as first deputy Foreign Trade Minister to conduct his dealings while his sister Galina enjoyed the merry-making of Moscow's bohemian set. She ran through lovers with the same alacrity as her father in his bygone years. The circus artist Yevgeny Milajev and the dancer Maris Lijepa were among her favourites. She finally married Yuri Churbanov, who was later arrested and sentenced to twenty years for corruption (!) by Brezhnev's successor Yuri Andropov. Galina's fate was also an unhappy one - she lost her mind and died penniless in a psychiatric hospital.

Since Nina Korovikova was gaining ever greater power over the malleable Brezhnev, Andropov offered her a generous pension if she would leave the Kremlin. She refused, but after her husband, a former customs officer turned General, died in a mysterious car crash, she accepted Andropov's offer.

This same Nina Korovikova was a neighbour of Sasha Obicka. After Nina's husband's death and Michail's secondment to Afghanistan, the two women grew close. It should be said that before these two significant occasions the two women had maintained distant relations. While Michail was being sent to fight in Afghanistan, General Korovikov was building his career in the warmth of General Staff headquarters. The two women were sitting in Sasha's living room, drinking tea with vodka and watching television. It was Monday, November 15, 1982, and a day of national mourning had been declared throughout the Soviet Union. The population was dressed in black and flags were flying at half-mast. Five days previously the USSR CP General Secretary and Chairman of the Presidium of the USSR Supreme Soviet Leonid Ilyich Brezhnev had died, and today was the day of his funeral.

Sasha and Nina opened a bottle of champagne - like the majority of the country's inhabitants; they were in a good mood. Needless to say, this was their private posture; in public, the nation was in mourning. Nina lit a cigarette. Although Sasha was a non-smoker, on such an occasion she decided to tolerate her neighbour's smoking. They were chatting while watching the state funeral, and as their drinking continued their voices got ever louder.

"Can't you keep it a little quieter?!" Josif reprimanded them. Neither of them had noticed that he'd come home. "The whole floor can hear you. What if Nina Sergejevna were to overhear you?"

The women stared at each other. Nina Sergejevna was the caretaker, officially in charge of maintaining order in the building, but everyone knew she was a KGB informer. Every apartment house in the Soviet Union had its 'caretaker', and people had long since got used to them. "There's a letter in the postbox," Josif mentioned, going into his room.

"It must have been there since Friday. The post doesn't come on state holidays. When you've changed your clothes, please go down and pick it up." Sasha nonchalantly took another drink of her champagne.

"Wow, how handsome you're becoming, Osja," Nina flattered the boy, looking him up and down. "I didn't realize you were growing up so quickly." Not yet fourteen, Josif blushed at her compliment. It was true that he was growing into a tall, strong boy. He'd been playing hockey for four years at an elite Moscow club, the Soviet Wings. Since the team was connected with the military, they enjoyed a number of advantages over the civil clubs. Although Josif showed great promise as an athlete, his doctors had initially advised against too much physical exertion, due to a heart murmur. Unfortunately the doctors were unable to advise Sasha and Michail on how to keep a strong, healthy lad on the leash. They had tried to restrict his activity, but Josif just didn't want to stay at home when all day long his friends were playing on the sports field between the apartment houses. It seemed that the more Josif ran, jumped and stressed his heart, the healthier he was. When at the age of ten he underwent a physical examination to join the Soviet Wings, the doctor told the family he'd found no trace of his heart problem.

"What are you doing home so early?" Sasha asked.

"I forgot about the day of mourning. Practice was cancelled." Osja took his favourite Pepsi-cola out of the fridge and sat down with the ladies in front of the television.

"Wouldn't you like to have a glass of champagne with us? Igristoje !" Nina continued her flirting with the boy.

"I'm going out running in place of our practice."

"It was Leonid Ilyich who brought us Pepsi-Cola." Now Nina was feeling sentimental.

"That's about the only good thing he ever did," Sasha objected. Suddenly she began to laugh. "Tell me, you were allowed to attend those politburo meetings, is it true that at every meeting Brezhnev asked the reason for Suslov's absence, and the poor guy had been dead for months? He-he-he..."

"People didn't have it bad back then..." Nina avoided responding to the comment. She looked doubtfully at Sasha, then at Josif. Everyone watched the television. Soldiers were just carrying in Brezhnev's coffin. The entire politburo walked behind with the heavy tread of the elderly. Nina had no trouble picking out Gromyko, Ustinov, Grishin, Andropov, Chernenko, all of whom she knew personally. The seriously ill Podgorny, who was himself to die in a few months, was having trouble keeping pace with the coffin.

"Disgusting old geriatrics!" Sasha commented. Nina and Josif were silent. "I truly hope that someone younger finally comes along and pushes these old-timers out. Look, they can hardly walk!" She looked at the picture of Brezhnev on the screen and suddenly burst out: "That son of a bitch sent your father to Afghanistan!" She turned and hugged her son.

"Don't curse him. You have a flat that the average Soviet citizen couldn't even dream of, you live in Moscow with your own car, your boy is in a good school and a top sports club... So don't complain, my dear..." Nina stopped for a drink.

"I'm surprised you're sticking up for him... he killed your husband and still you praise him!" On hearing this, Nina looked sad.

"My husband died in a car crash!"

"Ninocka, don't get upset. I know you're not going to say anything bad about Brezhnev or his monkey's eyebrows. You had it good with him - very good."

"Now you've gone too far, way too far! As if you were dying of hunger!" Nina angrily stubbed her cigarette out in the ashtray, stood up quickly and left the flat, slamming the door behind her.

"What a bitch!" Sasha was still angry. She glared at the television screen, where the procession was now approaching the wall of the Kremlin. The camera was filming the whole funeral from a bird's eye view.

"There are forty-five soldiers carrying Brezhnev's decorations on cushions," Josif commented sarcastically.

"I've been looking for cushions for the couch for the last two months. Now I know where they've all gone..." Sasha joked with a bitter laugh.

"Oh my gosh! They've dug the grave too short!" Josif laughed. Sasha leaned closer to the screen, and sure enough, when the soldiers began to lower the coffin of the highest official of the socialist world into his grave, they found the hole was not long enough. In their confusion the soldiers looked at one other for inspiration. In the end, the soldier standing by Brezhnev's feet loosened his ropes, and with an audible groan the coffin slid into the hole. The whole world was witness to Leonid Ilyich Brezhnev being buried on an angle!

"What a scandal! Those idiots aren't even capable of digging a grave properly!"

"It's as if the earth is refusing to accept him. He has thousands of deaths on his conscience. Thousands more are dying in Afghanistan."

"We haven't heard from your father in a while..." Sasha remarked quietly. "Run downstairs and fetch that letter. Maybe it's from him." Suddenly she had a bad feeling about it.

"I completely forgot." Osja eagerly grabbed the postbox key and ran from the flat. He was back in an instant, carrying the newspaper, a postcard and the letter. It bore the state emblem of the Soviet Union and the Ministry of Defence stamp. Sasha was at first excited, thinking surely it was from her husband, but then, reading the first few lines, her entire demeanour changed. Josif was by now looking on anxiously. The letter fell from her hands, and her world went black. If her son had not caught her, she would have collapsed onto the floor.

"Mummy, mummy... what's happened?" The boy, essentially still a child, eased his mother onto the couch. He remembered seeing in some film that when someone had lost consciousness, the best thing to do was to slap them gently and then sprinkle cold water over them. When he tried this, his mother slowly came around.

"Water, give me some water." Sasha drank it straight down, and tears began to flow from her eyes. Josif picked up the letter. The Soviet Union's Minister of Defence, Marshal Dmitrij Fjodorovich Ustinov, with the deepest regret informed her that on January 10, 1982 her husband, Colonel Michail Borisovich Obicki, died a hero's death in the fulfillment of his international obligations in the Afghanistan province of Badakhshan. His body would be returned home...

Josif placed the letter on the table and took his mother in his arms, joining his tears with hers. A strange feeling swept over him - not anger, more helplessness and absolute degradation, the degradation of being pushed right to the wall, and the consequent temptation to do things he would otherwise never do. The television was now playing the national anthem of the Soviet Union, with volleys of gunshot saluting its dead leader. In slow detail the camera panned over the country's supreme representatives. Josif grabbed a large copper vase and hurled it with all his strength at the TV screen. "You swine, you gang of pigs! You killed my father!!! You killed him..." Then he sat in front of the still smoking television and in frustration crushed the shards of glass under his shoes, as if they were the cause of his immense sorrow. Sasha swallowed the last of the champagne and leaned towards her son. They hugged each other and cried and cried and cried.

CHAPTER
FIFTEEN

BRATISLAVA 1977 – 1980

JUST before Christmas, 1971, a 'Judgment in the Name of the Republic' was issued by the District Court in Trnava. On the basis of a submission by the complainant, the Chirana state enterprise, Stara Tura division, Piestany foreign trade section, the right of the defendant, Ing. Jozef Balaz, to occupancy of a three-room service flat in the Piestany suburb of Sihot was cancelled. The defendant was obliged to vacate the stated flat within fifteen days of the provision of a replacement flat.

For the Balaz family this was the saddest Christmas ever. Beneath the lit-up Christmas tree, Martuska played with her new schoolbag and the many-coloured pencils and crayons Baby Jesus had brought her. She would be already in the first grade before next Christmas, so with typical foresight Baby Jesus had provided what the excited future scholar would need. Marta, whom Jozef had tried in vain to cheer up, watched on pensively. There were fewer presents under the tree than in previous years, but the average Czech and Slovak families would also surely be opening less that Christmas. The Communist Party Central Committee had declared a ten-percent rise in the standard of living, and they almost got it right... instead of the living standard, prices had gone up by ten percent.

A month after his ill-fated discussion with Winter, Balaz had been transferred to the Bratislava workplace of the Ministry of Foreign Affairs press section. His expulsion from Černínsky Palace was clearly in line with the dictum 'out of sight, out of mind' and represented a lessening of his chances of being sent abroad - the main goal of all East Bloc diplomats' careers. Such a placement meant a higher income than at home, greater social status, diplomatic immunity from prosecution, and a raft of additional benefits. In those times of 'real socialism', working in a capitalist country was the dream of every Czechoslovak diplomat. The workers' state would actually be supporting their capitalist lifestyle for four glorious years.

Balaz found himself in charge of three women at the Bratislava press office, the main function of which was to schedule meetings for foreign journalists arriving in Slovakia. The existence of the centre was the fruit of the efforts of the Minister, Bohuslav Chnoupek, and the ever-dependable Milan Kramar, who saw this as a way to use foreign journalists to increase the visibility of Slovakia in the world - an anonymity which was the natural result of the junior partner in the Federation standing in the shadow of the dominant Czechs. After some time Balaz realized that what he was mainly doing was taking onto his shoulders press relations for the Comrades in various Slovak institutions whom writers from abroad might like to visit. In the course of these years of 'tough normalization' no director of a national enterprise, no trade union boss, editor-in-chief or even a Minister himself would risk a visit from a foreign journalist on his own initiative. What if the resulting article appearing in the capitalist press reported something the Central Committee Comrades didn't like? After all, there were many examples of the persecution suffered by those daring to state their opinions out loud" - Dominik Tatarka and Hana Ponicka were crossed off the list of Slovak writers, Vaclav Havel was sentenced to three years imprisonment in Plzen-Bory, Jiri Dienstbier to three years in Pankrac, Alexander Dubcek was spreading his idealism among the trees in the forestry department; even Slovakia's premier comic Milan Lasica was forced to spend five years at Bratislava's opera theatre. There were thousands of cases of outspoken people being exiled to the nation's mines, forests or boiler-rooms.

In the press section Balaz was aware that in his relations with foreign journalists he would be forced to defend a regime that was blatantly suppressing human rights and freedoms. If he had managed to serve as a press attaché in some embassy, his tasks would have mainly consisted of sending home articles from the local press, while his contacts with their authors would be kept to a minimum. This was the unspoken rule for all Czechoslovaks seconded abroad, who spent their four golden years enjoying their advantages and toeing the Party line. In the press centre, however, he could not avoid daily meetings with foreigners, and moreover had to discuss topical issues with them. He had to do some thinking about solving tricky situations in such a way that both sides would be satisfied. It was clear that ahead of him lay a period of continuous skating on thin ice while trying to maintain as much as possible his own integrity. He understood why none of his colleagues envied him his Bratislava appointment. In essence the centre was a trap and Balaz, the scapegoat. What he didn't know then was that he would be frozen there for the next six years.

Something else he didn't know at the time the almighty cadre administration was decreeing his transfer to Bratislava was that a West German journalist by the name of Christina Karich, from the 'Meine Familie und ich' weekly magazine, had just applied for a Czechoslovak visa. She was doing a series of reports on the life of the average family in various European countries, and it was Czechoslovakia's turn. Despite Christina's earlier experience with East Bloc bureaucracy, she had never encountered such obstacles as with Czechoslovakia. The Federal Ministry of Foreign Affairs first informed her that she would have the chance to interview a family from Prague, but then changed the location to Brno, then Ostrava; until the West German Embassy in Prague got involved nothing was resolved. As it happened, the Czechoslovak President, Gustav Husak, had signed a bilateral memorandum on neighbourly cooperation which the Embassy now took advantage of. The result was that Karich was shunted to the Bratislava Press and Information Centre for Foreign Journalists and to Mr. Jozef Balaz. When he met Christina on September 13, 1978 he also learned that the problem was caused because no Czech family was daring enough to house a foreign journalist for an entire week - and now he was to find such a family in Slovakia. Again a difficult task was laid on Balaz's shoulders; he resolved it by turning in desperation to his older sister, Gitka Buranova, and getting her to host the German team.

At that time Balaz and his wife were renting one room, without windows or heating, from an eighty-year-old widow. As a result, little Marta had suffered from bronchitis all winter long. Balaz wrote in vain to the Communist Party Central Committee and to the national government, asking for their intervention. Since the German journalist and her photographer were looking at the living conditions of the average Slovak family, he had to stop himself from telling them that he and his family didn't even have a flat of their own.

Over their week together Christina Karich and her photographer got to know Balaz. The journalist began to feel his sincerity, which he showed to almost all the visiting reporters - barring those he suspected were agents of the Czechoslovak secret service, recognizable by their willingness to deride socialism, the Communist Party and its leaders. This was something the regular journalists never did, so this kind of behaviour put him on his guard. He told Christina openly that if she were to write everything he told her, he and his family could face serious problems.

When it came time for the Germans to go home, Jozef was tempted to ask Christina to try to find his friend Thomas Ankermann, but he came to the conclusion that it was pointless. Even if she did find something out, she couldn't pass the information on to him without the officials finding out about it. Mail from the West was regularly screened, as were telephone conversations.

Less than two months after her departure, Balaz was unexpectedly called to the Federal Ministry of Foreign Affairs press centre in Prague. The deputy director, Ing. Kaderabek, angrily waved in his face the December issue of the "Meine Familie und ich" magazine.

Also present in Kaderabek's office were two men whom he had never met and whom Kaderabek did not take the trouble to introduce.

"Read this!" Kaderabek commanded, holding the article under Balaz's nose. He read the lines underlined in red. At the conclusion of her six-page report from Czechoslovakia, Christina had written: 'We spent a wonderful week in Slovakia. We were made to feel right at home with the Buran family. The person most responsible for our great time was Jozef Balaz, the head of the Press Information Centre in Bratislava. My own father would not have received me more heartily than this young man did. He arranged five marvellous days for us. The tears were flowing when it came time for us to hug Margita, Ferko, Peter, Zuzana, Marta, Alenka and the other kind people goodbye. Jozef Balaz himself said: 'All people should be brothers and sisters. We should not be separated by borders.' We should think about these words more often.'

"What do you have to say?" asked Kaderabek in a raised voice.

"About what?" Balaz was confused.

"About you hugging an imperialist journalist. And about speaking of brotherhood with a bourgeois writer! Not to mention that stuff about borders!" Balaz felt his head spin, and decided to hold his tongue. "And one more thing, Comrade Balaz," one of the unnamed visitors added, "those journalists came on a visit to Czechoslovakia, but in this article only Slovakia is mentioned!"

Now Balaz found his voice. "Was I supposed to dictate to her what she should write? Or should I have told her she needed to have her article authorized by Prague?!"

"Calm down, Comrade, just calm down." Kaderabek accompanied his words with a soothing gesture. "The Comrade was speaking with the best intentions. You're still a young Comrade and he was only warning you not to make such mistakes in the future. Isn't that right, Comrade?" He turned to the unnamed man.

"Of course it is," he answered with a nod. Both of the visitors stood up. "Just follow the regulations Comrade." After shaking Balaz's hand, the two visitors left the room. Kaderabek was at him again as soon as the door was shut.

"You ass, what's wrong with you? Why couldn't you keep your mouth shut? When two secret policemen come to see you, it's serious business. Damn it, why can't you be careful?! How could you do this to me?! And this is not the first time. That Finnish journalist wrote that the two of you got drunk as Danes. Then the Danish Embassy complained!"

"It wasn't my doing..."

"Just be more careful. You must know that from the moment foreigners cross our borders the secret service records all their conversations!" Out of breath, Kaderabek stopped to light a cigarette. He offered one to Balaz, and the two men smoked in silence. "That bloody brother of mine had to run away to the West and now I, who shot at the Russians in sixty-eight with a shotgun, have to deal with relations with the secret police! It's enough to make you sick..." He stopped to think and continued in a fatherly tone: "Jozef, as a more experienced man I'm advising you to watch what you say. Obviously you can't control what they write, but you don't have to tell them things they shouldn't hear."

A couple of weeks later a delegation of journalists from the French Communist Party newspaper L´Humanité arrived at the Press Centre. They spent three days in Bratislava, with Balaz as their guide and interpreter. He practiced a newfound discretion even though they were from a Communist newspaper - or perhaps due to that fact. They visited a few factories and spoke to their managers, but saw almost nothing of Bratislava. On the third day, when they were scheduled to place a huge wreath at the memorial to the Slovak Uprising in the city centre, they asked Balaz to do it for them while they looked around the downtown. After agreeing to do so, he began to imagine the reaction of any of his friends if they noticed him standing alone and laying a wreath of roses in the French national colours on a war memorial. They'd think he'd gone out of his mind! That evening, Marta received the largest bouquet of roses she'd ever seen - in red, white and blue.

Two days later an upset secretary informed Balaz that a Comrade Mandak from the Regional Public Security Directorate on Victorious

February Street had called. Balaz was to report there the next day at ten o'clock.

This was the first time in his life that Balaz set foot in the public security headquarters. Comrade Mandak was called to pick him up from the vestibule. He was a man of about forty, and quite good-looking; he introduced himself and invited Balaz to follow him to his office. Balaz followed him into the lift, which dropped them on the third floor. To the right of the lift, the wide hall was cut off by a steel gate. Mandak pressed a button and murmured something into the intercom. A buzzer sounded, Mandak opened the meshed gate, and they continued down to the end of the hall. Here they were met by another metal gate, which Mandak opened with one of a ring of keys from his pocket. When they had both gone through the gate, he carefully locked it again. As he continued into a small office, a secretary politely stood up from her desk. Mandak signalled to Balaz to come in. They found a middle-aged man in a baggy suit sitting on a couch waiting for them. He was attempting to disguise his baldness by sweeping his gelled hair from one side of his head to the other. He looked slimy and unpleasant, and the hand he offered to Balaz was soft and sweaty. He didn't look Balaz in the eyes.

"Sit down, Comrade," said the agent, who had not introduced himself. "You sit down too," he instructed Mandak. Balaz figured he had to be some kind of senior official, but there was no name-plate anywhere to be seen. He recalled that there wasn't a name-plate on Winter's door in Prague either. He realized then that the Regional Public Security Directorate also housed the secret police. He also understood that they knew what was going through his mind. He was in a trap for sure. Not wanting to appear inquisitive his look around the room was as discrete as he could make it. The windows were covered in steel mesh and the walls were fibreboard. He also noticed the absence of a portrait of the Czechoslovak President Husak which he thought was obligatory in all state offices. He was overcome by the odd feeling that besides Mandak and the slimy man, there was someone else watching him. The secretary brought three cups of coffee, and although Balaz had not been consulted, he thanked her politely.

"So how are you doing?" the unknown agent began. "Did your wife like the roses?" This was said in a jovial tone of voice.

"Rose? What roses?"

"The ones those French journalists were supposed to be laying at the War Memorial." Balaz's hand, which was raising his cup to his mouth, shook, a fact which was noted with satisfaction by the other two. "Had she ever before received such a big bouquet?" Again that creepy smile. "Don't worry Comrade, your bosses up in Prague won't find out about your little trick - but really, after your problems with the German journalist, was it really wise?" The agent paused to light a cigarette and relished Balaz's growing discomfort. By now he was sure that everything that went on in this place was recorded and monitored by state security. He'd had the same impression when he was calling abroad and strange clicks and squeaks came over the line. Since he made international calls almost daily, he was well acquainted with the sounds.

"My name is Zurek. I'm quite a high official in this institution." His icy smile was also directed at Mandak, who nodded vigorously and gave a meaningless laugh. "The Press Centre is of course a federal body, but since it's located in Slovakia, you're under our jurisdiction. What you do there is of no interest to us, that's up to Prague to decide, but we're responsible for the security side of things. Your workplace is regularly visited by journalists from capitalist countries who may infiltrate not only anti-state materials but also anti-state ideas into our society. We would be glad if you would report to us any such ideas, matters or contacts which seem to you incompatible with normal relations. Of course you will not speak of these matters with anyone except for us. Comrade Mandak here will be meeting with you from time to time, whenever he judges appropriate. And if you yourself need or wish to contact us, not only about these foreigners but also about people you meet here, feel free to get in touch. Comrade Mandak will give you a number where you can call him." Zurek stopped, obviously waiting for a response from Balaz.

"But... but... of course I am a conscientious diplomat of socialist Czechoslovakia," Balaz stuttered out. His hands were shaking so much that he gave up trying to hold his cup steady. He wondered if his coffee had not somehow been doctored... that's what happened in detective films when the police wanted to soften up the person under interrogation.

"We know you're a conscientious diplomat, and we appreciate that. We're only asking you to let us hear any information that you don't want to put on paper... What you report to your ministry in Prague, those reports on discussions you've conducted, is usual practice, and of course they're then passed on to our colleagues in the capital. We would simply welcome closer cooperation." Now both Zurek and Mandak were looking at Balaz.

"Perhaps I don't quite understand you. I am obliged to hand reports in to the ministry. I signed on the register of cadre obligations that I would maintain confidentiality on state secrets. It's taken for granted that I will keep superior bodies informed of anything threatening our socialist structures..." That much Balaz managed to gulp out.

"Your superior bodies are up in Prague and it could happen that it is necessary to act rapidly. As I already mentioned, it is we who are responsible for security in Slovakia." Zurek produced a sheet of paper from somewhere and read out: "I confirm that I am conscious of my duty to maintain and protect state, economic and official secrets, and I am also aware that in the case of my divulging confidential facts I shall be liable to prosecution in conformity with Act no. 140/1961 Zb (Criminal Act), Prague, 31.1.1977." Zurek finished his reading and laid the document on the table. "Signed, Jozef Balaz." Balaz looked at the agent, not at all sure where this was leading. The sick feeling and spinning head came back. Even as an athlete he had never experienced such feelings. Plus, his heart was banging against his ribs. "So you admit signing this..." Zurek scowled at him.

"Of course I signed it. It's my duty as a socialist diplomat..."

"Look here Comrade, stop all this waffling on about socialism. You signed an obligation of secrecy, but you haven't been maintaining it. You informed foreign journalists about safety problems at the Jaslovske Bohunice nuclear plant, on so-called air contamination in the vicinity of the brown coal mines in Novaky and Handlova; you even gave them some nonsensical numbers on increased energy consumption allegedly showing that commercial consumption accounts for ninety percent of production and that the public consumes only ten percent. You told them we use outdated and worn-out technologies, that alcohol use is on the upswing, and that the average life expectancy is decreasing. Finally you have been taking an unhealthy interest in events surrounding the Solidarity movement in Poland!"

"I said that to those French journalists alone..." Balaz objected without pausing to reflect.

"And that's not going too far?!" Zurek raised his voice.

"They told you about it? But they were Communists..." Balaz showed his naiveté.

"That was none of your business!" Mandak, unhappy that Zurek had revealed that some of the French were working for them, cut his superior off. An immense discomfort flowed over Balaz. He suddenly felt like the earth was about to open up and swallow him, and he had no way to stop it. He didn't know how long the silence had lasted, how long the coffee on the table had sat there growing cold, how long it had taken the sun to move from one screened window to the next.

Zurek leaned forward and put his hand on Balaz's shoulder "None of all this is so serious. We still have faith in you. We only want you to confirm your faith in writing." He shifted a sheet of clean A4 paper in front of Balaz. "Be so good as to write on this piece of paper that you are committing yourself to inform us of all facts which could threaten the state and the social structures of our socialist homeland."

Balaz sat silent and unmoving. "But I already signed it in Prague," he objected in a low voice. Zurek thrust a pen into his hand and began to dictate: "Write. I, the undersigned Jozef Balaz, undertake that I shall inform the empowered employees of the XII Directorate of the National Security Corps of facts which could threaten...I have signed this undertaking voluntarily." Balaz heard and wrote down whatever Zurek dictated. He signed. "Date and signature," Zurek directed him. Balaz wrote the date and signed it. Zurek and Mandak looked at each other significantly.

"Can I go?" Balaz's voice was scarcely audible.

"Of course. Comrade Mandak will accompany you."

Balaz went out onto February Street. From there he continued up onto Pioneer Street and along the railway tracks, then up through the grape vines. He was travelling along the paths he and his father had once upon a time walked when they went to fetch grapes. He climbed right up to the top of Koliba Hill and into the Straw Hut restaurant, where he ordered Slovak gin. As he finished his fourth glass of this powerful spirit, he saw that the sun was going down outdoors. He would later have no memory of how he made his way down past the railway station to Defenders of Peace Street, where the Press and Information Centre was situated. Going into his office, he took an open bottle of vodka out of the fridge and drank off what was left in it. He took a sheet of paper and a carbon and wrote: *Federal Ministry of Foreign Affairs, Prague. Minister. Re.: Dissolution of Employment Relation with FMFA. In the sense of § 51, para. 1 of the Labour Code, I request the dissolution of my employment relation with the Federal Ministry of Foreign Affairs, CSSR as at 1. 5. 1980. Reason: Without statement of reason. Signed...*

Balaz carefully inserted the letter in an envelope, sealed it, and set off back to the railway station, where the only 24-hour post office in the city was located. He sent the letter registered. As he came out of the station he felt nothing but relief. Although he had no idea what would happen next, in particular where they would live, he found himself smiling. It was the smile of someone who had made a free decision.

His wife Marta was sitting at the end of the kitchen table, gingerly eating a pea omelette. The baby was sleeping in the windowless pantry which the landlady had put at their disposal. The only light it got was through the glass panes on the doors on either side of it. It contained two single beds along the walls, a wardrobe and a baby cot. After the court decision, Chirana provided them with replacement accommodation back in the Specialists' House in Stara Tura. It was clear to them both that if they went back there it would be the end of the line. Commuting from Stara Tura to Prague was practically impossible and there was no work for Marta in that town. Health care provision was at a miserable level and the nearest hospital was miles away in Piestany.

After vacating their Piestany flat, they had stored their furniture in an old musty room in the Statistics Office, where Jozef's childhood friend Milan Brezina was an economist. Their landlady was incredibly frugal, as a result of which the flat always smelled of re-used cooking oil. They were restricted to two baths per week in order to save on hot water. She found the gas bills expensive, even though the Balaz family was paying a generous share of them.

Marta was trying to eat silently and quickly so she wouldn't have to put up with the malicious tongue of their landlady. Her husband's arrival gave her a little more energy, and she rose from the table to give him a kiss. Then she made him an omlelette. After eating, they went to see if their baby was sleeping peacefully. Thankfully, she didn't have a temperature and was breathing freely. They stood by the cot and together watched their sleeping child. Jozef put his arm around Marta, trying to find the words to tell her he'd given his notice. If only he could think of some solution to their situation, but no other job was on offer. His wife sensed his unease and stroked his cheek. Jozef thought she too was trying to find the words to tell him something.

"Is there some problem?" he asked solicitously.

"Do we have anything but problems?" she answered with a smile. She paused, and taking his hand in hers, continued: "Nothing's wrong at the moment, but there could be a problem come October..."

"What's going to happen in October?"

"Another baby. I'm pregnant again!"

CHAPTER
SIXTEEN

BERLIN-NEUWIED 1982-1983

THOMAS walked through Plötzensee Park near to his house on Triftstrasse. It was a favourite place of his since he and Angelika moved to Wedding, and he was sitting on his usual bench by the pond. From a secret compartment in his pocketbook he took out a worrying photograph. It was of a young SS officer, Karl Joachim Lammer.

Again and again Thomas thought about an article in the Frankfurter Allgemeine Zeitung newspaper, in which a reporter named Franz Emmerich had written that Lammer's son-in-law was the Berlin senator, Thomas Ankermann. The two men argued practically every time they met, due to the fact that the older man refused to resign his position on account of crimes he hadn't committed. Angelika stayed out of their quarrels, but Thomas had the feeling she was on her father's side. He strolled through the park reflecting on whether he had the right to condemn his father-in-law. He himself hadn't lived through the Nazi era and couldn't judge the degree of Lammer's involvement. He'd been a member of the SS, but then again Thomas' own father had been in the NSDAP National Socialist Party. From the standpoint of principles, was there a difference between belonging to the Party and to the state security organ?

Along with these worries, he felt a weakening of his attachment to his wife. Partly he put this down to the fact that they hadn't managed to have a child, and partly due to her new involvement in politics. He himself was more and more reconsidering his political engagement. After the East German spy scandal, his political idol, Willy Brandt, had given up the chancellorship while retaining his post as head of the Socialist Party. His status in the party, however, had been damaged due to circumstances beyond his control. If Brandt had not acted according to his moral principles, he could still be Federal Chancellor today.

West Berlin was undergoing security restrictions due to the upcoming visit of the American President, Ronald Reagan, who was finishing up a ten-day European tour. The main item on Reagan's agenda was the NATO summit, to be held for the first time on German soil. In the national capital Bonn about a half-million people had protested against this meeting of NATO chiefs, while demonstrations in London and Paris had involved almost the same numbers.

Reagan was accompanied in Berlin by his Secretary of State, Alexander Haig, and the ailing West German Chancellor, Helmut Schmidt. After a short inspection of American soldiers at Tempelhof airport, Reagan delivered a speech before 30,000 people in the gardens of Charlottenburg Palace. From there he went on to view Checkpoint Charlie in Kreuzberg, the major crossing-point between the American and Russian sectors of the city. However, for security reasons it was not possible to get him back to Tempelhof by car since thousands of demonstrators had blocked the route; a helicopter was called in. Over 250 protestors were arrested. One of these was Thomas' old comrade, Reiner. Before the eyes of Senate Deputy Thomas Ankermann, the police beat him bloody. As he was being dragged along the ground by his legs, Reiner's glance met Thomas' for a few seconds. These were perhaps the longest seconds of Thomas' life.

He went home disgusted, and that evening failed to attend a reception staged by the Berlin Mayor, Richard von Weizsäcker. Somehow he had lost the desire to participate in such events. He was still dealing with the question as to whether politics was the right arena for him.

Early in October, the telephone rang in Thomas' flat. The voice on the other end of the line identified itself as Franz Emmerich, a journalist. Thomas immediately recognized him as the author of the article about his father-in-law. Very politely, he asked for a meeting with Thomas, and the two agreed on the old Berlin pub 'Tippel' for their appointment. Thomas arrived a little early and was passing his time reading the Berliner Zeitung when someone tapped him on the shoulder. Reiner stood looking down at him.

Thomas' instinctive reaction was to frown.

"Hi."

"Hi," Reiner answered in a voice holding more sorrow than malice. "What are you doing here?"

"I'm having a meeting."

"With a journalist called Emmerich?"

Thomas stared at him. "Are you him?"

"No way, I'm not a reporter, but that article... Do you mind if I sit down?"

"I guess we're not going to have our meeting standing up," smiled Thomas. "What are you drinking?"

"Beer. Berlin Weisse. You?" Reiner returned the question.

"The same." They called the waiter, and a silence fell between them.

"How's things?" Thomas finally asked.

"Normal. I deliver pizza during the day and work as a bouncer in the evening." Again Reiner had his comeback ready. "Doesn't it bother you, Mr. Politician, to be sitting here with a simple worker?"

"Why did you write that article?"

"I didn't write it, I just gave the background stuff to that journalist... Now I regret it... Sorry." Reiner spoke seriously.

"Don't be sorry. I've already broken with Lammer."

"And Angelika?"

"We're getting a divorce; it should be finalized any day now." Thomas took a drink from his glass.

"And politics? Are you still enjoying it?" Reiner finished his beer and ordered two more.

"Not so much, I have to admit. Since that nonsense when the Free Democrats left Chancellor Schmidt without support on account of the American rockets, I'm beginning to get fed up." Rainer watched him carefully for a second.

"We're organizing a protest demonstration against the approval of the stationing of the Pershing rockets on the twenty-second of October at the Government offices in Bonn." Thomas knew he was being tested, so wasn't surprised when Rainer continued: "Do you want to come along? Every well-known person will help the cause. The writer Heinrich Böll has promised to be present, a few rock groups and a lot of other people are appearing. Even some German soldiers want to join in, and that's in spite of being forbidden to take part in demonstrations..."

"I'll be there." Thomas' answer was quick and decisive..

Day and night, entry to the American air base in Mutlangen was blocked by over a thousand opponents of the long-range missiles. In more than a hundred towns across Germany, protests were held against the possibility of the German government allowing the rockets. Students, women's groups, workers, Church groups, all were all taking part. The apex was reached on October 22, 1983, when more than 200 000 German citizens made a human chain all the way from Ulm to Stuttgart - 108 kilometres. During that same week, two million of them took to the street. The Nobel Peace Prize holder and former Chancellor Willy Brand made an impassioned speech before 300,000 people. He called on the entire German nation to demand that the German government unequivocally refuse any Cruise or Pershing missiles whatsoever. After weeks of protest, word came down that the Federal Parliament was postponing a vote on the positioning of American rockets on German soil. The demonstrators hugged each other in joy at their success. After they had cleared the streets, the Parliament quickly approved the positioning of mid-range missiles. On November 25, 1983, the German media reported that the first hundred such weapons were being brought to Mutlangen. The next morning, Thomas sat at his desk with a cup of morning coffee and wrote to the SPD President of the Berlin Senate that he was withdrawing from the Party and ceasing all political activity of any kind.

After the end of the Bonn demonstrations, Thomas went home to his parents. He hadn't been in Neuwied for over two years, although he and his father spoke on the telephone. His mother was in a bad way, hospitalized in the intensive care ward at St. Elizabeth's hospital in Koblenz. Although it was clear her son's arrival cheered her up, she wasn't able to express it in words. She was only sixty-three and her heart was failing. According to her doctors, she had suffered three heart attacks, the most serious of which had happened a month ago.

She was lying in a pretty, well-lit room with an old lady. The room was on the second floor, and through the window she could see the massive crowns of some chestnut trees, on which the season's first flakes of snow glistened. Thomas sat at her bedside while her fellow patient went out into the hallway to converse with a visitor. His mother's favourite piece of music, Wagner's Tannhäuser, was playing quietly. It was music which always brought Thomas back to his childhood in Lückenwald. Doing her household chores, his mother had enjoyed listening to classical music concerts on their old Telefunken. Thomas' best memory was sunny afternoons in the courtyard when they still lived in East Germany.

The electric graph to which his mother was constantly connected suddenly began to show dramatic swings in her blood pressure. She turned white and gasped for breath, whereupon Thomas immediately rang for the doctor. She was given an injection that calmed her down and stabilized her blood pressure.

"I won't be here for much longer," she whispered, feebly squeezing her son's hand. After the doctor left, Thomas again took his place at her bedside and, looking into her half-closed eyes, attempted to buck her up.

"Mama, don't be silly, the doctors are optimistic..." Even to his own ears, the words rang false.

"How is Angelicka?" his mother asked.

"Pretty good, she's satisfied with her work." He was glad his mother's eyes were closed.

"No grandchildren on the way?"

"Not so far..." he answered diffidently, and his mother sensed this was not a pleasant topic for him.

"Have you been to Halbe?" With her question, she opened her eyes; she probably wanted to follow her son's reaction.

"Yes, yes, from time to time," he lied. He waited for his mum to bring up his dead brother Nicholas.

"At that time we got 400 grams of fat a month, and 100 grams of meat and half a loaf of bread a day. Nicholas was still with us, and we were lucky I was a 'Trümmerfrau'. They called us 'assistant reconstruction workers' in the newspaper. Your father was a prisoner of war and we were sent to Berlin to help rebuild. When I close my eyes, do you know what I see? Ruins, ruins, ruins... That image has always stayed with me, always. My whole life I've been dreaming of ruins!"

His mother squeezed Thomas' hand more tightly, and he returned the pressure. "We would pass along the dust and dirt one to the other in buckets,... hundreds, thousands, hundreds of thousands of buckets... Sometimes one of us would bring along some Knolly-Brandy, a spirit made from sugar beets. Luckily I wasn't a smoker, so I didn't need cigarettes. Your grandfather was a heavy smoker – he traded our old car for five cartons of American Camels. In the summer we got by okay; we made salads from thistles and dandelion. Do you know what Nicholas' favourite salad was? Daisies!.. Just imagine, my Nicholas loved daisy salad..." Tears squeezed from between her still-closed eyelids.

"Did you find him?" she asked.

"No, mama."

"I'll never forget that day; it was the seventeenth of November, a full half-year after the surrender. Nicholas was sitting next to me, helping to load the cleaned bricks into the buckets the strongest of us would take down onto the other side of the street, near Virchow Colony."

"Where!?" Now she had Thomas' full attention. He had heard her tale of Nicholas' death hundreds of times, but had never paid much attention to where it had taken place. But his mother, lost in her story, didn't hear his question, and went on: "Nicholas was shaking from the cold and suddenly noticed a piece of a coat sticking out below some ruins. It was number 64 Triftstrasse Street, and the bearing wall was still standing; some women were trying to move aside some timbers, under which they hoped to find some useful objects. At the same time, Nicholas was trying to free the coat trapped under some kind of stone. And that's when it happened – a sudden wind came up, the three-storey wall toppled, and not one of them got out alive. We all ran over and with our bare hands desperately tried to move away the stones and bricks covering their bodies when the side wall started to crumble and brought down the remains of the building. We stayed there digging without even picks, only with a few bricklayers' hammers, until the dark night came. The others gradually gave up the fruitless task, but I stayed there alone, digging and digging... Just before morning, the weather changed and a heavy snow began to fall. The demolition crew cordoned off the area and no-one was allowed on the site... Nicholas had no chance... Anyway, he didn't have long to live, he'd already contracted tuberculosis." His mother seemed to be trying to come to terms with the decision of Almighty God to take her son from her.

Thomas became aware of the two young doctors standing behind him and listening in. "They transferred us to Steglitz. Nicholas was classed as missing. He would have turned six the next week... I heard that they later buried all the missing in a mass grave in Halbe Teupitz, close to Berlin. You have to go there, perhaps you can find him. You have to go and look for him... Promise me..."

"Okay, mama, yes... I promise... I promise," he said, and stroked her hand and her hair. He thought this was probably the first time he had ever done so. Discreetly the doctors moved away.

"While I was trying to dig Nicholas out, I found this... please give me my handbag." Thomas took her bag from the side-table and gave it to his mother. "Open the side compartment, and there, right at the bottom, there's a kind of ... little medal... Do you see it?"

Thomas took out a small medallion on a chain. "There's something written there, I can't quite make it out... j... o... What is it?" Thomas asked.

"Ljubov. Love, in Russian... Probably some poor Russian soldier lost it... If one day you meet a Russian mother, give it to her... Maybe it belonged to her son..." Again the mother squeezed her son's hand, and Thomas could feel the tears running down his cheeks. At the same time he was struck by a strange coincidence - his older brother Nicholas had died three years before he was born. And the place he'd died, on Triftstrasse, was where Thomas was now living.

"And don't forget, Halbe Teupitz... don't forget..."

"No, mama, I won't forget..."

His mother smiled and closed her eyes. She seemed to have slipped into a sleep. The senior doctor came over to Thomas: "She's tired out, best let her sleep. Her body is worn out."

"Doctor, is it serious?" This was a question the doctor didn't want to answer. "I have to go to Berlin tomorrow afternoon; would it be all right for me to drop in during the morning?" Thomas pleaded.

"Of course."

It was the last day of November, four in the afternoon. Mrs. Ankermann died that night at eleven o'clock

CHAPTER
SEVENTEEN

BRATISLAVA – PRAGUE 1982

JOZEF and Marta Balaz returned to their rented room sometime after midnight. Their daughter Martuska was sleeping at her grandmother's and the walk home through the May evening was splendid. They were in a good mood, as were all the others who had spent the evening at the opening of the new Studio S theatre run by two comedians called Lasica and Satinsky. In those years of tough normalization, when prisoner number 9658 Vaclav Havel was serving his third year in Plzen-Bory prison, the return of this popular duo at a new theatre was surprisingly good news. After their years of being banned and re-assigned, regular appearances by Lasica and Satinsky were as welcome as the fresh spring air.

A few days after the wonderful evening at the new theatre, his friend Milan, the manager at the Statistics Office, came to tell Balaz that in February renovations would take place and that he would have to move his belongings out of the warehouse. Jozef broke out in a cold sweat. Luckily, the desperate situation was resolved by the services director of the Diplomatic Corps, who offered the Balaz family a new three-room flat in the suburb of Lamac. Since their stay there would be unofficial, it could only be at their disposal until someone with a stronger claim requested the accommodation. After that...

In the last week of May, the Balaz family moved into their new flat. Although it wasn't their own, it seemed like a miracle that they could take a shower whenever they wanted, that no landlady would be looking over their shoulders, that the flat would not smell of cooking fat, and, perhaps most importantly, that their child would have her own nursery with a window. It was the most beautiful spring they had spent in Bratislava. But their happiness was to be short-lived. In July, they were informed by the services director that they would have to vacate the flat, which was to be rented to a new foreign representation employee. They were offered an older, smaller flat in the centre of the city on Sokolska Street.

Martuska had just pasted pictures of her favourite animals on a board her father had put up in her nursery, and couldn't understand why he was now taking it down, along with her bed, cupboard and shelves. She went running to her mother, who, with tears in her eyes, explained that they were moving again. Marta didn't have the heart to tell her she might not have her own room in the new place.

Although the new flat had only two rooms, they managed to squeeze all their belongings into it. To make their happiness complete, the services director of the Diplomatic Corps gave them his word of honour that they could live there at least until the end of the coming year. This gave them a year and a half to work out something better.

One Friday afternoon near the end of June, Balaz was just preparing for his walk home, since his service Lada wasn't working. A mechanic friend had promised to have a look at it after the weekend. The phone rang as he was leaving, and Jozef heard the voice of the Minister of Foreign Affairs' secretary. When she had ascertained that it was indeed Comrade Balaz she was talking to, she connected him to the Minister in person. Balaz all but stood at attention.

"Comrade Balaz?" He recognized the voice of Minister Chnoupek.

"That's right, Comrade Minister..." he responded faintly, wondering what this could be about.

"Hello, are you there?" the Minister raised his voice.

"Yes, yes... please excuse me... I've never spoken to a government minister by telephone before..."

"Please sit down and relax... I have a request to ask of you... Tomorrow morning I'm going to a hunting meet in Záhoria, and will need to borrow a car... Hello, are you there?"

"Yes, Comrade Minister..."

"You have a service Lada, right?"

"Yes, that's right, but..." Balaz paused.

"So be so good as to drop it off at the Hotel Bôrik at eight o'clock, please."

"Yes, yes, I'll be there."

"So, goodbye until then," the Minister said, satisfied, and hung up. Now, the time was past four in the afternoon, and finding a mechanic on a Friday in socialist Czechoslovakia was almost as impossible as finding a housepainter on a Monday morning. Jozef begged his mechanic friend Gabo to at least have a look at the car.

" By when do you need it?"

"As soon as possible! I have to have it at the Borik tomorrow morning at eight!"

"No way. It's coming up to five, and I have to start my night job at six."

"What night job?"

"In a boiler-room. Since the first of the month I've been working as a boiler serviceman in addition to my job at the garage. I took a course, and it's as easy as pie. From time to time you turn a tap up or down, you check the boiler pressure, and the rest of the time you just lie around or invite some girl into the warm."

"Oh, I hadn't heard. Isn't the garage job enough for you?"

"It's not bad, but a friend offered me an old Mercedes, in great shape. I need the extra money to pay for it."

"Don't you know anyone who could help me out? It's a real problem... I'm willing to pay..."

"That's not the point, I simply have to go to work... Okay, I'll stop and look it over on my way to work."

"Super. I'll be waiting for you."

Gabo quickly discovered that one electric circuit kept shorting out, and to fix it they'd have to put it through the garage's tester... on Monday morning. In the meantime he had a way to make it run - he used a coin in place of the faulty fuse.

"You'll be able to drive it, but you'd better pray it keeps working. On Monday I'll fix it properly for you."

"And what if it breaks down again?"

"Don't worry, it'll go. It'll have to!" Smiling, he jumped into his old Skoda to drive to his night-job, leaving Balaz to work out what he was going to do.

"Comrade Minister, there's something I have to tell you," he began cautiously while handing Chnoupek the car keys. "It's a great car, but right now it has one small problem. I wanted to take it to the garage first thing Monday morning, but... you called me in the meantime. You can imagine how hard it is to find a car mechanic on a Friday afternoon..." Then he ran out of steam.

"What are you trying to say?"

"That it's really a great car, a top Soviet product, and since you're the Minister, surely you can get hold of some mechanic..."

"You can't be serious?" The Minister looked at him, confused.

"I really don't want to do this to you, but I'd rather tell you this now than to go to jail should something happen to you..." Chnoupek had heard that this young man was something of a joker, but he thought Balaz was going too far this time.

"Come on, you're pulling my leg, right?" He stared at Balaz.

"Comrade Minister, the Lada is a reliable car, but occasionally... like any car... it can have problems with the electrics. Instead of a fuse, we put in a coin." The whole truth finally came out, and the Minister sighed. "I'll show you what I mean," Balaz told him.

"If Kramar hadn't said so many good things about you, I'd think you were out of your mind... I only hope that they have mechanics working on a Saturday morning here at the Bôrik... Come back for the car tomorrow evening; I hope it'll be ready for you. When the clerk is not able to provide a car for the Minister, the Minister must provide a car for the clerk... I've been Minister for eleven years, and this has never happened to me...I can't believe this is really happening... Why don't I simply send you away?" He let out a cry like a wild Indian. "Nobody will believe this..."

„ Comrade Minister, sorry, but there's something I'd like to explain to you... I need only ten minutes... five minutes would do..." The Minister looked at him in curiosity.

"I don't have time... I have to go and find a mechanic... Be here tomorrow at four o'clock." Entering the vestibule, he turned and pointed at his forehead. Balaz shrugged his shoulders and started walking back home.

On Sunday at four, Balaz was back at the Borik. The Lada stood at the far end of the parking lot, covered in mud. The receptionist handed the keys to him and asked him to wait, then picked up the phone: "Comrade Minister will be right down."

A moment later, Chnoupek walked into the vestibule with a strange look on his face. He handed Balaz an empty bottle of Becherovka spirits. "If you wanted to give me this as a bribe, I can't understand why you drank part of the bottle first!" He remembered with a shock that when Gabo had come on Friday to look at the Lada, Balaz had thanked him with a bottle. Since Gabo was late for work, he had only poured one drink from the bottle. In his hurry, he must have left the bottle in the back of the car.

"This is so unbelievable I'm starting to enjoy dealing with you just to see what happens next," he said, shaking his head. Balaz apologized and explained what must have happened. Chnoupek examined him with a look. "I saw your play on television. It wasn't bad... Shall we have some coffee?" The offer took Balaz so much by surprise that he didn't manage to hide his confusion. This was the first time in his life he was speaking to a high state official. He managed a nod. The Minister called a waiter over and then said: "I have the feeling there's something you want to talk to me about..." Again Balaz nodded. He began slowly and circumspectly, then, when he saw he had the Minster's full attention, the intensity of his voice increased. By the end he was almost blaming Chnoupek for not responding to a single one of his letters. He told him everything, including his decision to quit the Ministry.

"I never saw any letters from you... If you want to be sure a letter gets through to me, send it by way of Danka Jurikova. You probably know her, she's from Bratislava too."

"I know her, but I didn't know..."

"Okay, don't worry about it. I'll have a look at your situation. My secretary will get back to you as soon as possible."

"As soon as possible," Balaz repeated in a sceptical tone.

"By the end of next week." The Minister smiled, and offered Balaz his hand.

The following Thursday, Chnoupek's secretary informed Balaz that the Comrade Minister would see him the following Tuesday at eleven in his office.

When Balaz entered the Minister's office, it was so huge it took his breath away. The Minister was seated behind his desk, reading something. Balaz addressed him politely. The Minister raised his eyes for a second, gestured towards a comfortable-looking leather armchair beside his desk, and returned to the document. Balaz sat down.

"Good morning. I'll be right with you..."

Balaz looked around this marvellous room and thought about a book he had in his library at home. It was a life of the former Czechoslovak Foreign Minister, Jan Masaryk. He occupied this office, as had his successor, Vladimir Clementis. Both of their lives had ended tragically. The Minister broke into his train of thought.

"What have you been up to?" he asked, looking over the papers. "It says here, 'not suitable for service in non-socialist countries'." He showed Balaz the hand-written comment in his cadre dossier. "It was written by someone on the Central Committee."

"Nothing. Really, nothing," said Balaz with a shrug.

"Well, okay... I don't have the time to look into it, and I don't feel like getting into a fight with Bilak's people over you," he said unabashedly. Balaz even had the feeling that what Chnoupek had revealed about the tension between himself and the Communist Party

Secretary for International Affairs, Vasil Bilak, hadn't been said deliberately. "I regret that the Comrades on the Central Committee have formed the opinion that you can't go to the West, but I did have someone look into where your talent could best be employed within the Socialist camp. Your German is on the highest level. The position of press attaché in the German Democratic Republic has become vacant... Would that interest you?" The Minister looked up at Balaz.

"Uh... well... yes... to tell the truth, I never thought... certainly, Comrade Minister."

"So, I'll write that you are to be prepared for secondment to the GDR in the position of press attaché. If they don't fire me in the meantime, you can count on going there." The Minister signed the order and looked up at Balaz with a smile. "So when are you expecting your second child?"

"You know about that? In October."

The Minister considered how to go on, and finally said: "So I guess it'll be born in your new flat." Balaz's eyes nearly popped out of his head. "Report to the Government Office International Section in Bratislava. They'll fill you in. So for now, goodbye... and take care." Balaz just stood there speechless. "Now, if you'll excuse me, I have another appointment."

Thinking back on it all, Balaz couldn't remember if he had even thanked the Minister for his kindness.

A few months later, he brought his wife home from the maternity hospital with another daughter, Anicka. Marta placed the baby in her cot in a brand-new three-room flat in the Bratislava suburb of Ostredky. When she heard the news, little Martuska tore home from school as fast as her legs could carry her. Her school bag bounced up and down on her back, but even so, Jozef could hardly keep up with her. Martuska ran right up to the little bundle of arms and legs which gurgled something, smiled up at them, and stuck her little fingers in her mouth. Martuska stared at her new sister for a long minute while her mother and father watched over both their children. They had the feeling that their lives were finally changing for the better. The silence with which they all looked at the gurgling new arrival was finally broken by little Martuska: "And here we all are."

CHAPTER
EIGHTEEN

MOSCOW, 1982 – 1987

THE Mi-8 helicopter with Michail Obicky on board was the first Soviet aircraft to be shot down by one of the five hundred Stinger rockets. By the end of the Soviet invasion, 332 helicopters had been destroyed by this weapon.

Two days after Brezhnev was buried, Andropov took over the highest state position. He would hold power for fifteen months, seven of which would be spent in bed at the State Hospital in Kuntsevo, from where he 'ruled' the largest country in the world. The USSR had fallen into a complex and dangerous crisis. After long years, famine had returned. Oil, cheese, butter and meat disappeared from the shops of Moscow. Corruption took over, and breaking the law became a normal facet of life. Theft, swindling, snitching and drunkenness were now part of the Soviet citizen's lifestyle. The desperate populace trailed from shop to shop in the hope of finding something they could use, or at least trade. Informers in shops, hairdressers, and even in funeral parlours reported every critical word, together with its author, to the secret police.

While the people were having trouble making ends meet, billions of dollars from the black economy were flowing into Swiss bank accounts. Mafia bands were formed, working hand in glove with the highest state and Party officials. The secret service was able to do practically anything it desired. Andropov, its former chief, initially tried to rid public *life of the thieves and bandits, but then his strength failed him. He died on February 9, 1984, to be succeeded by the seventy-two year old Konstantin Ustinovich Chernenko. This caused an even deeper spirit of apathy and impotence. The election of yet another old man was seen by the citizenry as a signal to adopt the slogan: 'Help yourself to as much as you can'. Of the thirteen months Chernenko was in power, he spent six of them, as had his predecessor before him, in the hospital.*

The citizens of Alma-Ata, Tbilisi, Baku, Vilnius and other cities took to the streets. The Soviet media met this wave of unrest with references to enemy actions against the USSR carried out from beyond its borders. The state was writhing in agony, industrial and agricultural production was dropping, the military-industrial complex consumed one-third of the economy. Whereas under the Czar Russia had supplied grain to half of Europe, cereal had to be imported by the Communist bosses. In 1985, a record fifty-five million tons had to be bought abroad. President Reagan's attempt to 'choke the USSR by arms' fell on fertile ground. The Soviet Union was being beaten down.

According to his wishes, Michail Obicky was buried in a cemetery in Irsava, Carpatho-Ukraine. Irsava lies just over the hill from the village of Kolodne, so many of Sasha's friends and relatives attended the burial. A military funeral and a tombstone with the standard inscription for Afghanistan veterans, 'he laid down his life in the fulfillment of international duties,' was refused. Sasha insisted that it be a normal religious funeral and rejected the participation of the army bigwigs from Uzghorod who had sat at home warming their bums while Michail gave up his life in a country most Russians and Ukrainians couldn't even find on a map. His parents and widow decided on a beautiful marble gravestone with his civilian photograph, the dates of his birth and death, and an Orthodox cross. Under Michail's photograph, Sasha had inscribed: 'He died in Afghanistan'. The inscription served as both an indictment and a warning for all who stopped at his grave. The only military official invited was General Sergei Gusev, who was the same official who had ordered a stop to Sasha Grycenko's KGB interrogation many years before. At the wake following the funeral, he told her that he and Michail had been classmates at the Secondary Military Academy in Mukachevo.

At the beginning of the eighties, Gusev was transferred from the KGB to GRU military intelligence. The commander of the GRU (Central Intelligence Administration) General Staff, General Colonel Piotr Ivanovich Ivashutin, remembered the penetrating intellect, dependability, independent thinking and chiefly the great energy, of his Kiev colleague, Major Gusev. Although he had remained a lifelong bachelor, Gusev had a rich social life. He knew a lot of influential people, both from his student days and from sporting activities. Due to his progressive and critical opinions on what was going on in the army, he was constantly a thorn in the side of his superior officers. Even as he approached his fiftieth birthday, his expression of his ideas remained open and fearless. For example, the GRU command knew he was not in favour of the Afghanistan invasion. He was proven right in 1984, when the Soviet Union discreetly attempted to negotiate with the Americans on terminating the incursion. The Americans, however, informed the Russians that they would leave the USSR to stew in their own juices at least as long as they had been forced to remain in Vietnam. Minister Ustinov and the other old men in the supreme command were furious.

The very fact that Moscow was trying to slide out of Afghanistan unofficially strengthened Gusev's position. The young Major General criticized the useless amount of armoured technology, and compared the USSR armed forces with those of the USA. For example, the Soviet Union used eight different types of fighter aircraft while the Americans depended on only three; they had twelve anti-aircraft missile models whereas the USA used only four; the USSR had eight classes of submarines as opposed the American's single class. Gusev went so far as to write a letter to the new Defence Minister, Sergei Sokolov, in which he pointed out that even though the USSR had four massive naval fleets, they were in a terrible state. He suggested that, instead of financing the largest army in the world, four and a half-million soldiers, the military should be made up of professionals and equipped with the latest technologies. Nobody paid any attention to his letter. Gusev became embittered, but refused to resign his commission. Since he had no family, he continued studying and playing sports. After Obicky's death, he occasionally met with Sasha, who shared his opinion on the crisis situation in the Soviet Union: unless changes were made, the country was on the road to ruin.

Sasha was sitting in her living room with her ear glued to the radio. Although the Voice of America signal was scratchy and interfered with, much of the program could be understood.

The doorbell rang; before answering the door, she quickly changed the radio frequency. At the door was Nina. After their quarrel around the death of Brezhnev, the women had resumed their friendship. They nostalgically reminisced about the good old days when bread, milk and even vodka were readily available in the shops. Nina had come to borrow an egg, but when Sasha looked in the fridge she saw there was only one left. When Nina saw her bitter smile, she apologized and turned to leave.

"What did you need it for?" Sasha asked, at the same time inviting her into her flat.

"I felt like making myself a snack."

"Listen, Ninocka, let's make something really tasty... Let's put our reserves together and come up with something good!"

"Fine, but first..." In a flash Nina was back with a bottle of quality vodka. "One of my souvenirs from the Brezhnev days," she laughed. Sasha joined in, and they poured themselves out a glass each. The first round was followed with another, and then they set to preparing some food. "Osja gets home from training at six, and I was getting ready to make something for him," said Sasha, taking some cheese, and salted fish from the fridge, and adding to it some bread, a tin of sardines, onions and garlic from the pantry. Nina contributed some smoked bacon and stuffed peppers. In the end, the table was covered with delicious things to eat. The women were just laying out cutlery for three, when Osja burst in, all excited. He tossed his sports bag onto the couch, clapped his hands, and ceremoniously exclaimed:

"Ladies, allow me to congratulate you!!!" They just stared at him in surprise. Coming over to his mother, Osja hugged her and then kissed Nina on both cheeks.

"Osja, what's going on? What's happened?"

"Maybe you're going to laugh, but the Soviet Union has again suffered a tragic event. Yippee!" When he saw how they were looking at him, he picked up the bottle, gave them both a drink and, to their surprise, poured one for himself. Then, raising his glass, he announced: "Chernenko is dead." He downed his glass of vodka. It was probably the first time in his life he'd drunk a whole glass in one swallow. Then he went over to the record player and at full volume played the latest hit by Alla Pugacheva, 'A Million Red Roses'. He finished up by dancing with both of the women.

"Wait, wait just a minute," said his mother, stopping the record. "Can it be true?" Sasha turned the radio on. Radio Moscow was broadcasting a program entitled 'From the Life of the Cooperative Workers', so instead she tuned into the Voice of America, where they heard: "... after a lingering illness, Konstantin Ustinovich Chernenko, General Secretary of the USSR Communist Party, died today in Moscow at the age of 74." Without a word, Sasha filled three glasses with vodka. The record player was again turned on, and the dancing continued. They sang along with the record: "Millions and millions of red roses you'll see from your window; when you're in love, life changes to roses..." They danced, they drank, they laughed, without caring if anyone could hear them. The death of the third old man in three years could do no other than build up hope that some younger, more dynamic leader would finally take over the highest position in the Party and the state.

The members of the Politburo met just two hours after Chernenko's death. Although during his illness the Politburo had been essentially run by Michail Gorbachev, his selection as Chernenko's successor was far from certain. The old men of the Politburo nomenclature were simply afraid of him. In the event, his confirmation was the result of two events – the orthodox Stalinist Kunajev was unable to travel from Kazakhstan, and the even more orthodox Scherbitski, from Kiev, was on a visit to the USA. As it turned out, his delay in returning home was deliberately delayed. It was the oldest member of the politburo, Gromyko, who found the courage to nominate Gorbachev. He made it clear to the members present that Gorbachev enjoyed the support of the army and the secret service. Nonetheless, the voting was close – four in favour, four against, and one abstention. So the deciding vote belonged to the Chairman, Gromyko. At the plenary meeting of the USSR Central Committee the following day, the politburo decision was unchallengeable. On March 1, 1985, Gorbachev was chosen to lead the Soviet Union. As soon as Chernenko was buried, Gorbachev outlined his program. One of the opening sentences of this speech read: "Our rockets fly to Venus, but our refrigerators don't work."

Perestroika had come to the Soviet Union. At that moment Gorbachev himself had no idea of the full extent of the problems his country found itself in. While in his time Lenin had chaired the Council of People's Commissars (the Government) with thirteen members, the current Soviet government was made up of 115 members, including 15 vice-premiers, 63 ministers, 23 government commission directors, and many more honorary positions besides. Gorbachev's ascent to his position was phenomenal. This jovial and smiling man, constantly accompanied by his charming wife Raisa, was a leader the like of which the inhabitants of the USSR had never seen before. Censorship was abolished, public opinion (glasnost) became the order of the day, and a total change of the old guard was instituted. Whereas the average age in the USSR under Khrushchev – thirty years before – was 67, nowadays it was 62. The reason: alcohol, against which Gorbachev declared an uncompromising war. Fighting alcohol abuse in the Soviet Union was, however, a cause bordering on self-destruction. On Gorbachev's instructions, the sale of spirits to those under the age of 21 was forbidden, as was its consumption at receptions and meetings. The mention of alcohol in films, theatres and books was outlawed. 300 000 hectares of grapevines throughout the country were ploughed under. The result was that while the official consumption of alcohol fell, sugar disappeared from the shops - almost everyone was making their own. People sought out any kind of liquor - aftershave, cleaning fluids, and when these were not available, they inhaled exhaust gases for their alcohol content. Thousands of people died from drinking low-quality alcohol. The new leader suffered the hatred of the people before he had the chance to gain their sympathy. The General Secretary became known as the

Mineral-water Secretary. The successes he was achieving on the international stage were of little interest at home.

But a greater catastrophe was still waiting for Gorbachev. On April 26, 1985, just after one o'clock in the morning, there occurred the greatest nuclear accident in the history of mankind. The fourth block of the Chernobyl nuclear power station exploded.

The production of electric energy in the fourth block started the very day it became operational. Usually, tests were carried out on a reactor's individual parts for a few months after the completion of its construction; only then was the power station certified to work at full capacity. Chernobyl, however, could not wait. The decisive factor was the almighty 5-year Plan, which called for the reactor to be in operation by the end of the year. And so on 31. 12. 1983, the director, Brjuchanov, was forced to sign a document on the successful completion of all tests, although this was patently false.

During the explosion, fifty times more radiation than that released during the bombings of Hiroshima and Nagasaki combined escaped from the reactor. Thirty to sixty thousand people died as a direct result of the explosion, while the results of the accident later killed a further six to eight hundred thousand people, most of them young soldiers. Twenty-five thousand of them were dead by the summer of 1987.

CHAPTER
NINETEEN

BERLIN 1983 – 1986

THE first time Balaz entered the new six-storey building housing the Embassy of the Czechoslovak Socialist Republic, located in the close vicinity of the Wall, was on October 1, 1983. The windows of darkened glass, the flat roof and the square shape of the building reminded him somehow of a mausoleum. From the back, the Embassy was bordered by the Otto Grotewohlstrasse metro station. Past that point the metro did not continue – well, it did continue, but its tunnel had been sealed off since 1961. Berlin carried on past that point, but as West Berlin. And that destination was farther than far away. Between the two parts of the same city stood a 165-kilometre-long wall. The most absurd and the ugliest construction in the capital of the country where Balaz was starting his diplomatic career was officially titled 'The Anti-Fascist Protective Wall'. He would look out on this wall almost every day for the next six years from his office on the Embassy's first floor.

The Balaz family was housed in a three-room flat on Lenin Square, not far from Friedrichshain People's Park. From their window they had a wonderful view of a massive statue of Lenin on a marble base about 20 x 20 metres square. It made a great place for Martuska to learn to ride a bicycle under the watchful eye of the leader of the proletariat. Behind the statue stretched a wood planted on hills artificially landscaped using debris from the devastated city dumped there after the end of the war. The park was large, with many pretty nooks and gravel pathways, along which the inhabitants of Berlin enjoyed walking or jogging.

One of Balaz's first strong impressions of the capital of the German Democratic Republic was the smell – the ever-present stink from two-stroke motorcars called Trabant and Wartburg. They were practically the only brands available to the ordinary citizen, with the odd Skoda or Lada thrown in for good measure. The only western cars on the roads were clearly the property of diplomats, except for the black Citroëns favoured by high-ranking members of the East German Communist Party. Czechoslovak diplomats on principle drove only Skodas, which made them the envy of the Berlin populace. But they didn't envy Balaz's car, for he drove a Trabant Kombi. He'd bought it for forty thousand crowns he'd borrowed before coming to the GDR. In fact his was the only Trabant in the city, perhaps in the whole country, with a diplomat's licence plate, CD 02 – 32. The diplomatic stink his exhaust put out was equal to the proletarian stink of his fellow Trabant drivers.

When diplomats from capitalist countries asked why he was driving a Trabant, he answered with a straight face that he was practicing proletarian internationalism by driving the same car as the working people of his host nation. From the employees of the GDR Ministry of Foreign Affairs press office, however, this remark was awarded only a sarcastic smile. Although they suspected that Balaz was pulling their legs, on ideological grounds they couldn't object to his words.

Balaz was a favourite among the East Berlin auto mechanics - on one hand because he seemed to be a regular guy, while on the other he had access to Versina, the special diplomats' shop where he could buy products GDR citizens knew only from Western television channels. Cognac, whisky, American cigarettes, chocolates and chewing gum were the main arguments that convinced car servicemen to find a place in their crowded schedules to look after the Czechoslovak diplomat's vehicle. Ordinary citizens often had to wait months to have their cars serviced. Because of this, many of them booked a date despite the fact their cars were still in good working order. If, when their turn came, their car didn't need any work done, they traded their appointment to someone who badly needed repairs. Appointments for the obligatory annual technical inspection were made once a year, on a Monday. For those unwilling or unable to give a bribe, the best thing to do was to park in front of the inspection garage on a Sunday evening and spend the night in a sleeping bag. This would ensure their being among those lucky ones managing to book an appointment.

Hunting down spare parts for cars or any home appliances was - not only in the GDR but in fact in any of the Communist countries - something of a national sport, a kind of 'socialist golf'. The goal of the sport was, however, much more materially rewarding than trying to hit a ball into a hole, and the 'players' covered a lot more ground in one round than did capitalist golfers. The joy that a Slovak, Czech, Bulgarian or Russian felt on securing a paper bag for a vacuum cleaner was far greater than an Englishman's pleasure in making even a hole in one. Moreover, the latter could have no comprehension of an East European's delight when he succeeded in 'scoring' windshield wipers or the right size bath plug.

Balaz was always driving the VoPo (people's police) crazy; he relished those situations when they'd pull his Trabant over for speeding, going through an amber light, or driving without lights. The VoPo were infamous for their arrogance towards the public, and when they stopped someone, the ritual was for the driver to immediately jump out of his vehicle and stand at attention before the police officer. If he did not do so, he risked being literally dragged out of his car. Balaz on principle stayed in his car, whose licence plate the police almost never noticed; never in their wildest dreams did they imagine a foreign diplomat behind the wheel of a Trabant. So when they screamed at him their traditional greeting – 'Papers' – Balaz would always smile and ask, "Why are you shouting?" Taken aback by this uncustomary behaviour, they'd usually shout even louder. On being handed his diplomatic identification, without fail they'd step back and finally look at his licence number. Then the papers would be returned, along with an apology. Balaz would then drive on, still smiling.

A Trabant was the waking dream of the East Germans. Maybe at night they'd dream of Volkswagens, Nissans or Fords, but in the daylight hours they hoped for a Wartburg or a Trabant. Their dreams were boosted by advertisements on East German television for the 'robust' Trabant – probably the only ad in the world for a product only a dream could fulfill. The ordinary citizen could, in the best of cases, expect a wait of twelve years to buy a Trabbie; in the worst case, he'd spend his whole life waiting in vain.

The more Balaz encountered the Prussian character of the East Germans, the more he was convinced that if any nation was fit to build socialism, it was this nation. In the times when Lenin proclaimed that socialism meant social order and electricity, he probably didn't realize that 'order' for these Germans was as mother's milk to a newborn. For example, it once happened that at two-thirty in the morning, a man was waiting at a red light at a deserted crossing not far from Frankfurter Allee. Along came Balaz, who calmly walked past the waiting pedestrian and through the red (it was minus five degrees outside). No doubt the man cursed Balaz, but he continued to wait obediently for the light to change. Then he caught up to Balaz, and gesticulated that Balaz had broken the law. Along came another deserted intersection, another red light; this time the other man angrily followed Balaz through the red.

Balaz turned to the unfortunate Berliner: "You just broke the law, you went through a red light. If you do that again, I'll call the police!" The poor man just stood there shaking with fright. It was encounters like this that reaffirmed Balaz's faith in the East German builders of socialism.

In the daily of the Central Committee of the United Socialist Party, Neues Deutschland, Balaz read that the Health Ministry was launching a campaign to support healthy lifestyles. The East German media regularly carried information on the wide opportunities for sport, healthy diets, and recreation; Neues Deutschland offered some great recipes for fruit and vegetable salads, along with a calculation of the vitamins in the individual ingredients. Everything was fine, except for the fact that at the greengrocer's, it was usually only possible to get woven vegetable baskets and decorations for them, garden tools, and other useful things - the only things you would have a hard time finding were fruit and veg! As regards fresh vegetables, there were always onion tops, which people bought when what they really wanted was onions. Once Balaz asked where he could get onions. The saleslady looked at him like he had just fallen from the sky, and asked: "Are you new to Berlin?" When he said he was, she answered: "Drüben... on the other side." 'On the other side' meant in West Berlin.

At the beginning of May, 1986 a leading interviewer from the Czechoslovak Rude právo newspaper came on a visit to the GDR. Part of his program was an interview with the Politburo member for culture, sport and education, the sixty-five year old Kurt Hager. The ill-looking Minister made use of the current local media campaign to impress on the interviewer that healthy nutrition was a part of everyday German culture.

"Our citizens have so many kilos of fruit and so many kilos of vegetables per head." Hager was reading out statistics from his background material. Jovially, he turned to Balaz and, no doubt counting on his agreement, said: "You live here, Comrade Attaché, surely you can confirm this." To his surprise, however, Balaz stared straight in front of himself and said nothing. "Oh, did I get my figures wrong?" Hager joked.

"In principle, Comrade Secretary, what you've said may well be true, but all I know is that every day I go to the Markthalle on Lenin Square, and very rarely do I find fruit and vegetables on sale. But I can always find onion tops..." Hager stared at Balaz in confusion while the interpreter studied the table in front of her.

"It can sometimes happen that there are delivery problems, but essentially things run smoothly," Hager objected.

"The saleslady there told me that our onions are exported to West Berlin."

"You seem to be badly informed, Comrade Attaché," Hager continued in a more assertive tone, "I go to the shops too, and in my experience everything is available." From that point to the end of the interview, Hager completely ignored Balaz.

Still wet behind the ears, Balaz was unaware of the fact that, although Hager did find what he wanted in the shops, the shops were all in the village of Wandlitz. He didn't know then that members of the Politburo and of the GDR Government lived apart from the ordinary builders of socialism in a leafy small town to the north of the city. In Wandlitz, which was surrounded by a high wall, barbed wire and an electronic alarm system, there stood dozens of houses with an average lot size of two hundred square metres. The normal three-room panel flat in Berlin, provided you were lucky enough to get one, was sixty square metres. Wandlitz had everything, but since there was no room for all the GDR's citizens, they were kept out, so as not to disturb the happiness of the town's inhabitants. Once allowed in, the townsfolk enjoyed special schools and kindergartens, a hospital, swimming pools and sports arenas, but best of all they had shops stocked with the best the country had. And the best the socialist country had was what was shipped in on a daily basis from capitalist West Berlin. Since every household boasted two servants, the wives of the bigwigs enjoyed shopping at subsidized prices, with free delivery to their nearby homes.

In order for the upper echelon to escape boredom, they engaged in various forms of entertainment: hunting in state reservations, recreation in luxurious exclusive resorts, shopping in West Berlin, and May Day celebrations. They enjoyed this last because it was an opportunity for them to show how much they loved, and were loved by, the working class. This was popular because they presented an opportunity for them to show how much they appreciated the rest of the population. Before donning their Sunday suits for lunch at the Government residence in Niederschönhausen, they appeared on decorated tribunes and waved to the delighted workers, and the grateful workers waved back. The May Day celebrations were organized jubilation in all the socialist countries, but nowhere were they so perfectly organized, and with such enthusiasm, as in the German Democratic Republic. In contrast to the other East Bloc countries, the East German comrades understood that if jubilation is concentrated in a smaller space, for a shorter time, and at a carefully calculated distance, its effect will be more powerful. In order for the participation of the working people to be as widespread as possible, they were attracted to the parade by a number of treats - fruit, cakes, pastries, sausages and even special beers were available at street stands. As a result, participation at the May Day celebrations in East Berlin was always high.

After the First of May celebrations, the second place the people of East Berlin gathered was in lines in front of selected shops. The foremost of these was Feinkost, where domestic delicacies were on offer, and at Intershop shops, where goods imported from the West were available. Jacobs coffee, 100 Pipers scotch whisky, chewing gum, cosmetics, jeans, Milka chocolate and Practica cameras were among the attractions at these outlets. Of course, these shops operated on the basis of Western currencies only. On special occasions, for example when asparagus was on sale, the masses gathering in front of the Intershops rivalled those at the May Day celebrations. It sometimes seemed to Balaz that the faces of those successful in getting hold of asparagus shone with even more jubilation than those who waved at Honecker, Mielk, Hager, Krenz and the other leading comrades who filled the tribunes on the wide Karl Marx Boulevard.

Since the majority of the May Day participants didn't know the joy of finding asparagus, the happiness shining from their faces was genuine, at least in the jubilation zone. The jubilation zone, as it was called by the people, was the area in front of the main tribune marked off by white lines drawn across Karl Marx Boulevard. The balconies on the panel buildings lining the street were dressed in red skirts, the tribune was draped in red cloth, and even the comrades on the tribune had red buds in their lapels. The young women in their red miniskirts and red blouses marching in the parade waved red flowers at the comrades above them. The sea of red was complemented by the East German boy scouts, the Pioneers, in white tunics with blue kerchiefs and pointed blue caps.

The seemingly endless parade of workers slowly moved from

Strausberger Platz up past the tribune. The GDR Television cameras, set up in front of the tribunes, filmed everything that went on within the zone. The weary and bored workers/marchers had been standing in the streets since early morning, gathered in the far distant Frankfurter Allee and in the streets parallel to it. The proletariat was united by one thought – to get it over with so they could retreat to the beer and sausages at the stands or in the garden restaurants. All this waiting about got on their nerves; the food was cheap and tasty, and while they were standing in line, some skivers might sneak in to the kiosk area and eat it all up. Things were arranged such that they had to show their jubilation before they got the sight of a sausage – the kiosks were on the other side of the zone. The workers could already smell the sausages; their nostrils flared, their mouths watered, their stomachs rumbled. When their turn came, they just had to wave, shout, chant a few slogans, and the sausages would be theirs. The closer they came to the line in front of the tribunes, the more they sped up, so as to get to the sausages in time. Those male workers with long hair combed it back neatly, smokers stubbed out their cigarettes, and women fixed their blouses and repainted their lips.

"Here come the world champions in sports and hypocrisy. They can't wait for their chance to shout out 'glory' at leaders they despise," Balaz commented, while watching the marchers approaching the zone. He felt scorn for them until the thought crossed his mind that in their place he would act just the same. 'You're just lucky they didn't send you out there,' he laughed at himself, 'maybe you'd even push your way into the front row so you'd be more visible!'

On entering the jubilation zone, the throats of those who a moment before were breathing out cigarette smoke began shouting 'Glory to the GDR, to Communism, to Honecker and the Comrades'. Nobody called out 'Glory to Gorbachev'. Whereas during the reigns of Brezhnev, Andropov and Chernenko the workers carried their pictures above their heads, the tradition of carrying such portraits suddenly disappeared when Gorbachev came to power. In their place they hoisted huge facsimiles of Party membership cards with slogans like 'I'm a Party candidate', 'We're fulfilling the objectives of the XI

Congress of the Communist Party', 'Forever united with the country of Lenin', 'For peace, for socialism', and lots of other catchphrases besides. Those charged with making the banners could freely choose from among the fifty or so slogans published in Neues Deutschland some weeks before the parade. It was forbidden to carry any other slogan. It had been decided that fifty choices were enough for even the most demanding sign writer. In addition to these, there were other banners carried on May Day that would please any censor: red flags and the national flags of any socialist country. With these, they showed their love to those up there on the tribune. Those above reciprocated this emotion to those below their feet. When the parade participants crossed the white line to the left of the tribune, they could be sure they were out of camera range. The jubilation zone was behind them, so the liberated workers tossed their props into the containers placed there for this purpose. The next day they were all to be found at the city dump. For Balaz, one main difference between this Berlin march and the May Day parades he'd known back home was that the mess left over following the parade stayed longer on Bratislava's streets.

Bärbel Hannes worked as a reporter for a weekly about life in socialist countries, 'Freie Welt' (Free World), and her husband Johannes was a violinist in the GDR State Radio Orchestra. They lived with their three-year-old daughter in a draughty two-room flat on Senefelderstrasse, in the Prenzlau quarter. There was no bathroom, a communal toilet, and their windows looked out onto a dark and dusty street. Balaz had met Bärbel after one of the press conferences at the Czechoslovak Culture Centre, on the occasion of the opening of an exhibition of contemporary Czech and Slovak graphic art. Bärbel was a fine art specialist, and Marta Balazova a ceramic artist, so the friendship that arose between the two families was the natural result of their common interests. Alongside his diplomatic duties, Balaz wrote television scripts and took an interest in art in general. Through their acquaintance with the Hannes family, they got to know other painters and artists. At first the meetings between the two couples were a little formal; it was as if they were sounding each other out. When Marta and Jozef were invited to the Hannes's flat for traditional German coffee and cake, the discussion moved from art to politics.

"Look at this," said Bärbel, pulling up Johannes' shirt to reveal a dark blue strip on his back. "He got this at a demonstration where we were chanting in support of Gorbachev and the Soviet Union. Then the police tore up my poster." With a bitter smile, she showed them a piece of white canvas, on which was written: 'Freedom belongs also to those who think differently. Rosa Luxemburg'. "They must be really worried when they won't tolerate people quoting the words of Communist thinkers!" Meanwhile, Martuska was playing peacefully with little Bärbel and Anicka was sleeping.

"Won't you get into trouble for knowing people like us?" Bärbel enquired.

"Why? Are you such anti-state elements?!" Balaz meant the question as a joke.

Without another word, Johannes left the room and came back in a strange grey military uniform. Balaz knew that the regular army uniforms were light green.

"What kind of uniform is that? That's one I haven't seen before... Do you mind if I wear it for a photo?" Johannes took off his grey military coat and hat; Balaz put them on, and a photograph was taken.

Marta looked at her husband uneasily. "What do you want that photo for?"

"Just for a laugh," Balaz replied nonchalantly, handing the tunic back to Johannes. "Where did you get it?"

Johannes lit a cigarette. "I'm a member of the labour militia..."

"What? But that's the punishment brigade!" Balaz wanted to be sure he was hearing properly.

"That's it... they drafted me even though I'd got an exemption. It was taken away when I was suspended from the Orchestra... My fingers are so damaged from working with chemicals, I don't count on playing the violoncello for a few years," Johannes explained with a resigned shrug.

"Why did they draft you?"

"Bärbel and I applied to emigrate from the GDR. She was immediately sacked from her job 'on the basis of a demand from the publishing house workers' collective'.

"So essentially you got it right, we're anti-state elements..." Bärbel added with a sad smile. "That's why I asked if you'd get into trouble for knowing us."

"I don't know, and basically, I don't care," Balaz reassured her.

Anyone who submitted a request to leave the GDR was in fact declaring officially their negative attitude toward the socialist system. The Hannes family was among the 383,000 GDR inhabitants who left or applied to leave. The approval proceedings took anywhere from a few months to a few years, and during this period the state authorities tried to break the applicants so they would withdraw their applications.

"They're back," said Bärbel, pulling the curtain back a bit. Two men were standing across the road, seemingly lost in a lively debate. One of them was carrying a camera, with which he took pictures of the roadway from time to time. "They're pretending to be tourists. They could at least change them from time to time... I guess they're short of manpower..."

"Dirty swine!" Johannes hissed between his teeth.

"And that's why you suggested we come on foot." Balaz nodded his comprehension.

"Right. I didn't want them photographing your famous diplomat's Trabant on the street where the scum of the GDR live," Bärbel explained. Now Balaz went to peek around the curtain at the strange men in the street. He felt sick, and partly because of his own conduct. He served this rotten system from which people were dying to escape, which was encircled by cement walls and barbed wire, where guard towers and border guards stood with their guns pointed at their own people. He realized that even if he excused himself on the grounds that he had never done anything to harm anyone else, he was still part of a system that repressed its own citizens. In his weaker moments he considered leaving diplomacy, returning to Bratislava, and finding some honest job. The next moment, he would cunningly reason that he wasn't doing anything wrong, that he went to vote every five years just like all his fellow citizens, and that if it wasn't him doing this job it would be someone else, someone worse, someone more cowardly. In essence, everyone was serving the regime in their own way. He flattered himself he was acting heroically when he chose the company of people like Bärbel and Johannes. He was simply a citizen of this ridiculous socialist Absurdistan, with its ridiculous pedestrian justifications and excuses.

Since meeting Bärbel and Johannes Hannes, the Balazes had met their friends, and gradually become friends with them too. For the most part, these were artistic types whom Marta made contact with first. She would go to their studios to bake her clay statues. Again, Balaz felt a certain wariness on the part of their new friends. He and Marta understood this as their suspicion that all diplomats were spies working hand-in-glove with the secret police. And essentially these people of the GDR were right: every diplomat is more or less a spy. His task is to provide institutions in other countries with information about his own country, and the reverse, to inform his own country about the country where he is serving. In the era of real socialism, being an East Bloc diplomat/spy in a so-called non-socialist country meant sense. But the German Democratic Republic was a socialist ally, and it would be nonsense to engage in espionage in a country where the highest Party and Government figures traded information which their diplomats had no way of knowing. This was especially true of countries whose secret services cooperated intensively with one another. To an extent, their new German friends were aware of this, but nonetheless Balaz had the feeling their trust didn't go all the way.

One day, Bärbel asked him to take some post to West Berlin and to mail it to an address in the Federal Republic of Germany. Balaz had a special pass which allowed him to visit West Berlin once a month. As a diplomat, he was exempt from searches at the border crossing, except in cases where the East German border police had direct information regarding a specific person. When Bärbel came to him with her request, Balaz reacted with hesitation. Bärbel noticed it: "Do you think I'm testing you?" she asked with a smile.

"Sorry, I know it's stupid, but if they were to catch me at the border, the best I could hope for would be sent back home as a worker – and that's the best scenario."

"Don't worry, I'm not a Stasi agent."

Balaz took the package, but thought it wiser to say nothing about it to his wife. On the border separating the Soviet and American zones – Checkpoint Charlie – he could feel a slight knot in his stomach. When he'd cleared the border, his first stop was a post office near Kurfürstendamm. To be on the safe side, he parked the 'diplomat's Trabant' with its GDR plates around the corner. Looking around nervously to check he wasn't being observed, he screwed up his courage and took two packets from his trunk, then entered the post office. He had the feeling that every person standing in the line was either a member of the East German Stasi or the Czechoslovak StB. He felt a little better as he left the post office, but his stomach was still aching. It was only two weeks later, when Bärbel told him the packages had arrived safely, that he completely regained his composure. From then on, he regularly carried mail for his East German friends – but he never lost that queasy feeling. It was years after the fall of the Berlin Wall that it finally went away.

The Balazes first met the Western German journalist Peter Greiner at the Hannes' flat. He was a kind, friendly and communicative person. Despite the fact that Eastern diplomats had been schooled that every Western journalist was probably working for his country's secret service, Balaz was not afraid to speak openly with Greiner. He had the feeling that he could trust him, and he sensed the same trust from Greiner. Although Balaz knew of the regulation compelling him to report any encounter with a Western diplomat or reporter, he never mentioned Greiner's name. He firmly believed that Greiner was on the level – if this wasn't the case, the StB would very quickly learn of their friendship. Although they continued to meet until Balaz's return to Slovakia, nothing happened in all that time.

At the end of the summer of 1987, the Balazes, together with their close and trusted friends took a Sunday outing to the woods near Müggelheim lake. They were all close friends, and trusted each other explicitly. With their whole families, they visited each other's' homes, celebrated birthdays, Christmas, and other holidays together, or just met to discuss and to cheer each other up. Friendship based on mutual trust was perhaps the most important part of the lives of these diplomats. Living for five years in an atmosphere of mistrust and hypocrisy could surely be endured, but it took its toll in terms of psychic strength. Over wine and with the record player turned right up in case the flat was bugged, they passionately debated the flow of events not just in the GDR but also at home and in the Soviet Union.

It was a beautiful summer's day. They spread blankets on the grass and unpacked their food baskets. Picnics were very popular with Berliners, whether at their cottages or right out in the meadows.

A week later, the baby, Anicka, developed a cough accompanied by a fever. At first, Marta tried to cure her using classic anti-flu methods. But after almost two weeks, a kind of apathy added itself to the fever. Anicka's neck became stiff, and even though she was eating next to nothing, she would regularly throw it back up. Her parents were seriously scared.

"Have you recently been out with your children somewhere in the countryside, some place with lots of trees?" asked the physician in the diplomatic section of the Charité hospital. When they nodded, the doctor informed them that Anicka had in all likelihood been infected by a tick bite. "We've given her a serological test which shows that she has a virus in her blood. In most cases, this is an infection which passes without danger. Unfortunately, it seems that your daughter belongs to the ten percent where chronic manifestations may be expected. They may take the form of epileptic attacks, Parkinson's syndrome or, in the worst case, paralysis. Children have the most dismal prognosis," the doctor informed the shocked parents.

"What can we do about it?"

"Well, that's the problem. To date, there are no medicines effective against this illness..."

"What does that mean?"

"It means that we can only prescribe classic medicaments from the class of penicillin, but the effects are not very strong... practically zero," the doctor confessed with a frown.

"I don't understand. How can there be no medicines?" Mrs. Balazova's voice was trembling.

"My dear lady, I'm so sorry... medical science can do many things, pharmaceutical development is moving forwards, but still there are still some illnesses for which cures simply do not exist."

"What does it mean, doctor?"

The doctor was deep in thought. "Are you religious?" They didn't answer. "Pray for a miracle..." was all he could find to say.

"This isn't possible, there must be something that can be done. A month ago she was a healthy child, doctor... Martha's voice failed her. She looked down at her daughter lying on the cot, her hands and feet covered in ugly brown spots.

"There might be one... theoretical possibility. We've been hearing about a medicine they've been working on in the United States. It belongs to the class of ceftriaxone and cefotaxmes. They are injected drugs, but, as I say, they're still in the stage of clinical tests." The physician handed them a tag of paper with the word Lendacin written on it. "That's what they're calling this new American vaccine. Your daughter would need at least twenty twenty-five gram ampoules. I have to tell you frankly that I've no idea how you could obtain it... Try for that miracle... But you don't have a lot of time..."

"How much time?"

"A week at the outside."

"Today is Sunday. So by next Monday?"

"Let's hope so." The doctor's tone was apologetic.

Balaz contacted everyone he could think of, both in Berlin and in Prague. The politicians, doctors, diplomats and journalists all gave him the same answer, however. Since the vaccine was still being tested, getting it here from America in three or four days was practically impossible. Even though many of his acquaintances promised to try their hardest, Balaz felt they were just humouring him. Anicka's state was steadily deteriorating – she could no longer move her head or her left arm. She seemed to have great trouble reacting to her parents. Marta, Martuska and Jozef prayed together at home.

As he was leaving work on Friday, the phone in his office rang. The porter informed him that someone was waiting for him downstairs. When he reached the porter's desk, Balaz recognized Peter Greiner. They went to sit in a funny circular meeting-room, where Greiner handed him two little boxes. Each contained twenty-five Lendacin ampoules.

"Here are the instructions on how to use it. The doctors here have no experience with it."

"Peter... How can I ever thank you enough?"

"Don't worry about that. My reward will be seeing your baby get well. Don't waste any time; get right over to the hospital! And who knows, maybe I'll need your help one day..."

Balaz, choked with emotion, pulled Greiner to his chest. "If there's ever anything I can do for you, you can count on me." Later that same time, the doctors gave Anicka the new medicine. Her condition improved dramatically over the next few days. The illness finally retreated, and in a month she was out of hospital.

Greiner had no idea how soon he would need Balaz's help.

CHAPTER
TWENTY

BERLIN 1987

PETER Greiner sat with Thomas in his favourite pub, 'Schupke', just a few steps from his flat on Triftstrasse. They were waiting for Heike, Thomas' girlfriend, whom he had met six months earlier. The year before, she had been living in East Berlin with her partner, Günter, and their two-year-old son, Peter. Günter Lorenz was an assistant registrar in the internal medicine department of the University hospital, Charité. He was an outstanding specialist on heart diseases, someone for whom every country in Europe envied the GDR. He wasn't a Party member, and therefore had to put up with the orders and instructions of the dilettantes who, thanks to their political connections, enjoyed higher positions than his.

Heike Klinsmann was employed as a primary school teacher. The children adored her because she had a different style of teaching from their other teachers. It wasn't in fact that she was 'different', she was simply more normal. Instead of rote memorization and the hammering of ideological nonsense into their heads, she tried to teach them things that would be of actual use in their lives. All the nonstop commands, instructions, meetings, forms and supervision finally got on her nerves; she had already been reprimanded a few times by her principal, but Heike had a mind of her own. The cup of patience ran over, however, when she ignored a daily ritual. Every morning, the class chairman had to give a report on the number of students present, absent, excused or truant, and this ended with the chairman saluting and reciting: 'The class is prepared for education'. Heike cancelled this exercise, and moreover told the children they needn't wear their Pioneer scout kerchiefs. While wearing the kerchiefs wasn't mandatory in the GDR, the principal had visions of being appointed to a position of inspector of schools which was coming vacant at the school board and didn't want to upset his superiors. In April, 1986 the head called Comrade Klinsmann in and told her to reinstate the practice of wearing the uniform scarves in her classroom. Klinsmann made reference to a speech Gorbachev gave to teachers in which he had recommended making the wearing of Scout kerchiefs voluntary. Her mention of Gorbachev drove the ultra-conservative principal to distraction. He advised Klinsmann to hand in her resignation; otherwise he would be forced to find some reason to fire her. Klinsmann had had enough.

Just at that same time Lorenz was also becoming fed up with the same treatment. That evening, they talked about a plan they had been hatching for some time: to apply for emigration. The idea was met enthusiastically by Heike, but Lorenz felt saddened. He still believed that after the new Soviet leadership came to power, things would get better in the GDR. For example, in the Soviet Union democratic voting was taking place in factories to choose head workers, and as a result non-Party members were being chosen for managing roles. They both agreed that Heike would leave her job immediately and they would file an emigration request at the internal affairs department of the Pankow quarter where they lived. To their great surprise, just before Christmas Heike was summoned to the Pankow Town Hall, where she was informed that in January, 1987, she would be allowed to leave. But for the moment the authorization applied only to her; the requests for her partner and their son would be considered only in February.

That Christmas was perhaps the most difficult one in Heike's life. The dilemma over choosing freedom or remaining with her son was almost unbearable. To make things worse, the Town Hall in its decision stated that if she did not accept this offer, no future emigration application would be entertained. It also stated that the application concerning her partner, Günter Lorenz, and their son, Peter, would be dealt with summarily and in conformity with a resolution accepted at the Security and Cooperation Conference in Helsinki and with an international treaty between West and East Germany. At the same time, however, she had to sign an affidavit that she gave her consent to the child remaining in the custody of Günter Lorenz, in the case of unforeseen complications. Trusting Günter implicitly, Heike signed the declaration. It was commonly known that the West German government had already 'bought' tens of thousands of would-be emigrants from the East Germans; moreover, they were both highly-qualified professionals. They assumed that the HUBACEK would value the services of a top neurologist. When Heike's mother agreed to move to East Berlin to help look after the child, the decision was cemented: Heike kissed Günter and little Peter goodbye, and left to join a friend in West Berlin. The plan was for her to live there with her until Günter and Peter could join her, and then they would continue on to Munich, where she had relatives.

At the start, she and Günter spoke on the phone every day. The question of whether anything had changed in their application process became ever more pressing for Heike, but Günter had received no news. More than that, she was starting to get a bad feeling that something about Günter had changed. Missing from his voice was that hankering for Heike; he sometimes didn't even bother to put Peter on the phone. Their calls became less frequent. Just at that time, Günter was appointed head consultant at the hospital and also Dean of the Medical Faculty at Humboldt University. This marked the first time that a non-Party member had ever held that position. He was also given a three-room flat, his salary was increased, and he was authorized to attend conferences abroad.

In autumn, 1987, he confessed to Heike that he had withdrawn his emigration application. At the thought of her separated child being looked after by her sickly mother and a man who obviously had no interest in her, she broke out in a cold sweat.

To make things worse, Lorenz declared that he was more capable of taking care of Peter in East Germany than she was in her unstable situation in the West, and therefore he was no longer prepared to consent to the child's joining his mother. Heike's world collapsed around her.

Even though she was only twenty-five, she looked older; her face was ashen, her hands shook, and she had begun to smoke. Pain and worry were legible on her aristocratic-looking features. The year away from her son was causing her serious health problems. In his desire to help her, Thomas turned to his former political contacts, but it was an almost hopeless case. After a six-month acquaintance, Thomas and Heike got married; he reasoned that if Peter was his step-son, it could make the case for immigration stronger. And above all, he and Heike truly loved each other.

But after this brief period of hope and happiness, Heike's depressions became more frequent. To combat her weeping fits, she took sedatives, and then a heart murmur was detected. It seemed the only times she was cheerful was when Peter Greiner came back from East Berlin with photos of her son taken by Heike's mother and the latest news. Peter was now living with his grandmother; from time to time Lorenz would drop by and bring Peter sweets from his travels abroad. This seemed to be the beginning and the end of his child rearing. Her mother admitted that she didn't feel strong enough to keep up with a lively child, and hoped Heike could find a way to get her son to the HUBACEK.

Greiner had enough experience with the East German authorities to realize that dealing with them was fruitless at best. When Thomas and Peter could no longer bear to see Heike's suffering, they decided the time had come to search out an illegal method of getting Peter out. Immediately, they both fixed on a diplomat's car, not liable to search by the GDR border guards, as the most secure route across the border. The problem was to find a diplomat willing to get involved in smuggling the boy over the border. Greiner had heard that they were installing X-ray machines at Checkpoint Charlie which were capable of detecting body heat. Once these devices were in operation, the possibility of using this method would be ruled out. They had to act fast! In his mind Greiner ran through all the diplomatic staff he knew in East Berlin, but didn't find one he dared approach with such a request. In the end, witnessing Heike's desperation decided the issue: he would turn to the only one who might be willing to help them: Jozef Balaz. After all, Greiner had almost literally saved the life of Balaz's daughter. Jozef would perhaps understand his friend's plea.

CHAPTER
TWENTYONE

BERLIN 1987

IN April, Michail Gorbachev made a visit to the GDR. Two days after he left, Balaz met with the Soviet press and culture councilor, Olutshkin, who was an ardent Gorbachev supporter. Balaz wrote a cipher for his superiors repeating what Olutshkin had told him: "At a meeting with chosen Soviet diplomats, Gorbachev stated that he had a strong feeling Erich Honecker had not correctly interpreted their past discussions to his political bureau. In consequence, Gorbachev requested that Honecker allow him the opportunity to meet with the entire politburo. At the meeting with this political elite, Gorbachev challenged them to an open discussion. In particular, he was addressing the younger members – Krenz, Schabowsky and Böhm. However, not one of the twenty politburo members and candidates present said one single word, leaving it to Honecker alone to do the talking with Gorbachev." Olutshkin also told Balaz that Gorbachev had complained to the Soviet diplomats: "What can we do? It's like hitting your head against a brick wall. The hardliners are in Berlin and Prague. It looks like we're going to have to give them a little help." When the Ambassador read Balaz's transcription, he asked: "Did Gorbachev really say this part about Prague and help?" Balaz just smiled.

"That's all right, then," Ambassador Roucek said, signing the cipher. Perhaps his equanimity was due to the fact that the Ambassador was already packing for his retirement, or maybe it was just because he was a normal person. Balaz was sad that this outstanding diplomat was finishing his term at the Embassy. One of his possible successors was the man who was Balaz's worst nightmare.

Balaz had long since shifted his desk so that he wouldn't have to constantly look at the Berlin Wall, but he turned it back after his visit to the 'War Museum', situated right next to the Checkpoint Charlie border point. Although he had been in West Berlin many times, he had never yet visited the museum. The Embassy corridors were full of 'authentic reports' that Czechoslovak diplomats were regularly followed during their visits to the West, either by secret service agents from the Embassy or by the CSSR military mission in West Berlin. Although nobody could guarantee the truth of such reports, nobody could prove that they were just rumours either. The staff was of the opinion that someone was spreading the reports for the purpose of making people afraid.

Perhaps inspired by Gorbachev's visit, Balaz overcame his fear and went to the museum. What he saw there was worse than his most horrible imaginings. The Berlin Wall, the most loathsome construction in the world – a three-metre high double wall with a rounded top that prevented hands or ladders gaining purchase there. Between the two lines of wall there were security facilities, guard towers, shooting embrasures, electrified barbed wire, guide wires for the watchdogs, and night-lights. The museum showed photographs of people shot while trying to escape from East Berlin and the symbolic graves of those shot dead on the Wall.

After his visit to the museum, something in Balaz changed. The thought that he had a hand in this machine of repression shamed him, while at the same time he was aware of being one of millions of prisoners of a social system hemmed in by barbed wire. He felt like apologizing to his East German friends for his having the luxury of a monthly visit to West Berlin, something they quite simply could not have. His only defence was that some of his colleagues were working full-time in Western embassies while he'd been relegated to serving in the GDR. Also, they had learned to keep their thoughts to themselves and their mouths shut; he at least was commenting, criticizing and agitating whenever he safely could. Within the circle of his trusted friends, Czechoslovak leaders like Husak, Bilak and Jakes were routinely pilloried and political jokes were exchanged, but essentially they dared go no further.

During his summer vacation, the family went back to Slovakia to spend time with their parents at the cottage in Vrbove. Marta was probably cooking in the kitchen since the air was full of tantalizing aromas. Balaz was sitting near the well peeling potatoes which were destined for potato pancakes for friends coming up from Bratislava for the weekend. The peelings fell in a monotonous rhythm onto the culture page of yesterday's Praca, the trade union newspaper. The time was passing slowly, so for something to do he glanced at the stories in the soggy paper. One report mentioned that a Slovak film, 'The Beginning of the Season' had won second prize at a film festival in Portugal. 'That's funny,' he thought to himself, 'that's almost the same title as the screenplay I wrote...' But when he read on and discovered that the award for lead actor was won by Karol L. Zachar, he started to get suspicious. Karol L. Zachar played the lead in his film, 'The End of the Season'. So he went over to the neighbours' to use their phone and called the film's dramaturge, Olga Feldekova. "It's stupid, I know," she explained, "the government censors thought the original title was too pessimistic. We had the choice of either changing the title or pulling the film from distribution. I hope you're not upset... And we also had to change the backdrop in the scene in the old people's bedroom. We had a picture of Jesus and Mary above their bed, but we had to reshoot it with a bouquet of flowers instead. Apart from that, it's all according to your screenplay. So, congratulations!"

Back at the Embassy, the staff was taking bets on who would be the new ambassador after Roucek. Numerous names were put forward, but as the time for the new appointment approached, one name was mentioned most frequently. On hearing that name, the hairs on Balaz's neck rose. He prayed that an act of God or of the Communist Party Central Committee would stop this man from becoming his new chief. A bad omen came in March – Paukovchin, a man Balaz knew to be the right hand of his old enemy, was named second secretary at the Embassy. He started to think about what he would do if his worst fears were realized.

His worst fears were confirmed when Ambassador Roucek called a working meeting to announce that the East German government had given its approval to a new Czechoslovak ambassador. Ambassador Jan Winter would take office effective from the following Monday.

CHAPTER TWENTYTWO

MOSCOW 1988

SERGEJ Gusev and Sasha enjoyed each of their meetings as if it was their first date. More and more often he stayed over at her flat. Her son Josif was living at the dormitory belonging to the Soviet Wings army club. Since Sergej was a keen hockey fan, the two quickly found a basis for their relationship. He had spent much of his life in the military, and it was only with Sasha that he realized that time was passing and so, along with divisions, rockets and flotillas, he also developed an interest in a woman. He was surprisingly shy in his relations with Sasha, and for her part she found this an attractive trait. At thirty-eight, Gusev was one of the youngest Major Generals in the Soviet army, and he was ready for love. Sasha always tried to steer the conversation away from politics and towards their private life. One day, he showed up with a bouquet of gerberas for her, which was in effect a double surprise for this flower was hard to find in Moscow. "A Georgian guy gave them to me," he explained with his shy smile.

"They must have cost everything you had!"

"So allow me to ask for your hand with everything I have."

It was a private wedding, with Nina and Sergej's superior officer, Piotr Ivashutin, as witnesses. After the wedding, he left the army barracks and moved in with Sasha for good. They got on well together, and for the first time in a long while Sasha was happy, although she wondered sometimes if it was love or the need to have someone beside her that drew them together. Two months into their marriage, Sasha informed her new husband that she was expecting. When their daughter, Ninocka, was born in July, 1988, Sergej was beside himself with joy.

Every day, the Soviet people learned more and more about the catastrophic situation their country was in. Sergej in particular flew into a fury when he read in the uncensored press about the latest secrets that were being made public. It seemed - even after everything - that thieving, fraud and shoddiness remained a normal part of life in the Soviet Union.

One day, Sasha started to laugh, showing Sergej the August edition of the union newspaper, Trud.

"So now you've started writing for the newspapers..." Sergej looked at her, surprised. "A certain Sergej Gusev is writing here about some man called Astachov, the economics director of a fish-processing plant on the Caspian Sea, in whose luxurious house five cars, gold bars worth 54,000 rubles, other valuables valued at 39,000 rubles and a bankbook with 310,000 rubles in it were found." Sasha put down the paper and commented: "And I have three hundred rubles a month at my job" Sergej was still waiting for more. "This was written by Sergej Gusev, the first deputy chairman of the Supreme Court. Another article talks about Brezhnev's son-in-law Tshurbanov being sentenced to twelve years in a work camp for fraud and corruption, and Brezhnev's secretary Brovin to nine years for corruption."

Like everyone else in the Soviet Union, Sasha and Sergej were shocked by the scale of the corruption. Such articles appeared almost daily in Trud, among the first unremittingly critical stories to be written after the end of censorship in the Soviet Union's newspapers. "I can't read any more of this!" Sasha said, disgusted, and handed the paper to her husband, who continued to read: 'Under General Secretary Brezhnev, positions in the Party hierarchy at almost all levels were for sale. A nomination as regional secretary cost

150,000 dollars (such elevated categories were available only for American currency), while the highest state decoration, the Lenin Prize, was available at the price of 750,000 dollars. The investigator Telman Gljan took the complete Central Committee of the Uzbekistan Communist Party to court. Buchara, Uzbekistan was known as the place where pure gold busts of Brezhnev were made.'

Sergej put down the paper and poured himself a glass of mineral water to combat his dry mouth. His blood was boiling, and if at that moment he had before him someone from the Party hierarchy, he would gladly have killed him. Sasha couldn't stop herself from reading on: "In the Soviet Union, the grain crop reportedly fell year after year. This, however, was far from the whole story. Grain often grew in record quantities, but no-one harvested it. While, according to statistics, Soviet agriculturalists had six to seven times more tractors than American farmers, sixteen times more combine harvesters. The problem was, out of one hundred machines, only between six and ten worked. In fact, the majority of them were non-operational even when they left the factory, and the others were either stripped for spare parts or directly for scrap'. This last caused Gusev to breathe deeply. "And now for the best!" 'The most shocking discovery for investigators was the simple people, who saw everything and knew everything. In one cooperative farm in Uzbekistan, where they had come to seize stolen property, wages hadn't been paid for six months. Still, nobody was complaining; on the contrary, many of them defended the very people who were blatantly impoverishing them.'"

Sasha finished her reading, and they sat in a stunned silence. "These are our people. This is our degraded and defeated character, whether we are Russians, Ukrainians, Uzbeks or Kazakhs, and it's been that way for a thousand years. They push our faces into the manure, and we pretend everything's okay; even when we can't breathe, we kiss our overlords' hand. To hell with it... Nothing's going to change here until we change our slavish nature.... I'm afraid it'll be too much even for Gorbachev."

Josif was losing his love for hockey. He started missing practices, and Sasha noticed a glow in his eyes – the glow that Soviet mothers and wives feared the most, the glow of alcoholic eyes. Josif had had an unhappy affair with a teammate's sister, and since she'd left him he'd been drowning his sorrows in vodka. His coach had at first coaxed him, then threatened him, and finally begged him to give it up, but nothing worked. He was dropped from the first team and, shortly after, from the juniors.

In early August 1987, Josif got his draft orders – reporting time and place: September 1, Camp 99, Engineering Regiment, Chernyhiv, north Ukraine. Chernyhiv was the capital of a region eighty kilometers distant from Chernobyl, a place anyone who could, fled from. Desperately, Sasha searched out all the information she could find about the catastrophe and its consequences. The Soviet media offered precious little, and even if they had written about it, nobody would have believed it. The Voice of America reported that a restricted zone had been set up in a radius of thirty kilometers around Chernobyl, that over 300,000 people had been evacuated, with many more awaiting relocation, and that the radioactive emission levels in the area were ten times the permitted dose. Experts were forecasting from forty to sixty thousand deaths in the coming two years around Chernobyl, and the surrounding areas. The land in these zones was contaminated with radioactive cesium Cs-137, with a half-life of thirty years. In other words, the contamination would drop to an acceptable level in three hundred years. Sasha's heart skipped a beat when she learned these facts.

Josif left home on the last day of August, coming to Chernyhiv as a sergeant thanks to his training in the army hockey club. He quickly proved himself a dedicated soldier, and the sight of the thousands of destitute people around him, deprived of their fields, farms, and the very roof over their heads, touched him deeply. In his naiveté, and under the influence of his political instructors, he believed that the sooner they could diminish the radioactive leaks from the reactor, the sooner these people could return to their homes. He quit drinking and, with the fanaticism of one who has been disappointed in love and sees no point in going on, threw himself towards the desolation the nuclear accident left behind. He volunteered to go into the most highly contaminated parts of the damaged reactor to pour tons of cement and iron into the almost infinite number of cracks out of which the radiation was leaking. After two months of this, he began to experience slight nausea. He got over it quite quickly since the body of a seasoned athlete seemingly resists radiation more readily than that of an ordinary person. He was awarded a medal for his bravery, promoted to second lieutenant, and reassigned to the outer part of the restriction zone.

"Our job is to deactivate the radiation in the contaminated area around Chernobyl and the dead city of Pripjať, which used to be a thriving city of fifty thousand. We bring in soil from the outlying contaminated area into the restricted zone. I spent a total of three months in the dead zone. Sometimes I suffered from nausea and felt really tired, but now I'm feeling a lot better. Our assignment is to shift four million cubic metres of contaminated earth and other waste into the eight hundred stores in the restricted zone. We hear it's dangerous here, and that our comrades are developing cancers and other illnesses. I don't believe this is true, because they look after us really well, the food is outstanding, and our accommodation is comfortable. I love you, mum. Your Osja."

His mother read his letter, and knew where the land lay. She knew her son. Osja always made light of problems, shrugged off hockey injuries, and overcame difficulties thanks to his strong will and self-discipline. Meanwhile, Voice of America was reporting that anyone exposed to increased dosages of this contamination would in the best of cases be subject to chronic effects throughout his entire life; in the worst case, he would soon die from a variety of tumorous illnesses. In explosions like the one at Chernobyl, an immense number of such cases were bound to appear. Sasha lost her head and screamed out loud: "I'll get you out of there! Even if they kill me, I'll get you out!" After her first husband, she couldn't bear to see her son too throw away his life for his ungrateful country. "You won't die there, my darling Osja, I'll get you out!!!"

Sergej felt that should such a fate befall Josif, his new wife would just wither away. As a Major General in the Soviet military intelligence, he knew what the true situation in Chernobyl was like. He was determined to do everything in his power to avoid this tragedy.

Of late, Josif was writing less frequently, and Sasha sensed that something bad was going on. She began to pray for him several times a day, and went to light candles in church and to ask God to spare her son. In late November, Gusev came home with joyous news: Josif was being transferred back to Military Intelligence in Moscow, effective immediately. Sasha was so relieved she couldn't sleep for the next few nights – her husband was bringing her son back home! Josif was sent on a special training course and housed directly at the GRU Academy. In comparison with the other students, he had the advantage of speaking German fluently. When the course was completed, there was news Sasha couldn't even have dreamed of.

Josif and Sergej came home in a good mood, and they invited her to sit down in the living room and to prepare herself to listen to their news. Josif announced that he was being promoted to the rank of lieutenant and assigned to Berlin as secretary to the Soviet Union military attaché in the German Democratic Republic. It was at that moment that Sasha began to believe in miracles. Snatched from a place where death was his likely fate, he was now on his way to East Berlin, the dream of every Soviet soldier. She smiled as she recalled encouraging Osja to learn German because it could come in handy one day. That day had come, and how!

At the East Berlin Soviet Embassy on Unter den Linden, Josif reported to Gusev's old army buddy, Colonel Vasilij Nikolajevich Tarkovsky.

CHAPTER
TWENTYTHREE

PRAGUE/BERLIN

THE head of the international section of the Czechoslovak Communist Party, a man from East Slovakia called Stofaník, expressed his surprise at Winter's decision to accept the East Berlin posting: "You're one of our most promising diplomats, someone right out of the Party apparatus. You already know there's nothing to stop you from getting to the top of the ladder. Chnoupek is coming to the end of his term, and we need you as the future Minister of Foreign Affairs. You have what it takes to show those Czechs and those spoiled brats from Bratislava where they get off. Of course, I'm not talking about your friend, Jan Husak... He's a special case, it goes without saying." This last part Stofaník added hastily, remembering that Winter was under the wing of the President's son. "From a political viewpoint, the position of Ambassador to West Germany is a key posting, not to mention the financial rewards are naturally higher in Bonn than in East Berlin. I simply cannot understand why you don't want to go there."

"I understand what you're saying, Comrade Director, but I think I still have time for the posting as Ambassador to West Germany. I think we should leave it to Comrade Hlavác. He's a seasoned professional, speaks good German, and he's one of us. He grew up in the east, in Krajna Poľana, a village near Krajna Bystra, where Comrade Secretary Bilak hails from. He has his complete trust. And also, I feel there is still work to be done in East Berlin. Our comrades in the GDR are having a tough time of it, as we are here. Moscow keeps pushing us towards greater transparency – glasnost, as they like to call it." Winter was at his most persuasive.

"Gorbachev's experiments won't turn out well. He doesn't understand that by loosening the reins on the media, he'll pull the whole structure down. What Bilak said at the meeting of the Czechoslovak Communist Party ideological commission was on the mark. We simply cannot automatically accept everything that is going on in the Soviet Union; each country has its own specific character."

"But all the same, we've always insisted that the Soviet Union is our model," argued Winter. Stofaník was surprised by Winter's open support for Gorbachev and his ideas; until now he had never voiced such sentiments. What Stofaník didn't know however was that Winter was connected to some key people in Moscow, and that one of their aims was to strengthen the pro-Gorbachev line in the Prague C.P. leadership.

"Don't make me angry. Of course Moscow is the model, but not in everything... certainly not when it means the destruction of socialism! You yourself know some people who want to have the Normalization Code rescinded. If our comrades in Moscow believe their reforms will strengthen socialism, that's their affair. Personally, I doubt it, but I'm not going to tell them that to their faces. You heard how Secretary Hager put it – just because your neighbour's painting his flat, that doesn't mean you have to paint yours. The main problem is that people still haven't grasped the true idea of socialism, haven't identified themselves with it. This is our main task: not to change socialism, not even to reform it, but to convince the people that it's the correct path."

Winter was beginning to feel sorry for Stofaník, for he knew that the man belonged to a dying breed. What he couldn't make up his mind about was whether Stofaník was serious about his relationship to socialism, if he was worried about losing his job, or if he was a complete idiot.

"Okay, if you're determined to go to Berlin, I guess you know why." The look he gave Winter revealed that he wasn't buying his reasons for turning down a lucrative posting to the West and preferring to work in East Berlin. "The Soviet Counsellor was in to see me, and he's enthusiastic about your appointment there. I can only wish you all the best there. Who knows, maybe you won't be there long before we call you back home here. I have the feeling we'll soon have to make some sharp personnel changes in the government." Stofaník gave Winter his hand and, for good measure, a paternal slap on the back.

CHAPTER
TWENTYFOUR

PRAGUE 1987

WINTER made friends with the Deputy Ambassador at the Soviet Union Embassy, Andrej Kirovkin, who had been sent to Czechoslovakia just a few months ago. In diplomatic circles, he was regarded as one of Gorbachev's men, and was also a personal friend of the Foreign Minister, Eduard Shevardnadze. Kirovkin had been informed that Winter often met with Jan Husak, and quickly came to understand the way the wind was blowing in the upper echelons. Kirovkin sought Winter out not only due to his opinions, but also so as to get from him valuable information on the situation among the leaders of the Communist Party, which was not at all sympathetic to Gorbachev's perestroika. He was astonishingly open to Winter, letting him know in no uncertain terms about Moscow's unhappiness with the trends developing in Czechoslovakia, the German Democratic Republic and Romania.

Winter was sitting in the Malostranska beseda restaurant in Prague, reading in Rude pravo that the Communist Party leadership had confirmed the validity of the so-called 'Lessons from the 1968 Crisis', and thus refused to re-evaluate the changes made in the 'normalization' period following the 1968 occupation of Czechoslovakia.

"What are you reading?" asked Kirovkin, whose arrival Winter had failed to notice.

"That our supreme comrades are painting us farther into a corner," he frowned as he folded up the paper.

"What do you think of Dubcek's letter?" asked Kirovkin with an assessing glance.

"What letter is that?" Winter replied.

"Dubcek wrote to the Party hierarchy and called for the democratization of Czechoslovak society, following the example of the USSR." Kirovkin placed a document on the table. "We received a copy at the Embassy."

"There's been no mention of such a letter in the local media..." Winter said disgustedly. The waiter brought two fresh beers and they toasted each other, then he continued: "Bilak is branding everyone who supports the reform of socialism a right-wing opportunist. His closest friends are Honecker and his supporters."

"Jan, what do you expect? We too would like to see changes both here and in the GDR, but we're not going to do it for you," Kirovkin gave Winter a long look, then completed his thought. "Mind you, we can help you a little bit on the way... especially if we have the help of people like you." This time it was the Russian who ordered the next round. "We're working on new ideas for global and European security. The balance between the power blocks has seen its day, the Brezhnev doctrine is dead; the unification of the two Germanys is the final step in the ongoing transformation of the continent's political climate." He registered Winter's surprised look and continued: "Of course I don't have to tell you the United States will try to take advantages of the changes we're putting in place. Europe will have to be strong, and the way for that to happen is a Berlin – Moscow axis, with the support of the French. The stronger this axis, the weaker the Washington – London alliance will be. So, naturally, for this model to work we need a unified Germany. For that to come about, we need deep-rooted change in East Germany, where things are not progressing as we had hoped. We'd definitely welcome your help!"

"How could I help you?"

"You're an outstanding diplomat, and your German is first rate. As you said, the biggest thorn in our side is the GDR. We can manage things in Prague... but Berlin is a tough nut to crack... And that's where you come in..."

"But I'm going... I'm supposed to be going to Bonn."

"You're supposed to be, but that doesn't mean you have to go. You could ask for East Berlin. Honecker has the firmest and most trusted relations with Prague and Bucharest. Since you're from east Slovakia, we can create the legend that you stand behind Bilak. This way they'll accept you more readily, and so put more trust in you. You know Stofanik believes in you, and he's Bilak's right-hand man."

"I still don't see what you're getting at..."

"So let me put it to you this way..." Looking around, Kirovkin placed on the table some kind of card with the Soviet Union emblem on it. Winter read the words slowly and solemnly: "Glavnoje razveditelnoje upravlenie..." Taking a gulp of beer to clear his mind, he put the card back on the table.

"GRU. The military intelligence..."

"Yes, military intelligence. After all, you are a 'Coat'.

Winter just looked at him, awaiting more. "Well, let's say a cooperator..."

Kirovkin watched a frown spread over Winter's brow. The latter was recalling his study times in Moscow where, along with his courses at the Institute of Political Science, he had taken a two-year special course in military intelligence. During his time at the university, he had been recruited by the largest Soviet secret service, boasting six times more agents than the KGB. They had sent him to the 'Conservatory', the pet name for the GRU Military-Diplomatic Academy. Its graduates worked as diplomats at Soviet Union representation offices abroad, or, as in his case, at the embassies of other socialist countries. It was said of the GRU that 'you got in for one ruble, but got out for two' – in other words, it was practically impossible to ever stop working for them. The GRU motto in fact was 'total secrecy'; anyone who opened their mouth at the wrong time could count on having their tongue cut off – in extreme cases, along with their entire head. The huge military intelligence headquarters stood on Choroshevsky Boulevard in Moscow behind a wall so high and long that it was almost impossible to see over it. Behind this wall was the legendary 'Aquarium', the main command centre for Soviet military intelligence. The complex also housed the construction centres for the Iljushin, Mikojan Gurevich (MiG), Suchoj and Jakovlev aircraft, the MAPO bombers, the rocket manufacturing factory, the Cosmic Biology Institute and the Military Aircraft Academy. The highest point of the complex was a large glassy nine-storey building called the 'K 200 Object'. Winter had never been inside it, for the Conservatory was situated in the facility closest to the 'October Fields' metro station. Its graduates were referred to as 'Coats' and were placed in representation offices abroad.

"Jan, I understand that what I'm asking has taken you aback, but... I believe your mission would be completely in line with your conscience. I am sure that socialist democratization and reform are close to your heart. And do you honestly think that those old men in Berlin and Prague are about to leave under their own steam? You wanted to know how Gorbachev could help you, and now you have your chance to help Gorbachev spread his ideas. Who better than you! Can we count on your help in East Germany?" Kirovkin gave Winter a conspiratorial look and added: "If things change in Berlin, they'll change in Prague, too." He held out his huge palm and, with a smile, Winter took it. Then they ordered another round of beer.

On his way back home, Winter considered how to logically explain to his wife that they'd be going to Berlin, and not to Bonn. He himself felt a certain personal disappointment, but when he realized he'd have Balaz under his control, he began to smile. This started him thinking about the old days in Moscow. He remembered one time at Sheremetevo airport when his flight was delayed and he'd found himself sitting next to a man of about forty with three empty shot glasses lined up in front of him. He turned out to be from Bratislava.

"I'm Horvath, Pavol Horvath," he introduced himself.

"Winter. Jan." And they began to chat, just to pass the time until their plane was ready for takeoff. It had been announced that the delay would last another two hours – in the Soviet Union, that meant five hours at least. Now, five hours is adequate time for two Slovak graduates of Moscow schools to become well-acquainted, and more than a little drunk. With the increasing number of vodkas inside him, Horvath became more and more talkative and less and less discreet. When Horvath began to suspect that he worked for the Soviet secret service, Winter simply smiled and said nothing.

"To hell with it... All of us studying in Russia are agent of one service or another, whether it's civil or military." Horvath followed up his words with another shot.

"So what do you do here?"

"I come here to embarrass myself... hik," said Horvath, nodding his head as if in agreement with himself. Winter waited for him to go on. "To shame myself before myself. In Bratislava I work in a specialized workshop at the Institute of Cy-Cy-Cybermatic Systems. We analyze the electronic systems Russian spies steal from American Pershing rockets. With these huge microscopes by Carl Zeiss Jena, we look and see what makes them tick."

"But where's the shame in that?"

"Because it embarrasses me, don't you see? I don't believe in what I'm doing... but that's life, what can you do?"

"Why do you do it if you don't agree with it?"

"That's the way things work out. Some time ago, I ran over an old lady when I was drunk... so instead of jail, they offered me this. From that time on, I've been working in Celinograd... a little way out of Moscow... It's a protected town... But what nonsense this all is... hik."

After four hours of this, they somehow managed to get onto the plane, with both of them sleeping all the way to Bratislava. At the airport, they parted with the uneasy feeling they'd said too much.

"Listen, what we were talking about stays between us, right?" Horvath wanted to get things clear.

,,"Well, of course."

When they said goodbye, they couldn't imagine the unlikely situation they'd find themselves in the next time they met.

CHAPTER
TWENTYFIVE

BERLIN 1987

JAN Winter, the new Czechoslovak Ambassador to the German Democratic Republic, was seated in the living room of Kurt Womatschka, the head of fraternal relations at the FDGB trade union organization. Kurt Womatschka's mother was a refugee from the former Silesia, which had become part of Poland according to the post-war Potsdam Treaty. His father had been killed on the Eastern Front. Kurt was two years old when they took the death march from Tesin to Bautzen in the Soviet occupation zone. The background of the Womatschk family was shrouded in mystery; their documents had been lost during the fighting and consequent resettlement. In the official biography it was stated that he was born in Slovakia, his father a German citizen of the Slovak Republic. As such, he was recruited into the Wehrmacht, and before that he was an activist in the German Carpathian Society in Slovakia. In 1920, he participated in organizing the DP, the German Party in Slovakia, led by the Fascist, Franz Karmasin.

The DP was organized according to the model of Hitler's Nazi Party, and just as the Nazi Party had its military wing, the 'Schutzstaffel', known by its abbreviation, the SS, so the DP had its paramilitary branch, the Freiwillige Schutzstaffel (FS). They proudly marched in their brown shirts with swastikas on their sleeves, and wearing black trousers and boots; their appearance sparked terror not only in the Jewish community, but also among those Slovaks unhappy with the German presence in their country. After the establishment of the Slovak State in 1939, the Hlinka Guard and the FS worked closely together.

After the suppression of the Slovak National Uprising in the autumn of 1944, captured partisans were interned in the dungeons of the Kezmarok Castle, along with many Slovaks of Jewish origin who were awaiting transfer to one of the railway wagons that would deliver them to Auschwitz. The castle was guarded jointly by the Hlinka Guard shock troopers and two regiments of the Einsatztruppe (ET). The commander of one of the regiments was Klaus Winter, Jan Winter's father.

In Womatschka's new flat in the Berlin suburb of Marzahn, Kurt Womatschka and Jan Winter kept putting on long-playing records. In the German Democratic Republic, the joke went that one-third of a wall was made of brick, another third of plaster, and the final third of Stasi bugging devices. Anyone employed at a higher state level could count on the fact that they were being listened to. Kurt was naturally aware of this, and so Wagner followed Beethoven and Bach. The truth was, he couldn't stand classical music. But he did appreciate the sound it created.

"Do you think this Balaz of yours could know about it?"

"I can't say for sure, but I have an uneasy feeling about him," Winter admitted.

"There was a war going on," said Womatschka, in an attempt to calm him down. "Forty years have gone by, and, since not one witness has come forward..." He waved his hand.

"Just Balaz's father-in-law." Winter ground his teeth. "It's unbelievable! I used to go out with his daughter, and now she's Balaz's wife. I had no idea back then that Marta Balecka was the daughter of the one man who saw it all!"

"When did you actually find that out?" asked Womatschka.

"In Vienna a while back, I was visited at the hotel by some guy. He was speaking Slovak, but he had a strong German accent. He handed me a photocopy taken from the Austrian State Military Archive. Unfortunately, some things on it were blacked out, but the names of the witnesses were legible, as was a photo of my father standing over a... dead man. When I asked this chap who else had this document, he said goodbye and disappeared. I haven't seen him since."

Winter sighed and took a sip of the whiskey Womatschka had poured him. "None of them are still alive: I checked it out. None except Balaz's father-in-law, damn it."

"Don't worry. You and Balaz have known each other practically your whole lives, and nothing has happened in all that time."

Winter was not so sure of this, and just shrugged. "The very thought that this could come out is so terrible... It would not only mean my career, but my family would also be destroyed. Can you imagine the headlines? The father of the Czechoslovak Ambassador, the potential Minister of Foreign Affairs, was an SS murderer."

"So if I've got it straight, you've decided not to go to Bonn, but to come here so that..." he stopped when he realized Winter wasn't listening, but was sitting lost in thought.

"Sorry, were you asking me something?"

"I asked whether you'd come here to find out what's going on with that document and about Balaz?"

"Yes, and I've already... moved forward on that," Winter looked determinedly into Womatschka's eyes.

"Something about it or about him?" Winter said nothing. "It's not going to be so simple to discredit him."

"I know..."

"Do you have some plan?" his host asked. Winter shook his head. Womatschka stared at Winter, who met his look with the feeling the other man was looking down at him.

Womatschka said slowly, "Even though it wouldn't be so difficult, it makes no sense to have Balaz liquidated. We don't know for sure he has that document in his possession. I think I see a way out of it." Winter couldn't hide his interest at these words. "In such cases it's always better to come to terms with someone by totally discrediting him. You have to lay one trap after another for him until he starts to make mistakes until his reputation is in tatters. I mean politically, you understand. A discredited man can come forward with any kind of accusation; no-one is going to believe him. Ideally, they would recall him to Prague in disgrace – on account of unreliability or infractions of work discipline, or... the best would be to set him up somehow. For example, spread the story that he's cooperating with an agent of the West or was responsible for some information leak. You're a smart guy, you'll think of something. The main thing is to pile up as much suspicion, or even better, proof, against him as you can. Once he's been recalled for political reasons, that'll be the end of your problems with him!" When Winter said nothing, Womatschka went on. "What are his political leanings?"

"He's completely behind Gorbachev."

"Couldn't be better. I'm sure the comrades on the Party Central Committee in Prague aren't delighted to have that kind of diplomat on board," Womatschka said with an evil smile. "So set your traps, collect your evidence about his anti-Party tendencies, and pass them on to the Cadre Department in Prague."

When Winter left Womatschka's flat, he was determined to get Balaz at any price. Balaz himself would give him ample opportunity for that.

CHAPTER
TWENTYSIX

BERLIN – MOSCOW 1989

JOSIF Josifovich Obicki was now a fresh young lieutenant in the Soviet army. He owed his rapid advancement to his outstanding marks at the GRU Academy, his decoration from Chernobyl, and chiefly thanks to his stepfather. It was Gusev who'd arranged his transfer to the GDR capital. The army and air force attaché, Colonel Tarkovski welcomed the arrival of his new assistant, and Josif, thanks in part to his excellent German, quickly oriented himself to both the Embassy and the city of Berlin. Tarkovski introduced him to his counterparts from the other socialist embassies and took him to the East German Ministry of Defence and of Foreign Affairs. Josif was also presented to the staff from the Military Missions Control Powers – the USA, Great Britain and France.

Josif was far from being the only Soviet soldier in the GDR who owed his secondment to contacts; roughly eighty percent of them enjoyed such preferential treatment. He was issued a diplomatic passport that allowed him into West Berlin to visit the Czechoslovak, Polish and Yugoslav military missions based there. Meetings followed, both formal and informal, and also social encounters with the Czechoslovaks and Poles, with whom Tarkovski had formed excellent relations. Josif's duties included delivering various official documents bearing the stamp of the Soviet Military Attaché to the

Czechoslovak attaché, Colonel Hlaváč, but that was not why he enjoyed crossing into West Berlin. He revelled in the opportunity to enjoy the free atmosphere of the city, and then there was the shopping. Soviet diplomats accredited in the GDR received a small sum in West German marks monthly to allow them to buy a few treats, some cosmetics or cheap clothing. They also found ways to afford pricier items such as electronic goods and even jewellery. There was always some shady character willing to pay cash for Russian vodka, champagne or caviar; the winding side-streets around the ZOO train station were lined with such Turkish, Yugoslav or Polish dealers.

Completely trusting the son of his old comrade, Colonel Tarkovski gave Josif an introduction to some of these 'entrepreneurs', in particular to Leszek, a young Pole who sold electronic devices from a small shop in Hardenbergplatz Square. Leszek was mainly interested in caviar, for which he paid Josif a hundred and fifty marks per kilo, and double or even triple that for more exotic varieties. The rates also depended on the number of video recorders, tape players and televisions the Soviet officer purchased. For one Sharp brand double tape player he charged 250 marks, the same retail price as the kilo of caviar Josif had traded him. When he was in the mood, he'd throw in a few video cassettes as a bonus. If the deal was big enough, he was also willing to let the newest porno videos go at a discount rate. The range of precious electronic devices in turn served as a fitting 'thank you' to the Soviet officials who'd made it possible for their young protégés to taste life in the West. Many a promising career was built on the back of electronics and dirty movies.

Czechoslovak diplomats and their families made a practice of going to the Soviet sports centre in the Berlin Karlshorst sector every Wednesday. Balaz and his elder daughter played volleyball while Marta and young Anicka went swimming in the pool. The Soviets had a number of excellent players, and so they were usually victorious in the volleyball matches. Finally it was decided to play mixed-squad games with the Czechoslovaks. Balaz noticed that a young good-looking man named Osja usually took up his position next to his daughter, Martuska. Well-built, black-haired and with a long nose, he was a good athlete, feared by his opponents for his vicious serves and high jumps. Balaz met him in the showers after one match, and started a conversation with the unknown young man.

"You're a good volleyball player."

"I've been playing for a while."

"Mind you, when you have hands like shovels, serving must come easy," the older man laughed.

"I've never played in a league. I used to play hockey for the Soviet Wings."

"Do you work at the Embassy?"

"I'm the Army/Air Force attaché's secretary."

"So, Vasilij Nikolajevich is your chief?" Osja nodded. "He's a good man to work for."

"I believe it."

"What is Osja short for?"

"Josif. Like your Jozef. Like you," Osja continued as he put on his uniform. Sitting down on the bench, he suddenly breathed in sharply; he was pale and a little blood trickled from his nose. Balaz handed him a paper tissue. "Thank you... and you can call me Osja, no need to be formal." After a few moments the bleeding stopped, and he finished dressing and said goodbye.

"That young guy has his eye on your daughter," Mihas, who was also showering, teased Jozef.

"Sure looks like it," Balaz laughed.

"And it's reciprocal. Better keep an eye on them."

"Know what? I finally understand why Martuska has suddenly developed a fondness for volleyball. She always looks forwards to coming here on Wednesdays!" Thinking it over, Balaz wasn't too concerned. The young officer seemed a pleasant, well-mannered young man. Their friendship continued for some time.

Martuska sang and played piano. On the occasion of a social get-together with the staff from the Soviet Embassy, she performed the song by Bulat Okudzhava, 'The Paper Soldier'. It was a legendary protest song by a singer who, in the aftermath of the 1968 occupation, vowed he'd never perform in an occupied country, and that he'd return to Czechoslovakia only when the Soviet troops withdrew. The diminutive brunette sang the lyrics with her whole heart:

'In the world lived a soldier, brave, fair and new,
But he got no respect, since he was made of paper.
He wished to change the world and live there happily,
But in a child's room he had to stay, he was only made of paper.
Ready to leap into flames, prepared to die for us.
Who would force him into a fire? He was only made of paper.
"You want me in the fire? Okay, then." Bravely he marched on
Till he burned up – a cheap victim of death – he was only made of paper.'

She sang the Russian so beautifully that those present had the feeling it was her soul that was singing to them. Balaz looked over at his wife and noticed the tears in Marta's eyes. A long moment of silence followed the end of the song, and then loud applause broke out. Everyone in the room was on their feet. In her confusion, Martuska simply stood by her piano and bowed and smiled. She knew she had never managed to sing her favourite song so perfectly.

A young Soviet officer emerged from out of the crowd, took her hand, and planted a kiss on it. She blushed scarlet, for Josif was the first man who had ever kissed her hand. "Thank you, you were singing about my father..." he murmured. Then he put his hand on his heart and bowed deeply.

When Sasha wanted to stop Sergej from talking about politics, she would take out a letter from Josif, and they would read it together. These were the golden moments that allowed them both to forget the disastrous situation that had, despite expectations, worsened since Gorbachev came to power. Needless to say, Osja wrote from Berlin more frequently than he had from Chernobyl. He praised his chief, and was enjoying life in East Germany. He told them about the Wednesday trips to the Karlshorst sports centre, and mentioned Martuska, a girl he'd met there, the daughter of the Czechoslovak press attaché. Her father was called Jozef, and was from Bratislava. He was forty years old, and a great volleyball player. He went on to speak of Martuska's beauty, and how she had sung Paper Soldier at the Soviet social club.

The letter describing this Jozef's background and talents found its way into Sasha's handbag. She would read it at work, on the metro, in the park she took her daughter Ninočka to. Again and again that phrase rang in her head - Jozef the volleyball player from Bratislava. She wrote back to Josif, telling him how glad she was that he was doing well. She was also worried about the pressure in his throat he'd complained of, and wanted to know why he was having trouble swallowing. Had he been to see a doctor? Then, changing her tone, she asked if he wasn't thinking of getting married to this young Slovak girl. In his next letter Josif enclosed a joint photo of the Soviet and Czechoslovak sports team; the forty-year-old attaché with the greying temples was clearly Jozef, her first love.

CHAPTER
TWENTYSEVEN

BERLIN 1989

IN April 1989, Peter Greiner invited Balaz to a gathering in his East German flat on Leipzigerstrasse. Balaz knew that he was obliged to report a meeting with a West German journalist to his Ambassador for approval, but his relationship with Winter was tense at best. Moreover, relations between diplomats and reporters had eased up significantly since Gorbachev came into office. He decided not to seek approval for his visit, and with his wife, Marta, called on Greiner with a bottle of Slovak gin under his arm. Greiner introduced the Balazes to all his other guests; the only person Balaz already knew was Mr. Grabbe, the West German Permanent Representation press attaché, and the only other names he managed to remember were Rainer Eppelmann and Markus Meckel. He didn't know who the other people were, but they certainly didn't look the type to attend diplomatic soirees. The conversation too was completely different to talking with Embassy types or GDR journalists, his usual conversation partners. In particular, he was taken by the words of Eppelmann, who complained openly that everywhere in the socialist camp change was in progress, except for in East Germany. Meckel and a few others, overhearing their conversation, joined in the debate. Balaz was conscious that he was the only East Bloc diplomat invited to the party by Greiner. In fact, he was wondering why the West

German had placed him in such a compromising and embarrassing situation. When the opportunity arose, Balaz discreetly steered Peter to a corner of the room and asked him the question directly.

"You're right, my guests are from the opposition – some Protestant priests, a couple of artists, a few emigration applicants..."

"You could have told me who would be here," Balaz reproached him.

"And would you have come? I only hope you haven't wet yourself! I simply wanted to show you that I trust you."

"But are you aware that I'm going to have to file a report about this gathering?"

"So write it. It won't cause problems for anybody here."

"Maybe not for you, but what about me?"

"Your problems will start when you write it up." With an ironic smile, Greiner waited for his reaction.

"Somebody once told me that located across the hall from every West German journalist is a flat full of Stasi agents." Now it was Balaz who waited for Greiner's reaction.

"Yeah, I heard the same thing."

"Jesus Christ!" Balaz drank down his wine.

"I have the feeling that this evening could soon stand in your favour... Jozef, I wanted to ask you if you felt like going out running tomorrow to Friedrichshain. I know that's your favourite route... I'm getting in shape for the Berlin marathon, and I don't like running alone."

"I don't know... okay, why not?" Balaz smiled. He had the feeling it wasn't company on his run that Greiner was really after.

The next morning, Balaz found Peter, in his running gear, waiting for him in the park behind the statue of Lenin. After a brief warm-up, they set off on their run.

"Well, did you report to your Ambassador?" Balaz nodded. His answer surprised Greiner. "Well, I couldn't risk him hearing it from your Stasi neighbours."

"What did he say?"

"That the story wouldn't go any further."

"He seems to be a reasonable guy," commented Greiner, aiming to elicit Balaz's real opinion of Winter. The next few minutes, they ran without speaking until Peter explained himself: "Sorry to drag you out here but, as you know, neither in my flat nor in the car can I be sure I'm not being bugged." At these words, both men instinctively looked around themselves. "Jozef, I have a favour to ask – a big favour. A good friend of mine in West Berlin has a friend who left here two years ago... Her son stayed behind, living with his grandmother, whose health is not too good... she's tried everything to get the boy out, but nothing has worked." As they ran on side by side, Greiner told Balaz the story of Heike, her son, and her partner, Thomas. As Balaz listened, he knew that the sweat breaking out on his forehead was not all due to the run. When Greiner asked if he could help in any way, his knees almost buckled. Greiner noticed how pale he had suddenly become. "Listen, I don't want to get you into anything that could put you at risk... I certainly didn't mean to suggest that you take him out yourself. I've heard they have special equipment at Checkpoint Charlie these days,"

"At risk!? You must be out of your mind... I wouldn't be at risk, they'd send me straight to jail... The Ambassador is already on my back... I can't even be sure we're not being followed at this very minute... Peter, I'd love to help you out... I know you helped me before, but this is really over the top."

They ran on for a while in silence. "Sorry if this is too much for you to take on board; forget I ever mentioned it. Our friendship can survive this." Greiner's final words before saying goodbye were: "Don't worry about it, we'll work it out some other way." Afterwards, Balaz was never able to remember how he'd arrived home after leaving Peter.

When he got home, he found Martuska sitting at the piano, playing a Liszt piano concerto. In a vase on the piano were the roses she had been given for her recent eighteenth birthday. Although she was legally an adult, for her parents she was still the little girl they loved so much. Her sister Anicka was at judo practice, and Marta was attending a German lesson. Jozef stripped off his sweaty clothing, took a shower, and nervously began to search the fridge for something to eat. Martuska noticed the state he was in.

"Is there something wrong?"

"No, no, I'm fine. What about you?"

"Me? I'm okay."

He finally spread meat paste on some bread, as his daughter mysteriously smiled to herself. She was thinking about her date with Osja the evening before – it marked the first time they'd kissed. Balaz was lost in his own thoughts, trying to find a way out of his predicament. It was obvious that Peter hadn't been trying to entrap him, and that what he'd told him represented a serious situation. Although he truly wished to help his friend, he was frankly afraid. If the GDR border police had even the slightest reason to be suspicious, they had the right to inspect his car. At the thought of them finding a child secreted in his trunk, chills ran up and down his spine. The whole idea was nonsense! They had that special X-ray equipment at the border, for heaven's sake!

The only one who could smuggle a child to the West with any chance of success was a member of one of the occupying forces, who had exclusive use of the Glienicke Brdge border crossing. Under no circumstances could the East Germans inspect a soldier's vehicle. The problem was that he didn't know any American, French or British military men. In fact, the only occupying force member he knew was Josif Obicki, the secretary to the USSR Embassy Military Attaché.

CHAPTER
TWENTYEIGHT

BERLIN – FRANKFURT ON THE ODER 1989

A two-day trip for foreign press attachés to the Frankfurt on the Oder region had been organized by the Press Section of the East German Ministry of Foreign Affairs. The group was accompanied by three section staff, plus five other people. Nobody knew exactly who they were, but everyone could guess.

The diplomats were escorted into a ceremoniously decorated meeting room. Behind the speaker's desk sat the district commissioner for agriculture, Mr. Neumann, the cooperative chairman, Mr. Steglitz, his two co-chairman, and Comrade Hartmann, the coop's best worker. The commissioner gave a lengthy address on the great successes achieved by the district's agriculturalists. Then Steglitz gave his speech.

"Dear Comrades," began the chairman in a shrill voice, despite the fact that the majority of those present were from capitalist countries. At first, they smiled at his terminology, but as they realized this was his normal way of addressing people, they let it pass. The Swedish attaché later joked that if he had known he was to be a 'comrade', he would have joined the Party before setting out. Nonetheless, there was a degree of hostility in the room – the hosts soon saw their foreign guests didn't believe these boastful references to their 'successes'. The Chairman went on: "Our comrades in the poultry division have achieved a doubling in egg production." After delivering this sensational information, the speaker looked out at his audience in expectation of the usual applause. Instead, the journalists simply exchanged knowing glances.

"This is even better than listening to Brezhnev's brother-in-law," Olutshkin whispered to Balaz, sitting next to him. He raised his hand: "Comrade Chairman, could you tell us how you achieved this success?"

The Chairman shifted uneasily in his chair, one of his co-chairman excused himself from the room, and the other man minutely studied the table in front of him.

"Through simplicity. In simplicity lies beauty," The Chairman gave a signal to his assistant, who turned on the slide projector. On the wall appeared cages, three hens to each one. On the next signal, this slide was replaced by another, this time showing six hens per cage. "That's how," the Chairman concluded, with a meaningful nod of the head. Laughter rang out throughout the room. Even the official guides couldn't stop themselves from joining in the merriment.

Olutshkin went on: "Comrade Chairman, there are now six hens in a cage designed for three. Don't you think they're a bit overcrowded?"

The Chairman looked uncomfortable, unsure how to answer. The district commissioner came to his aid, and in a bitter voice declaimed: "Perhaps it might seem to you that they are overcrowded, but we know the chickens feel all right!" These words were immediately followed by a sharp outburst of gaiety. This time, the five mystery men too began to laugh.

"The German Communist Party, the SED, executive knows that their hens feel good in their cages," one diplomat added, parodying Neumann's words. The unlucky district commissioner couldn't get it into his demagogic head that he had just stated the prize bon mot of the session. The entire rest of the trip was devoted to discussions about how many thousands of GDR citizens wanted to move out of their cages. Meanwhile, Neumann felt he wasn't being taken seriously and, in one final attempt as the journalists were leaving, said in all earnestness: "The people are happy; it's just that many of them haven't yet realized it."

In early April, an important visitor from Prague arrived at the Embassy. The Czechoslovak Communist Party General Secretary, Comrade Bilak, had come to East Berlin in order to shore up his allies in the SED 'in the difficult and decisive struggle against revisionists and opportunists'. When Winter announced that Comrade Secretary was interested in meeting the diplomats at a working lunch, Balaz was intrigued. He had never met in the flesh the man whose 'rhetorical skillfulness' was the stuff of legends.

Counsellor Hubacek, famed for his parsimoniousness, had been warning people all morning not to eat. "Today we're lunching with Bilak, we'll be stuffing our faces. Chef Pepík told me he's been to West Berlin to look for mutton. They say Comrade Secretary loves mutton, and so do I, believe me."

The lunch was held in the Ambassador's residence, and all twenty-five diplomats were seated around its giant table. Balaz was allocated a place on the corner opposite Hubacek. At the centre of the table was Bilak, with Winter opposite him. In order to save time, Comrade Secretary suggested the discussion go on while they were eating. This of course met with the approval of the hungry diplomats. Bilak requested their attention, and the stories about his rhetorical uniqueness were soon confirmed. The guests concentrated carefully on the food on their plates to keep from laughing. Bilak's combination of Slovak, Ruthenian and Czech was, thankfully, one of a kind. Due to its tricky form, the listener was less able to completely follow the content of the speech.

"...and so dear comrades, we must conclude that it is to the undying credit of Vladimir Iljich Lenin that he cleansed the revolutionary working class teachings of the slime of opportunism, and confirmed the timeless validity of the idea of Marxism!"

At that moment, a slight pop was heard in the room. Some thought one of the bulbs on the crystal chandelier had exploded, but Balaz and those seated near him recognized the sound as that of a fractured set of dentures. They belonged to counsellor Hubacek, who was too enthusiastic in his enjoyment of Chef Pepík's chicken noodle soup. Pepík was famous for the generous amount of noodles he added to his soups, and that was the source of the problem. They were so thick that even a diplomat with better sight than Hubacek would have had trouble locating a piece of his dentures in the bowl. He was also under time pressure – since everyone else had already finished their bowls, the waiters were waiting on him before serving the next course. "The motto Socialism with a Human Face was a mask which attempted to cover the face of counterrevolution in our country," Bilak prattled on.

"Did you enjoy it?" the waiter politely enquired of Hubacek, who was forced to give up the hunt for the piece of his dentures.

"Yes, thank you," Hubacek gulped, and with a sorrowful look saw the delicious soup, along with part of his dentures, disappear for good. The appetizer was ham with creamed horseradish filling; after a vain attempt to deal with it, Hubacek was forced to give in, for he was smacking his lips like a man with a broken dental plate in his mouth. After Comrade Secretary had sent a few annoyed glances in his direction, he put down his cutlery and just sat there. That made him about the only diplomat to follow Bilak's every word.

"Let us imagine this image, dear Comrades and lady Comrades," (there were no females in the room) "a house begins burning. The manager is too drunk or stoned to either put out the fire or to call for help."

"Did you enjoy it?" the waiter politely enquired of Hubacek as he swept away his plate of almost untouched ham with creamed horseradish.

"Yes, thank you, very good. For some reason, I've lost my appetite today..." he lisped through his slipping denture.

"We, experienced comrades, are not about to be duped so easily. As the old saying has it, a wolf remains a wolf even when dressed in a sheep's clothing."

Hubacek was right; the main course was indeed his favourite, mutton in sour cream. The chef had outdone himself on this occasion, and everybody dug in... except for Hubacek, who looked on stoically. His plate remained untouched.

"But his sons call for help, and the fire is extinguished."

"You really have lost your appetite today, Comrade Counsellor," the waiter joked as he took away the untasted mutton. "Pepik won't be pleased."

"There is no-one in the world capable of stopping the triumphant march of socialism!"

After the end of the working lunch, Comrade Secretary hurried back to Prague to save socialism. Balaz by pure chance got into the lift just as the Ambassador returned from seeing Bilak off. The two of them were alone in the small compartment. Winter, obviously deeply moved by the First Secretary's words, turned to Balaz and said: "What an ass that man is!"

The day following Comrade Secretary's departure, Balaz received a call from Peter Greiner, asking for a meeting. "Have you heard about our entertaining lunch with Comrade Secretary yet?" he asked with a laugh. But Peter's voice was serious as he requested they meet as soon as possible. "It's about our running together," he said. This made Jozef nervous – some time had passed since they were out together, and he'd hoped that in the meantime the issue with his friend's son had somehow been resolved.

When they met, Peter asked him to go to West Berlin to check the place the Soviet soldier would take the child. Now this meant a further complication for Balaz; until now, he had always visited with Marta, using his once-a-month pass. If he were to go alone to meet Greiner, he would have to do it unofficially or else lose the right to travel with his wife. In addition, the passes were issued by the Czechoslovak Ambassador, for statistical and recording reasons as much as anything. At Checkpoint Charlie, both the East Germans and the American border police had until now only asked to see his diplomatic pass and GDR accreditation, so the risk of being challenged wasn't great. Peter had asked him to join him at the corner of Zimmerstrasse and Friedrichstrasse, and then accompany him to a small restaurant near the Tiergarten.

Despite all this, Balaz was quite nervous travelling for the first time without his Czechoslovak authorization. He couldn't help imagining the Germans informing his Embassy about his 'black' crossing of the border. He saw himself as a worker at Dimitrovka, the vast chemical factory in Bratislava. But the crossing went without complications, and Peter was waiting at the agreed place. They drove along Bellevuestrasse and Tiergartenstrasse to a little pub called 'Zum Vogel' on the peninsula of the Neuer See lake. They crossed a dingy-looking yard sheltered from the street by thick boards. The back gate was opened for them and just as quickly closed after they passed through by Hans Vogel, the owner of the establishment. It was clear that he and Peter were old and trusted friends. They went into a separate room, from where they could hear voices and television noise coming from the main room. Since he wanted to get back as soon as possible, Balaz refused the offered cup of coffee. Vogel assured him he was in the pub from morning to night, and even lived in its rear section.

The men soon agreed the details; Balaz pleaded with Greiner that no-one must know who was behind the kidnapping. The cold look he got from Peter quickly reminded him that there was no need to even voice such a concern. They separated – in total Balaz had spent less than one hour in West Berlin. Coming back between the concrete barriers of Checkpoint Charlie, he was passed through the border with only a salute from the East German soldier on duty. He sighed in relief and drove back to the Embassy. No-one had noticed anything.

However, after seeing a Trabant with a 'CD' plate coming through his border-point, a senior passport control officer from the Ministry of State Security decided to have a look into the records book. Just for curiosity he checked at what time the rare diplomat's Trabbie with plate CD 02 – 32 had crossed the first time. He calculated a stay in the West of fifty-seven minutes. Looking back into the records, he saw that this same vehicle, limited to one crossing per month, had used Checkpoint Charlie just three days before. He called his supervisor, who came and made a few notations in his diary.

One hour later, Counsellor Mlejnek was seated in the Ambassador's office. Officially the Counsellor for Security Issues, it was understood by all concerned that Mlejnek was the senior StB secret police officer in the GDR. One of his main tasks was keeping an eye on the Czechoslovak diplomats.

Between the two men there lay a notification from the East German Secret Service, Diplomatic Representation Branch that a Czechoslovak Embassy First Secretary named Jozef Balaz had been in West Berlin from 14.03 to 15.00 on May 2, 1989.

"What do you intend to do about this?" Mlejnek asked the Ambassador.

"Leave it with me," replied Winter with a knowing look.

"Me, I wouldn't make a big issue out of it. The guy's going home next month, and lots of them go across unofficially." Winter was surprised by Mlejnek's speaking up for Balaz.

"It's all up to him," was Winter's considered response.

CHAPTER
TWENTYNINE

BERLIN 1989

On May 3, 1989, at two in the afternoon, Osja went into the garage at the Czechoslovak Embassy, on the corner of Mohrenstrasse and Mauerstrasse. Osja was familiar with the garage since he often parked there on his way to the army and air force section. Luckily, Balaz's parking spot was at the same end of the garage as the section's reserved parking places; moreover, there were no cameras in the vicinity. Should anyone notice them, it would seem perfectly natural for the father of a girl the young Soviet lieutenant was dating to be chatting to him.

Two o'clock was an ideal time for their meeting due to the fact that the Embassy's diplomats generally met with their partners during the morning, and social gatherings usually took place in the evening hours.

Balaz had placed a large cardboard television box in the trunk of his Trabant. Inside it sleeping peacefully was young Peter, thanks to some medicine Greiner had obtained from a pharmacist friend. They were assured that the injection would work for at least three hours. The day before, Osja and Balaz had gone through all the details surrounding the kidnapping, and although Josif wore a serious expression, he looked calm and self-assured. Together they transferred the box into a dark-green Opel Ascona 1.6 with a large luggage space.

After shaking hands, Josif set off for the Glienicke Bridge border-crossing. This, he recalled, was the same bridge where in 1962 representatives from the Soviet Union and the United States exchanged two spies named Rudolf Abel and Gary Powers.

Josif crossed almost the whole of East Berlin until he came to the border along Berlinerstrasse. The soldier on duty saluted politely, asked for his passport, and seemed to be studying it at length. Although he knew the man had no jurisdiction over him, Josif began to feel a little nervous. As he began to imagine what would happen should young Peter happen to wake up right there on the border, he felt the sweat break out on his forehead. The border guard finally handed back the passport and signalled to Josif to drive on. He had to manoeuvre through the concrete anti-tank blocks, which were decorated with paint of all colours from cars whose drivers hadn't quite managed the turns. The sight of Glienicke Castle on his left side calmed him down somewhat, and a few seconds later he arrived safely in West Berlin. The trip to the Tiergarten park didn't take long, and soon he noticed a sign advertising the 'Zum Vogel' garden restaurant. He was there!

Again the back gate was standing open and, after Josif drove through, it was immediately closed. Hans Vogel indicated for him to carry on into a spacious garage where Peter Greiner and Thomas Ankermann were waiting. Hands were quickly clasped, the trunk was opened, and the cardboard box removed. When Thomas picked up his end, his hands were shaking so badly that Josif had to use his massive hands to hold it up. They carried it into the pub's back room, and there sat Heike. When she caught sight of her peacefully sleeping son, however, her legs buckled and she fainted away. As her friends sprinkled her face with water, Josif stood back and grinned at the shaken Germans. When things were under control, Thomas came over and, without speaking a word, hugged him tightly. He then tried to give the young Russian an envelope, but Josif politely refused to take anything. Instead, he said he had to get back, and sat back into the car. Vogel opened the gate, and the Opel Ascona disappeared down the street.

The ZOO Garten shopping streets were a short distance away, and Josif was soon buying from Leszek the items on a list given to him by Colonel Tarkovski. His next stop was the Czechoslovak Military Mission in the American sector of Berlin, where he handed over his sealed mail to the service officer before heading back to Glienicke Bridge.

Meanwhile, after seeing Josif leave, Balaz retreated to his office and quietly closed the door. He then fell to his knees and began to pray. He prayed that the pub owner Vogel would be at home, that Josif was safe, that the child had not by any chance awakened prematurely, and that his phone would soon ring with the message: 'I'll see you at the next volleyball match'. It was at that moment that Balaz realized that he loved the young Russian – his feeling was one he was unable to define rationally, but it felt somehow paternal. He had his two daughters of course, but he had never experienced the bond between a man and his son; he reckoned it felt something like what he was now feeling.

Josif parked in the garage belonging to the Soviet Embassy on Unter den Linden and went up to his office. The first thing he did there was to pick up the phone and dial Balaz's number. "I just wanted to tell you how much I'm looking forward to our next volleyball match," were his words.

Had someone walked into Balaz's office at that point, they would doubtless not have understood why a rational adult discussing sports was laughing so hard. In his joy, Balaz was actually beating his hand against the wall. He felt such a strong wave of relief after replacing the receiver that he felt the tears damming up in his eyes.

CHAPTER
THIRTY

BERLIN 1989

ON June 4, 1989 a ceremonial atmosphere reigned in the large meeting-room at the Czechoslovak Embassy in East Berlin. The diplomats' meeting at which Ambassador Jan Winter would bid farewell to his staff was about to begin.

"Comrades," he began, "today marks my last day of service in the German Democratic Republic. Even though I've only been with you for two years, your outstanding work has made a strong impression on me, and I thank you for this. As you no doubt know, I'm being recalled to Prague in connection with other important tasks that have been delegated to me." There followed, in Winter's native Slovak for a change, a series of clichés about the great collective and their excellent cooperation. Then he looked directly at those staff members who, during the two years he'd ruled over them with an iron fist, had gotten most into his hair. "And now, Comrades, since I'm leaving and nothing will come of it, feel free to speak your minds. How do you perceive my time here? I sincerely beg you to be frank; it will be to your benefit and to mine." The Ambassador looked out at the almost thirty people who were looking back at him with frightened eyes. Asking diplomats for their honest opinion on a man who was soon to be their minister was like asking a condemned man, just before his execution, how he felt about the hangman.

One after the other, the diplomats thanked the Ambassador for the wonderful two years fate had allowed them to spend with him. Balaz was the only one who kept his mouth shut throughout.

After it was all over, Winter sat in the leather armchair in his office looking at his packed-up books and documents, feeling somehow gloomy. The supreme GRU officer in Berlin, after consultations with his colleagues in Prague, had decided to bring Winter back to Czechoslovakia. It was necessary for dependable cadres to be prepared to take over positions of power in the period which was slowly but inevitably coming.

"Sit down," Winter invited Balaz when, on his request, he came to his office. "What are you drinking? Just name it, there's all kinds of alcohol left over."

"Thanks, but I don't feel like a drink."

"You also didn't feel like being at a meeting... I hope you're at least going to sit down. Damn, the air-conditioning's broken down again. What are you staring at?" the Ambassador asked.

"You're speaking Slovak today."

"I've stopped noticing. And then again, a person shouldn't be ashamed of where he comes from."

"You mean you used to be ashamed of being a Slovak?"

"Certainly not, but sometimes I ask myself the question if children should be ashamed of their parents," Winter continued, examining Balaz's reaction. Balaz had no idea where this was going. He was ignorant of the fact that Winter was looking for some sign revealing that he knew the secret concerning Winter's father.

"That depends on what the parents did wrong."

Winter scowled and then, unlocking his attaché case, withdrew some papers from it.

"It looks like there's a fifty percent chance they're going to appoint me the next minister. It's true that Jakes is not in my corner, but his position is weakening." He gave Balaz a meaningful look, and went on: "And there are other people behind me... If they do make me minister, I wanted to ask if you'd serve as my spokesman, in other words, the Ministry of Foreign Affairs spokesman." Balaz stared at him in surprise - Winter suddenly needed the guy whose ass he'd been kicking since they'd both joined the civil service. As regards the job, only a fool would try to make sense of Czechoslovak foreign policy with Jakes as Communist Party First Secretary.

"I'm not sure I'd be a suitable candidate... you're aware that my opinions are not always in line with what the Party leaders are saying."

"That's precisely the reason why. We need people who are not afraid to present their own opinions, and we both know you're that kind of person. Look, I know a lot of things about you, and I value your attitude... in short, I'd be glad to have you at my side... I trust you." Winter was speaking in a tone Balaz had never before heard from him. It was almost as if he was apologizing for something.

"Jozef," he said in a suddenly jovial voice, "perhaps there's been a certain amount of friction between us in the past, but the times are changing... we have to help each other: nobody knows where we'll end up... and I'm willing to help you, too... for example, like this." On the table he placed a Stasi secret police report including all the occasions on which diplomatic vehicle 02 – 32 had crossed the border between East and West Berlin. Balaz found himself blushing under Winter's penetrating gaze.

'So that's the way it is,' he thought to himself. 'We suspected that all of our crossings were being recorded. And that's exactly what they were doing!'

"When was the last time you crossed over?"

"You've got it written down right in front of you!" Balaz wondered how much Winter knew about his last crossing. He felt his heart thumping – if they knew about Josif, it meant not only the end of his career, but he would also be facing criminal charges.

"Fifty-seven minutes exactly," read Winter, shaking his head. Balaz would give anything to know how much the Ambassador knew!

"I'm going home next week, and just wanted to pick up some treats. My monthly limit was used up..."

Winter looked him up and down. "You're aware that this is a serious breach of working discipline calling for your immediate recall to the Foreign Ministry in Prague and all that that implies..." Balaz said nothing. "You could have come directly to me, I'd have approved your shopping trip. Now everybody up on the sixth floor knows about it... But you're lucky; I took the note away from Mlejnek. Since you're leaving anyway, we decided we'd keep it under our hats. Otherwise you can just imagine what they'd do to you for an unauthorized border crossing!" Balaz nodded his understanding. "Do you need to go over again?

"No, I bought everything I needed,"

"So this," he continued, waving the Stasi dossier, "stays between us."

"Thanks a lot!" Balaz couldn't keep the relief out of his voice – it was clear Winter knew nothing of the reason for his trip.

"That's all right," smiled Winter, and he rose to give Balaz his hand. His final words were: "Think about that spokesman position. Really, I'd appreciate it. At least promise me to accept the posting if I'm appointed minister."

On his return to Prague, Ján Winter was appointed First Deputy Minister of Foreign Affairs of the Czechoslovak Socialist Republic.

CHAPTER
THIRTYONE

BERLIN – BRATISLAVA 1989

BALAZ sat in his office deep in thought, surrounded by the pile of boxes, cases and cartons ready to be packed into the moving van. Today would be his final day in the GDR. A few days before, at the farewell dinner at the Stadt Berlin hotel, the head of the press section of the GDR Foreign Affairs Ministry, Wolfgang Schleyer, had awarded him the Friendship between Nations medal for strengthening ties between the GDR and the CSSR. Balaz liked Schleyer because when he spoke it was always to the point. In addition, he was sensitive to the difference between Czechs and Slovaks. In his acceptance speech, Balaz joked that if his friends in East Germany knew what he had reported about them to Prague, they would never have given him the medal.

"But about you I said only good things," he said, looking at Schleyer.

"I don't know if that's such good news," Schleyer laughed in reply.

"I've been working among you for over five years, and I've learned that Germans, both from the West and the East, are people just like anywhere else, with their good and bad sides, their strengths and weaknesses, hopes and disappointments. From my heart I would like to thank you for this medal for strengthening the friendship between Germans, Czechs and Slovaks. I'm deliberately not saying East and West Germans; I sincerely believe that before very long, you'll once again be one Germany." There was a deathly silence in the hall – Balaz had stated what everyone present was thinking, but no-one else had the courage to say out loud.

Two weeks later, Gyula Horn and Alois Mock cut the wire on the Hungary-Austria border. The Iron Curtain had begun to be pulled open.

Balaz looked around his living room and in his mind bid farewell to it. His glance fell upon the open shoe-box where Martuska had carefully packed her letters and photographs. He would never normally look at his daughters' private things, but he was drawn by the photo of Josif at the top of the box. He had given it to her when they said goodbye, along with a bouquet of pinks and a typically Russian set of Matryoshka dolls. Martuska had nobly concealed her sadness at their parting. The last few times she'd been together with Osja, she'd noticed how often he was swallowing and clearing his throat. She thought he might have an enlarged thyroid, but he blamed it on a cold and a slight fever. They'd promised to write to each other, but nonetheless Martuska felt that her first love affair already belonged to the past. Her Osja was a professional soldier after all, and could not predict where he would be sent in a year or even in a month.

Balaz held in his hand the photo of this exceptional Soviet soldier. He had never dared ask him his date of birth, but he recalled Josif once saying that the day he was born was a special day; everyone in Carpatho-Ukraine was crossing their fingers for the Czechoslovak hockey team in their game with the Soviet Union. His mother remembered that the Czechoslovaks had won 4: 3, that memorable victory in March, 1969. Balaz and Sasha had had their night of love in Kiev in July, 1968...

His wife Marta and the girls went straight back to Bratislava, while Balaz remained in Prague. He had been summoned by Ing. Karasek, the head of the press section of the Federal Foreign Affairs Ministry, who informed him that the Ministry had decided to nominate him as spokesman. Exactly who in the Ministry had suggested his name was not made clear. Essentially this was only a formal nomination, for his appointment had already been confirmed. Balaz requested a week to think it over, but his chief refused, saying that in light of the evolving situation the job was to start at once. The number of foreign journalists who were coming to Prague was rising exponentially. The prime task was for someone to explain to them the decisions and steps that the CSSR government and the Party Central Committee were taking. This person should be jovial, educated, multi-lingual, and known to display independent thinking. One of those who fulfilled these criteria was Jozef Balaz.

The tension was increasing and the courage of the people growing in direct proportion to developments in the Soviet Union, Poland and Hungary. The Czechoslovak leadership reacted to the demands of the society only through formal declarations, and Balaz had absolutely no interest in being the one to decipher, far less justify, them. He turned down the offer from Karasek. Six months ago, he could have expected serious consequences from this refusal, but as things stood, he was told only that if he didn't plan to accept the posting, he had no reason to stay in Prague.

On the first of July, he found himself back in the Bratislava Press and Information Centre. This occurred just a few days before foreign radio stations broadcast into Czechoslovakia the anti-government 'Few Sentences' declaration attributed to Havel and his group. Only a few of the signatories, men like Knazko and Carnogursky, represented Slovakia. The resolution called for the enactment of immediate reforms, the freeing of political prisoners, respect for religious freedom, the annulment of censorship, open debate about the 1950s and the Prague Spring of 1968, and private enterprising – things that no-one could disagree with.

The flood of foreign journalists was also deluging Bratislava. Balaz had the opportunity to meet many top European journalists whose names he recognized from foreign journals. Perhaps chief among them was the reporter for the Austrian daily Der Kurier, Franz Eder. Balaz helped him jump over many of the bureaucratic hurdles so as to allow his readers to find out what was happening in the country next door. He and Eder thought about establishing a joint Austrian/Slovak radio station, CD International. Needless to say, their discussions ranged far beyond the limitations set upon Balaz by his signing of the Declaration on the Conservation of State Secrecy. Also taken for granted was that the foreign journalists' visits were being monitored by the StB.

One August afternoon, Jozif and Franz were seated in Senkvitska, a traditional wine restaurant, enjoying home-made sausages and a litre of good wine to wash them down. Balaz noticed a man with a camera sitting alone at a nearby table, which struck him as strange since the restaurant was not a usual destination for camera-carrying tourists. Lunch over, Franz got into his car and started back to Vienna. The next day, his old nemesis Mandak came to see Balaz. He was interested in what happened during Eder's visit. Balaz of course realized his friend's presence in the country was recorded by the secret police, but he didn't know how closely his movements inside Czechoslovakia were monitored, so he gave an account of their visit to the Gabčíkovo/ Nagymaros hydro-electric station. Mandak, however, wished to know more.

"How much wine did the two of you get through?" From this, it was clear to Balaz that the 'tourist' in the restaurant was indeed an StB agent.

"How much? Oh, one glass each."

"What about your meeting at the radio station? I hear you were discussing a new broadcast station... Austrian/Slovak... and that you were the interpreter". Mandak waited for him to answer; Balaz could only react with horror to the idea that they had spies everywhere.

"Well, yes, we discussed the idea, but nothing came of it."

"Give me some details about your talks!"

"From what I'm hearing from you it would seem you already have the facts. All you want is for me to confirm them," Balaz retorted angrily. Mandak simply stared at him.

After a moment, Mandak took Balaz by surprise: "Everything's coming to an end, believe me – it's even spread among the secret police officers, in case you don't think there are normal people in StB". Again he paused, and then went on: "If I had the courage, I'd blow up the whole Central Committee!" Balaz was unsure if what Mandak was saying reflected his true opinion, or if it was just another secret police provocation. Suddenly the other man was on his feet, his hand out to Balaz. "If we don't meet again, I wish you all the best."

He never set eyes on Mandak again. Seventeen years later, Balaz was told by the Nation's Memory Institute (UPN) that in the 1980s several dozen secret service officials were either fined or expelled from the police corps. Their offences included making up 'black souls', either agents or collaborators whom they allegedly hosted at a variety of restaurants and pubs, or who were paid off with expensive alcohol. They had no receipts for these bribes, simply honourable declarations concerning their 'hospitality' expenses. The bottles of alcohol were of course shared among the policemen, and the expense money made up a second, sometimes even a third, salary for them. Mandak was one of these officials. Despite the fact that the UPN had enough evidence, they never published any details of the case. Obviously they didn't want to cast doubt on the trustworthiness of the Institute, which gained its information solely from StB assertions.

CHAPTER
THIRTYTWO

BERLIN 1989

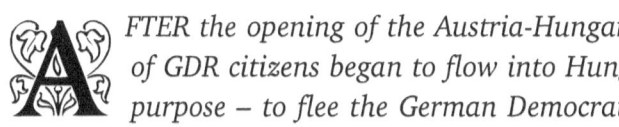FTER the opening of the Austria-Hungary border, thousands of GDR citizens began to flow into Hungary with one single purpose – to flee the German Democratic Republic. According to the West German constitution, every GDR citizen was automatically also a citizen of the FRG. On August 19, 1989, during the "Pan-European Picnic" near the city of Sopron, about 900 East German citizens managed to cross into Austria. Immediately following this event, waves of refugees started to appear at the FRG embassies in Czechoslovakia and Hungary. After complex negotiations, the Hungarian and CSSR governments allowed these citizens to travel to the FRG. However, a further quarter-million resolute applicants still awaited authorization to leave East Germany. At this time the greatest and probably also the strongest GDR representative, Erich Honecker, paid a visit to an electronics factory in Erfurt, where he managed a joke: "Not even five oxen can brake the rise of socialism." Following this, he praised 'the massive working initiative of hundreds of thousands of citizens in support of the upcoming celebrations of the 40th anniversary of the founding of the GDR'.

On October 6, 1989, the sky over Berlin was lit up by the rays from a laser show. The lights were free and could, even without the agreement of the official East German bodies, shine over West Berlin. When *the inhabitants of both parts of the divided city followed the effects of the colours on the horizon, they had no idea that the time was drawing near when not only the lights but they themselves would be able to cross the Wall. The laser show was organized by the SED Central Committee on the evening before the GDR's 40th anniversary as a part of a gala celebration by the Free German Youth organization, whose members were brought to the country's capital in hundreds of buses. Above their heads flew GDR flags and the blue banners of the FDJ, and hundreds of torches were lit. When Erich Honecker and Mikhail Gorbachev appeared on the tribune, the crowd roared: 'Gorby, Gorby, Gorby!' Not even Honecker's most loyal youth party supporters called out his name.*

After the ceremonial events, the guests moved into the Palace of the Republic, where Erich Honecker gave the jubilee address. He turned towards Gorbachev and began to read: "I can assure you that socialism on German soil, in the homeland of Marx and Engels, stands on unshakeable ground." The interpreter translated it for Gorbachev and his wife, Raisa. They were seated on the left of Honecker, who was speaking in an old man's squeaky tone with a voice which kept cracking. Gorbachev was clearly bored. Perhaps he was thinking of those who, at the very moment of the speech by their highest official, were standing literally a few metres from the Palace of the Republic on the banks of the River Spree and were chanting "Freedom, Freedom". This crowd was steadily increasing in number and was spreading towards the Red City Hall. In spite of the high-quality sound bafflers, the noise from the street could not be ignored. Honecker finished his speech, then stood up and toasted Gorbachev and Raisa. He reached across his wife Margot to toast the Czechoslovak Party boss Jakes and the Romanian dictator Ceausescu.

This marked Honecker's last toast. Ten days later, during 'GDR Fire Safety Week', he stepped down from the post of SED General Secretary 'at his own request'. His successor, Egon Krenz, turned out to be simply a younger edition of his predecessor. The protests only got stronger.

On the 4th of November the GDR artists' unions called a demonstration, at which they demanded freedom of expression, travel, and assembly and, most importantly, free and democratic elections. Stefan Heym,

Christa Wolf, Christoph Hein and more than twenty other leading GDR artists lent their support to the over one million citizens demonstrating throughout the nation. The GDR leadership could not handle the situation. The true revolution had begun. It was not just an uprising by a part of the German nation, it was a civil rebellion. The people were declaring that they wanted to be treated not as 'masses' but as citizens with human dignity and with civic responsibility.

Egon Krenz, the new SED Central Committee Secretary General, authorized Günter Schabowski, a member of the politburo, to call a press conference for six p.m. on November 9, 1989 at the East German Press Centre. The public was expecting a definitive statement. There was scarcely enough air to breathe in the hall. GDR Television carried the press conference live. A correspondent from the Italian ANSA Agency, Ricardo Ehrmann, arrived late and had to sit in front of the podium, literally at Schabowski's feet. No-one was aware that at this moment history was about to be written. Schabowski spoke for almost an hour in his typically vague manner about the expansion of the opportunities for GDR citizens to travel to the West. The hall began to hum, and he came under pressure from the impatient journalists. Finally he said in an uncertain voice:

"Travel to the FRG may be undertaken by GDR citizens." The hall went mad. Ehrmann, seated one meter away from Schabowski, was the first to raise his hand.

"Does this also apply to West Berlin?"

"Well... yes," Schabowski answered after a moment's hesitation.

"When will this come into force?" The key question resounded through the hall. Schabowski looked Ehrman right in the eye. Who knows what was running through his mind at that instant, but in a suddenly firmer voice he answered: "Immediately." Then he seemed to freeze, but the genie was out of the bottle.

At that moment jubilation broke out in both parts of Germany. Thomas and Heike hugged each other. The news was picked up by the Reuters Agency and was broadcast on all West German television and radio stations. They announced that with immediate validity all border crossings were open. Even though GDR Television made an attempt to backtrack on Schabowski's statement, masses of people were already on their way to the border. The most popular of the crossings was the Bornholmer Bridge in the populous Prenzlauer Berg quarter.

When it was announced on the RIAS radio station that the inhabitants of West Berlin were gathering at the border crossings to East Berlin, Thomas and Heike couldn't stay away. The crossing in fact was only a few blocks from the house in Wedding where they were living. Heike asked a neighbor to keep an eye on little Peter, who was still sleeping. They quickly put on their warm quilted jackets and hurried out. The streets were crowded, but not as packed as on the eastern side of the border. The crowds were chanting: "Tor auf, Tor auf!" ('Open the gate!'). The border police were clearly shaken. The people at the front were arguing with the border guards. The tension was tangible. Nobody knew whether the supreme leadership would resort to violence after all. The police guns were loaded, and machine guns and water cannons were at the ready. Then the commanding officer, Lieutenant Jäger, telephoned Stasi headquarters. He received a puzzling order: "Try to force the people back as much as possible. Let the most aggressive ones go over..." Bemused, Jäger put down the phone. It was clear to him that the almighty secret police were at their wits' end. They had probably received orders not to use force. He quickly analysed the situation: if there was no such order, he would surely have been commanded to use 'all means possible'. But he had received no such instruction. It was up to him to decide how to proceed. Again he called headquarters to request permission to cancel the controls on the border. The enflamed citizens of East Berlin were by now beating at the window of his wooden barrack office. On the other side of the border the people of West Berlin were calling: "Let them go, let them go." The telephone continued to ring, but no-one would pick it up. He put down the receiver, thought for a second and made his own decision. He went outside and raised the barrier. The time was precisely eleven o'clock in the evening. The Bornholmer Brücke checkpoint and its commanding officer had become the classic weakest link in the chain which had to snap for all the other links to be relaxed.

It became clear that the chickens in the cage known as the GDR were not satisfied with their confinement. People swarmed into West Berlin to dance, to hug each other, to cry. Their brothers and sisters from West Berlin came out to greet them. Hundreds of Trabants and Wartburgs squeezed in among the crowds of pedestrians heading west. Thomas and Heike embraced each other and then their brothers and sisters from the East. By two in the morning all the other crossings to the FRG and West Berlin were open. The pubs on the Kurfürstendamm served beer free of charge. Thomas went with Heike to the Brandenburg Gate, the symbol of a divided Germany, where hundreds of people were already standing on the Wall. Thomas just stared at them – he would never have believed that one day it would be possible to dance on the Berlin Wall. Heike could not resist, and went running along Unter den Linden Boulevard, a place she hadn't been in for years. In a kind of frenzy, she hugged everyone she met. She had long since ceased to believe she would ever see her beloved boulevard again.

It was nearly morning when a megaphone sounded in Paris Square before the Brandenburg Gate. An officer of the GDR border police forcefully requested that the citizens leave the square. The area in front of the Brandenburg Gate slowly but surely became a closed zone. But only for a few hours; on December 22, the Brandenburg Gate was opened permanently. New Year's Eve was celebrated there by half a million Berliners.

Next morning at nine, the telephone rang in the office of General Secretary Egon Krenz. The operator connected Soviet Ambassador Vjaceslav Kochemasov. "Comrade Krenz, I wish only to express Moscow's surprise that you have unilaterally opened the border crossings to West Berlin."

"With respect, Comrade Ambassador, this was agreed to by your Minister of Foreign Affairs, Shevardnadze."

"Yes, but not the crossings to West Berlin, only those between the GDR and the FRG. In doing so, you violated the status of Berlin." Kochemasov finished his statement and put the phone down. Krenz sat

at his desk and began to read that morning's secret service reports. After a minute, he distractedly put them aside. He leafed through the newspapers but found he could not concentrate. The call from the Soviet Ambassador kept echoing in his head. They had done exactly what Minister of Foreign Affairs Fischer had agreed with Shevardnadze. He called Fischer, who confirmed that crossings to Berlin were explicitly included in the oral agreement between Shevardnadze and himself. In Moscow, however, no political decision had been taken. In the statement he sent to Fischer, Shevardnadze agreed with Gorbachev that the Supreme Soviet leadership knew nothing of such an arrangement.

Kochemasov called back one hour later. Krenz apprehensively lifted the receiver and heard: "Comrade Krenz, I would like to send to you the warmest greetings from Mikhail Sergeyevich. He congratulates our German ally. He considers what you did last night a daring step." Krenz thanked him. He wondered what had happened in Moscow that had caused the Ambassador to present two diametrically opposed opinions in the space of one hour. Just ten days before, during an official visit to Moscow, in answer to Krenz's question concerning the place of the FRG and GDR in Europe, Gorbachev had clearly said: "I don't know why you are asking this. I can't name one responsible politician in the world who would wish for a united Germany. We stand behind you." Then he had shaken Krenz's hand firmly.

Something had happened in Moscow during that one hour that changed the Kremlin's perspective on Berlin. They had come to understand that the GDR was lost. Gorbachev, for some as yet unknown reason, now favoured the unification of Germany. In the final analysis, this was also the will of an overwhelming majority of the East German citizenry. Krenz caught himself wondering if he himself wanted it too. It was clear to him that this was the beginning of his end.

Thomas and Heike couldn't sleep. It seemed strange to them that their best friend, the journalist Peter Greiner, who usually called them up two or three times a day, was remaining silent at this sensational moment. This thought had just run through Thomas' mind when the phone rang. On the line was Gabi, Greiner's wife. She told him that things were bad with Peter. After the press conference, he'd managed to get his report off to his editor and had subsequently lost consciousness. He was taken directly to the hospital, where a severe heart attack was diagnosed. Gabi was crying into the telephone. Thomas hurried over to see her: "It was too much for his heart... I told him to take it easy... And he was planning to go to Prague next week," she sobbed.

"Don't worry, everything will be all right... he has a strong constitution... He's a marathon man!" Thomas tried to calm her down.

"If only... I didn't want to upset you, but lately he's fainted on a number of occasions..."

On the afternoon of November 17, student demonstrations took place in Prague. Peter Greiner knew nothing of this; he died that same evening at eight o'clock.

Part III

CHAPTER
ONE

PRAGUE – BRATISLAVA 1989

THE President of the Republic, Gustav Husak, was watching the television news in the President's Residence, situated in the gardens of the Prague Castle. As a result of the third stroke that he'd suffered in June, he tired easily and found it difficult to concentrate. Sometimes he had seizures and fainting spells. He also wrestled with the question of whether his steadfast belief in the values which his country had long since abandoned was justified, but found he no longer had the strength or courage to analyze his life or reevaluate the decisions he'd made in his career.

The television was showing clips from his native Bratislava, where the day before, on the sixteenth of November, several hundred people had congregated in Peace Square to celebrate International Students' Day. The young people had then moved to the Ministry of Education, where they had debated with the Communist Party Ideology Secretary, Gejza Slapka. The irony was that the majority of the students had no idea who Slapka was, and why they were bothering to argue with him. Husak shook his head at the dumpy figure of the Party official and thought: *"Why did it have to be him!"* Next on the screen was the Central Committee First Secretary Milos Jakes, and the sight of him was enough for Husak to nervously light up a forbidden cigarette. Another one he couldn't stand! In fact, he realized that in the entire leadership of the Party there was nobody capable of undertaking real reform; even the young Party radicals were primarily interested in power for its own sake.

For the last few days, the President had been watching television from morning to night. Nobody was bringing him secret reports, and so he was reduced to the being kept informed by the media. He poured himself a glass of his favourite cognac, and switched the radio on to Free Europe. He'd considered resigning all his posts, but he couldn't face leaving the running of the country to the likes of Jakes, Bilak and Indra.

Thus it was that the President of the Republic learnt of the ten thousand students gathered in the courtyard of the Prague Medical Faculty from Free Europe Radio. 'Ten thousand!' he thought.

'Good thing we stopped blocking this station; otherwise, I wouldn't know what's going on in the country I'm President of,' he reflected with a sarcastic smile. The students' gathering had been organized by the Young Socialists' Union SZM to commemorate the fiftieth anniversary of the uprising of Czech students against the German Nazis, and had been approved by the Prague City Council. Husak wondered if the timing of the march was somehow connected to the upcoming Malta Summit between presidents Bush and Gorbachev.

A change in the atmosphere at the Medical Faculty was brought about by Dr. Josef Sarka, present back in 1939 at the funeral of an anti-Nazi demonstrator, Jan Opletal. Dr. Sarka called on the gathering to renew the fight for freedom. The plan was to march to a park in front of the main railway station, lay a flower tribute to Opletal, and then disperse. However, due to pressure from the security forces, the organizers decided to march to the Vysehrad cemetery and leave the tribute on the tomb of the poet, Karel Hynek Macha.

Alexander Dubcek, in Prague to be interviewed by an Italian reporter, was invited to speak at the demonstration. However, the secret police tapped the telephone over which the hero of the 1968 Prague Spring was told of the change of route, so instead of addressing the students, Dubcek spent three hours at police headquarters.

After the flower-laying ceremony, a group of the students moved along the Vltava River in the direction of the National Theatre. The inhabitants of the nearby streets were surprised by the interruption of the trams in both direction; they were all the more shocked by the order to keep the entry doors to their buildings locked. The riot police of the National Security Corps and the Rapid Response Squad, known as the Red Berets, were dispersed throughout the neighbourhood around National Boulevard.

Earlier that day, the Interior Minister had complained of health problems and flown to his home in the city of Ostrava. The running of the ministry was thus delegated to the head of the secret police, General Lorenc. At the time when the student march was coming down National Boulevard, Lorenc was dining with a delegation from the KGB, the Russian secret service, headed by General Viktor Grusko. The meeting, planned well in advance, was to discuss cooperation between the Soviet and Czechoslovak intelligence services.

But nobody could say when the visit of another Soviet general, Gennadijo Teslenko, had been planned. It is known that during the demonstration on National Boulevard, he was in the control headquarters with Lieutenant Colonel Danisovic, who was directing the police action against the demonstrators.

On November seventeenth, both delegations signed the final protocol. Before joining the Soviets for dinner, General Lorenc called Party First Secretary Jakes and gave him an oral report on events at the demonstration. His interpretation was that it represented an attack on the state with clear political ends. Jakes thanked him for the information and promised to think the situation over.

"What do you think we should do?" Jakes continued after some reflection.

"I've issued an order that force is not to be used – in any case, it wouldn't solve anything for anybody."

Jakes again weighed all his options, and came to the conclusion that it would be best to wash his hands of everything: "Fine, do as you think best. I'm going to my cottage. Call me if anything comes up." With that, he hung up the phone.

On the morning of that day, Vaclav Havel left Prague for his cottage in Hradecek. In fact, most of the Charter 77 leaders and their families were out of the city: none of them wished to find themselves back under arrest. This meant that neither Havel nor any of the other Charter 77 organizers actually took part in the dramatic events of November 17, 1989.

The dinner between the Czechoslovak and Soviet secret police delegations was constantly being interrupted by updates on the situation, so at eight thirty Lorenc finally made his excuses to Grusko and left. He made his way to National Boulevard to see the situation for himself, and found about five thousand demonstrators facing a cordon of police. Lorenc could hear them chanting: 'Our hands are empty, Our hands are empty'. Those in the front row were actually giving flowers to the armed policemen. After about an hour, the riot police got the order to disperse the crowd, and out came the truncheons. Various estimates later set the number of wounded at between fifty and five hundred.

General Lorenc went back to his office and tried to connect to the Minister of the Interior, who failed to answer his phone.

In an attempt to find out what was happening, President Husak again turned on the television. From Czechoslovak TV he learnt that the demonstration on National Boulevard had been broken up, with fifteen lightly injured by the forces of law and order. It was only the next day that he, along with the entire nation, was taken aback by radio reports on the Voice of America, the BBC, Deutsche Welle and Free Europe, as well as Austrian and German television stations, speaking of armoured personnel carriers and the death of a student named Martin Smíd. Despite the fact that no such vehicles were seen on National Boulevard and that Smíd was interviewed that day on Czechoslovak television, the populace was mobilized. It was later discovered that the legendary student was in fact an StB officer called Zifcak. In this case a lie served the truth, and the news was broadcast around the world. The Communist regime's days were numbered.

That Saturday, Vaclav Havel and the other Charter 77 members hurried back to Prague. At a meeting in the Theatre Club, the newly-founded Civil Forum stated their rather modest demands: they de-

manded the resignation of the most corrupt politicians, the immediate freeing of political prisoners and the calling of a general strike – small potatoes for a revolution. Power lay within their grasp, but instead of grabbing it firmly, the Chartists called for negotiations. So the people took things into their own hands, and on Monday November 20, 1989, a meeting on Wenceslas Square was attended by 100,000 citizens and no proclaimed leaders. The leaders would only appear the next day, when Havel appeared in public for the first time to address 20,000 demonstrators. On Saturday the 24th, the complete Communist Party Central Committee, headed by Milos Jakes, resigned. The unknown Karel Urbanek was appointed in his place; it was rumoured that he became the Communist Party strongman only because he was the only person around at the time.

The Slovak actor Milan Knazko found himself in Prague on Sunday, the nineteenth of November. He attended the Theatre Club meeting, signed the Civil Forum declaration, and took the first train back to Bratislava. That same evening, about 500 members of various artists' associations met to hear Knazko read out the protesters' demands, and the Public Against Violence (VPN) movement, an offshoot of the Czech Civil Forum, was born. A follow-up meeting at Bratislava's Comenius University, undisturbed by police action, saw a group of conservationists headed by Jan Budaj join the VPN group. On the twenty-first, the first VPN Coordinating Committee was created.

Further steps toward a new order were taken on November 21 and 22; this time, the venue was the Bratislava Courthouse, and the demand was the release of Jan Carnogursky, charged along with his group, with subversion. The next day saw the Bratislava protests spread to other Slovak cities. On the twenty-third, a Bratislava City Court tribunal freed Carnogursky. On SNP Square in Bratislava, the writer Lubomir Feldek read out the 'Declaration of Ordinary Communists', calling for the annulment of Article 4 of the CSSR constitution; this was the clause enshrining the primary position of the Communist Party in society.

The largest meeting to date was held on November 25 at Letenska plan in Prague, with 750,000 people in attendance. This time both Vaclav Havel and Alexander Dubcek addressed the crowd. This was *followed two days later by a symbolic general strike throughout the country. That same week, the Federal Assembly revoked the unpopular Article 4, the guarantee of the leading role of the Communist Party in society. On December 7, President Husak appointed Marian Calfa Chairman of the Federal Government; since Calfa was a Slovak, it was clear that the Czech Vaclav Havel would become the new Czechoslovak President. Since the public in both the Czech and Slovak republics had anticipated the appointment of the revered Alexander Dubcek as head of state, this decision came as a surprise. Husak himself declared that he would step down from the presidency on December 10. On December 28, Dubcek was elected Chairman of the Federal Parliament, and the next day this same body named Havel as President. February of the following year marked the beginning of negotiations on the removal from Czechoslovakia of Soviet troops, and by year's end their twenty-two year occupation of the country had come to an end.*

In April, 1990 Pope John Paul II visited Czechoslovakia. On June 8 and 9, 1990, the first free elections since 1946 were held, with a voter turnout of 95.39 %. In August of that year, during the celebrations in honour of the pre-war Slovak nationalist Andrej Hlinka, slogans for an independent Slovakia were heard for the first time. Czecho-Slovakia was on its way to dissolution.

CHAPTER
TWO

BRATISLAVA – PRAGUE 1989

IN early November of 1989, Balaz and his wife, for the first time in their lives, applied for permission for a one-day trip to Austria so that Marta could visit a ceramics exhibition in Vienna. A few days later, Jozef was contacted by the editor of the New Word weekly, who asked him to write a report on events in the German Democratic Republic, which was celebrating its fortieth anniversary. The paper's local correspondent was apparently not sufficiently critical of the Honecker regime.

"You spent five years there, so please write something worth reading," was his brief. His article was a half-page essay entitled 'Jubilation Zone'. It was strongly critical of the GDR's refusal to adopt Gorbachev's reforms and described the atmosphere of fear and hypocrisy that was driving many thousand East Germans to leave their homeland. After reading the article, the editor called Balaz. "It's pretty strong," he commented, "but I'll print it. Either we'll be applauded or we'll be sacked!" The article appeared on November 16, the day before the Prague demonstration. A few days later, Comrade Deputy Minister Winter telephoned: in light of a complaint from the GDR Embassy about the New Word article, he would like Balaz to come to Prague for a meeting.

Balaz's wife, a ceramics artist, was a member of the Association of Slovak Artists. Wearing a serious expression, she explained to Jozef that the Association had invited her to sign a declaration by a movement calling itself 'Public Against Violence'. "You are a state employee after all, so I don't know if..." she continued.

Balaz thought it over. By this point, it was obvious that sitting at home in front of the television was more than an escape from reality: it was sheer cowardice. "Do you want to go down to the Association?" he asked.

"Certainly," she answered.

"So let's go together."

An exhibition was underway at the Artist's Association, and the place was packed. A meeting where Milan Knazko spoke had just ended; one after the other, artists were leaving the hall to sign the 'VPN Declaration'. Jozef and Marta signed, then went to the nearby Krym café for a beer. They had reason to celebrate: their application for the Austria trip had been approved by the Public Security office. It was true that two weeks earlier the Czechoslovak government had torn down the Iron Curtain and was now allowing people to travel freely, but the Balazes had never before received official permission to go to the West, and they wanted to savour their success.

As public meetings were spreading throughout the country, Balaz got a call from a friend of his, the director of the town theatre in Trnava. He invited him to speak at one of the meetings being held at the theatre. His speech would be given from the exterior balcony, which formed a sort of natural tribune.

So it was that on November 22, Balaz stood on a tribune for the first time ever; he had also never addressed a crowd of twenty thousand. But his speech must have met with the organizers' approval, for he was invited back two days later. The weather was gloomy – rain mixed with snow – but the spotlights shining on him kept him warm. He smiled confidently and exchanged waves with some familiar faces in the crowd. Below the balcony stood a group of noisy, half-drunk fans of the town's football team, Spartak Trnava. Balaz lost his sangfroid, and as a result the crowd took to chanting: "Who caused it? Who caused it?" Caught off guard, Balaz just stood there for a bit, then made a gesture that took even him by surprise. Maybe it was a case of mass psychology, he'd never know, but he first raised his arms to quiet the crowd, then he unzipped his leather jacket, pointed to himself and declaimed: "Us Communists!" For a second the square remained silent, and then exploded into an unbelievable uproar. One part of the crowd applauded his honesty while the rest shouted and spat, and someone tossed an apple core that landed on the balcony. The noise died down only when the next speaker approached the microphone.

"You're completely out of your mind! Trnava is a bastion of the most conservative Communists – they're all around you – and you want to take the blame all by yourself?!" His director friend couldn't understand what had possessed Balaz, and Balaz had no satisfactory answer to give him. So he lit a cigarette instead. Suddenly one man pushed his way through the crowded foyer and approached Balaz, pointing his finger. Then he burst out: "I know this guy well. He's a regular pig!" Then he came right up and went on: "You've got no right to be up there on the tribune; you deserve the people's boos. You were a Communist and you have to bear responsibility for what you did. We're going to chase you out like the dirty dogs you are!" Balaz tiredly lifted his head, and realized this man's face was familiar from somewhere. "Don't pretend you don't know me, we both worked at Chirana!" It was Remenar, the vagabond and cheat, the creep Balaz had voted against when the former applied for Party membership. Giving it all up for lost, he made his way through the crowd back to his car, got in, and drove back to Bratislava.

The meetings in the city's main square continued over the next few days, and Balaz was there almost constantly. He encouraged his colleagues in the press centre to attend: "The more of us there are out there, the sooner the whole thing will collapse."

"Don't be too optimistic; the Party's got it all under control. I'd be a little more careful if I were you," was the flip opinion of his new colleague, Vrablec, who a few days earlier had mysteriously been transferred down from the Prague office. "I personally don't have time for these senseless meetings!"

November 23 was the date the poet Feldek read his 'Declaration of Ordinary Communists' from the tribune at a Bratislava meeting. His words, "We, the ordinary Communist signatories, have studied the declaration by the Public Against Violence association, and without reservations we support their demands!" rocked the square. "The government has branded the reform attempts as the work of anti-state elements... It is our feeling that governments that label the population, and especially the youth, of their country 'anti-state' have lost the moral right to govern... We are sure that if one wants to search out anti-state elements, the place to start looking is at the top... The Czechoslovak Communist Party can be cleansed in one way only: by giving up, voluntarily and immediately, its illegal and violence-backed status in society!"

As Balaz's name was read out among the signatories and he heard the applause that greeted it, he felt rather satisfied with himself. He felt less heroic the next day, however, when he found the signed declaration pasted on the wall of an underpass, with a large headline: "Traitors!" When Feldek brought the Declaration of Ordinary Communists to Prague, Havel is said to have remarked, 'The Slovaks are ahead of us'.

The latest reason for the citizens' disappointment and protest was the formation of a new government in which there was still a majority of Communists. After arriving home from one such protest, Balaz sat at his typewriter and wrote to the Chairman of the CCP organization: he was resigning from the Party in protest against the trickery of the high Communist Party officials. He felt the old guard was unteachable, completely incapable of understanding the situation engulfing them. The next morning, December 5, he posted the original letter, plus a copy to the cadre section of the Ministry of Foreign Affairs. To collect his thoughts, he took a stroll in his favourite woods, Sitina. Whenever he was going through a tough patch, it was in this valley that he found a meditative peace among the wise yet silent trees. He was glad that the political system in which spirituality was buried in nonsense and bureaucracy was coming to an end. Yes, he was glad, although at the same time conscious that when you cut down trees, small chips like himself could get lost, become unnecessary and be forgotten. He was aware that he himself was part of the very mechanism he was fighting. He had accepted the crumbs thrown his way by the power-mongers he despised. And were they really only crumbs? Being a diplomat, albeit one assigned to East Germany, was not a bad fate under socialism. He had his own Lada, even if he'd had to save for four years to afford it. He had bowed down before the mighty so that he might have a flat and promotions at work. Bowing and scraping to fools was degrading, but they held power in their hands, and he did not. This was not because a share had not been offered to him, but because he had never lusted after power; he had an aversion to those he would have to share it with. He justified his own actions to himself, quieted his conscience, and trusted that the new order would create possibilities for the honourable, the wise and the civilized. Being the idealistic dreamer that he was, he failed to foresee that in democracy power would be as pitiless and treacherous as it had been under totalitarianism. Power's temptations remain the same, always and everywhere.

On the ninth of December, Jan Winter sat in his large office in the Federal Ministry of Foreign Affairs and smiled at Balaz, sitting across the small table from him. Winter was reading from a photocopy of the 'Jubilation Zone' article attached to the letter of complaint from the GDR Ambassador. The Embassy noted that the author, one Jozef Balaz, was a Ministry employee, and demanded to be informed of the sanctions that would be taken to ensure that such stories would not be repeated. After reading the note aloud to Balaz, Winter laughed aloud.

"You never told me about the chickens and the cages, that's a good one! We didn't have it easy back then, but now it seems a new chapter is beginning and things are finally moving in the right direction." Winter nodded in satisfaction. "The Germans want me to keep them informed about the measures that will prevent this situation from happening again..." He placed the article and the letter on his desktop: "Got any ideas?"

"I have," Balaz replied. "Tell them to go to hell."

"You're pretty steamed up!" Saying this, Winter called in his secretary. "Eva, take a letter please: 'The Federal Ministry of Foreign Affairs respectfully sends its greetings… blah-blah-blah… and begs to inform Comrade, no, make it Mister, Ambassador that the author of the article, after a serious discussion, has promised to do everything in his power to help the situation in the German Democratic Republic evolve in the correct direction.'" He turned to Balaz: "Sound okay?"

"What does 'the correct direction' mean?"

"Let them decipher it for themselves."

"Sounds good."

His secretary left the room and Winter took a bottle of Chivas Regal from his bar and poured out two glasses.

"What's going on in Bratislava?" he asked straightforwardly. "I've been informed you're arranging interviews for foreign journalists with Dubcek, that you're using state money and state telephones to incite Western reporters against us, that you're out demonstrating all day long, that you're setting up a Slovak/Austrian company, and that you're moderating some sort of meetings with Austrians… And worst of all, the Comrades complain, you're not keeping them informed about all this…"

"I'd only like to say that I'm through with all this. I've left the Communist Party," Balaz retorted, handing Winter a copy of his official letter of resignation. The Deputy Minister took it calmly, and only asked, "Is this not premature?"

"In what way premature?"

"To leave the Party. See how it all plays out. The Communist Party has always been here, and it always will be – it's just a question of getting the right people into positions of power. Why in the world didn't you warn me? We were counting on you, but I'm afraid that if you're now outside the Party, there'll be no chance of you getting a key job. And we need people like you, damn it! Can't you rescind your resignation or something?"

"If you take my advice, Jan, you'll do the same, and don't waste any time about it. Get your secretary back in here, and dictate an abdication notification, then step down as Deputy Minister!"

"Now, just when Calfa is forming a new government and is looking for a Foreign Minister?"

"What are you thinking? Don't you know that Civil Forum has long since agreed with Calfa that Dienstbier will be named Minister? Do you really think that an Ambassador who was a member of the CPC Central Committee Presidium has a chance to make a career in the new government?"

Winter thought it over. "What you're saying makes sense, but there are things you don't know, and sorry, but I'm not in a position to talk about them." Winter considered his words, and then called Eva in. To Balaz's astonishment, he dictated a letter to his Minister to inform him that he was stepping down from his position.

"Take this right to the Minister's secretariat and bring me back confirmation of acceptance," he instructed his secretary.

"Well, congratulations. I wasn't sure you'd take my advice, smiled Balaz, offering Winter his hand. The smile was returned, but Winter was already thinking of other things.

"Well, I guess I'll be leaving."

"No, no, hang on a minute, there's something I wanted to clear up." Balaz saw that Winter was having trouble getting started. "For some time I've been wanting to ask you how you and Marta are getting on."

"Marta?" he looked at his old rival in surprise. "Fine, I guess... Why?"

"And your father-in-law? Decent kind of fellow?"

"Nice guy, yeah," Balaz replied, wondering where all of this was leading.

"Did the two of you ever talk... about the old days?"

"I don't follow... what old days?"

"You know, about his time in Kezmarok back then..."

"He told me some things... his mother was in charge of the post office."

"Right, right... she was a nice old lady... Did he never mention my father? His name was Klaus," Winter went on testing the waters. Balaz didn't know what to say to this.

"Doesn't ring a bell?"

"Sorry, nothing comes to mind. Why are you asking?" Their glances met, and Balaz had the feeling he was being X-rayed, that what Winter was after was something Balaz might know about his father.

"So, let's just leave it. Sorry. Forget I ever mentioned it."

"Why are you so interested in the past right out of the blue?"

"I just thought he might know something about my dad... I never knew him: They say he left home in the summer of 1944, maybe to take part in the Warsaw Uprising. From that time, my mother never heard from him again. Then I was born in the spring of 1945".

"Why did you think my father-in-law might know what happened to him?"

"Listen, just forget it, okay?" He thanked Balaz for coming. They shook hands. "Until next time, all the best." As he left the room, Balaz felt Winter's eyes bore into his back. Then Winter opened a drawer and began to pack his belongings.

CHAPTER
THREE

MOSCOW 1989 – 1991

IN the autumn of 1989, the Gorbachev-appointed KGB Chief Vladimir Krjuckov warned of unfavourable developments in the German Democratic Republic, where the call for German reunification was strengthening. Gorbachev understood that there was no alternative to the reunification, and so, despite the opposition of France, the United Kingdom and the USA, he refused act against the will of the German people. At the end of the day, the only counter-strategy rested on mobilizing the Soviet Armed Forces stationed in East Germany, and the last thing Gorbachev wanted was an armed confrontation.

Krjuckov and the other hardliners in the Soviet hierarchy were deeply angered by the diplomatic support Gorbachev and his Foreign Affairs Minister Eduard Shevardnadze were providing the USA in its war in Iraq. They also disagreed with his soft policies on Germany. Even West German Chancellor Helmut Kohl, prepared for tough and lengthy unification negotiations, was surprised by Gorbachev's agreement to the GDR joining West Germany and even NATO.

At the same time, the opposition to reform within Russia was following Gorbachev's moves with interest. Led by Boris Yeltsin, the Chairman of the Russian Federation Supreme Soviet, they saw that the sun was setting on the Soviet Union, and the new rising star would be Russia *itself. Yeltsin, with his square shoulders and human touch, had quit the Party and in so doing won over the Russian people. It was against this backdrop that the Party conservatives and the KGB urged Gorbachev to slow down the reform process.*

Anti-Russian sentiment was fomenting in the Baltic states, Ukraine, Georgia, Armenia and Azerbaijan, and Yeltsin was among the first to acknowledge the irreversibility of these processes. Furthermore, the dissolution of the USSR would make a switch to a market economy in Russia more rapid and effective. Another setback for Gorbachev was the resignation of Shevardnadze, his closest ally, who two years later became President of Georgia. In his farewell speech to Parliament, Shevardnadze warned against the possibility of a return to dictatorship: 'I cannot agree with the coming of a dictatorship. Nobody knows who might become dictator'. His words were met with thunderous applause.

The KGB was indeed pressuring Gorbachev to declare a state of emergency and the formation of a hard-line government. Gorbechev walked the halls of the Kremlin, lamenting "I'm a bad Czar. A good Czar would not shy away from killing. I'm no dictator!"

In mid-January, the elite KGB strike force, Alfa, made an attempt to overthrow the independence-minded governments of Lithuania, Latvia and Estonia. While Gorbachev covered for them, Yeltsin travelled to Lithuania in support of its claim to national independence. On June 12, 1991, Boris Yeltsin was elected President of Russia; the former Party politburo member pledged the Presidential Oath to the Moscow Patriarch, accompanied by music from Glinka's 'Life Under the Czar'. The dissolution of the Soviet Union was at hand.

The KGB lost patience. On August 5, while Gorbachev was holidaying in Crimea, its head, Krjuckov, met with the Interior Minister, Boris Pugo and the Minister of Defence, Dmitrij Jazov in a Moscow sanatorium to establish the Committee for an Emergency State. The KGB went so far as to vacate two floors in Lefortovo Prison to house expected prisoners from the country's government.

In an attempt to convince him to hand over his authority to the Committee, the conspirators met with Gorbachev two weeks later, but in vain. In consequence, Gorbachev was interned in Crimea and declared unfit to hold office due to health problems. The plot leaders convened in the local office of Gorbachev's Vice-president, Gennady Janajev, the man spearheading of the coup. By an irony of history, this same office, number 49, was previously occupied by the head of Stalin's secret police, Beria. In contrast, Janajev was himself a weak man and a chronic drunkard; in fact, these reactionaries turned out all to be cut from the same cloth and incapable of radical action. Their decree stripping Gorbachev of power was ignored by most of the senior KGB.

What definitively sank the putsch was the resoluteness of Boris Yeltsin. He came to the Parliament building and took over activities against the plotters. His masterstroke was to address the public in front of the world's TV cameras from the turret of a tank. Then he shrewdly contacted the regional KGB bosses. He began in Petrograd, where the local KGB head, one Vladimir Putin, refused to join the plotters. Latvia and Estonia saw their chance in all this confusion and declared their independence. Interior Minister Pugo then committed suicide and two days later Yeltsin banned the activity of the Communist Party within Russia. The next day, Mikhail Gorbachev resigned as Party General Secretary.

In their anger over the political irresponsibility, an enraged crowd of Muscovites gathered in front of KGB headquarters on Lubianka Square and toppled a huge statue of the founder of the secret police, Felix Dzerzhinsky, from its pedestal.

The death throes of the empire continued for another four months. On September 6, 1991 Moscow recognized the independence of Lithuania, Latvia and Estonia. A referendum in Ukraine confirmed that country's secession from the Soviet Union as well. Mikhail Gorbachev chose Christmas Day to announce he was stepping down from the USSR Presidency. The next day, a final session of the Supreme Soviet Upper Chamber met with only one item on its agenda: a Declaration of the Annulment of the Soviet Union. Of its 374 members, only 24 showed up to approve the resolution. In place of the USSR red emblem, the Russian flag suddenly fluttered atop the Kremlin. Seventy-four years of Communist rule had come to an end.

CHAPTER
FOUR

BERLIN 1989

FTER fifty days as head of the SED, Egon Krenz resigned, along with the entire party leadership, on December 6, 1989. The new executive renamed the party the Democratic Socialism Party. Once the borders opened, the slogan 'We are the people' evolved into 'We are one people', and 'Germany, our only homeland'. The population didn't want a new East Germany, but a united Germany.

During Gorbachev's meeting with the West German Chancellor, Helmut Kohl, in Moscow on February 10, 1990, specific steps in the reunification process were discussed. Kohl was under the impression that NATO would not be permitted to extend its authority into the territory of the former GDR.

For the first time in almost sixty years, free elections were held in East Germany on March 18, 1990. In Premier Lothar De Maizier's cabinet were two Protestant priests: Markus Meckel, the Minister of Foreign Affairs and a socialist, and Rainer Eppelmann, the Minister of Defence. On the first of July, the economic, monetary and social union of the two Germanys took place. The beloved West German mark finally became the currency in the GDR as well. During a visit to Russia by Kohl and Hans-Dietrich Genscher lasting from July 14 to 16, the

Soviet side dropped its objections to NATO membership for the new united Germany.

From October 3, 1990 the German people were again living in one country.

Thomas and Heike, along with three hundred thousand other fans, took in the wonderful atmosphere in Potsdam Square in Berlin. The popular rock band Pink Floyd presented their mammoth project 'The Wall' in July, 1990, less than a year after the fall of the Berlin Wall. Never before had so many people attended a rock concert. Invited by the band's Roger Waters, another twenty rock stars also appeared, performing Pink Floyd songs either solo or together. Thomas was finally living out a dream from his student days, to attend a Pink Floyd concert. His only regret was that the band's guitarist, David Gilmour, was absent. Even so, seeing Roger Waters, Van Morrison, Bryan Adams, Joni Mitchell and the Scorpions live was fantastic. The crowd of three hundred thousand was hushed as the first notes of 'Mother', as sung by Sinéad O'Connor, rang out. Her voice sent shivers up and down spines, and some fans were even in tears. Along with the rock groups, Pink Floyd enjoyed the support of the East German Radio Choir and Philharmonic Orchestra, the Marching Band of the Combined Soviet Forces in Germany, and the Red Army Chorus. So much energy was produced that it seemed the Wall would tumble down for a second time. Among the millions watching on screens was Bärbel Hannes, who couldn't hold back her tears. On the stage, her husband Johannes was playing cello in the orchestra. They weren't allowed to go to freedom, so freedom came to them.

As the sun set gradually behind the stage, a huge hairy creature appeared against the red clouds. Swung by a crane, the giant bug crawled onto a virtual wall and looked down at the people. It then supervised the plastering of the last bricks in the wall that the sun's rays were lighting up. When at the end of the concert the wall gradually crumbled, and the Soviet military musicians bade farewell to Berlin forever, millions of souls were made conscious of the impermanency of power and the patient humility of the powerless.

Thomas' and Heike's hands, together with those of many thousands of others, waved them goodbye with surprisingly little resentment. Rather, they felt a little sorry for them – and for themselves. Who could return to them the liberty their youth had been deprived of? Who was responsible for its absence – those who had denied freedom or those who had tolerated its denial?

For a few hours, Potsdam Square, a demolition site near the abominable wall, where the Anhalter railway station had once stood, was the centre of the world. Thousands of throats joined in: 'We don't need your education...'

Accompanied by deafening cheering, the symbolic wall came crashing down. Its dust spread everywhere, but nobody cared. In a soldier's suit, Roger Waters sang: 'I want to go home and take this uniform off!' As the end of the concert drew near, thousands of crosses appeared among the debris of the wall that was scattered over the stage, the Soviet drums crashed, and the last brick fell. Soviet military vehicles arrived to take the soldiers away. Waters sang: 'Bring the boys back home'. Thomas unconsciously pulled Heike closer. They swore they would never let their children grow up to be soldiers.

CHAPTER
FIVE

BRATISLAVA 1989

THE Balazes were spending their first Christmas in the old vineyard house in Bratislava they had saved the money to buy. After midnight, the women and children went to bed, leaving Jozef alone with his father-in-law.

Although Balaz had been waiting for the opportunity for them to talk, the charged Christmas atmosphere had prevented them from being alone together. Now, after a little hesitation, he asked his father-in-law if the name Klaus Winter meant anything to him. The older man thought for a bit, nodded, and began to speak.

"I've been expecting you to bring up the name of your lifelong 'friend's' father," he smiled sourly. "I thought about mentioning him myself, but somehow the occasion never came up, so I left it to fate." Sighing deeply, as if to collect his thoughts, he began his tale: "After the suppression of the Uprising in '44, the captured partisans, along with a number of Jewish Slovaks who were to be transported to Auschwitz, were held in the cellars of Kezmarok Castle. The Castle was guarded by Hlinka Guard divisions and two Einsatztruppe (ET) platoons. The commander of one of these ET groups was Klaus Winter, the father of Jan, your former Ambassador." Balecky hesitated.

"What happened?" Balaz encouraged him to go on.

"This is all fifty years in the past..."

"I get the feeling something's weighing on your mind." He stared at his father-in-law as if trying to see inside his soul.

"What they say about old man Winter is not the truth. That's the most important thing to grasp. The evidence is in this packet." Balecky took a thick sealed envelope out of his jacket pocket and handed it to Balaz.

"You were ready for my question, it would seem."

"You could put it that way," Balecky avoided a direct answer. "Give it to Jan Winter after my death; till then, keep it in a safe place."

"I don't know what they say about Winter's father."

"That he shot the owner of the Podolinec sawmill, Müller, in the Castle forecourt."

"So that's what was making Winter nervous, he thought I knew about it..." He turned brusquely in Balecky's direction. "Why were you carrying this envelope today?"

"I always take it with me when I know I'm going to meet you, but I've never had the courage to give it to you... I have the feeling I won't be around much longer... Your knowing the truth will be a comfort to me when I'm lying in my grave." Balecky took a drink from his glass.

"You couldn't trust me enough to tell me something so serious?"

His father-in-law spoke slowly and quietly: "You know, Winter was in the Slovak German Party, which was something like the Nazi Party in Germany. And me... I was in the Hlinka Slovak People's Party..."

"Does that bother you? After all, everybody belonged to the party, during the Slovak State it was the only official party."

"Yes, but just like the German Party in Slovakia had its SS, the Freiwillige Schutzstaffel, so the Hlinka Party had its storm troopers, the Hlinka Guard." Balecky seemed to have trouble telling Balaz this.

"But..." he began, but Balecky silenced him with a wave of his hand and went on.

"The most fervent Schutzstaffel members were selected for the ET, their storm troopers. Winter was chosen to join it... and the

Hlinka Guard had its Emergency Brigades... I was in one of them." On hearing this, a frown spread over Balaz's forehead. Balecky reflected, and then went on as if unwillingly. "What happened next, you'll find in this envelope. Maybe Winter will feel like telling you the story in the meantime. I don't have a lot of time left, the cancer has spread to my intestines. My doctor wants to operate, but I don't want to go to the trouble..."

"Listen, you know I like you and respect you. As far as your illnesses goes, we'll do everything we can so you can be with us as long as possible... And excuse me for saying it, but I think you'd go to heaven more peacefully for having spoken about this thing... What do you have to fear? You have my word that anything you tell me will go no further... I wouldn't even say anything to your daughter." Balaz added this last as he realized that Balecky was probably worried that his two daughters would find out something about their father to change their image of him as a wonderful, generous and loving family man.

Balecky considered all this, and in a sudden flowing outburst said: "I was also present in the Castle's forecourt, not as a paver like it says in the report, but as a member of a Hlinka Guard Emergency Brigade. Together with the German Party storm troopers, our job was to send the Jews to the concentration camps."

This revelation brought about a lengthy silence, during which Balaz felt that now was perhaps not the right time to force the old man into further confessions. Despite his better judgment, however, he commented: "You told me you were a Democratic Party member up to 1948, when you joined the Communist Party, but you never said you were in the People's Party..."

"Are you reproaching me? Yes, I was in the Hlinka Party, because I believed that I could do the most to serve my country there. I wanted to do my utmost for Slovakia. In forty-three, I started studying law so as to be able to administer justice... ha, ha..." Again Balecky's cynical smile. "After the war, when the Democratic Party voted to allow ordinary Guard members to join the party, I took out membership. I joined mainly because I saw how aggressive the Communist Party was becoming; I didn't want my country to fall into their hands. I had always been in favour of Christianity, order and democracy. We resoundingly won the 1946 elections, and then the end came – the Communist putsch of February, 1948. There followed pressures, repressions, imprisonments. When the Democratic Party leader Lettrich escaped to Austria in June of that year, it was clear that no hope remained... I had been married for three years, your sister-in-law, Eva, was two years old, and I was about to graduate from the Law Faculty with a first-class degree. We were looking for a flat.... About a month before my graduation, I was called in to see the Dean of the Faculty. He told me the Communist Party needed new members... The Democratic Party no longer existed, and those who hadn't managed to flee to the West and were in a similar situation to mine had renounced their membership. Moreover, the Dean hinted that he knew something of my past... suddenly I, someone who had been against Communism all my life, was in the Party. A year later, after passing my bar exams, I got a two-room flat... For my family and me, it was a sort of liberation. Until then, we'd been sharing a one-room flat with my mother." Balecky stopped to pour himself another drink.

"Are you still a Party member?" Balaz asked.

"I don't really know, but I don't think so. When I retired, I stopped paying my membership dues, stopped going to meetings. At first, they called me up, but I just ignored them. I haven't heard from them in ten years."

"I left the Party three weeks ago."

"Good for you!"

"Never again will I belong to any kind of political party... Never again," Balaz concluded resolutely.

"Ha, ha," Balecky laughed.

"What's so funny?"

"That's exactly what I said when I left the Hlinka Party... Do you know what the worst thing about belonging to a small nation is? It's that while throughout history big countries have always behaved like gangsters, we have always acted like prostitutes. The difference is that while prostitutes at least ask for money, we Slovaks have always put out for free, and willingly! Excuse my language, please. And don't forget that packet... but remember, give it to him only after I'm gone!"

CHAPTER
SIX

BRATISLAVA 1989 – 1991

JUST after Epiphany, the phone rang in the Balazes' flat. Petr Horacek, who Balaz knew from the Berlin Embassy, was calling. He was a good friend, one of those people you could share your most personal experiences with. In the current atmosphere of fear and suspicion, their closeness strengthened both of them. His was one of the five families Balaz and his wife spent a great deal of their free time with, including the Christmas and Easter festivities. They made for each other a kind of island where all involved could breathe freely. But now Petr sounded anxious and worried. He asked to meet Balaz for ten minutes the following week.

"What do you mean, ten minutes? Come to stay with us for a few days if you like," Balaz suggested.

"Unfortunately, that won't be possible – I'll have to get right back here. What I want to see you about is really quite urgent."

"Can't you tell me anything of what it's about? Do you need my help?"

"No, but thanks anyway."

He and Horacek met in the hotel Krivan, just below the main railway station. Petr had said their meeting would be brief, but surprisingly he began by discussing their friendship and cooperation back in Berlin. Balaz figured this wasn't the reason for Petr's trip, but he waited patiently. And then he came out with it: "You know, Jozef, there are situations a person can't come to terms with, even if he lives a hundred years. I... I... you remember how we used to tell each other everything, how we used to fight with Winter... It helped me a lot... but the fact is, I was assigned to keep an eye on you - on you and Honzo and Vlasto and Juro and a few others... I swear I never told them anything that could harm you, but all the same... Forgive me... I just couldn't bear it... I couldn't start a new life with that on my chest... I had to come and tell you... Forgive me..." Petr's eyes were red.

Balaz just sat there stunned, not knowing what to say, then: "I want you to know that I still consider you my good friend. The times have changed, but I know you'd never do anything wrong."

"Forgive me," Petr burst out, and quickly left the café. They never met again.

Balaz was watching the news; they were reporting on prisoners who had been released from jail and were already back in custody. It was less than three weeks since President Havel had declared a general amnesty, freeing recidivists and thousands of people accused of serious crimes. Balaz just shook his head, and said to Marta: "If he'd learned anything from history, he'd never have done that. When the American forces liberated Italy, the first ones to claim they were victims of fascism were the biggest criminals. They had been sentenced under Mussolini for murder and other serious crimes for which they'd have been jailed no matter what government was in power."

"Take that dog out," she called from the kitchen. "Don't you hear her whining?"

Balaz took Pesina out for a walk through the snow-blown pathways of the valley where they lived. His head was full of the information he'd heard that day from his friend Vasek in Prague: that Jaromir Komorous was going to be nominated as the new Czechoslovak Ambassador to Austria. Balaz didn't need to hear any more; he knew Komorous from his time in Prague, and he was an unpleasant man who didn't like many people. Most of all, he didn't like Slovaks. Balaz understood that if this man was appointed to Austria, Slovakia's only direct link with the West would be compromised.

He continued his walk through the valley's pathways and wondered what he could do. He knew one thing clearly: Komorous must not be named Ambassador to Austria! If there was any hope of stopping the nomination, someone else had to be found for the post. He ran a series of suitable names through his head, then remembered the pleasant evening he and his wife had spent recently with Hana Kunova. At that time, Hana had spoken about giving up the theatre and seeking something new and interesting. He knew she understood politics, she was a popular Czechoslovak actress, and her German was first-rate. Damn, he should have thought of this before! Hurrying home with the dog, he wondered if the fact that she had been a favourite artist under the wing of the Communist Party and had signed the Anti-Charter Declaration would spoil her chances with the new power elite. On the other hand, he had faith in their tolerance and sympathy. Still, Havel could nominate Komorous any day now, so he would have to get going on his campaign. He left the dog in her kennel and raced to his typewriter. It took all his courage to write to the Foreign Minister, Jiří Dienstbier, and suggest he consider the actress Hana Kunova for Ambassador to Austria. He read the letter over a number of times, made some minor changes, and sealed the envelope. He only hoped his daring would not disappear with the morning, and that he really would send the letter. To make sure, his first stop the next day was the post office, where he sent the letter registered mail. Next, he called in on his friend Kamil, the VPN spokesman. In the hallway of their headquarters, he ran across Gabo, the man who had long ago looked after his Lada. "Hello, Jozef – welcome to the coordination centre."

"Aren't you working in the boiler room anymore?"

"Nope, now I work here," Gabo called back as he ran down the stairs.

Kamil told Milan, at that time a counsellor to President Havel, about Balaz's idea. At first Milan wasn't thrilled with the plan, but in the end he passed the suggestion on to Havel.

At the beginning of February, 1990, Hana Kunova was invited to the Federal Foreign Affairs Ministry. The Public Against Violence Centre had officially proposed Kunova as Ambassador, and her nomination was supported by Dienstbier. A few days later, her nomination was approved by the President.

The authorization document was submitted to Austrian President Kurt Waldheim on April 10, 1990 in the Hofburg Imperial Palace. From the beginning of her diplomatic career, Balaz had stood behind Kunova both as her deputy and as her guardian angel.

On March 14, 1991, radical nationalists celebrating the fifty-second anniversary of the wartime Slovak State attacked President Havel in Bratislava's SNP Square. The demonstrators spat and swore at the President. Among the most active in the crowd was Balaz's one-time colleague, Vrablec, the man who, at the start of the Velvet Revolution, had had no time for 'senseless meetings'. Strange to tell, there were an unusual number of foreign journalists and television crews in front of the podium that day; it was as if they had been tipped off that something was about to erupt. The next day, the world was told the chauvinistic Slovaks were out to break up the Czech and Slovak Federal Republic.

The CSFR Minister of the Interior, Sacher, abolished the StB Security Service on February 17, 1990. This abolition was strictly formal however; most StB personnel had already found their way into new organizations. The Foreign Information Administration, responsible for espionage abroad, now became the Office for International Relations and Information (UZSI), and needed new figureheads – and one of these was Jan Winter. After walking away from the Foreign Affairs Ministry, he walked into the UZSI. When he was called to meet his new chief in the latter's office, he found it hard to mask his shock. The man sitting behind the desk was the same man Winter had got drunk in the Scheremetevo Moscow Airport!

"I guess you're a little surprised to see me here," Pavol Horvath smiled, offering Winter his hand.

CHAPTER
SEVEN

BERLIN 1991

REINER, Bodo, Walter, Dietrich and Thomas were sitting in a beer garden talking about the old days when as students they had rebelled against the American war in Vietnam, the Soviet invasion of Czechoslovakia, the university system, the Bonn government, and practically anything else that was 'protest-friendly'. Thomas was a little surprised that his old friends still kept in touch with each other. Following his entry into politics, their relationships had cooled off. They'd been talking and joking for almost an hour, but Thomas felt the reason for their reunion hadn't yet come out. He looked at his watch.

"Sorry, guys; it's been nice talking about the old times, but the clock is running, and I have another meeting in Charlottenburg in half an hour." Hearing this, the others looked to Reiner, who shifted in his chair.

"Look, Thomas, we know you're not in politics any longer, but you still have a good name with the public... and it's a shame you're not still active. I'm talking about this gross rip-off that goes by the name of privatization," he began cautiously.

"I don't get you."

"Don't you see what's going on in the former east zone? More than eight thousand East German enterprises with four million workers are being passed around by mafia gangs as if they were candy. The whole Treuhand privatization agency is a fraud."

"What makes you think that?"

"If the factories were being privatized in order to increase production, that would be one thing, but in most cases they're being run in such a way that they stop producing. The operation goes downhill, and just before it goes bankrupt, a few good men from Treuhand sell it off to their friends for next to nothing ... And then thousands of people are put out of work." Thomas had the feeling his old gang was somehow taking advantage of the injustices in the privatization process to show the public – and themselves – that the remnants of the RAF and other groups were still active.

Thomas thought it over: "I'm not saying there are no fiddles going on, but I'm sure the Ministry of Finance has things under control." The men began to laugh out loud at this. "And I hate to say it, but the majority of the GDR national enterprises are simply not competitive."

"You're talking as if you had a hand in it yourself. You don't see, or don't want to see, that these Treuhand crooks are putting directly into their own pockets millions of marks from the federal government intended to support privatization and ensure new employment opportunities!"

"What do you expect me to do about it?"

"Just what we said before. If someone with your reputation were to discuss the issue in public, maybe someone in government would take it serioously. They say that the Treuhand boss, Rohwedder, has become one of the richest men in Germany in just a few months. Maybe it would be enough just to have a heart-to-heart discussion with him."

"But I don't even know the guy! And you're exaggerating my position. I'm not in parliament any more, don't forget. And what exactly are you lot planning to do?"

"Perhaps we'll give him a thumping; if he survives it, he'll remember the lesson for the rest of his life... But maybe that won't be necessary..."

"Cut it out with these silly threats. Even if he was impeached or if you did kill him, what would that change? They'd put in a new chief, and..."

Reiner cut him off: "And when the new boss steps in, he'll have been warned. But we don't want to go that far... That's why we need you. You have the public's trust, and your opinion is still respected in political circles."

Thomas thought about it, then answered: "Boys, I'm not saying you haven't got it right, but what you're planning makes no sense. It won't change anything. In any kind of large-scale privatization there's bound to be abuses. The thieving will only end when the privatization ends."

"I can't believe what I'm hearing – this is Thomas Ankermann, the one-time revolutionary?" Bodo tried a little moral pressure.

Reiner chipped in next: "Everyone knows you're one of the few people who left politics on the basis of his own decision, without scandal or financial trickery... In fact, your hands are clean... Even your divorce with Angelika was on account of her father," he said persuasively.

"We didn't divorce because of her father; we just weren't getting along. Just as with politics and with you guys, we broke up because we didn't see eye to eye."

There was silence for a time, which Reiner broke: "Well, you know, that time when on television you called us 'a criminal element', that wasn't very nice of you. And that time in Kreuzberg, when Mr. Deputy just looked on as the police were breaking my head with their truncheons, that wasn't so nice of you either... But it's all behind us now."

"Excuse me, but that show you put on in Kreuzberg was pure futility. You knew it, but you needed to draw attention to yourselves. When you organized that demonstration in Mutlangen against the American rockets I came because I believed in what we were doing. Sorry, boys, don't think badly of me, but it's just not on." Thomas said nothing more, just shook his head and looked Rainer right in the eye.

He thought about the big order from an international corporation, Alumetall, his wife's consulting company had received for a five-year order to prepare management employees in the thirty-two countries where the corporation had branches. Alumetall was one of the firms that had come into existence through the privatization of the East German VEB Aluminiumwerke conglomerate.

Reiner was not yet done: "Is that your final word?" he asked. Thomas nodded. "Okay. But you could have saved him."

With that, the others left. Thomas watched them go with an uneasy feeling.

On the evening of April 1, the head of the German National Property Fund (Treuhand), Detlev Karsten Rohwedder, was sitting in his study in his villa in Düsseldorf. His curtains were not drawn, and as he rose from his desk he was hit by a bullet fired from an estimated distance of sixty metres. His wife was also shot, but in contrast to her husband, her wound was not fatal. Rohwedder's murder has to date not been solved. According to investigators, this may have been the final terrorist act of the Red Army Faction in Germany.

The privatization balance under Treuhand was catastrophic – an income of sixty million marks was offset by expenses amounting to over three billion. The greatest theft in Germany's recent history, however, was soon forgotten. As in Poland, Hungary, the Czech Republic, Slovakia, Russia, Bulgaria, Romania and Ukraine, those who were in the right place at the right time got the property which the sweat of millions of people had built up over several generations.

CHAPTER
EIGHT

VIENNA – PRAGUE 1992

THE Federal Assembly, despite objections from many deputies, on October 4, 1991 passed the disclosure act which banned one-time Communist Secret Service collaborators from holding higher political office. However, Alexander Dubček, the Chairman of the Federal Assembly, refused to sign the act into law, explaining that since it was based on documents collected by the StB, essentially a criminal organization for which lies, fraud, scandal, blackmail and murder were standard working practices. Lists of reported secret police collaborators began to appear in the press and were used by political opponents to mutually discredit each other. The mud-slinging even caught President Vaclav Havel, who was identified as a secret cooperation agent. Although the police reports were full of information on those who were reportedly recruited by the secret police, nobody objected to the fact that those who were carrying out the recruiting were never identified. In other words, the public never found out the names of the StB officers. One newspaper ran a cartoon of two men talking in front of the Parliament building in Prague: 'I'm not afraid of disclosure,' one of them was saying, 'I was never an informer; I was the one who issued the orders'.

At the end of March, 1992, Deputy Ambassador Balaz was invited to a discussion with Deputy Foreign Minister Langer, a Civic Forum nominee who knew nothing of diplomacy. This well-meaning fellow compensated for his ignorance by drinking too much, and thus eagerly accepted the bottle of good whisky Balaz brought him. At least he was honest enough to open it right away, as opposed to the majority of his colleagues.

"I have some unpleasant news for you," Langer began. "On the basis of the disclosure act, I have to inform you that we have received documentation of your erstwhile cooperation with State Security."

"Please don't refer to it as cooperation," Balaz objected. "Cooperation implies initiative. I was simply summoned to the StB; I never went there of my own volition. Before going to Vienna, I informed the relevant people in the ministry that under the old regime I had been interviewed by the StB when I served as head of the press centre in Bratislava. I was the one who asked the personnel department to check my dealings with them."

"Unfortunately, new facts have come to light."

"New facts? No new facts could come to light other than those I personally introduced during my interview with the former head of the personnel administration. There's a record of that interview."

"Apart from anything else, the problem is that Doctor Zíhal himself was found to have been cooperating with the StB... He is no longer in his post."

"Could you tell me one specific thing I've been accused of?"

"Well, I'm sorry to say, I can't... the fact is... I don't know." Langer again poured them both a drink and quickly swallowed his. "I have all your documentation over there in that metal cabinet."

"So show me it!"

"I can't do that," Langer said uncertainly. Balaz had a feeling the cupboard was empty. "I don't have time to read all that nonsense. It was all written by the cops..."

"So you're talking about some information written by unreliable people, and you're judging me on that basis..."

"I'm not judging anybody! I don't really give a damn. I can honestly say that in my opinion, you're one of the most competent diplomats we have... But all the same, there are those issues." Langer sighed and took another drink.

"Sorry, but in my opinion, it's all irrelevant."

"And what is relevant, then?" He looked at Balaz in bewilderment.

"Mr. Langer, I'm not some greenhorn; I see what's going on around me. It's clear that the republic is coming apart."

"Don't even whisper such things! I won't allow Czechoslovak diplomats, even if they are from Slovakia, to even consider such an eventuality!"

"Then why are various ministry commissions, composed solely of Czechs, coming to Vienna to make inventories of our property? So far no-one has come from Bratislava."

"They couldn't. Bratislava isn't authorized for that."

"Mister Deputy, this is a process which cannot be halted. It's clear they are going to divide up the holdings – and in Vienna there are a lot of them... And it's clear that for... Prague, it's unacceptable that in a significant embassy like Vienna the top two persons are Slovaks. I expect the Czechs also want to have a list of the property." Balaz gave Langer a lengthy glare.

"Well, you've put it in a nutshell... Thank you for saving me from beating around the bush."

"So it's clear that I'm finished in Vienna. Not on account of this StB mystification, but for these political reasons... By the way, Lado Korecky will make a good Deputy Ambassador."

"Up to now, no specific names have been mentioned."

"Sorry, but I've been in this ministry a few years longer than you. These names are known long before they're mentioned out loud. I'm not going to make things complicated for you; I'll submit a request for termination of my contract."

On the last day of July, 1992, Jozef Balaz finished his activities at the Federal Ministry of Foreign Affairs of the Czech and Slovak Federal Republic.

On the seventeenth of July, 1992, the Slovak National Assembly issued the Declaration of the Sovereignty of the Slovak Republic as the basis for the sovereignty of the Slovak nation. That same day, at six in the evening, the President of the Czech and Slovak Federal Republic, Vaclav Havel, resigned from office. One week later, the Chairmen of the respective governments, Vaclav Klaus and Vladimir Meciar, agreed on the division of Czecho-Slovakia, effective from 1. 1. 1993. The promised referendum on this issue was never held.

CHAPTER
NINE

MOSCOW – KIEV 1991 – 2005

FTER the demise of the Soviet Union, most of the high-ranking officials of the Communist Party became democrats from one day to the next. The democratization process was supported by the Party leadership, the state administration, the KGB and even by the mafia. Former Party officials suddenly became bankers and businessmen.

Like his Communist predecessors, President Boris Yeltsin was away from the Kremlin more often than he was in his office. The ailing President spent most of his time in the state recreation complex at Sochi, in the Black Sea area. He was receiving anti-depression medicines and regular back massages while the country was being run by his daughter, Tatiana Djatshenko. This unofficial chief of the Kremlin, and therefore of the whole of Russia, operated from her workplace, known as room 262. According to the well-informed former KGB agent Vladimir Putin, running the country meant overseeing the illegal transfer of twenty billion dollars every year from 1991 to 2000.

During that first year, all the former Union countries declared their independence. The largest of these, Ukraine, took this step on August 24, 1991. As a result of this, it was necessary to find every experienced administrator to build up the new state's governing bodies. This was complicated by the fact that most of these people opted to remain in Moscow as fresh Russian citizens.

Sergej Gusev was called to Kiev at the beginning of 1992 to help in the formation of the Ukrainian military intelligence. He was one of the few Ukrainians who were ready and willing to give up their comfortable lives in Moscow and come back home. General Gusev and Sasha returned near the end of May and were given an official flat close to the centre of Kiev near Bessarabskaja Square. Sasha's parents were overjoyed that after so many years away, their daughter and their granddaughter Ninocka would be closer to them.

Sasha's father was an old friend of an outstanding banker called Vadym Hetman, and when he was appointed Chairman of the Board of the National Bank of Ukraine, he chose Grycenko's daughter as the head of his secretariat. Sasha brought experience and energy to her new position. When in 1993 Hetman resigned his post (he was assassinated in 1998), Sasha was kept on by his trusted successor, a young economist named Victor Yushchenko. Over time, the ambitious new Chairman grew to appreciate Sasha's diligence and sense of responsibility. However, despite having just been elected for a second term of office in 1997, Yushchenko was surprisingly chosen by President Leonid Kuchma as his Government Chairman. In 2001, the Supreme Council declared its non-confidence in Yushchenko. He reacted by forming a new political party, 'Our Ukraine', which, even though it won the most seats, was forced into the opposition.

In 2004, President Kuchma finished his term of office, and the election of a successor was contested by two men named Victor – Yushchenko and Yanukovych.

In early September, 2004 Yushchenko dined at his cottage with the head of the Ukrainian Security Service, Igor Smeshko, and his deputy, Volodymyr Sacjuk. They were there to discuss the neutrality of the Special Service during the upcoming election. The next day, Yushchenko complained of a dramatic decline in his state of health. He was immediately transported to a specialized clinic in Vienna, where the local doctors suspected dioxin poisoning. During this most crucial episode in his life, his wife Katarina, his five children and his closest allies were summoned to his bedside.

Despite his serious health complications, Yushchenko narrowly won the first round of voting, but without achieving the fifty percent of the ballots cast necessary for an outright victory. He faced Yanukovych in the second round and was narrowly defeated. Amid suspicions of electoral fraud, the Central Elections Commission refused to accept 300 objections from Yushchenko's election committee. Yushchenko subsequently declared a general strike for November 25, at which hundreds of thousands of Ukrainians took to the streets. This was the first step in the so-called Orange Revolution, which mobilized the camps of both of the Victors. Despite the chill November weather, thousands of Yushchenko supporters camped out on Kiev's main square, Majdan, and the fresh winner of the Eurovision contest, a popular singer known as Ruslana, declared a hunger strike in support of Yushchenko. Finally, a rerunning of the election was announced – Yushchenko took 52 percent to Yanukovych's 44 percent, and was inaugurated on January 23, 2005.

Sasha, her family and a few neighbours followed the election results in the living room in their parents' house in Kolodna. Spread out on the table were the tastiest snacks available in a Ukrainian village during the winter: sausages, cheese, piroshky, vareniky,potato pancakes, smoked fish, borscht, Horilka liquor, Sergej's favourite Obolon beer and the finest Crimean wines. More and more neighbours kept dropping by, and the room was thick with smoke. Everyone was laughing, discussing their nation's future and the stormy past few months. Here in West Ukraine, Yushchenko was the clear winner, and Yanukovych's supporters were loudly criticized. Also debated was the division of the country, which certain political powers, especially in the East Ukrainian area, had proposed. The idea was roundly rejected; preserving the unity of the country was judged to be the most important task facing the new president.

"Sasha, Sasha, are you listening? You have to tell Viktor Andryjovich Yushchenko that we're all in his corner, but that he has to find a way to come to terms with Yanukovych. And that we don't want to get into any quarrels with Moscow!" Sasha sat next to her husband and smiled absently in reply. She looked at her joyful neighbours and friends, and thought back over the stormy weeks she had gone through in Kiev. She would have laid down her life on the streets of Kiev for her longtime boss, Victor Yushchenko. Those cold and stressful days when Ukraine teetered on the edge of civil war were finally over, and the country was following the televised account of the new President's inauguration with relief. But she personally found it hard to concentrate on the moment the whole world was watching. When he saw the tears dropping from her eyes, Sergej tenderly pulled her to him.

"Now, now, my dear Sasha, come on... we'll get through it." When her friends noticed her distress, Sasha decided she couldn't tinge their delight with her sorrow. In her need to be alone with her heart-wrenching grief, she made her way into the hall. Sergej followed along, knowing where she was headed. He helped her into her winter clothes, and put on his own coat.

They walked in silence for about ten minutes, making their way beyond the bounds of the village. They went down a slope lightly covered with the year's first snow, then across a wooden bridge over a stream. Beyond the bridge was a cemetery, and in that cemetery was one freshly-dug grave.

CHAPTER
TEN

BRATISLAVA 1992 – 1999

FOR the Balaz family, as for many Czech and Slovak families, New Year's Eve, 1992 was strange indeed. Czechoslovakia had split up, and although the cities' squares were full of celebrants, the majority of the population did not feel like celebrating. They still were unsure if the division of the republic was a good thing or not. Slovaks certainly felt relief and a sense of excitement from attaining national independence, but at the same time they feared economic difficulties; the media were predicting a rapid decline in the status of the economy. But while the nation's birth was greeted by some with sadness and nostalgia, others were expecting Europe's newest state to show its worth.

Balaz listened to the pathos-laden New Year's addresses by the Slovak Parliament Chairman and the Premier to a backdrop of fireworks and merrymaking. His daughters, Martuska and young Anicka, watched on as their parents discussed whether the new national borders would affect their visits to Marta's family. Her sister Eva had studied medicine in the Czech Republic, in the city of Olomouc, and had married a merry and personable local man, Eman Stanek. When they telephoned the Balazes after midnight, nobody had much to say. There were thousands of mixed families on both sides of the new frontier who were probably equally at sea. As it later turned out, except for waits at border crossings, the relations between the two new neighbours did not pose very many complications – Slovak and Czech farmers were even allowed to continue ploughing fields suddenly situated in a foreign country.

"They broke up the republic just because they couldn't agree on who would be the boss. This way, they all get a piece of the two smaller pies," was the angry opinion of Mr. Balecky. Although he had lost a good deal of weight and his eyes were going, he still retained a ready wit and a sharp tongue. Nowadays he regularly followed and commented on the news from the standpoint of someone whose days were essentially coming to an end. "All those dirty dealings throughout history were allowed to happen not due to the daring of the power-grabbers, but because of the cowardice of those who were afraid to say no to them. In this case it's not the greedy on the one side and the civilized on the other – they're all greedy! They've been practicing thievery for forty years, but at least then it had to be clandestine; now they can do it out in the open."

"Quiet down, someone could be listening," his wife warned. This type of warning flourished in the new democracy – under totalitarianism, she would have been afraid to even warn him. Nowadays there was no-one to fear, so such warnings were the kind of joke she enjoyed. His wife was one of those who, when something bad happened, took pleasure in saying: "I told you so..."

"Now you're going to tell me when and what I can say! That's all I need!" Balecky stopped to pour himself another glass of wine, then continued his emotional expose.

"Jozef, take that bottle away from him, he's getting drunk!" Now his mother-in-law was getting Balaz involved in it.

"Better let him get on with it. He's got his Slovak state back."

"So this is what your Velvet Revolution comes down to – the start of the race towards the trough? The starter raises his pistol, but when he looks at the starting line he sees just the backs and the dust of the sprinting runners. Off they all go together: careerists, communists, anti-communists, churchmen, secret servicemen, policemen, soldiers, actors, swindlers, money-changers and... these characters for example." Balecky placed the in-house law gazette on the table: "The authors' collective analysis of our new constitution. Lovely!" He read out a few sentences: "'Citizens have the right to establish political parties and movements which are independent of the state. The legal arrangement of all political rights and freedoms, and their application, must allow for and preserve the free competition of political powers in a democratic society.'" He put down the gazette: "The free competition of political powers. Great!"

"Where did you pick up the legal gazette?"

"I buy it from time to time. I am a lawyer after all!"

"What have you got against the free competition of political powers?" Balaz couldn't see what he meant.

"Nothing. It's just that Mister Academician, member of the collective of authors of the democratic constitution, tried to fill my head with this back in the early eighties..." Balecky pulled out another publication. 'Historic Lessons from the 1968 Crisis.' Twenty years ago, Mister Academician insisted that 'the most dangerous feature of rightist revisionism consists in the rejection of the leading role of the Communist Party in a socialist state. The chief aim of the right-wing opportunists was to replace socialist democracy with a so-called pluralistic conception of democracy which was to manifest many of the features, institutions and techniques of the bourgeois democratic system, chiefly the free competition of political powers!" Angrily, Balecky slammed the brochure down on the table. "It's enough to drive a normal person mad. Mister Academician kicked people out of the review commission for stating then what he's trumpeting now. Today he's a celebrated co-author of the democratic constitution, and those he threw out are still crying for justice. He was a big-shot then and he's a hero today ... These Johnny-come-lately heroes make me sick! When the battle's over, they're sitting in the front row and acting like heroes. Before November, I had never heard of one Slovak dissident, and now they're as thick as flies. It was the same thing with the partisans during the war; the longer ago the Uprising, the more of them there were. I won't be surprised if in a few years the list of Anti-Chartists will be added to that of the Chartists. At least then there'll finally be some Slovak Chartists! And that old boss of yours, Kunova! The biggest star of socialist cinema, a Party Central Commission protégé with a daily salary equal to a worker's monthly pay, crying how she suffered!"

He looked at Balaz in disgust. "Thank God there are still a few idiots in politics. They had no chance because like true idiots they were standing at the starting line waiting for the pistol to be fired. Everyone was crowing on about democracy and justice, and at that same time the Church and Party bigwigs were crowding around the finish line. Both teams have the widest experience in grabbing property. They only hated each other because they couldn't get at what the other one was grabbing. Now we can see as clear as day that religious anti-communism wasn't a struggle for democracy but a fight to get one form of totalitarianism out of the way in order to replace it with church totalitarianism. In place of Moscow, we have the Vatican. It's a simple trick since the country is already used to genuflecting before the mighty; now it can bow down to the almighty! And it doesn't bother them in the least that Jesus would never take part in such a race. They kicked him off the team because he was standing in their way. To hell with the lot of them!" This time it was the newspaper that slammed down on the table.

Marta had had enough of it, and groaned, "Do we have to talk politics even on New Year's Eve?"

"Exactly. Listen to how nicely Habera is singing." Her mother turned up the volume, and not only because she was getting hard of hearing. *'It's the last time I'll be standing here at the crossroads... you hide your face in the newspaper, love is not compulsory...'*

"That guy could do with a haircut," was Balecky's comment on the singer and his song. Then he fell silent and gazed morosely at the television screen. Balaz's gaze fell on the headline in the 'New Times' newspaper that had knocked the Gazette onto the floor: 'They were the iron fist at Chirana.' He began to read the article, in which some journalistic rookie was uncompromisingly condemning on principle the actions of the people's militias in the production/administration branch of Chiran. At the end of the commentary was a list of the members of Chirana's people's militias. Among them was the name of Balaz's unlucky colleague, Julius Grajtak. Next to his name was the remark that Engineer Grajtak had attempted suicide as a result of the senseless accusations.

In January, Slovakia was accepted into the United Nations. In February, Parliament elected Michal Kovac as President of the Republic. At midnight, February 8, a new currency was adopted – the Slovak Crown. Those who had a large amount of Czechoslovak Crowns at their disposal deposited them up to the last minute in Czech banks in the expectation of a serious decline in the exchange rate between the two countries. Many people became very rich in this way. The Slovak citizens' social situation became dramatically worse as prices rose for almost everything. For example, the price of a Skoda Favorit automobile was 70,000 crowns at the end of the socialist era. When a few months later its price jumped to 130,000, people shook their heads. When it later cost 230,000, then 330,000 crowns, they stopped reckoning.

Balaz finished his six-month training course at the Vienna leasing company, Raiffeisen Leasing and as of January, 1993, he was authorized to establish a new company, Tatra Leasing, in Bratislava. At the same time he was appointed its first director. The firm needed clever people and at least one true expert on cars. Balaz thought of Gabo.

"Hello, this is Jozef, how are you getting on?"

"Fine, you?"

"Fine. I'm setting up a new leasing outfit, and I need someone who understands cars for the technical operation. Are you interested?"

"It's nice of you to think of me, but I'm in business for myself. Some friends and I privatized Cooperative Service."

"Cooperative Service?" That used to be the biggest garage network in the city. How did you manage that?"

"In the right place at the right time... If you have any car troubles, my technicians will look after you. In the meantime, take care."

CHAPTER
ELEVEN

PRAGUE – BRATISLAVA 1992 – 1998

SHORTLY before his abdication, President Havel named Ján Winter as the Czech and Slovak Federal Republic Ambassador to Argentina. A few days before his appointment, Winter met with his Russian contact Kirovkin in the Na Vikarce restaurant, one of Havel's favourite wine cellars.

"The Argentina appointment is in the bag, but I would advise you to cut out your pro-Czech rhetoric when you get there. It won't sit well with the Slovaks living out there. The breakup of the Republic is inevitable. According to our sources, the two republics are going to establish diplomatic relations on the last day of the year. Slovakia is a key ally of the Russian Federation in Central Europe. We understand the mentality and opinions of the Slovak people, and we're counting on you. Good relations between Germany and Russia are key for a stable Europe. For various reasons, we can't rely on the Czechs, Poles or Hungarians, but the Slovaks have always enjoyed the trust of both Germany and Russia."

On the first of December, 1992, Jan Winter received approval from the Argentinean government, and two weeks later he took up his post in Buenos Aires. From the very start he spoke only Slovak and quickly found favour with the local community. His good reputation for professional, civil and personal skills also spread back to influential politicians back in Slovakia. Winter spent almost six years in Argentina, which is longer than is customary in diplomacy.

He would have represented Slovakia even longer had he not been recalled by the government during its hour-long session in the Presidential Palace on March 3, 1998. On his return from Argentina Winter entered the Ministry of Foreign Affairs as the head of the Department of Strategic Events, one of the ministry's most crucial sections.

Shortly afterwards, he met with the counsellor from the Embassy of the Russian Federation, Nikolaj Ivanovich Borzov, who told Winter straight away that he had been informed about him by Kirovkin. He hinted that it would be wonderful if a diplomat with such a good name were more involved in politics. Since Winter had been considering this for some time, he didn't need much persuading from Borzov. A few days later, all the Slovak newspapers announced that the internationally acclaimed diplomat Jan Winter was joining the newly-established Slovak Civic Party. His long diplomatic experience with communicating half-truths was now paying off. His smooth manners, smile, joviality and willingness to answer reporters' questions gradually won the public over. He rose up the ladder of popular politicians, and the door to a successful political career opened ever wider.

CHAPTER
TWELVE

BERLIN 1990 – 2005

THOMAS, as a former politician, was well suited to found the Institute for Political Analysis and Prognoses (IPAP). His feeling was that active political activity was for people whose moral threshold was a great deal lower than his own. But political science still interested him and he was excited by the possibility of providing the media, schools and institutions with objective analyses. Thanks to his good reputation, interest in his company increased, his client base grew, and he was able to take on new employees and make IPAP a recognized international player.

From the birth of their twins, Marlies and Claudie, in November, 2000, Heike became a dedicated mother, in addition to successfully running her own legal consulting firm. On the German human resources consulting market, she managed to establish her firm among the most highly respected.

Neither Thomas nor Heike had the power to dissuade the young athletic man Peter had grown into from a career as a professional soldier. From his youth, he had shown a desire for adventure and an interest in faraway countries. He became the Berlin student champion in karate, and while his schoolmates were running after a football, he was at home training with sticks, chains and his bare hands.

He was firm in his intention to continue his education at the Land Army Officers' Institute in Dresden.

After completing his studies, he enrolled in a two-week special training course for soldiers destined for Bundeswehr foreign operations. On the exercise field at Altmark, he underwent preparations in mine clearing, communications technologies, basic mountaineering, searching persons and vehicles, disaster relief and, of course, anti-terrorism. Thanks to his long years of martial arts training, he completed the course with top marks. Before the 2005 Christmas holidays, Peter travelled to Potsdam and filled in an application for foreign secondment. Early in the new year, he and several of his Dresden schoolmates were invited for an interview consisting of psychological and physical testing. He got the best results in all of them, and things moved quickly after that. The commander of the Dresden Officers' Institute promoted him to the rank of lieutenant and immediately ordered him to report to the Provincial Reconstruction Team in Feyzabad, the capital of the Afghanistan province of Badachschan.

Peter came home to say goodbye to his parents and sisters near the end of February, and it wasn't the easiest of partings. Heike was on the brink of tears throughout, and Thomas stubbornly repeated: "It's your decision..." Peter remained the calmest of the three of them.

On March 1, 2005 he and his friends Hans and Joachim took off from Berlin to Cologne, where they reported to Major Diestel, the commander of the squad going to Kabul. As they arrived at the airport, an Airbus A 310 full of the soldiers Peter's brigade was to replace was just landing. Tired-eyed yet smiling, it was clear to see their joy at being back home. Amidst the confusion between the returnees and their welcoming families, Peter spied an older schoolmate from Dresden named Erich Lummer. He made his way over to him, they hugged each other, and Erich asked the obvious question: "Are you going out next?" Peter just nodded.

"Where to?"

"Feyzabad."

"I made the same mistake; I let myself be lured by the money... But they'll never get me back there again. Take care!"

That afternoon at two, a huge military Airbus left Cologne for Termez in Uzbekistan, the base of the German and Dutch forces. The plane touched down at eleven p.m. local time. Peter's squad transferred to a four-prop Hercules and continued on to Feyzabad, about three hundred kilometers further. When the plane hit an air pocket, Peter felt his teeth rattling in his mouth. "We're lucky the Russians built a runway here, otherwise NATO would have nowhere to land," Joachim grinned.

Badachschan province turned out to be relatively quiet. After four months, as Peter's assignment to the Provincial Reconstruction Team was coming to an end, he developed stomach cramps and chronic diarrhea. The doctor prescribed bed rest, and so instead of him, Joachim flew off on a standard reconnaissance mission in the direction of Kunduz. The four-man crew lifted off in their BO 105 M helicopter at eleven in the morning. A half-hour later their aircraft was hit by a Stinger missile fired by the mujahidin, one of those supplied by the United States to use against the Russian occupying force fifteen years earlier. No-one survived.

On his return from Afghanistan, Peter applied for release from service in the Bundeswehr.

CHAPTER
THIRTEEN

BRATISLAVA 2001 – 2004

SOMETIME in the spring of 2001 Balaz saw the feature film Gandhi, and left the cinema with the feeling that all the Slovak political scene needed in order to be perfect was – himself. He almost regretted that the country was not occupied by British colonial forces like in India, for then his entry into the struggle would be all the more impressive. So Balaz gladly accepted an invitation, at least for coffee, from the head of a large private television station. After a number of such meetings, where they convinced each other that without them Slovakia was headed for catastrophe, he resigned his job as the industrial policy director of one of the country's largest firms. In April, together with a number of other idealists, they formed a political party called PALO –True Alliance of Liberal Citizens. Balaz had decided to become a politician, to experience the magic of power and controlling others. He failed to realize at that time that while politics indeed meant gaining power over others at the same time it meant losing power over oneself.

Establishing a liberal party in populist Catholic-Communist Slovakia was a daring move, but Balaz was motivated by the belief that having a party which would stand for personal freedom and individual responsibility was of crucial importance in the country. People who for generations had been indoctrinated with the idea of collective irresponsibility could have neither self-respect nor self-confidence. He was at the same time aware of the power of an influential private television channel, Angelika, which the PALO party chairman owned. This media element proved to be decisive. The party got stronger and stronger until, when it was registering a constant public opinion score of between seven and nine percent, a number of influential people overcame their initial scepticism and joined up. It often happens in life that those who look on in safety run fresh onto the track late in the race and easily overtake those who have been setting the pace from the outset.

The date for the next National Council elections was fixed for the one day Balaz could be relied on to remember: his own birthday. On the basis of the elections of September 27, 2002, True Alliance not only made it into parliament, but into the government. The National Council elected Balaz as head of the NR SR Permanent Delegation to the NATO Parliamentary Assembly, and later as head of the NR SR Permanent Delegation to the European Council. Thanks to his life-long activities in foreign trade and diplomacy, he worked his way up to stand among the foremost experts on foreign and security policy.

On November 15, 2002 Balaz headed the NR SR delegation for the first time at a plenary session of the NATO Parliamentary Assembly in Istanbul. With butterflies in his stomach, he walked the seemingly endless halls of the Congress Centre to the room where the political commission was meeting. While he was still orienting himself in the huge space, the session was called to order. Balaz found his place at the table with the bilingual sign Slovakia/Slovaquie, and tuned in to the speaker's words. A man with short greying hair and a thick beard was analyzing the international security situation in good English, switching to fluent German when he couldn't find a word or two. His name was written on a card in front of him, but it was lost beneath a pile of documents. Balaz kept trying to remember where he knew the fellow from, and finally went to introduce himself during a break.

"My name is Jozef Balaz, the new head of the Slovak delegation."

"I'm Markus Meckel, the head of the German Parliament delegation."

Balaz had the feeling that Meckel too was looking at him and trying to place him.

At a joint dinner for the delegation heads that evening, both of them smilingly recalled a strange meeting at Peter Greiner's in a country that no longer existed. After the fall of Communism in the GDR, Meckel had served as Foreign Minister, and after German unification had automatically become a member of the Federal Parliament. It was in part due to Meckel's friendly support and lobbying that Balaz later became one of the five Vice-Presidents of the NATO Parliamentary Assembly.

In the National Council he concentrated on foreign policy and security, not getting involved in domestic and economic issues. Gradually, however, he realized that in politics, 'not getting involved' in something was not an option, since he had to at least vote on these matters. He found moreover that for a politician, stating one's own opinion was not only unwelcome but could even be risky. Political parties are organized in such a way that the opinion of the party leader, and therefore of those who finance the party, is paramount. He was careful not to be drawn into any 'deals' that would leave him open to blackmail. It's a sad rule of politics that the one who is most successful is the one who knows the most about the other politicians. Political stability is in fact built on mutual blackmail. If a rookie politician has no skeletons in his closet, someone is sure to try to create some guilty secret. In Balaz's case it wasn't so simple, for he had never stolen, privatized, bribed or been bribed. His hands were clean, and he was therefore free, but in politics a free man is considered unreliable. Reliable deputies vote according to the instructions of the party leader without thinking twice about it; the issue of making a free decision doesn't even enter into it. Not only is this a safer path, but a more comfortable one. The citizenry regards anyone who has been in politics as a part of a powerful engine in which each component contributes to the movement of the machine with one goal: to get rich quick.

People are wrong in thinking that ordinary deputies, or even ministers come to that, have power. This is an illusion created by the media. Power is enjoyed by those outside politics – those sitting in industrial and business consortiums, in banks, or in developers' offices: investors, privatizers, lawyers, media brokers, those who found themselves in the right place at the right time. Politicians bow down before them, and the citizenry, under the mistaken impression that politicians make the decisions, bow down before politicians.

One of the saddest things Balaz witnessed was the governing and opposition deputies meeting in the members' salon to decide how to argue in front of the television cameras so as to make an impression on their respective electorate. Then they buy each other a drink and await the results of the newest public opinion survey to see how many more popularity points their 'conflict' brought them. Almost as depressing was the sight of government deputies bragging to each other what they managed to arrange from some minister and what they would get from those they'd arranged it for. It made him sad when an opposition politician came forward with a reasonable suggestion and he himself was told to vote against it simply because the idea came from the opposition. The self-interest and greed of sponsors, parties and individuals came far ahead of the service to the citizenry they had so resoundingly promised on election day.

He regretted the irrational behavior of the present and future premier, and their reciprocal personal resentment. He rejected this hatred, and rather sought compromises and cooperation with the opposition. It bothered him that when a difficult situation arose and he was fighting for his honour, he got the support of the entire opposition while his own Christian and democratic colleagues in government turned their backs on him.

Sometimes it came into his mind that if he wasn't enjoying politics, he should simply resign. His immediate reaction was to persuade himself that he ranked among the civilized, and it was good that some such people remained in politics. Perhaps the best thing about the political life was the money he earned without working too hard to attain it. He also enjoyed the opportunity to travel. Some journalist came up with data showing that Balaz travelled more than any other politician in the National Council.

In April, 2004, Marian Lagovic, an editor with the Domino Rum weekly, asked Balaz for an interview. He knew of Lagovic as a young journalist trying to uncover the truth. In fact, under a number of editors-in-chief, Domino Rum had built up the image of itself as uncompromising in the fight against Communism. Although it had actually joined the fight against Communism rather late, its reputation had obviously left an impression on the naïve young reporter. Balaz ordered coffee for the two of them, and smilingly asked after Lagovic's boss. For the young man, his Editor-in-Chief was something of the prototype of an anti-Communist fighter.

"You know my Editor-in-Chief?" Lagovic asked, obviously surprised. Clearly, for him Balaz was, in contrast to the Editor-in-Chief, the prototype of a man without character.

"Of course we know each other: for over thirty years."

"Where from, if I may ask?"

"We did our military service together at the Klement Gottwald Military and Political Academy," Balaz smiled, looking at this young fighter for the truth. "You didn't know he was at the Academy?" Lagovic looked at Balaz in shock. "Or that his deputy editor was a Communist Party official and signed the Anti-Charter... twice in fact." Lagovic had nothing to say to this. "So say hello to the two of them for me." Now the silence was becoming embarrassing. "Do you know what I can't stand?" Balaz went on, looking Lagovic straight in the eye. "It's people like your bosses pretending they came into the world in November 1989. They act as if they themselves singlehandedly overthrew the Communist regime. Look on the internet and you'll see that their biographies start in 1989. And I guess we know why. Don't get me wrong – you're a young man and that's all the more reason for you to ask your older colleagues what they were doing in the old days. Under totalitarianism I never heard that their type was doing anything to bring down the regime – quite the contrary."

Lagovic's interview with Balaz appeared in the edition that came out on the seventh of May. A full half of the discussion was made up of questions referring to events and personalities from thirty years ago that Balaz had only a faint memory of. However, the naïve Lagovič mentioned precise names, dates and times. It was obvious that he was drawing his questions from Balaz's dossier which, according to the Nation's Memory Institute, was 'in the stage of preparation for release'.

One of the NMI staff finally admitted that the Deputy Chairman of the NMI Board of Directors, Pavol Horvath, had leaked his dossier to the media on his own initiative, referring to it as a 'treat for the media'. Balaz received his dossier on September 13, 2004, four months after Horvath provided it to Lagovic. On the basis of this, Balaz proposed in the National Council that Horvath be removed from his function as a member of the NMI Board of Directors. He backed up this motion by revealing something from Horvath's past to prove that his own hands were far from clean. The motion was defeated by three votes; Horvath's Christian Democrat friends kept him in office.

Of his eighty-five page dossier, he found sixty pages of falsified claims that he was unable to disprove. Fortunately, the dossier also contained one letter with his alleged signature on it. It was clear at one glance that the signature – from twenty-five years before– was completely different from the way Balaz signed his name at that time. He had numerous samples of his signature from that time from which any hand-writing expert would conclude that the dossier signature was a fake. The problem was that to run this test he would need the original rather than the photocopy he'd been given. Horvath categorically refused to surrender the original, from which Balaz concluded that it was Horvath himself who was behind the campaign to discredit him. Since in Parliament Balaz had hinted that he was aware of Horvath's activities under Communist rule, Horvath was now determined to discredit this source of negative publicity through the media.

When the influential newspaper could find nothing scandalous in Balaz's dossier, the prime evidence left against him was the interview conducted by StB captain Mandak, where Balaz had informed him that he and the Austrian reporter Eder had been drinking wine together.

Balaz kept on agitating for the publication of the original document, challenging Horvath in the media to publish it. Even Horvath's supporters could not comprehend his stubborn refusal to surrender the document. Rumours started to fly that some people in Horvath's institute were selling off the originals of documents while others had actually been lost. As a National Council deputy, Balaz had the right to a face-to-face interview with the NMI head, but every time he showed up at Horvath's front door, Horvath went out the back way – at least that was what the doorkeepers at the Institute told him.

Once the two men met be chance on a street in Bratislava. Balaz started right in: "Mr. Horvath, what are you afraid of? If you're right, give the original to an expert and show it's my signature! It's your big chance to neutralize me. But you know I didn't sign anything, and so you don't want the document out in public. You're using your institute for political ends, you're blackmailing and discrediting people on orders from your political sponsors. Why don't you act like a man..." Balaz never finished his rant, for Horvath jumped onto a tram that was just pulling away. Balaz realized he'd never be able to clear his name.

Balaz tried one last time to get in to see Horvath. State officers are, after all, obliged to accommodate Members of Parliament. When he arrived at the institute at the appointed time, however, the secretary informed him, not without an ironic smile, that Mr. Horvath had been called away unexpectedly, and had no idea when he'd be back.

"Tell that wanker that this was his last chance," said Balaz angrily, "Tell him I've stopped fooling around!"

"Is that a threat, Mr. Deputy?"

Balaz slammed the door on his way out.

CHAPTER
FOURTEEN

BRATISLAVA 2004

JUST before the elections in 2002 when Balaz became a deputy, his in-laws moved from Presov to their house in Bratislava. Balecky and his wife were both over eighty, and Marta didn't want to leave them alone in their old age. They put up a partition to divide the space in two, and moved the Báleckies into the smaller half. They were in relatively good health, although he was losing his sight and she, her hearing. In a certain way their handicaps were complementary; the wife described what the actors on television were doing and her husband shouted out what they were saying. The worst part was the six o'clock news – she wanted to watch the visually more interesting news on the commercial channel, Markíza, while her husband preferred the more informative reports he could hear on the state-run Radiojournal. Their dispute was only resolved by the old man listening to the news on a transistor radio in the bathroom. At half past six, they discussed what they'd heard and seen, and then watched the news at seven with the feeling they'd heard it all before. At seven thirty, the trouble started again: one of them wanted to watch another popular station called TV JOJ, and the other to listen to the second national network. Since they had only the one television set, the wife usually got her way. Not wanting to admit defeat, Mr. Balecky spread a blanket on the floor in front of the TV and, stripped down to his underwear, began to do his yoga exercises. He claimed that this was the only space in the flat large enough to lay a blanket, while she complained she couldn't see the television through his stretched-out legs. She didn't have the strength to move the mahogany armchair, and her husband refused to help... he was too busy doing yoga! The problem was that he couldn't keep his legs in the air throughout the entire program, so his solution was to shift to yoga exercises, which somehow managed to interrupt the signal from the TV antenna.

"Can't you do those exercises in a way that doesn't block the signal?" she would ask petulantly.

"No, I can't! You'd be in my way," he retorted triumphantly. "Anyway, what do you need to watch the news for? You've already seen it three times." Suddenly changing his posture, Balecky managed to knock over the rabbit-ears antenna, and the picture disappeared from the screen.

"You're impossible! It took so long to catch the signal, and now you've gone and lost it for us," the old woman cursed. In such situations, Mrs. Balecky often went to complain to her daughter. Of course, at that time of night Marta was either making oatmeal, watching the clock so the boiled eggs wouldn't be hard, or doing the washing. While their younger daughter Anicka was still living at home, Marta would trust her to keep her grandmother occupied, and so Mrs. Balecky would learn the latest gossip from the world of show business. Later, the old woman would parade her 'insider's knowledge' before her husband. But since Anicka had moved out, Marta had to pacify her mother on her own. She started by quickly explaining that she and her father had to be more tolerant of each other, and finished by telling her not to be so childish. Mrs. Balecky usually ended up sniffling that granddad got all the sympathy due to his 'imaginary' cancer while she, with her peptic ulcer, got no sympathy at all.

In the end, his disease was unfortunately not imaginary at all; Balecky's doctor informed them that his illness had progressed to a more critical stage. He stopped doing yoga and rarely went out of the house. He lost interest in gardening, and even politics didn't get him angry in the way it always had before. He closed within himself and practically ceased interacting with those around him.

Meanwhile, Jan Winter was gaining more and more public support. In April of 2004, during a discussion program on Slovak Television, he declined to rule out running for President. Less than three weeks after his interview, the Slovak Courier newspaper published a lengthy report on the shipping of Slovak Jews to the concentration camps during the Second World War. Winter read the article with interest, and came away with an uneasy feeling, because the author had promised a follow-up piece the following week. This second article dealt with the transports from the East Slovak town of Kezmarok, and caused Winter a sleepless night. The reporter had mentioned a certain Klaus W. as one of the commanders of the deportation depot. To Winter's mind, the articles had one clear goal: to discredit him before the start of the election campaign. He picked up his telephone and called Balaz.

"I need to meet with you... as soon as possible... right now if you can." Winter was unable to hide the anxiety in his voice.

"I'm afraid I won't have time today," Balaz answered in a flat, almost sad tone.

"What could be more important than helping out an old friend?" Winter asked peevishly.

"I have to go to a funeral: my father-in-law just died. But it's good you called, because he left some kind of parcel for you. I can bring it to you tomorrow if you like."

"Fine then, tomorrow. But I'd rather not meet you in my office, if you don't mind. I can reserve a room at our club."

"Have you any idea what it could be?" Winter asked nervously. The wax seal was so toughened by age that he had to bang it against the table edge. He had already asked the waitress not to disturb them; with a slight bow, she closed the padded door behind her.

"Just read it: I promise not to interrupt you."

Winter opened the packet, which contained only two sheets of paper. "Give me a minute, will you?" He looked thankfully at Balaz, who tactfully left him alone.

"Dear Mr. Winter! I feel a little silly addressing you like that, but many years have passed since I called you little Jano. I wrote the following letter on May 15, 1987, when you were appointed Ambassador to Berlin. I knew that sooner or later the time would come when it would be necessary to speak out, in the interest of both the truth and the good name of your father. I'm only sorry I put it off for so long.

'In February 1953, I was called as a witness at the trial of the District National Council Secretary in Kezmarok, Jan Mlynar. This took place two months after Clementis, Slánsky and thirteen others were sentenced to death in show-trials, and two years after Horakova, the only woman involved, was hanged. These were probably the most difficult times in my life and in the lives of many other people, I'm sure. Trials seemed to be taking place constantly, both those of high officials and also those of ordinary people. The Communists had decided that it was necessary to show the people that 'class enemies' existed both in high places and in their everyday lives. Mlynar was one of the latter, a decent chap, truth be told. He was one of the 'lucky' ones who were not executed, 'only' sentenced to fifteen years of hard labour. They released him in 1960, but the poor chap died from the deprivations he'd suffered in prison. At his trial, he was accused of participating in the deportation of the Jewish population of the Kezmarok region to the concentration camps.

Allow me to quote from the prosecutor's speech: 'After the suppression of the Slovak National Uprising in the autumn of 1944, captured partisans were interned in the dungeons of the Kezmarok Castle, along with many Slovaks of Jewish origin who were awaiting assignment to one of the railway wagons that would transfer them to Auschwitz or Majdanek. The castle was guarded by jointly by the Hlinka Guard storm troopers and two regiments of the Einsatztruppe (ET). The commander of one of the regiments was Group Leader Klaus Winter'.

Winter read the record of the trial, which he already knew from the StB dossier, but even so he was excited. He breathed out and took a sip of his brandy.

'Among the incarcerated Jews was one Leo Müller, the owner of a sawmill in nearby Podolinec, along with his wife and son. The fate of the prisoners depended entirely on the will and mood of their guards, who were often drunk. One afternoon, a group of Hlinka Guard and ET soldiers was on the lookout for some Jewish women who had been detailed 'for entertainment'. This simply meant that the soldiers raped the unfortunate women. One of these was Elsa Müllerova. When they drove her out of the cellar, her husband stuck to her like glue, refusing to let go. The other captives trembled in fear as the drunken soldiers began to beat the couple with heavy wooden posts they'd found in a corner of the cellar. The couple's three-year-old son, Leo, witnessed this and began to cry, not understanding why his parents were being beaten. When even after this the guards couldn't separate them, they forced them both out into the courtyard. The brigade commander, Klaus Winter, pulled out his pistol and ordered Müller to let go of his wife. The Müllers, still clinging to one other, knelt in the dust. Some of the Hlinka Guard members roared with laughter, others turned their eyes away, while still others quickly left the yard. Jozef Balecky, the leader of a squad of pavers working nearby, was present at the disgraceful scene. "Klaus, have you gone mad?!" Balecky cried out. Winter hesitated for a bit, but realized everyone in the courtyard was looking on – as commander, he didn't dare risk his authority by backing down. Again he shouted at Müller to release his wife. Winter raised his arm, which was shaking visibly. He hesitated for a time, his arm shaking more and more. Then a shot rang out. Müller fell dead on the wet, stony ground, and Winter went over and began shaking him. The accused, Mlynar, at that time head of the Hlinka Guard storm troop, came forward.

"He's dead," Mlynar announced. Winter shook Müller a few more times; when he saw the man wasn't breathing, they dragged the body into the cellar together.

'Mr. Witness, is that the way it happened?' the prosecutor asked me.

"After hesitating for a time, I nodded my head."

"Dear Mr. Winter, at that moment my head began to spin. I couldn't speak, only nod, because just prior to the trial I'd been taken to the police headquarters and, under the threat of a beating and the revelation of my past, I was forced to agree to commit perjury. The actual truth is that your father did not shoot that unfortunate man. The one who pulled the trigger was an SS major who had been transferred to Kezmarok just the day before, a man nobody knew. While your father was present in the courtyard, he didn't kill anyone. I myself was so close to the action that I swear I could see the smoke rising from the German major's gun-barrel. But I wasn't the head of the squad of pavers, as the prosecutor claimed, but a Hlinka Guard soldier. I was too terrified to tell the truth in that courtroom.

I don't wish to justify my own past before you, please understand that. The main thing for you to know is your father didn't kill that man. The witnesses were exclusively members of the various militias active at the Castle, and although some of them are still alive, I have no right to name them as witnesses. In the end, nothing can now change the fates of the dead or the living.

When the rumour that your father had killed Müller started going around the town, he lost his nerve and absconded without even saying goodbye to your mother. We never saw your father again; we only heard that he had gone to Warsaw, where he volunteered to join the partisans.

Dear Mr. Winter, perhaps you will now reproach me for not sharing this information with you sooner. Practically, there would have been no point in doing so, because there are no witnesses to the truth of what I'm telling you: Morally, I never had the courage to reveal my guilt to you. I can't ask you not to tell my son-in-law what you've just discovered – I can only hope that you're as decent a man as your father was. Yours truly...'

Winter replaced the letter in its envelope, then called Balaz back into the room. He told Balaz as much as he felt necessary, and followed it with a confession: "I owe you an apology. I thought you were the one behind these stories in the newspaper. Forgive me,"

They ate their meal in near silence.

Winter stood up and put on his jacket. "I must be going, I have a meeting at two." Together they left the club and parted on the sidewalk. Back in his office, Winter called the Nation'sl Memory Institute, where he was told that Deputy Chairman Horvath was in his office. "Tell him I'll be there in ten minutes," was his curt message.

"Mr. Winter," said the secretary, showing him into Horvath's office.

"Welcome! What brings you here so unexpectedly? Would you like some coffee?"

"Well, my friend, I'm onto your tricks," Winter burst out with an ashen face. He tossed onto the desk the article from the Slovak Courier. "They got this from you!"

"Are you out of your mind?!"

"The only place they could have got this stuff is from your institute. So listen, my man, this second installment is the final installment, got it?"

"What? What are you saying? That I'm out to discredit you?"

"Who else could it be, you dirty rat?!"

"Please, calm down; think about what you're saying." Horvath was still trying to keep things from getting out of hand.

Winter suddenly got to his feet. "I'm not going to tell you twice. There's nothing to stop me from calling for your impeachment again, and this time it'll go through – you can count on that!" Winter was almost shouting by now.

"For God's sake, I had nothing to do with this!"

"Tell it to that reporter guy you dictated it to!"

Horvath burst out laughing.

"What's so damn funny?"

"I was in parliament myself, so I'm familiar with the code. The National Council can reopen the debate on a motion only six months after its introduction. That will be after the Presidential election... Ha, ha."

"Again I'm warning you, stop this campaign!" With these words, Winter turned and left the office. Horvath poured himself a shot of vodka and drank it down with the thirst of an alcoholic. His long, greasy hair stuck to his forehead, and there was a malicious smile on his lips.

Three days later, on the fifth of October, the Slovak Courier ran the third in its series on the fate of the Spiš Jewish community. The storm trooper commander was again identified only as Klaus W. At the conclusion of the article, however, the author promised to seek out the full names of those involved before the fourth installment.

On October 8 2004, the nation's media reported a serious car crash in the east of the country. The driver, the deputy head of the Nation's Memory Institute, Pavol Horvath, was pronounced dead at the scene of the accident.

CHAPTER
FIFTEEN

KIEV 2005

THE weather was gloomy in Kiev on October 20, 2005. A light rain fell on the windowsill of the President of the Republic's reception hall. On one side of the long white table sat President Viktor Juščenko along with his Foreign Minister, Boris Tarasjuk, the head of the delegation of the Ukrainian Supreme Council to the NATO Parliamentary Assembly, Oleg Zarubinský, the interpreter and minutes-taker. Opposite them were seated the NATO Parliamentary Assembly delegation - the President, Pierre Lellouche, two Vice-presidents, Vahit Erdem from Turkey and the Slovak Jozef Balaz, the General Secretary, Simon Lunn, his deputy, David Hobbs, and Svetlana, the Ukrainian responsible for Parliamentary Assembly relations with Ukraine. Viktor Yuschenko signed a few documents which his personal secretary had laid before him, and, looking up, gave his visitors a friendly smile.

"Excuse me for being late, discussions with the Georgian Prime Minister, Mrs. Nino Burjadze, took longer than anticipated. I can assure you that we will have ample time for our meeting." And he favoured them with another small smile. It seemed that his facial muscles were somehow strained, as if from pain. His ashen face was still marked by the effects of the reported poisoning attempt, and his features seemed stiff, wooden. Despite his scars Viktor Andrejevič was an elegant man in his black suit with a burgundy tie and handkerchief. His deformed ear was covered by the well-styled greying hair around his temples.

"Mrs. Burjadze is a charming woman, so we can understand your predicament," commented Pierre Lellouche with the smile that opened doors for the Frenchmen that were closed before many. He informed the President of the arrival of the NATO fleet in Sevastopol, and thanked the Ukrainian side for its gracious welcome. President Yuschenko was evidently in good form. He spoke deliberately, using clear argumentation peppered with humour. Lellouche, Erdem, Lunn and Hobbs paid close attention to the words of the man who had headed the Orange Revolution from a tribune in Kiev's Independence Square during the winter of 2004.

Balaz sat as a man enchanted, but not by the President's rhetoric. His head was full of images from August 1968, when the streets of Bratislava were blocked by Soviet tanks. He felt that shiver of fear that overcame him whenever he recalled the concrete barriers of Checkpoint Charlie – the crossing between East and West Berlin. The images came and went through his head, but she remained, sitting opposite him. Balaz could not take his eyes off her.

She looked a well-preserved fifty with a chestnut rinse, a still attractive woman. He followed her hand as it recorded a shorthand version of the debate, and he had the impression that she was writing unessential words just so that she would not have to raise her eyes from the page. When she did, he felt as if she was examining him, those green eyes fixing on him for a heartbeat before again being lowered to her work.

The discussions were coming to a close. The President had allotted them twenty minutes more than originally planned. The Head of Protocol accompanied them to the entrance of the Presidential Palace, where they retrieved their coats from the cloakroom. Passing the Palace ceremonial guard outside, Balaz instinctively looked around. From beside one of the massive marble columns on the first floor, he felt the unforgettable turquoise eyes of the minutes-taker, Sasha, looking out at him. When their glances met, he was sure she was smiling. Then she turned quickly away and retreated back onto the gallery.

The trip back to the hotel seemed to take forever. The service BMW had barely stopped before Balaz was dashing up the stairs. He leafed through a pile of papers on his desk until he found the packet which had been distributed by the Ukrainian Supreme Council. It outlined the program for the visit and included the names of the Ukrainian delegates. The last name on the list was that of the President's protocol assistant, Alexandra Josifovna Guseva. It was her, beyond all doubt.

He sat in wonderment on the duvet covering the bed. After thirty-seven years, he had again met his first love! With shaking hands, he checked the register, picked up the phone and called the delegation secretary, Svetlana. He asked her to try to connect him with the President's secretary, Alexandra Guseva.

"If I may say so, that's a rather strange request, Mr. Vice-chairman," Svetlana responded.

"I know it is, Svetlana, but you would be doing me a big favour. It's of great importance to me."

"Does Mrs. Guseva know you?"

"Well, I think so... Yes, I'm sure she does," Balaz insisted.

"I understand. I'll do what I can. I'll get back to you"

Balaz lay back on the bed and absently looked out at the façade of the building across the road. He felt as if his head would burst from the tension. What if it turned out not to be her? No, he was sure it was! The look they had exchanged in the vestibule was crystal clear proof of it. Why else would she have looked at him for so long? Twenty minutes had gone by since his exchange with the delegation secretary, and when his phone finally rang, Balaz quickly picked up the receiver.

"Mister Balaz?"

"Yes."

"This is the receptionist; please hold the line, I'm connecting you with President Yuschenko's office."

Balaz's heart was pounding, and although he tried to stay cool, it was beyond his powers. For about the twenty-fourth time, he rehearsed what he would say to her. Happily, his Russian had come back to him after appending the last few days in Ukraine.

"Hello," a woman's voice came over the line. Subdued, sentimental, sad – only 'hello' in the Russian/French style, without the 'h'.

"Hello... this is Jozef... Jozef Balaz from Bratislava..."

A long silence, confirming that it was indeed Sasha.

"Zdravstvuj, hello Osja... Sasha speaking..."

'Osja. My goodness, Osja.' The last time she had called him that was buried thirty-seven years in the past.

"Forgive me for not having been in touch for such a long time, but..." He was conscious of the fact that his phrase was completely idiotic.

"I know... You couldn't... I'm sorry too... I couldn't... I didn't know how to... "

Jozef heard Sasha's voice tremble on the other end of the line.

"I'd really like to see you... I don't even know how you're getting on, if you're single, married, divorced."

"Married, my dear, married, to a wonderful man... I want to see you, too, but today is impossible. You'll still be in Kiev tomorrow; I have your delegation's program in front of me. If you can skip the reception with our parliament at seven, my husband could pick you up at your hotel. His name is Gusev, Sergej Gusev."

"Yes... fine... I'm really looking forward to seeing you."

"Me too... me too... dear me..." Sasha's sigh was audible as she put the phone down.

Gusev took Jozef to their spacious flat near Bessarbska Square. Sasha was wearing a suit similar to the one she had on at the President's reception, and she looked very nice in it. Balaz had brought a bouquet of roses and a bottle of Slovak gin for them. When they met in the hallway, Sergej sensed that this moment should belong to Jozef and Sasa, so he left them alone and continued on into the flat.

"Welcome," Sasa said.

"Thank you." Jozef presented the bouquet to her.

"They're beautiful." Balaz leant forwards to give her a kiss on the cheek, but she shyly moved aside. "Won't you come in?"

The dining room table was set for three. Sasha noticed his surprised expression and explained: "My daughter is at her grandmother's in Carpatho-Ukraine... Please sit down" They sat at the table.

Gusev was the first to break the awkward silence. "Sasha has told me all about you... and the strange times we've all lived through. To your health!" They raised their glasses and drank a toast. Sasha brought in some borsch soup to go with the typical Ukrainian snacks on the table.

"But these are Slovak sheep-cheese piroshky," Balaz laughed.

"Yes, my Slovak grandmother taught me how to make them."

"Right, I remember your grandmother was Slovak..."

"Listen, you two are old friends, so let's drop the formalities. I'm Sergej," smiled Gusev, turning to Balaz. My friends call me Seryoscha."

"I'm Jozef - to my friends... Osja," Balaz laughed heartily. Then he noticed the expressions on the others' faces: "Sorry if I've said something wrong..." he was quick to apologize.

"No, no, that's all right... Osja... that's fine," Gusev reassured him.

Soon they were all talking together. Sasha explained how she came to be working for President Yuschenko. As the evening progressed and the level in the gin bottle went down, they kept interjecting, laughing, and reminiscing. No-one could explain how life could have brought such a coincidence to them. Balaz was amused that Sasha could still remember so many details from their time at that long-ago volleyball tournament.

"That boy with the booming voice nobody could shout over - what became of him?"

"Brblos? He's a hotel director in the Tatra mountains."

"And that good-looking guitarist you played together with?"

"Juro Chochol. He's still just as good-looking."

"Who was the fat one who was sweating so much? We felt he was constantly watching us. He had really curly hair; you had a silly nickname for him."

"Tubby... Winter... He's a big shot these days; in fact, he's running for president..." Gusev looked at Balaz in surprise, started to say something, then instead stood up and went over to a desk. He took a packet of photos from it.

"Really? He wants to be president?" Sasha was bemused. "Is he really that special?" But it was Gusev who answered.

"I know that Winter a little," he said. "His first name is Jan, right? Here he is. A really clever man... very clever indeed." Gusev handed Balaz a photograph in which he was standing with Winter on some kind of cruise ship. Balaz felt the blood rushing to his face.

"Hold on... what is this photo?"

"I really shouldn't be talking about it, but those times are over now... Besides, you're on a NATO body, and Yuschenko's government wants to join NATO as soon as possible, so we have to learn to trust each other... At that time, I was on the General Staff in the Soviet Army... We were in charge of the GRU – military intelligence, you know. I was teaching at the Military/Diplomacy Intelligence Academy. Winter was a student of mine for about a month... But this photo is from about five years ago, when Winter came to visit me in Moscow." Gusev paused and looked at Balaz. "Sorry, but I can't go into details. I remember he was a strong supporter of Perestroika. He was a clever guy." Balaz looked amazed, then gave a shrug. "So come on, drink up! Give him this photo, along with my best regards."

Sasha and Sergej sensed that Balaz was somehow on edge, as if he wanted to ask something but couldn't find the words. He looked at Sergej as if waiting for him to say something more.

Sasha decided a change of subject was in order: "We're going to have a wedding in the family next September." She smiled proudly.

"Your son's getting married?" Balaz asked.

"Son?" Gusev looked at Balaz in surprise. "Our daughter, Ninocka."

"The wedding will be in Carpatho-Ukraine, in Kolodne, the village where I was born. My mother still lives there, in a lovely little house. It was Ninocka who wanted to get married in Kolodne... village weddings are very much in style here," Sasha added.

"So, your daughter, Ninocka... congratulations!"

"Osja, you have to come to the wedding! You must. Have you ever been at a Ukrainian wedding?" Gusev was delighted with the idea.

"No, never."

"So it's settled. You're invited... the second Saturday in September next year, in Kolodne. Don't forget. The greatest village in the world – two cows for every inhabitant. Ha, ha! Write it down and we'll send you your invitation when the time comes. And no excuses! It'll be a great honour for us to have a Slovak deputy and member of the NATO Parliament at our wedding."

"I'll come, with pleasure... I only hope nothing will get in the way of my being there..."

"Nothing could be more important than our daughter's wedding!" Gusev grabbed Balaz around the neck and planted a kiss on him, Eastern European style. It was obvious that the alcohol he'd drunk was getting to him. When Gusev started to nod off on the couch, Balaz reckoned it was time to go. He stood up and made his way into the hallway, followed by Sasha. Again he was struck by her beauty and charm. She waited for him to put his shoes on, then politely handed him his coat and gloves. He deliberately took his time getting dressed, searching for a way to ask the question that had been most on his mind since they'd arranged his visit. He felt that Sasha too was aware of things unspoken; their paths had taken them far from each other, and a lot of dust had settled in the meantime.

"Sasha! Sasha! Where are you... where the hell are you? Bring me some pickled cucumbers, I feel bad... Do you hear me? " Gusev could be heard moving quickly to the bathroom, from where the unpleasant sounds of vomiting were soon heard.

"And your son, Osja? How is he doing? " Balaz couldn't stop himself from asking.

"I have to go... Come to the wedding. Osja will be in Kolodne too."

"Sasha, where are you?!" Gusev cried out.

"Come to the wedding. Say you'll come!"

"I'll be there." She offered him her hand in parting. Again he tried to kiss her on the cheek; again she gently pushed him away.

CHAPTER
SIXTEEN

BRATISLAVA 2005

THERE were less than two weeks to go to the election of the President of the Slovak Republic set for early December, 2005. The country's streets were decked out in the candidates' posters. One candidate wished the citizenry 'a Happy New Year', another announced that he'd 'be right there for them', the third 'thanked the citizens for all that they'd managed to achieve together', the fourth claimed to have 'the courage to take tough decisions', the fifth simply wished everyone 'Good day', the sixth informed the people they 'were not alone', and the last declared he would 'always stand by them'. They were all handing out plastic bags or pencils, cooking goulash, serving tea, pouring out beer or grog, visiting hospitals, hockey games, church services and homeless shelters. Any time a camera came in sight, they were posing before it.

Singers, actors, TV moderators and athletes were publicly declaring their support for the candidate who paid them the most. Winter's face, however, appeared less frequently than his rivals' on billboards and in the print media – evidently his campaign didn't have their large budgets. But despite this, he was capturing media attention. For someone who two or three years ago had been almost unknown, he was steadily picking up public support as time went by, and now ranked among the frontrunners. The analysts were putting this down to the public's distaste for old political hacks; Winter's was essentially the only fresh face in the race. Although his rivals played down his seriousness, the press, along with trying to discover who his backers were, gave him a good chance of winning. Public opinion polls placed him in fourth or fifth place, but he was the only candidate whose support was constantly increasing – the gap between him and the top was by no means insurmountable. Even his Communist background didn't seem to put people off; after all, of the seven men in the race, five were former Communist Party members.

In the televised debates, he appeared to be an experienced politician and a specialist in foreign affairs. His role in bringing down the Communist dictatorship in East Germany was mentioned often. One journalist, however, hinted at possible connections between Winter and the Soviet, later the Russian, secret service. When he read this particular article, Winter had to laugh.

Since his return from Kiev, Balaz was occupied with a serious dilemma; whether to force Winter to withdraw from the race or to forget about the whole thing. Sergej Gusev's photograph played on his mind during the day, and kept him from sleeping at night. The idea of his country's potential President being an agent of a foreign intelligence agency was abhorrent to him. He asked himself constantly if he himself was in a position to moralize and condemn another man whom he personally disliked. Moreover, he was aware that some of the other candidates had more to hide than did Winter. But about them he had no evidence. And then, maybe the Winter affair belonged to the past; Gusev, his controller, was now retired. But the threat of blackmail still remained current.

Finally, he came to a decision.

"What's up?" Winter's voice on the telephone was cold.

"I need to talk to you."

"I'm really busy, you know. Meetings, appearances... Couldn't it wait until after the election?"

"No, it can't. It's urgent."

"I'm afraid it's totally impossible before then."

"I need only five minutes of your time; I have something to show you – something of great importance to you."

"I thought we'd already resolved that Kezmarok affair!"

"It's not about Kezmarok."

"Well, then. Come to my headquarters at eight tomorrow morning. I can give you five minutes."

Balaz made a scan of Gusev's photograph, then enlarged it. When he got to his office, Winter was waiting with his jacket folded over his arm as if to symbolize how precious his time was.

"Sorry to be in such a hurry, but if you want to overtake the big guys, you have to work twice as hard. So what can I do for you?"

"I've come to advise you to drop out of the race."

"To do what!?"

"To call off your campaign."

Winter sat down, folded his jacket over the back of a chair, and gave Balaz a searching glance… "And why would I do that?"

"Because of this," said Balaz, handing him the photo. Winter first felt his skin grow cold, then a hot sweat bathed him.

"Where did you find this?" He looked daggers at Balaz.

"That's irrelevant. You notice it's just a copy; I have the original stored away in a safe place… Just in case something should happen to me, my colleagues will open the sealed envelope I've given them and have this photograph published."

Winter looked at him in shock. "You've had it all this time and said nothing about it?"

"No, I just got it."

"And where did it spring from all of a sudden?"

"Hmm… As they say, I found it by the wayside. But that's beside the point – the main thing is, it's genuine."

"This doesn't prove a thing."

"But I know about it, and I know the fellow with you in the picture."

"What else do you know?"

"Drop out of the race." This time Balaz's voice had more of an edge to it.

"I can't do that. Can you imagine how many supporters, sponsors, journalists, analysts, advisers and all the rest are involved in the campaign? Do you know how much money, time and energy have been invested in me? I'm on the way up, the latest numbers show four hundred thousand people plan to vote for me; I have a real chance to pull it off. And now you come in here and tell me to just write off all those people?!"

"If they were to find out what you are, they'd do more than just write you off, they'd run you out of town!"

Winter considered the whole thing for a bit, then leaned closer to Balaz: "Jožko, nobody but the two of us knows anything about this. We've been walking the same path together almost all our lives... These are things that are way behind us... They're skeletons we can leave in our cupboards; they don't mean anything anymore."

"This isn't about you, it's about the Slovak Republic. It's just not possible for the President to be open to blackmail."

Winter asked his secretary to cancel his next appointment and to bring them coffee, and then poured out two generous shot of cognac. "Your health," he toasted. Balaz's glass remained on the desk.

"So you're serious with this threat – or more accurately, this blackmail? Who was it sent you here?"

"Nobody. Sorry, but I don't see any way around it. If it was someone else who held this information, maybe you could skate. But you're out of luck: I'm the one who knows your secret. That's the way it is." Balaz stared straight in front of him.

"Again, to your health." Winter raised his glass, but still Balaz made no move to raise his. "Is that your final word?" Balaz nodded. "I'll ask you again: is that your final word?" His voice had risen, but Balaz simply stared him right in the eye. The veins in Winter's temples stood out; he sighed deeply.

"I thought I wouldn't have to fall back on this, but as things stand..." Winter moved over to his safe, opened it, and drew out an A4-size envelope. He hesitated for a moment and then passed it over.

"For a change, this is something that will be of interest to you!" Balaz, intrigued, took out a sheaf of papers about one centimeter thick. It was decorated with a coloured ribbon and bore the official state stamp.

"But this is... " He couldn't find the words to express his feelings.

"Yes, it's your original dossier from the Nation's Memory Institute."

"But this is what I ran after Horvath for like an idiot for three years, demanding he hand it over to me!" Balaz quickly turned over the pages until he came to number forty-four... He read out loud: 'The Director of the Press and Information Centre for Foreign Journalists, Jozef Balaz, on May 1, 1978, received from Captain Mandak the sum of 1,000 Czechoslovak Crowns. Signed, Jozef Balaz.' Balaz felt his throat constrict, and in one swallow drank down the cognac. "So this is the original dossier?" He spoke as if in a trance.

"Yes, it's the original; the one you hounded Horvath for in vain; the one the papers used to blacken your name."

"But it was on account of this that I had the law changed, don't you see? The National Council changed the law to force Horvath to give it to me. And still the guy refused to publish it. Did he give it to you?"

"I swiped it from him. He lent me your dossier and I simply kept it."

"And didn't he ask for it back?"

"Of course he did." Winter sneered, blowing cigarette smoke out of his nostrils. "I really enjoyed watching the two of you go at it!"

"So the reason he couldn't have it examined by handwriting experts was that he didn't have it in his possession?!"

"Exactly."

"And we too kept meeting, and still you didn't tell me about it? I can't believe it! It's... I can't find the right word for it! You knew I was fighting for my honour, how important the original document was to me. You had it all the time and didn't tell me?!"

"How the hell could I give it to you? Yes, I regret it. I borrowed that file at a time when I was convinced you knew about my father's past. I kept it as an ace in the hole, just in case you decided to blackmail me. But thanks to your father-in-law, it wasn't needed. In the end, it wasn't necessary."

"What do you mean it wasn't necessary, you great fat pig! For whom wasn't it necessary?" By this time Balaz was almost hysterical. "You knew how much I needed that document!"

"What are you so upset about? Yours wasn't the only dossier that got lost!" Now Winter too was shouting.

"That's the dirtiest trick you've ever played on me, you bastard!" Balaz shook his head in disgust. "And Horvath didn't dare tell me the truth; otherwise he'd have had to admit that he'd given you the original dossier illegally... This is too fucking much! And what am I going to do now with your damned original?"

"I'm offering it to you. Take it to a handwriting expert and have it evaluated. I'm giving you the chance to finally clear your name. It's the chance of a lifetime. I'll trade you your file for the original of that photograph!"

"Listen to me." Balaz couldn't control the shaking of his hands. "You're even a bigger asshole than I thought. What do you imagine I'll tell the expert when I hand him this file? Where will he think I got it from? According to law, the Institute can only submit original files to other institutions, not to private persons. The only way would be for you to return the dossier to the N.M.I. That's it; you have to give it back to them." Balaz finally saw a light at the end of the tunnel. "Then I can request a handwriting analysis from the Nation's Memory Institute, and I'll give you the photograph in return."

"Are you out of your mind? A presidential candidate admits he is in possession of an N.M.I. original file, and...?" Winter hesitated.

"... and that he's a thief! Just so. If you own up, I'll give you the photo. It's the only way for you to do me a favour and mainly to help yourself at the same time!"

Winter poured himself another glass of cognac and lit up a cigarette. "I'm sorry, truly sorry. Understand, I didn't want to blackmail you, that file was simply a last resort. I thought you knew about my father's wartime activities and... could use it against me anytime you saw fit... Sorry... Now I regret it." Winter was sweating and hyperventilating.

"I could use it against you anytime I saw fit... Do you honestly believe everyone thinks the way you do?"

"Look, find some handwriting expert who's willing to swear the file mysteriously turned up on his desk. Stranger things have happened." It looked to Jozef as if Winter was really grasping at straws.

"Not only are you stupid, you're completely without morals. Only a truly evil person would be capable of thinking like that; and you are one evil person. You're an utter swine!" Balaz buried his face in his hands. "So you had it all the time. You read how the papers shamed me and disgraced my family... and you were killing yourself laughing at me and that loser Horvath. You're an utter asshole!"

"Just calm down. It wasn't me who started this blackmail stuff. You came here this morning to blackmail me! So which of us is the swine? It takes a thief... I don't care if you're a Member of Parliament or not, I'm not out to wreck your career; you ruining me!" Nervously, Winter reached for another cigarette.

"Back there in Berlin, I should have cracked your skull with an iron bar!"

"You didn't have the courage to do it!"

"You're right, I didn't have the courage," said Balaz reflectively, and nodded his head as if in sorrow. "Nor did I have the balls when we were teenagers playing volleyball in Kezmarok and you wouldn't own up to your foul. I should have beat you up when you snitched on us in Kiev and in Germany. I should have hit you in the head with a rock when you threw that Molotov cocktail into the Russian command centre in Bratislava... My God, and you have the nerve to run for President! A right-thinking man would rather hide his head in shame!"

"And you truly think you have the right to moralize?!" Both of them were quiet for a time, then Balaz got to his feet. "So you're carrying on with your blackmailing?" There was a distinct menace in Winter's voice.

"No doubt about it. If I don't see a story about your withdrawal in tomorrow's papers, the next day the media will be flooded with reports of everything the GRU man told me about you. It should make for good reading! See you around." Winter giggled strangely, dropped his head and concentrated on his drink and cigarette.

Standing in the half-opened door, Balaz looked back at Winter: "That car crash that killed Horvath? That was a really strange accident!"

Winter sat on, trying to bury his grief in the bottle of cognac. The next day, all of the country's newspapers ran the same headline concerning the unexpected withdrawal of one of the favourites, Jan Winter, from the Presidential campaign.

CHAPTER
SEVENTEEN

BERLIN – BRATISLAVA 2006

AFTER the fall of the ruling coalition, new elections were called for June, 2006, so the NATO Plenary Assembly that spring was the last Balaz took part in. In the Subcommittee for Trans-Atlantic Defence and Security meeting-room a lecture by the IPAP Institute was taking place on the theme: 'New quality in USA/Europe relations following the 2003 crisis'. It was a topic of particular interest to Balaz, and he was curious about the opinions of the renowned institute's speaker. As an Assembly Vice-Chairman, he was entitled to sit in on the deliberations of any NATO committee or sub-committee. Quietly he made his way into the hall and sat down in the last row. At the podium, a good-looking man of about fifty was speaking absorbingly about the future prospects for relations between the United States and Europe.

"A key question is whether following the war in Iraq relations between Washington and Europe can return to the pre-war level or will remain weakened for many years to come. There are two camps on both sides of the Atlantic: – the optimists maintain that the Iraq war has, with the exception of Britain, distanced Europe from the USA in the same way that the stationing of medium-range weapons did some time ago. But, despite the heightened tensions that caused, NATO survived. The speaker stopped to take a sip from a glass of water, then with a smile, added: 'I know what I'm talking about because I too protested against the rockets." A wave of laughter coursed through the audience, and Balaz paid closer attention to the speaker. He was somehow familiar, and trying to place him took Balaz's attention away from the contents of his address. He ran through all his former German contacts, both professional and personal. He tried to picture the faces of previous lecturers at training sessions in Reemstma Hamburg or at NATO and Council of Europe seminars. Still he drew a blank. Going out of the hall and over to the nearest table, he scanned the day's program till he found what he was looking for – the IPAP Institute's lecture was to be read by its director, Thomas Ankermann. Jozef returned to the hall, and watched the speaker closely. There was no mistake; it was Thomas. When Thomas had finished his speech, he went into the vestibule for a cup of coffee and watched as the Assembly participants move to the large congress hall. In twenty minutes, the concluding plenary sitting, hosted by the NATO General Secretary, would begin.

"Excuse me, my name is Jozef Balaz. I'm an Assembly Vice-Chairman." Thomas didn't recognize him.

"I'm Ankermann. IPAP Company." He was obviously waiting for Balaz to say something relating to his lecture.

"You used to play volleyball in Neuwied, right?" This made Thomas put down his coffee cup and nod, surprised by the comment. "How did you know?"

"And you used to play the banjo."

"Yes, I did." Now a smile was beginning to form in his eyes.

"And you were in Czechoslovakia in August, 1968."

"Yes, I was! Um Gottes Willen. My God... Seppi... This can't be happening..."

"You're right, it can't be... But nonetheless it is, Thomas."

The two old friends stood and looked each other up and down.

"Dance, dance, twirl around..." Thomas sang the Slovak folk song, grabbed Jozef, and began to dance with him. They embraced, and tears came into their eyes. Passers-by looked on in amusement as two grown men in turn danced, hugged, laughed and banged each other on the back. Jozef's Vice-Chairman's seat remained vacant during the assembly meeting. The Slovak delegation's plane from Berlin to Vienna was due to take off at two thirty, which meant that Thomas and Jozef could only spend two hours together. As they had said only a fraction of what they wanted to, it was decided that Thomas and Heike would come to Bratislava that summer.

In the end, Thomas was able to come to Bratislava only on September the sixth. He couldn't manage it earlier since he had to complete a seminar for forty clients. Heike had to stay at home because her daughter was going into the first grade and Heike's didn't like leaving her for her aged mother to look after.

That evening, Jozef made a fire and Marta prepared some Slovak specialties. Their daughter Anicka came with her boyfriend, Balaz's sisters with their husbands, and a few neighbours. They talked, they drank, they laughed, and reminisced. Jozef took out his guitar, and they sang 'Dance, dance, twirl around', of which Thomas remembered the whole first verse. When the guests left, Jozef and Thomas remained alone. Marta felt this was a moment both these grey and balding fifty-something men had been looking forward to. The fire crackled on that warm September night, and Jozef's favourite star, Venus, shone brighter than ever. The crickets stopped and everything was quiet, as if nature was allowing these two old friends to remember in peace.

"This is unbelievable... We've said so much and yet we are just beginning to talk," Thomas commented. He told Jozef about the volleyball players from Neuwied, about his university years, about the fall of the Wall, about his family and about his political career. Then it was the turn of Jozef to speak of his life; they cut into each other's stories, filled them out for each other, and didn't notice the time passing. When Jozef started to speak about his time working in East Berlin, Thomas was reminded of the young Soviet soldier who had daringly smuggled Thomas' stepson into West Berlin.

"Did you meet that soldier?" Jozef's question was seemingly out of the blue.

"Why do you ask?"

"Was he tall and dark?"

"As I recall, he was. When he handed the child over to me, we were both extremely nervous, so I can't say that I remember him very clearly. But what I do recall is that he had extraordinarily large hands, and that he wouldn't accept the money I offered him. I didn't even manage to thank him properly; he got back into his car and drove away. But if I ever had the opportunity to meet him again..." Thomas' voice dried up. Balaz looked at him in silence.

"I also experienced something similar... We've been talking for two days, but to speak about the recent history of Europe, you'd have to stay here a month at least."

"I'd love to, but the new semester starts next week... Is this the Slovak gin you once gave me for my father?" asked Thomas.

"It's from the Spis region; it's my favourite."

"My dad only offered it to his closest friends."

When the sky began to lighten a couple of hours later, the friends were still speaking as if they had just begun. Thomas' banjo and Jozef's guitar lay crossed over each other on the lawn. The instruments were silent, just as their owners now enjoyed each other's quiet companionship. When two friends meet who haven't seen each other for forty years, they have so much to say to each other that sometimes the words cannot be found to express all their thoughts.

But next day, when their daughter Anicka came for lunch with her friend Tomáš, the conversation regained its former tempo. The young people kept asking about past events which seemed obvious to Thomas and Jozef.

Marta came in with a stack of letters the postman had just left. Most were for their daughter, who, even though she didn't live with them, still used her parents' postal address.

"There's something here for you from Ukraine," said Marta, handing Balaz an unusual-looking envelope.

"That'll be the wedding invitation!" Excitedly he tore the envelope open and read: 'Nina Alexandrovna Guseva and Yuri Grigorjevich Schevchenko have the pleasure to inform you that Saturday, September 9, 2006 will be their wedding day. The wedding will take place at the Church of St. Basil in the municipality of Kolodne, Isava region, Carpatho-Ukraine.' Jozef Balaz and his family were cordially invited. Attached to the invitation was a letter in which Sasha and Sergej reminded Jozef of his promise to attend the wedding.

"Why did it take so long to get here?" wondered Balaz, shaking his head. The postal stamp read September 1, 2006.

"You know how it is, they don't rush things like we do here," Marta smiled.

"So let's go to Carpatho-Ukraine!"

"I told you before, I can't go. I have hardly any holiday time left this year – You're retired, you can do what you want."

"My dear Thomas, a pensioner is the freest person in the world. I can't wish you anything better than to stand in your own garden growing strawberries while your wife supports you and all the citizens of your country contribute to your pension. Great deal!" Balaz laughed. Then he turned to Thomas: "I really, really want to be there. And I have the feeling you're going to want to be there too. Have you ever been to Ukraine?" Thomas shook his head. "You told me your new course starts next week. When do you have to be back in Berlin?"

"Tuesday evening, at the latest."

"So come with me. You have your passport and Germans don't need a visa. I'll let them know an international delegation is on its way."

"But it will eat up three days! And what will the people say when I turn up unannounced?" Thomas tried to find objections to the idea.

"Let me explain something. Last night you told me your story about a certain Soviet soldier bringing you a little boy in a television carton in 1989, right?"

Of course I mentioned it – that's the kind of thing you don't forget. I'll always be grateful to that lad."

"Do you remember how Peter Greiner organized it all?"

"Damn right I remember; I've already told you about it a couple of times over. Greiner probably helped my family more than anyone else in the world!"

"Do you know whose wedding I'm talking about? The sister of that Russian soldier who helped you out in Berlin. And he'll be there too!"

"Who'll be there?" Thomas wasn't sure he was following all this.

"The soldier who smuggled your friend's son over to you!" Balaz looked pleased by Thomas' look of surprise.

"Jozef, would you kindly explain what's going on here? Do you actually know that Russian who saved my son?"

Jozef thought how best to tell his tale. "I know him..." he began in a low voice, then changed tack: "You left out that was the day Heike fainted from happiness..."

"My God, however could you know that? Did the soldier tell you the story?" Thomas burst out in surprise.

"No, it was Peter Greiner who told me. I had no idea the person we'd decided to help was you! I never saw Peter after that... nor the soldier. Our paths never crossed again."

Then Balaz had no choice but to tell the whole story to Thomas, Marta and their daughter. It was, after all, one of those episodes that seem too unbelievable to be true. "Completely by chance, I ran into the soldier's mother in Kiev about six months ago." Balaz continued with the latest chapter in that decades-long saga. The tale was so engrossing that nobody thought about the meal waiting for them inside.

"Peter Greiner died just as the Berlin Wall came down." A silence fell over the little group which lasted until Thomas and Jozef again exchanged memories of their good friend, Greiner. Then Jozef added that he and the young soldier had met while playing volleyball in East Berlin.

Thomas was still unsure about attending the wedding in Ukraine: "All of this happened almost twenty years ago, and everyone has gone their own way since then... It's so unexpected... I don't know if going there is the right thing to do... But I would definitely like to shake that man's hand."

"So let's go. There's nothing to worry about, you'll see." Balaz picked up his phone and a moment later was talking to Sasha. Of course she had no objection to Jozef's bringing a really nice German man, his very good friend, whom he had met thirty-seven years before, just at the time when Sasha and Jozef had first met. Thomas, Marta and Anicka were all ears as Balaz continued merrily speaking to his Ukrainian friend. "Fine, we'll phone as we're nearing the Berezovo border crossing... Sergej will wait for us there? Excellent... It's only sixty kilometers from the border to your village? Excellent!... Yes, we're coming, and greatly looking forward to it! Tell Ninocka and Josif how much we'll enjoy meeting them... Bye for now."

Balaz hung up and announced they'd be setting off for Ukraine at five o'clock that Friday morning.

"But how did you meet this person? Is it really him? How do you know it's him?" Thomas was clearly caught up in the adventure.

"We'll have time to talk about it in the car," Jozef reassured him.

"Never in my life did it occur to me that I'd be on my way to Ukraine with Jozef Balaz! But isn't it too risky? I've heard there's a lot of car theft there..."

"No risk at all. Waiting for us on the border will be a man who is a general in the Ukrainian army. We couldn't ask for a better guide!" Balaz laughed.

"Why will a Ukrainian general be meeting us?"

"Because he's the father of the bride, and a good chap. Relax, everything will work out fine!"

"Okay then... I think I'll wait till we get back to phone Heike to save her from worrying. Up the Ukraine!" Thus, Thomas heartily joined Balaz's wedding trip.

On the Thursday before their departure, they went to visit Jozef's old, frail mother, whom Thomas had expressed the desire to meet. She was under excellent care in a hospice where the doctors and nurses had succeeded in returning a little colour to her face. For Thomas' part, he was finally meeting the first Czechoslovak he had talked to on the phone following the 1968 Soviet invasion.

The old woman lay on her bed and stared out into the unknown. Although her long-term memory was still functioning well, names, events and relations slipped easily from her mind. Her time was coming to an end, and in fact the doctors weren't giving her many more days. Occasionally she would have a lucid moment and remember some past moment with surprising precision.

Old Mrs. Balazova was from a well-rooted Bratislava family and, like a true daughter of the city, spoke Slovak, Hungarian and German. Jozef was long accustomed to calling her 'édesanyám' or 'Mutti' in place of 'Mama'. But on more formal occasions, he used Slovak. As they approached her bed, they saw that her eyes were closed. When Jozef called to her, she didn't react, so he took her hand. She returned his pressure although her arm was bloated and blue from the needle pricks.

"I've brought someone to see you… This is Thomas, the German boy who couldn't come to visit us when we were teenagers… You remember how we waited for him." His mother looked vaguely around, first at the ceiling then in the direction from which her son's voice was speaking to her. "He was delayed a little, but now he's here." This prompted Thomas to step nearer and take Mrs. Balazova's other hand, even though he wasn't sure if she would register his presence. She squeezed his hand, and in a quiet voice said: "Weinen sie nicht… Hat er gesagt…" ('"Don't cry, he said".)

"Ja, genau das habe ich damals gesagt…" (Yes, that's exactly what I said then…") The old woman painfully tried to raise her hand to touch Thomas, but she couldn't manage it. Her eyes closed, and a tear ran out from under one eyelid.

They all stood around her in silence until the doctor said "She's tired". Then they left the hospice.

That afternoon, Jozef went to the shops to buy some plum brandy, Slovak gin, a selection of Slovak cheeses, and gifts for the newlyweds and for Sasha and Sergej. Not knowing what to expect in Ukraine, he added a carton of cigarettes and a few staple groceries. He remembered that young Josif was a keen photographer, so he bought the latest Olympus camera, a model with six thousand pixels. He imagined that the young man was probably married, so he bought a red garnet for his wife. Without knowing quite why, he also imagined two children, and so bought a laptop on the advice of a friend who worked for a computer company. Reckoning it up, he realized he'd got something for everyone except Sasha's daughter, the bride, Ninocka. The shops were gradually closing, and he suffered a moment of panic until finally the ideal gift dawned on him.

The ivory and turquoise dress! He'd almost forgotten about it and wasn't even sure where he had stored it. In the end he found it in a trunk in the attic, well protected by the plastic KaDeWe carrier bag. It looked just the same as the day he'd purchased it in Neuwied.

"What do you think?" he asked, showing it to Marta.

"Where did you pick that up?"

"I found it in that Austrian shopping centre in Parndorf," he lied.

"It's lovely, very stylish."

"It's a present for the bride."

"You're buying things as if they were for your own children," his wife commented, shaking her head.

"My dear, it is a wedding I'm invited to. I'm a Member of Parliament; I can't go with just a bottle under my arm!" Balaz smiled to himself, thinking how close Marta had come to the truth. He was thinking again of what Josif, his wife and children could look like. He had the idea that their son may well be called Josif too. "I'll find out soon enough," he thought in eager anticipation.

Early that Friday morning, Jozef and Thomas climbed into his Nissan Almera and started off for Kolodne.

CHAPTER
EIGHTEEN

KOLODNE 2006

THE trip was pleasant and speedy, and Jozef and Thomas scarcely stopped talking the whole time. At one point, looking out at the splendid landscapes they were passing through, Thomas exclaimed, "I believe I'm starting to enjoy this trip." When they approached Krivan Mountain near Liptovsky Mikulás, he couldn't contain himself, and asked Jozef to pull over for a minute. Jozef turned off the motorway, and Thomas took out his camera and took a few pictures of the majestic peak crowned with golden autumn sunshine.

"I'm sure I have this same shot at home on a black and white postcard I bought at some souvenir stand. What is the mountain called?"

"Krivan."

"Right, Krifan," said Thomas, attempting to pronounce its name as well as he could. "I remember it due to its Indian head."

"Yes, that's what it looks like."

"Thanks, we can drive on now."

Despite Thomas' promise not to ask to stop again, Jozef detoured to show him Spisska Sobota, Levoca and Spis Castle. Sergej phoned twice to check on their progress. It was nine at night when they reached the border crossing at Ubla. The customs controls took Jozef back to socialist times, whereas Thomas nearly went into hysterics over the wait of almost two hours – there were after all very few cars entering Ukraine at that time of night. They passed the Slovak border smoothly, but the Ukrainian officials examined the German passport as if under a microscope, hinting there were ways to speed up thee the process. A twenty-Euro banknote finally turned the key to open the country, and the customs guard smiled as he wished them a peasant stay in Ukraine. Although the lights were dim, they easily spotted Sergej Gusev jumping up and down and waving to them. After hugging and kissing Jozef, Sergej turned the same attention to Thomas. Even though the German was somewhat taken aback, Sergej's friendly intent relieved Thomas of any fears he might have had concerning Ukrainians.

"Jozef's friends are my friends," Sergej declared categorically, and then asked if they were hungry.

"No."

"Thirsty?"

"Thanks, but we had time enough to have a snack during the wait at the border crossing."

"We could stop in Perecin; from there, home is a little over an hour's drive."

"We're fine, there's no need to stop."

"Sasha has prepared supper. As you can imagine, the whole village is upside down; it's only a small place, and they don't celebrate many weddings... especially with such esteemed guests. So, guys, I'll go in front, and if anything goes wrong, we can phone each other. When we turn off the main road it'll get a little bumpy, but as I said, Kolodne is just a little village and the last time they laid fresh asphalt was back in the Khrushchev era," Sergej laughed.

Both travellers were surprised that the villages and small towns they were driving through boasted no street lights: in fact, they relied on the car's high beams most of the way. At Mukachevo, Sergej turned off the main road and they blundered along back roads with potholes pitting the asphalt surface. After a few kilometers of this, they rejoined the highway, which was of much better quality than the side roads. The two foreigners were intrigued by the large number of police patrols along the way despite the late hour. Mostly they were situated a few dozen metres behind road signs announcing reduced driving speeds. Although Sergej had warned them that foreign cars were the police's primary victims, their luck held and they weren't stopped once. After passing through a village called Zaluzie, they turned left at a pond and Sergej's brake lights lit up.

"Now we'll go for a little adventure tour through some woods, and shortly afterwards we'll arrive in Kolodne."

Not even Kolodne's oldest inhabitants could remember a wedding to equal this one. The village was abuzz from early Saturday morning, and Stepan, the local militiaman, went so far as to proclaim an exemption from the ban on driving under the influence of alcohol. The good news quickly spread throughout the settlement. When asked if this might not cause a shock for motorists driving through, Stepan answered laconically that since this was the wedding of the century, they would have to risk it.

The Municipality Chairman personally welcomed the esteemed foreign guests – the Member of the Slovak Republic Parliament, Jozef Balaz, and the German 'biznesman' Thomas Ankermann. The courtyard of Sasha's mother, Olga Ivanovna, had been outfitted with tables from which the guests had since morning been refreshing themselves with an assortment of domestic and foreign drinks. Even the ages-old well with its winch were decorated with white balloons. There were so many guests staying in the widow's farmhouse that Jozef and Thomas had to share one room in the back part of the building.

Right from the start, the outhouse was the most visited part of the property. If it happened to be occupied, the men relieved themselves on a conveniently located manure pile. Those cows and pigs not being sacrificed as the wedding meats mooed and oinked their relief at still being alive. On the other hand, the calf Malina and Júlia, the heaviest sow, were already being portioned and placed on the groaning boards. The village women, with Sasha's help, carried off the remains of the slaughtered animals to the village culture centre, where the actual wedding party was to be held. Sergej, the proud father of the bride, was dressed in his ceremonial general's uniform.

He was so engaged in greeting and toasting the many guests that at around eleven a.m. he decided he'd just go for a little lie-down in the summer kitchen.

Perhaps Sergej's choice of location was not the most fortunate, since the trio from Irsava was rehearsing their wedding repertoire directly outside the kitchen's windows. Not only that, but their merry neighbor Vasja added the clash of his grandfather's cymbals to the rhythm section.

The bride, Ninocka, was seated in front of a large mirror in the middle room with the hairdresser working on her perm. Despite the fact Ninocka was four months pregnant, white ribbons, symbolizing innocence, were strewn throughout her coiffure. The bridesmaids had made her a beautiful wedding gown, while her white carnation bouquet had come all the way from Mukachevo. The clement weather, warm as a summer's day, perfectly suited the beginnings of her new married life.

Thomas, in a splendid humour, sat in the yard and managed to communicate very well with the native wedding guests. He was introduced to Rudi Schuster, the driver of the co-op tractor, who came from the former German colony of Zwidau/Zavidovo. In halting German, Rudi explained that his parents, Alois and Maria, were Austrians who had come there as young children prior to the First World War. His father, a master blacksmith, now reposed beside his wife in the German cemetery up in the hills.

The 'Germanec' quickly made friends, and drank to peace, to Stalingrad, to the cooperative, and even, on the instigation of some cycling fanatic, to Uwe Ampler. Thomas had no idea who this could be, but willingly drank his health.

"Alles gut, gut," the locals smiled at him.

"Karacho, karacho," Thomas smiled back.

Balaz trained his Russian fluency throughout the morning, superficially with the neighbours and at length with Sergej. At the same time he kept his eyes on all the male guests around the age of forty, wondering if one of them was Josif. He felt that the almost twenty years since last ther last meeting could not have changed him beyond all recognition. None of the men, however, reminded him of Josif. When Sasha came out of the house, he went over to her and, without attempting to disguise his anxiousness, asked her when Josif would be coming.

"Don't worry, you'll see him. This afternoon..."

"But where is he now? Is he coming with his family?"

Quickly Sasha turned and hurried back towards to the house. Then, with a soft and sad smile, she halted to say: "Later, later... Please tell Thomas to be ready to go to the church at one o'clock. It's only for the immediate family, but you two are exceptions. You are our special guests." Then she was gone.

Meanwhile, ten friends of the groom ran into the house and, in line with tradition, kidnapped the bride. They loaded her into a Skoda Superb parked in front of the house, and drove off, followed by two other cars. The groom, Yuri, was being 'held captive' at some friends' house, and so could not come to her rescue. When he received the message that his bride had been stolen, he jumped into an old Fiat and set off to find her. The village people kept sending him off in the wrong direction, killing themselves laughing as he dashed away. Yuri politely thanked each of them for their help, poured them a drink, and took off again. According to the tradition, the bride had to be hidden in one of the houses in the village. Although the settlement was small, by the time Yuri found the right house the whole village was in a jolly mood. In fact, if the local militia had not allowed drunk driving, Yuri would never have found Ninocka within the allotted time. As it was, he brought her to the bride's parents for the traditional custom of requesting their daughter's hand in matrimony. The groom listed all the good qualities of the bride's parents, and swore he would care for her nobly until death do them part. The women wept, and the men had red eyes. Jozef quietly translated everything for Thomas. This was a significant part of the marital tradition, for which the entire family should be present. Only Josif was absent. Since Sasha had promised Jozef they would meet that afternoon, he surmised he couldn't be ill.

Saint Basil's Church was about one hundred years old. A signpost next to the main entrance commemorated the reconstruction and blessing of the church in 1999. Although it lay at no great distance from Sasha's mother's house, the family made the trip in six gaily decorated Skodas, while the bride and groom were transported in a new Volvo. This had been borrowed by Sergej from the Regional Military Administration in Uzhgorod. Its licence plate was covered with a red sign, 'Vesilija, Wedding', and it too flew white balloons. Once there, Ninocka and the best man, Yuri and the bridesmaid, the groom's parents and sister, Sasha and Sergej, Jozef, Thomas, a few godparents, grandparents and the churchwarden Hrehor nervously awaited the arrival of the priest – Pop Feodosi. Finally, the sound of Pop Feodosi's scooter, on which he had driven all the way from Irsava, announced his arrival. He then disappeared into the sacristy, from which he quickly emerged clad in the ceremonial red tunic with white surplice. Also immediately, Hrehor, with obvious gusto, began the singing. His sonorous voice rose to the building's ceiling and on up to the sunny heavens, where he hoped God was listening. Feodosi tactfully signalled him to turn down the volume, and the two of them sang what reminded Balaz of some sort of Gospel duet.

"Gospodi, pomyluj ny. Žiju krs te, pomiluj ny! Gospodi, glasy naše. Daj nám wšem, Gospodi, žizň a mir v zemi!"

"Gospodi, pomiluj ny..."

Their singing continued all the way to the end of the wedding service.

Jozef looked around the splendid, icon-decorated white church. The main aisle leading to the altar was decorated with flags bearing the portraits of Orthodox saints. The bridesmaids and male attendants were by this time obviously trembling from the weight of the golden crowns they held over the heads of the bride and groom. From time to time, Jozef met the eyes of Sasha, seated among the women in the left front row. The men occupied the pews to the right of the altar.

As the ceremony was drawing to an end, the sound of a mobile telephone was suddenly heard throughout the church. Pop Feodosi glared at the congregation, who as one raised their eyes to the Crucifix. But the ringing tone did not stop until, after some time, the priest realized it was his own phone that was ringing. He furiously tore it out from beneath his robes, pressed a button, and angrily chanted into the receiver: "Sejcas nemogu... I can't talk now!" Laughter broke out in the church, and Pop Feodosi himself joined in, and so the service ended on a merry note.

On the groom's request, the wedding guests moved on to the Irsava hospital to visit Yuri's grandmother, who due to her ill health could not be present at the service. The next destination was the Culture Centre; Jozef took the opportunity to speak to Sasha, who seemed to be taking a break from her duties.

"Josif wasn't there... did something happen?"

"Yes, it did. Come with me."

"Thomas would like to come too." Sasha stopped to think this over, then shrugged her shoulders. She started off, waving them to follow along.

"We're going to meet your Russian soldier," Jozef explained to Thomas. The two of them went after Sasha, sharing an uneasy presentiment. For ten minutes the trio moved along in silence until they reached the end of the road. Then they dropped down a hillside to a stream, which they crossed over a small wooden bridge. On the other side of the bridge was a cemetery. Sasha led them to a tasteful marble gravestone with a photograph of the young man Jozef had known well. On the headstone he read the inscription: Josif Josifovic Obickij. Born 28. 3. 1969. Died 5. 1. 2004.

The end, koniec, Ende, amen. A pretty little bench had been built close to the gravesite, and a wreath and some fresh red flowers lay on the marble. Sasha knelt down and straightened out some small imperfection.

"He died from leukemia," she commented, and went to rest on the bench, Jozef wordlessly joining her. Thomas felt this was a time just for Sasha and Jozef, and started back towards the cemetery gate. Fearing he would get lost trying to find the village, went off to the far side of the graveyard. He saw crows flying overhead, and heard the whistle of some distant train.

The heavens above them were blue, without a hint of cloud; its splendor stood in sharp contrast to what the two former lovers were now feeling. Sasha took a plastic envelope out of her apron pocket, and in a slow, choked voice began to read a letter written by Josif.

'Dear mum, I often go with my commander to the sports hall in Karlshorst. Even though soldiers aren't really supposed to play with their superiors, he has invited me to play volleyball with our friends from Czechoslovakia. Every Wednesday I have the joy of meeting Martuska, the daughter of the Czechoslovak attaché. He is from Bratislava, and his name is Jozef, just like mine. The father is a great volleyball player, and the daughter is a beauty. I've fallen in love with Martuska, and I have the feeling she might love me in return. She plays the piano, and sang Okudzhava's Paper Soldier at a concert in the Soviet club not long ago'.

Sasha folded the letter and drew another from its envelope. Tears ran down her cheeks; Jozef pulled her to him. She didn't resist.

"You can't imagine, mum, what a fine family the Balazes are. We went together to a nice restaurant called Koliba on the bank of a lake a little way east of Berlin. Mister Balaz played a number of Slovak folk songs for us on his guitar, and then sang some in Russian. His wife and Martuska joined him in singing some Hungarian songs, which we all sang along to, Russians and Czechoslovaks together. Since the restaurant was rather smoky (you know how cigarette smoke bothers me) I went outside for some fresh air. To my joy, Martuska came out too, and we went for a long walk together. Mum, she let me hold her hand, and when she began to feel the chill, I lent her my uniform jacket. We both laughed at this, and felt wonderful in each other's company." When she finished reading, they sat in silence.

"How did he live his life?"Jozef asked after a while.

"Do you mean, how did he die? He simply faded away before our eyes. He was constantly exhausted, he lost weight... Near the end, he couldn't even manage to climb up his favourite hill, Lysa. He suffered from fevers, nosebleeds, bleeding gums, swollen glands and an enlarged liver... How my poor son suffered! It was all because of that damned Chernobyl! He was such a lovely boy, so good-looking... My God in heaven... "

"He went through a lot, the dear boy."

Sasha said nothing, but took out another three letters addressed in a rough, unformed hand: Miss Martuska Balazova, Bratislava, Slovakia. "Here are three letters Osja wrote to your daughter but never posted. Still, I think he'd have wanted me to hand them over to you... I would like to meet your daughter one day; for Osja to have loved her so much, she must be a wonderful person. Please give her them."

"Sasha..." Balaz began, but had trouble continuing. He stopped for a deep breath and then got his question out: "Was he our son?"

They heard steps approaching from behind them. Thomas, his eyes red and obviously moved, came up to Sasha. He asked Jozef to translate for him.

"Alexandra... it's... it's hard for me to express my gratitude... I once had a brother, Nicholas. He was six years old at the end of the war, in November, 1945. Our father was a British prisoner-of-war and our mother was one of the thousands of German women, called Trümmerfrauen, who cleaned up the destruction caused by the falling bombs. Nicholas used to go to help her stack the salvageable bricks. A wall toppled down on him. My mother and the other women tried to dig his body out, but they couldn't find him... But she found this object, and she gave it to me, saying that I had to give it to a Russian woman who had a son as wonderful as hers. I..." Thomas' voice faltered. "I know what your son did for my son... So I have to give you what my mother found under that wrecked building. I suppose it was lost by one of your soldiers..." Thomas produced a small case, and from it he withdrew a chain with a piece of tin with the word: 'Ljubov, Love' inscribed on it. He placed it in her hand and then kissed the hand. Her eyes full of tears, Sasha gazed down at Thomas' gift.

Next he knelt by the grave and, in a low voice, prayed: 'Vater unser im Himmel. Geheiligt werde Dein Name. Dein Reich komme...'

He was reciting the Our Father in German, and Sasha and Jozef joined in, each in their own tongue.

In front of the House of Culture a crowd of people were standing, talking, smoking, drinking, laughing and dancing. In Kolodne it was a custom to place well-stocked tables in front of the Culture Centre for those who weren't invited to the banquet inside. Of course, as the evening progressed and people moved in and out freely, it became impossible to say who was or was not an invited guest. The co-op headquarters, where the newlyweds underwent a civil marriage directly after their church wedding, was only a stone's throw from the House of Culture, a fact which had certain advantages - the wedding banquet could be held in the Culture Centre, which had a separate toilets for each sex. In those years, only selected Ukrainian municipalities had their own Culture Centre, and only a few of them boasted two toilets.

According to the records-keepers, the Kolodne Culture Centre has two toilets because in 1958 the Soviet Union General Secretary Nikita Sergejevich Khrushchev passed through the municipality. As a native Ukrainian, Khrushchev loved to drink kvass, and everyone knows that this particular beverage produces a great deal of urine in the body. The highest-placed USSR official felt a pressing need for the toilet just as his motorcade was passing through Kolodne; his car pulled to a stop in front of the House of Culture. Nikita Sergejevich ran to the latrine, but as someone was already sitting there Khrushchev was forced to pee out behind the outhouse. Before getting back into the government ZIL, Khrushchev wished to know why the Culture Centre had only one latrine. He was sure that he had been assured by the Central Committee Culture Secretary that every Culture Centre in the Soviet Union had separate toilets: "Lying to me as usual," he is reported to have remarked in disgust before being driven away.

To be on the safe side, the Municipality Chairman had a second latrine built; after all, no-one could be sure the Supreme Leader wouldn't feel a pressing need to use the facilities the next time he was passing through the municipality. However, this second, relatively luxurious, latrine was kept permanently locked in case Khrushchev might one day need it. But since the years had gone by, and Khrushchev was long gone from politics, the members of the local Soviet democratically decided that the second toilet could be used on ceremonious occasions. The marriage of Nina Sergejevna Gusev and Yuri Grigorievich Shevchenko was one such occasion.

Inside the hall, the musicians from Iršava alternated with the deejay Semion, who tried in vain to choose music that would get the wedding guests onto the dance floor. Almost everyone, however, was calling for the songs of Verka Serdjucka, Ukraine's greatest star, a man who dressed in strange female costumes. His songs had the wedding guests dancing close to distraction. Balaz had the honour of being the fourth to dance with the bride, after the groom, Sergej, and Yuri's father. Thomas was next in line. He no longer needed Rudi's translations – alcohol and good humour made him capable of communicating with all comers.

By eight o'clock, the wedding celebration was following the usual dynamic: the women were dancing with other women, and the men, including the Municipality Chairman, Pop Feodosi, the Village Party Chairman and Stepan the militiaman were already incapable of sensual perception. The last conscious act by the local law and order official was taking away Matvej's driving licence. He had senselessly provoked Stepan. If, totally drunk as he was, he had discreetly slipped behind the steering wheel in an adjacent parking lot, no-one would have batted an eye, but he tried to drive in front of the assembled wedding party, right under Stepan's nose. The militiaman couldn't risk a loss of authority, so he ran a breathalyzer test. When Matvei finally managed to get the testing tube into his mouth, it turned as green as spring grass.

"This calls for the suspension of your driving licence, my boy!" Stepan declaimed with authority, and put out his hand. Matvej took his licence from his back pocket and humbly handed it over to Stepan.

"This is the second one you've taken from me this week," he complained, leaning for support against the hood of his car. "But no matter, I still have one more, hee-hee-hee."

"Where did you get it from?!" Stepan wanted to know.

"Don't you remember? You gave it to me for my birthday."

Stepan obviously had no memory of this, but then again his memory was not too functional at that point in time. Rather, he asked Matvei to drive him home.

"But I've been drinking!" Matvei reminded him.

"Don't worry, no-one is going to catch you. I'll be in the car with you!" Since Stepan's wife had stayed at the wedding, it was Matvej who put him to bed.

The traditional dance, where the girls place their handkerchiefs before their chosen partners, curtsey and invite them to dance, took place with almost exclusively female participation. The young men were almost without exception sleeping off the alcohol on the benches in front of the Culture Centre, their heads supported by the tables. The few who were still conscious stood around smoking or ran off to vomit behind the latrine. As is usual at such gatherings, the wilder element was fighting it out on the so-called parking lot. This parking area was almost unused most days; the few functioning automobiles in the municipality were usually parked in their owners' yards. But on occasions such as this one, it came in handy. The Municipality Chairman proudly pointed this out to his subordinates with the comment: "Wasn't it clever of us to build it?"

Sergej, clearly the worse for wear, was led home by his neighbours. Jozef remained by Sasha's side, sensing that she was glad of his company. They danced and sang together, and sometimes they clandestinely held each other's hands, enjoying their few remaining moments together. Verka Serdjucka's emotional ballad was playing:

'Kto sogrejet, neznaju, bez ľjubvy zamerzaju, Who will keep me warm? Without love I will freeze'

So they danced and danced and twirled around. They were as merry as two people can be who have the feeling they'll never again have such an opportunity.

Just after midnight, the new bride, Ninocka, changed out of her wedding gown, entered the hall.

Sasha gasped in appreciation – her daughter literally shone in her wonderful ivory and turquoise dress. The bride and groom made their way over to them, and Ninocka kissed and hugged Jozef. "Many thanks for your gift. It's beautiful," she enthused in a fetching blend of Russian and Slovak. Her husband also firmly gripped his hand in thanks. Then the newlyweds went off to dance.

Suddenly it was five in the morning, the sun was appearing over Lysa Peak, the wedding guests were dispersing, and Jozef and Thomas went off to their beds. Jozef got up around eleven, dressed, and went out into the courtyard, where Olga Ivanovna was already tending to her livestock. He spied Sásha seated under a leafy chestnut tree.

"Couldn't you sleep?" he inquired.

"What about you?" she asked calmly in return. It was as if she had been waiting for him to appear. "I was helping mum with the milking. It's starting to be too much for her. I suggested she just keep the pigs, but you know how stubborn old people can be... they'd rather work themselves to death."

"It's the work that keeps them alive."

"Where are you off to?"

"Nowhere really. It's a beautiful day, and I thought I might take a walk down to the stream. Would you care to join me?"

"Just hang on; I'll put on something more suitable and be right back." When she returned, Balaz noticed she's gone to the trouble of applying a touch of makeup. She was still a beauty; her hair had started to grey, but those turquoise eyes still radiated that indescribable shine and goodness. Together they strolled through the dewy meadow.

"So you'll be leaving this afternoon..."

"I have to. And Thomas has to be at work tomorrow... But it's been marvellous!"

They walked on by the stream, sharing with each other all they hadn't managed to say the day before. In less than two hours they spoke of everything about their lives, knowing it could be a long time before their paths crossed once more.

"There's something I want to read to you," she said all at once, and took out a letter written on an old yellowed piece of paper. She put on a pair of old-fashioned glasses and began: 'Dearest Sasha,

I'm sending you the glasses I promised and only hope they're all right. I chose the prescription exactly according to your specifications. I hope they suit you and make your exquisite turquoise eyes even more striking – but not so much so that other people will pay too much attention to them. I don't know what happened to me, but I've been completely different since I got home from Kiev. You really surprised me with your knowledge of Slovakia, our literature and our history. I have taken the liberty of sending you the latest edition of Sládkovic's 'Marina'. Its first verses should read like this:

'I sing of a thirst for beauty, besotted with loveliness... but the centre, the element, heaven, unity, of beauty is for me, my Sasha' Forgive me my directness, but I have fallen so deeply in love with you. I hope we will meet again soon."

She took off her glasses and, with a deep look full of love and unfulfilled desires, stared straight into Jozef's eyes.

"Are these those same glasses?" he asked.

"Yes, but the prescription is a little stronger."

EPILOGUE

BALAZ was appointed Ambassador of the Slovak Republic to NATO in Brussels. His wife remained in Bratislava, unwilling to devote four years of her life to attending senseless receptions, premieres, exhibitions and concerts. She preferred to spend her time with her beloved ceramics, for which she obviously had a talent. Balaz participated in sessions of the North Atlantic Council, the supreme body of the largest military organization in the world. Each member had a veto right, but no-one ever took advantage of it. When voting, Balaz kept an eye on the American Ambassador, and voted as he did. Sometimes he would have to smile, remembering how during his time in the GDR he would vote in concert with the Soviet Union delegate at international meetings. Both then and now, he voted 'correctly', as did most of the other ambassadors.

Sometimes he felt like a puppet, but took solace in the fact that he wasn't the only one in this situation... and every month he received a salary most Slovaks couldn't even dream of. He constructed his own zone to which he could retreat, coming out only when it was time to applaud or be applauded.

His younger daughter, Anicka, successfully completed university and began work as a television and radio host. His older daughter, Martuska, got married in a legendary recreational facility in Bratislava – the same hall where, two weeks prior to the August 21, 1968 Soviet invasion, Brezhnev, Ulbricht, Gomulka, Kadar and Zivkov reassured their Czechoslovak allies that all would be well. Martuska's daughter, Natali, was born on the very day her grandfather completed this novel.

Winter turned into a prosperous businessman who was said to financially support all of the political parties in Parliament.

Thomas continued his career as a political science lecturer at a private Berlin university. Some of the students were so thick that Thomas would have gladly expelled them from the school. But the Rector, a co-owner of the institute, made it clear to him that the tuition these children of the rich were paying was supporting Thomas and his family's lifestyle.

Sasha closed in upon herself. Sergej became more interested in drinking and nostalgia for the USSR than in his work, and so lost all contact with his military past. Sometimes Sergej was too quick with a slap, but compared to what other women suffered from their husbands, Sasha couldn't condemn him. She looked after him with loving care.

After their time at the wedding in Kolodne, Sasha and Jozef exchanged a few letters and postcards, but their communication gradually dwindled and finally ceased. Thomas attended the launching of this book in Bratislava, and he and Jozef keep in loose touch via email.

Those who have walked the roads of friendship often haven't the time or energy to brush away the dust that gathers where their feet once trod. I only hope their children never forget the time when, once upon a time, their parents lived in the jubilation zone.

Jozef Banáš
Bratislava 23. 4. 2008

Jozef Banáš
Zóna nadšenia

Jozef Banáš
Jubilation Zone

Translated from the Slovak original Zóna nadšenia (an imprint of IKAR, a.s., 2008) by Kevin Slavin, 2008

English Edition Published by Hybrid Global Publishing, New York and co-published by Global Slovakia, Bratislava Slovakia, a.s. in 2021

Printed in the United States of America, or in the United Kingdom when distributed elsewhere

WWW.GLOBALSLOVAKIA.COM

THE PUBLISHING OF THIS BOOK WAS MADE POSSIBLE, THANKS TO:

1400 Inspiration Place SW Cedar Rapids, IA 52404
319-362-8500

https://ncsml.org

The NCSML preserves, presents and transcends unique stories of Czech and Slovak history and culture through innovative experiences and active engagement to reach cross-cultural audiences locally, nationally and internationally. The NCSML is an innovative leader in lifelong learning, community building and cultural connections. We encourage self-discovery for all ages so that the stories of freedom, identity, family and community will live on for future generations.

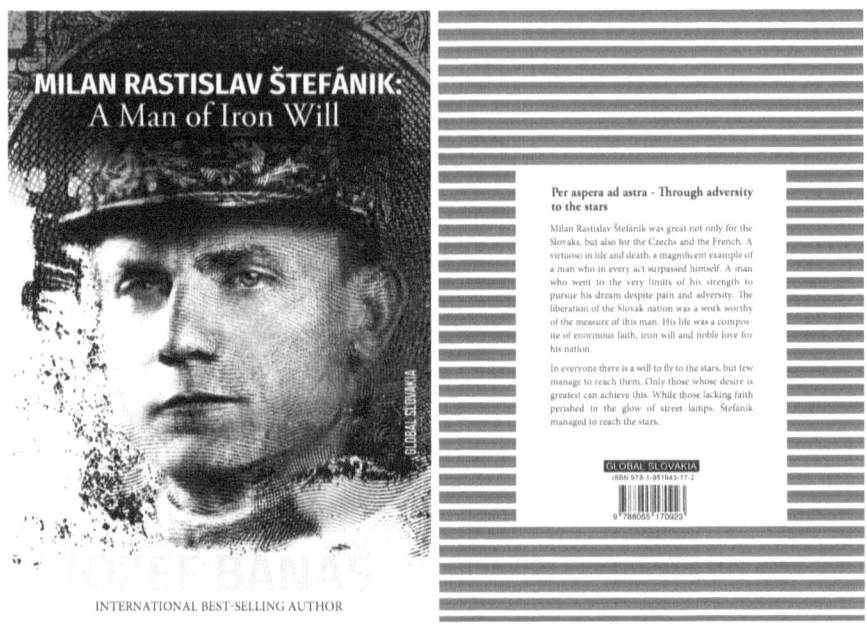

Milan Rastislav Stefanik: A Man of Iron Will - English

Per aspera ad astra - Through adversity to the stars
Milan Rastislav Štefánik was great not only for the Slovaks, but also for the Czechs and the French. A virtuoso in life and death, a magnificent example of a man who in every act surpassed himself. A man who went to the very limits of his strength to pursue his dream despite pain and adversity. The liberation of the Slovak nation was a work worthy of the measure of this man. His life was a composite of enormous faith, iron will and noble love for his nation.
In everyone there is a will to fly to the stars, but few manage to reach them. Only those whose desire is greatest can achieve this. While those lacking faith perished in the glow of street lamps, Štefánik managed to reach the stars.

BY THE SAME AUTHOR

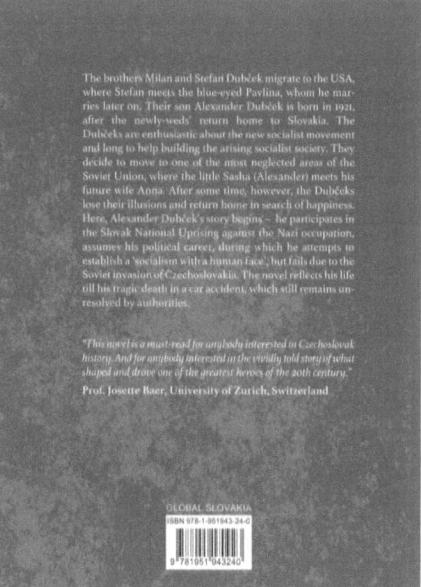

Stop Dubcek! The Story of a Man Who Defied Power

The brothers Milan and Stefan Dubček migrate to the USA, where Stefan meets the blue-eyed Pavlina, whom he marries later on. Their son Alexander Dubček is born in 1921, after the newly-weds' return home to Slovakia. The Dubčeks are enthusiastic about the new socialist movement and long to help building the arising socialist society. They decide to move to one of the most neglected areas of the Soviet Union, where the little Sasha (Alexander) meets his future wife Anna. After some time, however, the Dubčeks lose their illusions and return home in search of happiness. Here, Alexander Dubček's story begins – he participates in the Slovak National Uprising against the Nazi occupation, assumes his political career, during which he attempts to establish a 'socialism with a human face', but fails due to the Soviet invasion of Czechoslovakia. The novel reflects his life till his tragic death in a car accident, which still remains unresolved by authorities.

"This novel is a must-read for anybody interested in Czechoslovak history. And for anybody interested in the vividly told story of what shaped and drove one of the greatest heroes of the 20th century."
Prof. Josette Baer, University of Zurich, Switzerland

BY THE SAME AUTHOR

www.ingramcontent.com/pod-product-compliance
Lightning Source LLC
Chambersburg PA
CBHW030900080526
44589CB00010B/85